Mental Health Interventions with Preschool Children

Issues in Clinical Child Psychology

Series Editors: **Michael C. Roberts,** *University of Kansas–Lawrence, Kansas*
Lizette Peterson, *University of Missouri–Columbia, Missouri*

BEHAVIORAL ASPECTS OF PEDIATRIC BURNS
Edited by Kenneth J. Tarnowski

CHILDREN AND DISASTERS
Edited by Conway F. Saylor

HANDBOOK OF DEPRESSION IN CHILDREN AND
ADOLESCENTS
Edited by William M. Reynolds and Hugh F. Johnston

INTERNATIONAL HANDBOOK OF PHOBIC AND ANXIETY
DISORDERS IN CHILDREN AND ADOLESCENTS
Edited by Thomas H. Ollendick, Neville J. King, and William Yule

MENTAL HEALTH INTERVENTIONS WITH PRESCHOOL
CHILDREN
Robert D. Lyman and Toni L. Hembree-Kigin

A Continuation Order Plan is available for this series. A continuation order will bring
delivery of each new volume immediately upon publication. Volumes are billed only
upon actual shipment. For further information please contact the publisher.

Mental Health Interventions with Preschool Children

ROBERT D. LYMAN

University of Alabama
Tuscaloosa, Alabama

and

TONI L. HEMBREE-KIGIN

Early Childhood Mental Health Services
Tempe, Arizona

PLENUM PRESS • NEW YORK AND LONDON

Library of Congress Cataloging in Publication data

On file

ISBN 0-306-44860-2

© 1994 Plenum Press, New York
A Division of Plenum Publishing Corporation
233 Spring Street, New York, N. Y. 10013

Printed in the United States of America

To Kathy and Meghan

—RDL

To my parents, Jim and Jean Hembree, and to the loving memory of my grandparents, Dave and Lillian Hiebert

—TLH

Preface

Preschool children have been largely neglected in the mental health treatment literature, although research has established that many behavioral and emotional disorders in children result from events occurring during the preschool years or are first manifested during this period. This has occurred for several reasons. Traditional psychoanalytic thinking has considered preschoolers to be too psychologically immature for complete manifestations of psychopathology, and the limited language abilities of young children have complicated assessment procedures and made them less appropriate for treatment approaches that are largely verbal in nature. In addition, the developmental complexity of the preschool period has deterred many researchers from investigating clinical issues with this age group.

Partly as a result of the lack of information on preschoolers in the literature, practitioners have historically been uncomfortable in conducting assessments and initiating treatment with young children. They have often adopted a "wait and see" attitude in which formal mental health diagnosis and treatment are not implemented until after the child's entry into school. Unfortunately, such a delay may mean wasting the time during which mental health interventions can be maximally effective. Recently, this attitude has changed and practitioners now recognize the need for assessment and treatment of behavioral and emotional disorders early in life. What they require to assist them in the timely delivery of such services is information about assessment and treatment procedures specifically designed for preschoolers and with demonstrated efficacy with that age group.

With this book we are attempting to provide such information and to focus attention on the unique aspects of mental health assessment and treatment with preschoolers. Our intended audience includes mental health practitioners who have the opportunity to work with preschoolers but may have hesitated because of inadequate information about the unique clinical features of mental health conditions in preschoolers or the specific approaches that have been found to be effective in treating these conditions. In addition, we hope that this book proves useful to academics who are interested in researching clinical issues with a preschool population and need a specific compilation of clinical research findings with that age group. We also feel that graduate and undergraduate students in a variety of mental health disciplines can benefit from the research and clinical findings collected in this volume.

We have organized this book by clinical conditions rather than by diagnostic and treatment approaches for several reasons. First, we hope that the book will be a useful continuing reference for clinicians and that this organizational schema will help them to efficiently find the section on a specific condition when they are confronted with it clinically. Practitioners are less likely to ask "When should I use the K-ABC?" than to ask "How should I assess this five-year-old with suspected learning problems?" Therefore, we have organized the book by clinical conditions as they present to the practitioner. Second, we feel that assessment and intervention are interrelated activities and that it is a mistake to view them in isolation from each other. Assessment procedures should be tailored to the condition to be assessed rather than structured as a "standard assessment battery," which contains the same components regardless of the referral question, age of the client, or possible diagnoses. Thus, the assessment procedures discussed in this book for autistic children vary greatly from those presented for use with children with psychosomatic disorders. Assessment should truly be the initial stage of treatment and we feel that by linking assessment and intervention for a specific condition in each chapter we have emphasized the important relationship between the two.

The topics covered in this book include clearly defined clinical conditions such as autistic disorder and psychosocial dwarfism as well as other topics such as bed-wetting and food refusal, which are frequently seen in preschoolers and may not be indicative of significant psychopathology. We intend this book to be useful in helping practitioners differentiate serious psychopathology from "normal" developmental difficulties and hope that many interventions discussed in these pages will have applicability for children whose problems fall in both categories.

Soon after the manuscript for this book was finished, DSM-IV was released. Although many of the statements in the book reference DSM-III-R diagnostic categories that have been slightly changed or relabeled in DSM-IV, we have reviewed their applicability to DSM-IV and feel that their underlying validity is intact. In some chapters, we had information about the changes in diagnostic nomenclature or structure that would result from the release of DSM-IV and have incorporated that into our coverage.

No book is written solely by its identified authors and we are indebted to a number of individuals who contributed in various ways to this book. We would like to express our gratitude to the following people, who provided us with critical feedback on specific chapters: Kathy Andrews, Barbara Burgess, Sheila Eyberg, Beverly Funderburk, Lani Greening, Anne Griffin, Jean Hembree, Yo Jackson, Tim Kigin, Lisa McElreath, Sandy Osborne, Joy Ott, Jane Silovsky, and Wendy Stone. The book is much improved as a result of their input. Thanks are also due to Teri Chisholm and Dona Rhone for their clerical assistance.

Special thanks are extended to our friend and colleague, Michael Roberts, who labored over a much-too-long first draft of the full manuscript, and to our long-suffering Editor at Plenum, Mariclaire Cloutier, for her patience during "trying" times.

Most of all, we would like to thank our families for their support when we were preoccupied, unavailable, irritable, and overwhelmed.

ROBERT D. LYMAN
TONI L. HEMBREE-KIGIN

Contents

1

Introduction

It is paradoxical and uniquely frustrating that even as mental health practitioners and educators recognize and emphasize the need for early detection and treatment of mental health problems in children, there is little focus in the research and clinical literature on how to go about doing this. Many practitioners are unfamiliar and uncomfortable with preschoolers, and in the absence of clear guidelines in the literature, often advise parents to "wait and see if the problems continue," thus squandering the opportunity for intervention at a time when it may be maximally effective. It is hoped that this volume can provide guidance in the assessment and treatment of mental health problems in preschoolers and, therefore, help practitioners with timely and appropriate intervention. Before we address individual disorders and syndromes that occur in preschool populations, however, it is important to discuss the necessity of considering preschool behavior within a developmental context.

The years between birth and age 6 constitute an unparalleled time of change for a child. Although children initially can make only a few innate behavioral responses, they gain the ability within this time span to enact highly complex motor behaviors, to communicate, to engage in high levels of abstraction and problem solving, and to socialize meaningfully with adults and their peers. Many mental health problems in this age group are first recognized as deviations in this developmental process; therefore, it is important that practitioners and researchers have an accurate and clear understanding of the "normal" developmental process and the factors that affect it.

GENETIC VARIABLES

Within recent years, we have greatly increased our knowledge of genetic transmission of behavioral traits and, consequently, our estimates of the importance of genetic variables in mental health problems. Current evidence strongly suggests that a wide range of behaviors are at least partially genetically linked. Recognition of such genetic causality means several things to practitioners. First, it means that behavioral deviations may occur in even very young preschoolers, before environmental factors could be expected to have much impact. Second, the evidence for the importance of genetic factors in childhood mental health problems means that practitioners (and researchers) must obtain complete information concerning the occurrence of mental health and medical problems in the child's extended family. Finally, practitioners must be aware of continuing developments in medical science, and the possibilities that genetic or biological markers for mental health disorders may be discovered through physical examination or laboratory tests.

PRENATAL VARIABLES

Just as in recent years we have increasingly recognized the importance of genetic variables, we have also begun to understand the importance of prenatal variables. One of the best examples of this understanding is the recent recognition of fetal alcohol syndrome (FAS) as the leading known cause of mental retardation in the United States (Abel & Sokol, 1987). The effects on the fetus of moderately excessive alcohol ingestion by the mother were largely unknown 15 years ago, and few medical or mental health practitioners recognized the behavioral patterns or physical anomolies associated with FAS. Recent literature suggests that other important prenatal factors include maternal and paternal drug use, maternal smoking, and prenatal exposure to environmental toxins such as lead. In addition, a recent area of tremendous concern is the number of HIV-infected children in the United States, most of whom are infected prenatally or at the time of birth. Again, practitioners in this area are obligated to obtain adequate history relating to these variables and to know when referral for medical evaluation is indicated.

PERINATAL VARIABLES

There are a number of factors that occur or become apparent at the time of birth that can produce mental health problems during the preschool years. Physical trauma can produce cerebral palsy, with resulting motor and cognitive deficits. Premature delivery and low birth weight, although often resulting from factors occurring throughout the prenatal period, become apparent at the time of birth. Low-birth-weight babies generally are more likely to be developmentally delayed and at risk for such disorders as attention-deficit disorder. Also, premature births account for a disproportionate percentage of physically abused children, possibly because of the separation and diminished parent–child bonding that results from placement of the child in a neonatal intensive-care unit or high-risk nursery or because of the high incidence of prematurity among teenage mothers.

Recent advances in fetal monitoring capabilities have greatly improved the opportunities for intervention in cases of fetal distress. Interventions such as cesarean section can now be implemented in a more timely fashion to prevent fetal damage from such perinatal complications as crimping of the umbilical cord or breech presentation. One widely used perinatal assessment procedure is the Apgar score (Apgar, 1953), which is used in most hospital delivery rooms to assess infant health and development at the time of delivery. This 10-point scale assesses infant capabilities in the areas of heartbeat, breathing, muscle tone, skin color, and reflex irritability at 1 minute and 5 minutes after birth and assigns a score of 0 to 2 for each area. Infants with a total score below 4 on the Apgar scale are viewed as being at risk and are usually accorded intensive medical care, including oxygen and other respiratory support. Children scoring between 4 and 7 at the 1-minute assessment are usually carefully observed for possible medical problems.

NEUROLOGICAL DEVELOPMENT AND IMPAIRMENT

In the past, mental health practitioners have often known little about neurological development of young children and, therefore, have been unable to evaluate or consider this factor in their assessments. Fortunately, however, the growth of the fields of pediatric neurology and neuropsychology has triggered a corresponding growth of interest in neurological and neuropsychological function in preschoolers and their significance in mental health problems. Development of such formal assessment techniques as the Brazelton Neonatal Behavioral Assessment Scale (1973) has greatly increased practitioners' capabilities to assess young children, and such advances in medical science as the magnetic resonance imaging (MRI) and positron emission tomography (PET) scans have enabled us to relate functional neurological deficits more clearly to anatomical and physiological dysfunction. Increasing numbers of psychologists and other mental health practitioners now receive formal training in neurological development and are aware of such clinically relevant facts as the failure of the cerebral cortex to significantly affect behavior for the first 6 to 9 months of a baby's life, or the lack of significant myelination of nerves serving the sphincter for a year or more after birth, meaning that toilet training is not even physiologically possible before that age. Interventions for neurological conditions have been increasingly studied in recent years as well, and it is important for mental health practitioners to be familiar with this literature. For example, long term use of seizure medication during the preschool years has a number of significant cognitive and behavioral sequelae, and it is important for a practitioner to be familiar with these, both for purposes of assessment of a child who has been on such a medication and for helping parents and physicians assess the risks and benefits of such treatment.

The development of the human nervous system is a process that begins during the fetal period and continues during much of early childhood. Although this process is genetically driven, it is vulnerable to environmental factors throughout its course. During the first 4 weeks of gestation, nerve cells differentiate and migrate to form the neural tube, which further develops to form the spinal cord. The brain develops out of the anterior portion of the spinal cord over the third through tenth weeks of gestation, with basic development of the cerebral cortex occurring from the seventh week through the seventh month. Myelinization, or the development of a fatty insulation layer around neuron axons that enhances transmission efficiency, begins in the spinal cord during the third month of gestation and reaches the brain during the sixth month of gestation. At birth, only a few brain areas are fully myelinated. These are mostly brainstem areas concerned with instinctive behaviors such as sucking. Sensory neurons generally become myelinated before motor neurons, which accounts for the superiority of infants' sensory capabilities to their motor capabilities (Brierley, 1976). Myelinization of the fibers connecting the cerebral cortex to the cerebellum is often not completed until around the age of 4 and complete myelinization of the nervous system often is incomplete until after 15 years of age (Kolb & Whishaw, 1991). Post-natal nutritional deficiencies have been linked to disorders of myelinization in the brain (NINCDS, 1979). There also appears to be considerable postnatal development of dendritic connections between neurons. By the time a child turns 2 years of age, his or her brain has reached about 75% of its adult weight and by the time the child turns 5 the brain has achieved about 90% of its adult weight (Yeterian & Pandya, 1988).

Abnormalities in neurological development during the prenatal period can include failure of the neural tube to close properly, resulting in a condition called spina bifida, in which the spinal cord does not develop properly to the lower extremities, resulting in paralysis of the legs and hydrocephalus. This condition can result in significant cognitive as well as motor impairment. Such failures of neural development can be caused by environmental factors (such as rubella, exposure to radiation, hypoxia) as well as by genetic factors.

Neurological problems occurring at the time of birth are most often the result of mechanical trauma, hypoxia, hypoglycemia, or subarachnoid bleeding. The most common neurological disorder seen in neonates is seizure disorder. Premature infants have seizures 15 times more frequently than full-term infants and 70% to 90% of preterm infants who have seizures die (Holden, Mellits, & Freeman, 1982). Eriksson and Zetterstom (1979) found that 13% of full-term infants who had neonatal seizures died, with 30% of the survivors suffering severe psychomotor retardation and only 15% considered developmentally normal at 1 year of age. Children with nonfebrile convulsive disorders generally demonstrate mild to moderate behavioral and cognitive deficits later in life. For example, Bolter (1984) found a mean IQ of 92 in a sample of such children, with only 13% obtaining IQs over 110.

A more positive prognosis is attached to the occurrence of febrile convulsions, defined as seizures occurring between the ages of 3 months and 5 years, associated with fever but without evidence of intracranial infection or disease (Millichap, 1968). The incidence of these convulsions in the preschool population is approximately 29/1,000. Only 30% of children who experience one febrile convulsion ever experience another. The recurrence rate is higher for children whose first febrile seizure occurred before 18 months of age than for those who were older than 18 months when their first seizure occurred. Nelson and Ellenberg (1978) found no IQ deficits at 7 years of age in children who had experienced febrile seizures, although Schiottz-Christensen and Bruhn (1973) reported increased behavioral problems and a 7-point Performance IQ deficit in children who had had febrile convulsions when compared to their unaffected twins.

SENSORY DEVELOPMENT

Visual Abilities

Visual tracking abilities are present even in newborns, although speed of tracking and ability to track a stimulus in the periphery of the visual field are not equivalent to adult performance. Visual acuity is poor at all distances until about 1 month of age, when it becomes approximately as good as adult vision when the stimulus is 8 to 10 inches from the eye. Vision for greater distances continues to be poor throughout the preschool period. An infant can generally see at 20 feet what an adult can see at 200 feet, while 2- or 3-year-olds see at 20 feet what adults see at 30 or 40 feet (Acredolo & Hake, 1982). Fantz (1961) determined that by 8 weeks of age infants were able to discriminate between visual patterns and preferred complex patterns (particularly faces) to simple ones. Infants as young as 2 months old are also capable of depth perception, and Cohen (1977) determined that infants as young as 7 months old demonstrate "shape constancy," or the ability to perceive an object as unchanged even when its orientation to the subject, and therefore its image on the retina, is changed. Investigations of color vision in infants (Bornstein, Kessen, & Weiskopf, 1976) have shown that infants as young as 4 months of age are capable of differentiating essentially the same colors that adults perceive as different hues.

Auditory Abilities

Although hearing is intact at birth, neonates are neither able to detect low-volume sounds nor able to differentiate between sounds as well as adults can (Schulman-Galambos & Galambos, 1979). However, some of this deficit may be due to the fluids that are often present in the ears of newborns. Young infants do demonstrate the ability to discriminate between sounds of different pitch and appear to have a preference for lower pitch sounds (Eisenberg, 1976). They also demonstrate greater response to human voices than to nonvoice sounds (a bell) of the same pitch (Freedman, 1971). Infants are also able to roughly localize the source of sounds soon after birth (Butterworth & Castillo, 1976). Auditory abilities appear to improve until the age of 12 or 13, at which point they stabilize until middle adulthood (Pick & Pick, 1970).

Tactile Abilities

Pain perception appears to be poorly developed at birth but increases greatly over the first few days of life (Anders & Chalemian, 1974). Touch sensation appears to be largely intact soon after birth, but like other sensory modalities shows gradual improvement over the preschool years (Gliner, 1967).

Olfactory and Gustatory Abilities

The sense of smell appears to be highly developed in neonates as young as 1 week old (Rieser, Yonas, & Wilkner, 1976). For example, 1-month-old infants have demonstrated a preference for the odor of their own mother's breasts (MacFarlane, 1977). The literature suggests that sensitivity to odors is fairly well developed by age 6, continues to improve until middle age, and then declines.

The ability to differentiate tastes is grossly present at birth, and neonates appear to have innate preferences for certain tastes. For example, they prefer sweeter substances even when they are less nutritious than alternatives (Bower, 1977). Some evidence (Pick & Pick, 1970) suggests that children's taste sensitivity continues to improve throughout childhood.

MOTOR DEVELOPMENT

Neonates are born with over a dozen innate reflexes, many of which have significant survival value and which are controlled by subcortical areas of the brain. The presence of reflexive behaviors in neonates is often used as an indication of neurological and developmental integrity. Gradually, beginning between 2 months and 1 year of age, the cortex assumes more and more control of motor behavior, resulting in the disappearance or diminishment of these reflexes and the emergence of voluntary motor behaviors (Capute, Accardo, Vining, Rubenstein, & Harryman, 1978).

Even before reflex behaviors diminish, neonates can engage in a number of voluntary behaviors. The emergence of these behaviors in early infancy follows a fairly predictable course and can be used as a rough indicator of developmental progress, although it is important for both practitioners and parents to realize the considerable individual variability in this process. By the age of 1 month, most infants can lift their heads up when they are lying prone. By 2 or 3 months of age, 50% of infants can roll over, and by 5 or 6 months of age, 50% of infants can sit without support. By the age of 7 months most infants begin crawling or creeping, although it is not uncommon for children to remain nonambulatory until they begin walking around the age of 1 year. Walking is often preceded, at the age of 9 or 10 months, by a period of "cruising," or walking with the support of furniture, adults, or other structures. Several months later, infants develop enough balance and coordination to be able to walk backward. The abilities to hop on one foot and jump in the air with both feet are generally not seen in children until the age of 2 or more. By the age of 5, most children can jump a considerable distance across the ground as well as up in the air. Development of stair climbing follows a fairly predictable course. At first, children climb steps by moving one foot to a higher step and then bringing the second foot up to that same level. Not until children are 3 or 4 years old do they begin to climb steps by each foot on an alternate step, as adults do.

Ambulatory abilities continue to improve throughout the preschool period and in most cases reach essentially adult levels by age 6.

Motor development in the use of the hands also proceeds in an orderly fashion. Even neonates will reach for objects placed within their visual fields, but their actions are poorly coordinated and appear to be reflexive in nature. At 4 or 5 months of age, infants begin engaging in more purposeful reaching for and touching of objects within the visual field. At this age, there is little or no independent finger manipulation; objects that are grasped are "scooped" up or held with the whole hand. From 6 to 12 months of age, infants develop more precise and sophisticated finger control, culminating in the development of effective pincer movements (opposition of the thumb and forefinger) at around 1 year of age. Throwing and catching a ball are abilities that are present in many children by the age of 2; however, these behaviors consist largely of gross trunk and arm movements. Only by age 4 or 5 do children become very skillful at these activities, using their fingers and hands more and their trunks less. Finger and hand coordination continue to improve throughout early childhood.

The research literature suggests that the process of motor development is the product of both physical maturation and experience. A classic study by Gesell and Thompson (1929) demonstrated that although children could be taught basic motor skills (climbing steps) at an earlier age than untutored siblings, their superiority in these abilities quickly disappeared when the untutored children were given the opportunity to practice the task. Cross-cultural studies (Kagan, 1984) have also demonstrated that culturally determined expectations and opportunities for practice influence the age at which infants achieve such motor milestones as walking. Again, however, these differences appear to be rather modest and to have little effect on motor capabilities at later ages.

COGNITIVE DEVELOPMENT

Even at birth, infants appear to have considerable capacity to learn and remember. Siqueland and Lipsitt (1966) demonstrated that children as young as 2 days old could learn a head-turning response to an auditory stimulus when reinforced with dextrose, and infants 6 months old have been shown capable of remembering visual stimuli for a period of 2 weeks (Fagan, 1973). Despite this evidence of impressive early abilities, preschool children do have significant limitations in their cognitive processes. Their memories are not as good as they will become. At 3 years of age, a child can hold only three items in short-term memory storage, as opposed to six items for a 10-year-old and as many as eight for an adult (Case, Kurland,

& Goldberg, 1982). Time delays appear to interfere more with younger infants' problem-solving abilities than with those of older infants. One study (Kagan, 1979) found that 7-month-old infants could solve a toy-finding problem if they were delayed 3 seconds before being allowed to search for the toy, but were unsuccessful if they were delayed for 7 seconds. Ten-month-old infants could solve the problem even with the 7-second delay.

Piaget (1963) described cognitive development during the first 2 years of life as occurring primarily through integration of sensory perceptions and motor responses. He viewed development during the "Sensorimotor Stage" as progressing through six discrete phases. Piaget believed that, during the first month of life, neonates interact with their environment primarily through reflexive response patterns and that initial cognitive development consists of modification of these reflexes in response to biological maturation and environmental demands.

Piaget described the second phase of cognitive development, occurring from 1 to 4 months of age, as focused primarily on what he called "primary circular reactions." These are motor responses based on reflexes that are actively repeated because of the stimulation and pleasure they produce. These motor responses are modified and elaborated, and the initial coordination of different motor actions is seen. Over this time period, motor responses begin to appear less reflexive and more purposeful, although the infant's primary concern continues to be with his or her own body rather than the external environment.

The third phase of cognitive development, according to Piaget, is marked by the development of "secondary circular reactions" during the fourth to eighth months of life. These behavior patterns are similar to the primary circular reactions exhibited during the prior phase of development except that the major focus of stimulation and pleasure is the effect on the external environment rather than the effect on the infant's own body. A focus on the external environment marks the beginning of the development of the concept of "object permanence," or the recognition that objects and other people have a continuing existence separate from that of the child. Piaget also noted the development during this phase of the beginnings of a sense of "anticipation" in infants for regular or clearly signaled events in their environment. This sense of anticipation serves as the foundation for the development of an appreciation of cause and effect at a later point.

Piaget characterized the fourth phase (8 to 12 months) as consisting primarily of the combination and coordination of secondary circular reactions into more complex and efficient behavioral patterns, which continue to be elaborated and modified by environmental demands. The purposeful nature of behavior increases, and anticipation and understanding of causality improves. Piaget described behavior during this phase as being stereotypic and lacking in flexibility. An example of the type of cognitive errors infants make during this phase of development is the "AnotB error," in which infants perseverate in a previously reinforced behavior (looking in an adult's left hand for a toy) even though the conditions of reinforcement have clearly changed (the toy has been visibly transferred to the adult's right hand).

Piaget described the focus of the fifth phase, occurring between 12 and 18 months, as being on what he termed "tertiary circular reactions." These are purposeful variations and combinations of earlier, simpler behavioral responses that are implemented in a trial-and-error fashion in response to environmental events. Although the child's abstraction and problem-solving abilities are still limited during this phase, cognition is less stereotyped and rigid than before and the understanding of object permanence is further developed. For example, children at this age will no longer make the "AnotB error" they made in the previous phase if the toy is visibly transferred to the other hand. They will, however, continue to choose the wrong hand if the transfer of the toy is not visible to them.

From 18 to 24 months, according to Piaget, children in the sixth phase of cognitive development first begin to engage in symbolic thought. This means that children can "try out" solutions to their problems mentally rather than engaging in overt trial-and-error problem solving and that solutions that have never actually been attempted may be successfully implemented on the first try. Because of this newfound ability to engage in symbolic thought, children are now capable of "true" object permanence, in which they can infer the location of an unseen object, even when they have not observed it being moved. Another characteristic of this phase of cognitive development is the capability for "deferred imitation," in which children duplicate behaviors of others that they have observed at an earlier time.

Piaget considered children to be in what he called the "Preoperational Stage" of cognitive development, from the age of 2 throughout the preschool period. He believed that, during this stage, children became more adept at representational or symbolic thought and developed better understanding of relationships and variations in their environment. However, Piaget still saw children below the age of 7 as being largely "egocentric," or unable to appreciate the perspective of others. Two other cognitive characteristics of the preschool period, according to Piaget, are "animism" and "artificialism." Animism is the attribution of human or animal-like characteristics to inanimate objects. Children this age may blame their toys when they become broken, or they may tell the clouds to stop raining. Artificialism is the conception that the entire world has been created by humans (or a human-like deity) and arranged for human use. Frequently, a child this age will ask questions such as "Why are they making it cold today?" reflecting the belief that humans are in charge of all natural phenomena. Another related cognitive misconception of this age group is called "immanent justice." This is the belief that there is an innate system of justice in the world and that good and bad outcomes are meted out according to reason. When misfortune occurs to someone, it is the result of some wrongdoing on that person's part, and conversely, positive events occur as rewards for some laudable action.

One aspect of preschool cognition that has been extensively studied is classification skills. Preschoolers can generally classify objects accurately according to one dimension. They experience difficulty, however, if asked to classify objects that vary on more than one dimension or if the classification task is a more complex one. An example of a more complex classification task with which preschoolers experience difficulty is the class inclusion task (Piaget & Inhelder, 1969). Although preschoolers are easily able to separate white buttons from black buttons, they may have difficulty accurately answering the question "Are there more black buttons or more buttons?"

In his early observations (Inhelder & Piaget, 1958), Piaget noted that preoperational children did not grasp the concept of reversibility and its corollary, conservation. These preschoolers usually cannot follow a set of procedures backward (either actually or mentally) and see that two apparently dissimilar conditions are actually equivalent. Piaget's classic example involved pouring liquid from a tall, thin container into a wider container and asking children if the amount was the same. Piaget found that a majority of children under the age of 6 responded incorrectly that the amounts were different. By contrast, questions involving nonreversible phenomena (Is a candle the same candle after it burns to a stub?) can usually be accurately answered by age 5 (Flavell, Green, & Flavell, 1986). Preschoolers tend to have changing and imperfect concepts of quantity as well. Three- and 4-year-olds who were asked to sort the numbers one through nine into the categories small, medium, and large responded very differently. Three-year-olds tended to classify one as a small number and all others as large. Four-year-olds classified one through four as small, with the other numbers variously considered as medium or large (Murray & Mayer, 1988). Similarly, time concepts are developing throughout the preschool period, with 3-year-old children having little ability to differentiate much more than "now" and "later," and 6-year-olds being able to understand such concepts as "this afternoon," "tomorrow," and "next week."

LANGUAGE DEVELOPMENT

The precursors of language in infants appear fairly soon after birth. Infants as young as 1 month of age are able to differentiate between different phoneme sounds (Eimas & Miller, 1980). Sanger (1955) found that infants responded to the sound of the human voice before the age of 2 months, and beginning between the ages of 2 and 4 months they stopped their own vocalizations in order to listen to adults' speech.

Infants' vocalizations consist largely of grunts and crying for the first few months of life. Beginning in the third month, cooing, a more articulated sound, begins to be produced. This is followed, between 4 and 8 months of age, by more complex patterns of babbling, which often appear to mimic adult speech in their intonation and pacing. Babbling usually persists into the second year of life and often continues even after real speech has emerged. Research has shown the importance of adult language stimulation during this stage on later language capabilities.

Children's first words generally appear somewhere around their first birthday; however, there is considerable variability in this schedule, and parents may have difficulty differentiating true first words from babbling. Usually children are able to understand the meaning of a number of words before they begin speaking themselves. Most children's first words are concrete nouns that describe food, toys, animals, and people that are present at the time of utterance. Words may be voiced initially without much understanding of their meaning. From the point of speaking their first words, most children rapidly add to their expressive vocabulary. By the age of 18 months, the average child uses between 3 and 50 words with considerable accuracy and has begun to use pairings of two or even three words (DeVilliers & DeVilliers, 1978). These pairings are often not true sentences when initially used, but usually by the age of 2 they evolve into "telegraphic sentences" with more complete structure, even though they lack prepositions, conjunctions and tense endings. Children as young as 2½ years old demonstrate the ability to form plurals by adding "s," even for nonsense words they have never heard before (Berko, 1958). By the age of 3, children are capable of carrying on complex conversations on a variety of topics. Speech at this age is characterized by errors caused by overgeneralization of speech rules. For example, children will attempt to use regular tense endings even when an irregular form is correct ("I buyed this toy"). By age 4, the telegraphic quality of children's speech largely disappears as they begin to make greater use of conjunctions and prepositions.

SOCIAL AND EMOTIONAL DEVELOPMENT

Infants appear to have innate socialization tendencies. Soon after birth they demonstrate a preference for human voices and faces over nonhuman auditory and visual stimuli (Brazelton, 1976) and are able to distinguish their mother's face from a stranger's (Field, Cohen, Garcia, & Greenberg, 1984) and maintain eye contact with their mothers (Tronick, 1989). Although reflexive smiling occurs in infants during the first month of life, it is not until the second or third month of life that true "social" smiling occurs, usually as a greeting to a caretaker or in response to pleasurable environmental stimulation (Lewis & Coates, 1980). From the fourth to the sixth months of life, occurrence of this social smiling becomes more selective, and anxiety and withdrawal from unfamiliar people begins to occur (Smith, Eaton, & Hindmarch, 1982). Until this time, infants are fairly indiscriminately attached to whomever they are with. After this time, however, they show increasing preference for particular people, especially their primary caretakers. By 6 months of age, most infants are capable of some interactive play, with elements of social imitation and turn taking evident.

Ainsworth (1979) investigated attachment in young children (those old enough to crawl or walk) and found that infants varied considerably in the extent to which they were attached to parental figures. She classified children as being "securely attached," "anxious–resistant," or "anxious–avoidant." Securely attached infants (70% of all infants studied) would turn to their mothers for comfort as needed, but they also moved away from their mothers and explored the environment on occasion. They exhibited little anxiety when their mothers were away for short periods of time but became happily excited when their mothers returned. Anxious–resistant infants (10% of all infants studied) did not move away from their mothers to explore the environment and became upset when their mothers left them, even for brief periods of time. These children often did not appear to be pleased when their mothers returned, sometimes even pushing them away. Anxious–avoidant infants (20% of all infants studied) appeared to have little attachment to their mothers and demonstrated little distress when their mothers left them alone. They also demonstrated little emotion when their mothers returned, often ignoring them completely. Research has shown that these patterns of attachment are fairly stable. Londerville and Main (1981) found that securely attached children complied better with parental rules at 2 years of age and were more willing to accept parental help with problems. Securely attached children have been found to be more likely to seek attention in positive ways in preschool at age 4 (Sroufe, Fox, & Pancake, 1983). By contrast, insecure attachment has been found to be associated with behavior problems in preschool (Sroufe et al., 1983).

Bowlby (1969) has described early social attachment as occurring in a series of discrete phases that appear to coincide fairly well with empirical observations. Bowlby's first phase, which he titled "Indiscriminate Sociability" was described as lasting from birth through the first 2 months of life. During this phase, infants demonstrate a number of social behaviors, but they are displayed indiscriminately and without much sense of reciprocity.

The second phase of social development, which Bowlby called the phase of "Attachments in the Making," was envisioned as lasting from 2 to 7 months of age. During this phase, infants begin to demonstrate social preferences for certain individuals, usually the primary caretakers. Temporary separations from these preferred adults are usually tolerated fairly well, however, and anxiety at attention from strangers is not well developed.

The third phase, which Bowlby called the stage of "Specific, Clear-cut Attachments," lasts from 7 through 24 months of age. During this phase, attachments for specific people become strongly developed. This results in the emergence of both separation anxiety and stranger anxiety.

Bowlby called the fourth phase, which lasts from 24 months on, the phase of "Goal-Coordinated Partnerships." During this phase, children become more capable of flexible and appropriate attachments and true cooperative play. They are better able to appreciate the needs and perspectives of others and begin developing the ability to tolerate caretaker absences.

Waters and Sroufe (1983) described the development of social competence in preschoolers as progressing through six phases. During the first 3 months of life, issues of physiological regulation are primary, and the role of the caretaker is to meet the infant's basic needs. From the third to sixth months, issues of basic tension management are foremost in importance, with the caretaker aiding this process by engaging in sensitive, cooperative interactions with the infant. The interaction during these two phases optimally achieves something similar to Erikson's (1963) "basic trust." From 6 months to 1 year of age, infants are focused on establishing rewarding attachment relationships, with responsive availability on the part of caretakers crucial to the process. From 12 to 18 months of age, exploration and mastery activities are of primary importance in the development of social competence. During this time period, it is important that caretakers provide a secure and reliable "home base" from which these explorations can be launched. During the period from 1½ to 2½ years of age, Waters and Sroufe (1983) view the primary task of social development to be that of individuation, with caretakers providing firm support and feedback. Finally, the sixth phase, from 2½ to 4½ years of age, is concerned with learning how to control socially unacceptable impulses, gender-role identification, and the development of peer relationship skills. Caretakers are important during this time period for the modeling and instruction they can provide in the areas of social roles and values, and for the firm but flexible control they exert over the child's behavior.

Sigmund Freud (1965) also discussed emotional and personality development during the preschool years, with a focus on sources of pleasure and gratification. He viewed the first 2 years of life as being a period during which gratification was derived largely through oral activities such as sucking, eating, and during the later part of this phase, biting.

For children ages 2 to 4, Freud viewed the focus of gratification as shifting to the process of elimination, with pleasure resulting from both the production and retention of feces. This stage also marked for Freud the first application of adult standards of social behavior (toileting) to children, and he believed that parental management of toilet training was critical to the child's personality development.

Freud believed that from ages 4 to 6, the critical element of children's emotional development was their awareness of their genitals and the derivation of gratification by manipulating them. Freud saw this as the age at which sex-role identification and primary identification with the same-sex parent emerged.

Another theoretical conception that focuses on social and emotional development during the preschool years is Erik Erikson's psychosocial theory (1963). Erikson believed that during a child's first year of life, either a basic trust or a basic mistrust in the benignness of the world develops. Trust results from the dependability of caretakers in meeting the child's fundamental needs (food, warmth, affection) and in not allowing unreasonable amounts of pain or discomfort to occur. Mistrust results from neglect of or delay in meeting these basic needs, or other insensitivity to the child's demands. Abuse or punitive discipline can also result in the development of basic mistrust. Erikson viewed the first year of life as a critical period for the development of basic trust and believed that if children did not receive appropriate nurturance at that time, they would have extreme difficulty later developing open and trusting attachments, regardless of their life experiences after the first year of life.

Erikson's second stage of psychosocial development, which occurs between ages 1 and 3, concerns the conflict between autonomy and shame or doubt. During this stage, children become aware of their autonomy from parental figures, but also become aware of their limitations and dependence on parents. At times, the child's desire for autonomy creates conflict with parental standards of behavior, and the resulting negative feedback and/or punishment can create self-doubt and a sense of shame.

The third of Erikson's stages of psychosocial development occurs between the ages of 3 and 6 and is focused on the conflict between initiative and guilt. Children at this age become more active in planning and undertaking their own activities and are even more independent of their parents' direction. Parents can support this initiative, or they can undermine their child's newfound sense of independence, creating guilt over autonomous activity. Erikson viewed this psychosocial developmental process as a cumulative one, with resolution of the basic conflict at each age leading to the next level of psychosocial development.

CARETAKER AND FAMILY VARIABLES

Caretaker and sibling interactions play a critical role in shaping preschoolers' personalities and behavioral patterns. Among the important elements in these interactions are the degree of guidance and instruction the child receives, the quality of emotional interactions, and the type of discipline employed. Research from the Harvard Preschool Project (White et al., 1973) established that some children could be described as socially and cognitively "competent" by age 3 and that the mothers of these children demonstrated certain characteristics in contrast to the mothers of "incompetent" children. The mothers of the competent preschoolers appeared to enjoy their children and talked to them frequently on a level they could understand. They allowed their children to develop autonomy and engage in mildly risky behavior, and they set reasonable limits. Mothers of incompetent preschoolers provided less stimulation for their children and were often either overprotective or ignoring of their child.

Becker (1964) investigated the consequences on children's personalities and behavior of being raised by mothers who varied on the two orthogonal dimensions of acceptance–rejection and permissiveness–restrictiveness. He found that children raised by permissive–accepting mothers were generally independent, outgoing, creative, friendly, and active. Children raised by permissive–rejecting mothers were generally aggressive, hostile, and noncompliant and frequently demonstrated delinquent behaviors later in childhood. Children raised by restrictive–accepting mothers tended to be dependent, obedient, and compliant. Children raised by restrictive–rejecting mothers tended to be socially withdrawn, inhibited, and quarrelsome, and to demonstrate self-hostility.

Baumrind (1980) has characterized several styles of parental discipline. He described "authoritarian" parents as enforcing a rigidly set code of conduct, with an emphasis on obedience and punitive discipline. He described "authoritative" parents as also firmly directing their children's behavior, but in a more rational, interactive fashion. Finally, "permissive" parents were described as being nonpunitive, with child involvement in rule setting, and a great deal of tolerance of child misbehavior. Research has shown that the authoritative parenting style is more likely to yield children who are independent, self-confident, and sensitive to the needs of others (Baumrind, 1980), while authoritarian parenting may yield conformity and submissiveness, or rebelliousness, and permissive parenting may produce selfish and immature behavior in children (Kochanska, Kuczynski, & Radke-Yarrow, 1989).

The presence or absence of the father in the home appears to exert a significant effect on the development of the children. Children raised in homes without fathers do less well on IQ tests than children raised in two-parent homes (Biller, 1974), and the presence and involvement of fathers also appears to be important in the development of appropriate sex-role behaviors (Langlois & Downs, 1980).

Children's interactions with siblings and peers during the preschool years are also extremely important. Younger siblings often try to imitate the behavior of their older brothers and sisters and may learn both cognitive and social lessons through this modeling (Dunn, 1983). Children who have been exposed to same-age peers in day care as infants have been found to be more demanding, independent, and assertive, and less willing to comply with adult directives than children who have not been in day care (Clarke-Stewart, 1989). Shea (1981) observed 3- and 4-year-olds during their first 10 weeks of preschool and found that they gradually became more independent of the teacher, more playful and outgoing, and less aggressive with each other. These changes in social behavior were more significant for children who attended the preschool 5 days a week than for those children who attended only 2 days per week.

Socialization abilities during early childhood are a fairly good predictor of these abilities later in life. Roff (1974) found that preschoolers who are consistently rejected by their peers run a much higher risk of emotional disturbance later in life, although the direction of causality is uncertain in these findings. Socialization abilities during the preschool years do appear to be somewhat amenable to remediation, however. Kerby and Tolar (1970), for instance, found that they could increase the social contacts of a withdrawn 5-year-old boy by giving him a bag of candy that he was directed to distribute to his preschool classmates. After distributing the candy, he was praised and rewarded for his efforts. After several days, observations during free play indicated that the boy had become more outgoing and cooperative with the other children.

GENDER IDENTITY

By age 2, most children are clearly able to identify themselves as "boys" or "girls," even if they are somewhat unclear what these designations mean (Money & Ehrhardt, 1972). By age 3, clear sex differences in toy selection and play patterns are evident, and by age 5, children often can express stereotypic opinions regarding the gender appropriateness of adult occupations and activities (Huston, 1983). Preschoolers like same-sex children more and prefer them as playmates. Jacklin and Maccoby (1978) found that, even when all children were dressed identically and adults had difficulty determining their gender, preschoolers were more likely to play with children of their same sex. They also found that girls were more likely to withdraw from play and watch if their partner was a boy and that boys were more likely to physically dispute ownership of a toy with other boys than with girls.

Research suggests that gender identity is greatly influenced by parental attitudes. For instance, Tauber (1979) found that fathers respond more positively to physical activity in boys than in girls, while mothers respond more positively to affection and physical contact from girls than from boys. Fathers appear to be more active in establishing and maintaining stereotypic gender-role behavior than mothers, particularly with boys. Langlois and Downs (1980) observed parental reactions to preschoolers' play with stereotypic male or female toys and found that fathers rewarded gender-appropriate play and terminated gender-inappropriate play, especially with boys. In contrast, mothers were inconsistent in their reactions to both gender-appropriate and gender-inappropriate play. Parents tend to have higher expectations of boys than girls and to require more independence of boys (Block, 1979). They respond more quickly to requests for help from girls and focus more on the interpersonal aspects of activities than on the skill aspects (Rothbart & Rothbart, 1976).

FOUNDATIONS OF PSYCHOPATHOLOGY

It is apparent from the above material that the preschool years are critical in the development of basic cognitive, social, and behavioral capabilities. It is during these years that mental health problems often first become evident in children. Jenkins, Bax, and Hart (1980) studied parents' concerns about their preschoolers in a nonclinical sample and found significant reports of behavioral problems. During infancy, the number of concerns expressed was fairly low, with the primary areas of worry being infant crying, eating, and sleeping patterns. During the second year of life, expressions of parental concern became more frequent, with eating and sleeping patterns still the primary focus. From age 2 to 3, the primary focus of parental concerns became bowel and bladder control, while after age 3 social behavior and discipline became the major concerns. Richman, Stevenson, and Graham (1982) found that approximately 13% of English 3-year-olds were described by their mothers as restless and overactive, and almost 11% were described as difficult to control. Follow-up demonstrated that behavior problems persisted in a significant percentage of the children identified as having difficulties at age 3. At age 4, 63% were identified by parental ratings as still having problems and at age 8, 62% were still described as problematic. Teachers also rated the 8-year-olds who had been identified as being difficult to control at age 3 as having more behavior problems than children who had not been described as problematic as preschoolers.

Other longitudinal studies have confirmed the stability of behavioral problems from the preschool years to later childhood. Teachers rated hyperactive preschoolers as more aggressive and hyperactive than other children at ages 6 and 7 (Campbell, Endman, & Bernfeld, 1977). Later research by Campbell (1990) suggests that two-thirds of hard-to-manage 6-year-olds will continue to have problems at age 9. Fischer, Hand, and Russell (1984) found that preschool reports of aggression were associated with parental reports of behavior problems 5 to 7 years later. Lerner, Inui, Trupin, and Douglas (1985) also reported that severe behavior problems in preschool were predictive of a variety of behavioral problems during adolescence. Parental psychopathology, harsh child-rearing practices, and marital discord are associated with a poorer prognosis for continued behavior problems in preschoolers who are difficult to control (Wallander, 1988).

Other forms of psychopathology also clearly have their roots in the preschool years. For instance, research by Solyom, Beck, Solyom, and Hugel (1974) has suggested that preschool anxiety problems may continue until later in life. Similarly, autism usually first becomes apparent in the preschool years (Kolvin, 1971), and psychosis and conduct disorders may be first noted during this time period (Wenar, 1990).

PREVENTION PROGRAMS

A number of programs have been implemented during the preschool years that attempt to prevent the occurrence of later mental health problems in either unselected or "at-risk" children. Perhaps the best known of these programs is Project Head Start, begun by the U.S. federal government in 1965. Head Start is discussed in Chapter 2. Jason (1977) developed a preschool prevention program that has demonstrated benefits in academic skills, social interaction, and motor skills. This program involved both children and parents and used sessions in the child's home as well as at a health center. Children were taught a series of lessons that emphasized language development, while parents were involved in group sessions in which child-rearing issues were discussed.

Risley also developed a preschool prevention model that emphasized the development of language and social skills. Techniques used in this program were effective in increasing children's spontaneous speech, response to teacher questions, and social skills (Risley, Reynolds, & Hart, 1970). Similarly, Spivack, Platt, and Shure (1976) were effective in increasing interpersonal problem-solving and adjustment abilities through a preschool prevention program that emphasized language and cognitive abilities applied to social situations.

It is apparent from the above discussion that many mental health problems in children first become evident during the preschool years, if we are observant, and that the foundation for later childhood and adult mental health problems is set. Significant mental health problems in preschool children are seldom "outgrown" without intervention. Fortunately, there exist a number of assessment and intervention techniques with demonstrated effectiveness with preschool children. In the following chapters, we will discuss a variety of mental health problems as they present in the preschool child, with an emphasis on the developmental context within which they occur, the assessment of significant versus nonsignificant deviations from normality, and the design and implementation of effective intervention programs.

2

Learning Problems

Learning problems in preschoolers generally separate into two categories. First are the global disabilities in cognitive processing that are labeled mental retardation or developmental disabilities and that usually manifest themselves fairly early in the child's life and affect a broad range of cognitive skills. Second are the more specific and limited learning problems that affect only a narrow range of cognitive tasks and are usually not detected until the child enters an organized academic environment. These are labeled specific learning disabilities.

Assessment and diagnosis of learning problems in preschoolers must be accomplished within the context of familiarity with cognitive development during the preschool years and with knowledge regarding the significance of deviations from expectations for normal cognitive development. In this chapter, we will briefly discuss the normal process of cognitive development during the preschool years and discuss etiological factors involved in both mental retardation and learning disabilities. We will then discuss assessment instruments and procedures and their use in diagnosing and differentiating these conditions. Finally, interventions that have proven effective with mentally retarded and learning disabled children during the preschool years will be presented.

COGNITIVE DEVELOPMENT

As outlined in Chapter 1, the process of cognitive development is fairly similar in most children, with responsiveness to sensory stimulation and ability to recognize and remember stimuli as significant indicators of cognitive progress during the first months of life (Siqueland & Lipsett, 1966). Progression of motor responses from simple reflexes to complex volitional patterns also serves as a significant indicator of cognitive progress during the first year of life, with the average child walking alone by his or her first birthday (Bayley, 1969). Following the first year of life, cognitive development is indexed primarily through an assessment of language. Children's first words usually appear around 1 year of age and consist primarily of concrete nouns. By age 2, most children are combining words into short sentences and have a vocabulary of up to 300 words (DeVilliers & DeVilliers, 1978). Also by age 2, most children have begun engaging in symbolic thought (Piaget, 1963) and are, therefore, able to problem solve mentally rather than overtly. They are also capable of deferred imitation and object permanence. Children throughout the preschool years, however, are largely unable to appreciate the perspectives of others or proceed from hypothetical premises (Piaget, 1963). Preschoolers also usually experience difficulty understanding the concepts of reversibility and conservation (Inhelder & Piaget, 1958) and have problems with more complex classification tasks (Piaget & Inhelder, 1969).

There is tremendous variability in the ages by which children achieve cognitive developmental milestones, and practitioners should be cautious about diagnosing developmental problems based solely on a child's inability to accomplish a cognitive task by a certain age. Some researchers in the field (Satz & Fletcher, 1981) differentiate among "developmental deficits," "developmental delays," and "developmental lags." Developmental deficits are defined as deficits in level of performance that persist past the stage during which a behavior or concept is being learned, while a developmental delay is viewed as a delay in the onset of the process of learning a behavior or concept that may not result in any deficit in the final level of performance. Developmental lags are defined as deficits in the rate of learning a behavior or concept that may or may not affect the final performance level.

MENTAL RETARDATION

Definition

Over the years there have been a number of definitions of mental retardation. Some of these definitions rely almost entirely on evaluations of a child's performance on standardized intelligence tests, while others also include consideration of social and functional variables (Grossman, 1983). The American Association on Mental Retardation (AAMR) currently uses a definition that focuses on both measured intelligence and adaptive behavior and requires that significant deficits in both of these areas be present prior to the age of 18 for mental retardation to be diagnosed. This definition has been incorporated into the American Psychiatric Association's *Diagnostic and Statistical Manual of Mental Disorders* (DSM-III-R; APA, 1987) and used in Public Law 94–142, which mandates special education services for exceptional children.

Classification of degrees of mental retardation has also focused on impairment in measured intelligence and adaptive abilities. The AAMR classification schema (Grossman, 1983) includes four levels of retardation that are differentiated by tested IQ and behavioral competencies. This classification schema considers mild retardation to exist when IQ scores range from 55 to 69 (for IQ tests with a standard deviation of 15) and when affected individuals can develop social and communication skills and are only minimally affected in sensory-motor areas. Mild mental retardation is often not distinguished until school enrollment. Moderate retardation is characterized by IQ scores from 40 to 54 and the ability to talk and/or communicate. Individuals with moderate retardation usually have fair motor skills and poor social awareness. They can profit from training in self-help skills but usually require some degree of continuing supervision. Severe retardation is characterized by IQ scores ranging from 25 to 39 and poor motor development and minimal language and communication skills. Individuals with severe retardation often show little benefit from training in self-help skills and require close supervision. Profound retardation is characterized by IQ scores under 25 and minimal capacity for motor and sensory functioning. Communications abilities are largely absent, and intensive care is necessary. Educational agencies often use a similar classification schema in which mild and moderate retardation are termed "educable" and "trainable," respectively.

Prevalence

Because of the varying definitions of retardation and classification schemas used over the years, it has been difficult to arrive at consistent estimates of the number of preschool children who are mentally retarded. In addition, a number of retarded children are not identified until they enter school. Overall, approximately 3% of the U.S. population is classified as mentally retarded (Grossman, 1983); however, one study found that only 0.45% of children below the age of 5 were so classified, compared with 4% of children aged 5 to 9 and 8% of children aged 10 to 14 (New York State Department of Mental Hygiene, 1955). Mental retardation has also been shown to be more prevalent in males, in minority group members, and in the poor. Children in the mild range of impairment make up the vast majority of those classified as retarded. Grossman (1983) estimated that of the total retarded population, 86% was mildly retarded, 10% was moderately retarded, and 4% was severely or profoundly retarded.

Cultural–Familial Retardation

Over 75% of all retarded children are diagnosed as having retardation resulting from environmental influences or other unknown conditions, with the majority being classified as having cultural–familial retardation. This means that their retardation is not attributable to specific biological or genetic factors and that they have at least one parent or sibling who is mentally retarded. Well over half of the children classified as culturally familially retarded are in the mildly retarded range of functioning (Hutt & Gibby, 1979). Cultural–familial retardation appears to have both genetic and environmental causes. Such environmental factors as early verbal stimulation, parent–child relationship, and family structure and size have been shown to be related to child intellectual functioning. However, research has also shown that natural parents and their children have more similar IQ scores than adoptive or foster parents and the children, even when the children are removed to adoptive or foster homes early in their lives (Horn, Loehlin, & Willerman, 1975). Thus, it appears that both genetic and environmental variables are significant.

Retardation Associated with Genetic Abnormalities

Specific genetic abnormalities make up the next largest group of retarded children. Down syndrome, the most common specific genetic retardation syndrome, is not the result of a genetically transmitted trait, but rather the result of an aberration in the chromosomal replication process. This aberration can result in an extra 21st chromosome (trisomy), detachment of genetic material from one chromosome and reattachment to another (translocation), or a mixed pattern of normal chromosomal material in some cells and trisomies in others (mosaicism). The mosaic form of Down syndrome results in the highest IQs, while trisomy results in the lowest IQs. Trisomy is the most common form of Down syndrome, accounting for over 90% of the cases. It is strongly correlated with maternal age, occuring in almost 7 births out of 10,000 for mothers in their early 20s and in over 180 births out of 10,000 for mothers who are 40 or older (Cahalane, 1989). The parents of Down syndrome children are usually genetically normal, although when mothers with Down syndrome bear children, approximately half are affected with the syndrome (Crome & Stern, 1967).

The clinical manifestations of Down syndrome include skeletal, joint, muscle, and organ abnormalities in addition to intellectual deficits. Usually, stature is small, with the head also small and flattened in the rear. There is an upward slant to the eyes, often with speckling of the iris (Brushfield spots) and epicanthal folds, or skin flaps, on the inner corner of the eyes. The tongue often protrudes because of a small mouth cavity, the ears are commonly small with absent lobes, and the bridge of the nose is flattened. Other common physical stigmata include short, spade-like hands, with a curved little finger and a single palmar crease, and a wide separation between the first and second toes. Down syndrome children usually demonstrate a deficit in muscle tone and hyperflexibility of the joints. Congenital heart deficits occur in over one-third of Down syndrome infants, resulting in a 43% mortality rate during the first year of life (Baroff, 1986). Down syndrome children are also more likely than the general population to have leukemia and are more susceptible to respiratory infections.

Intellectual deficits in Down syndrome children are usually recognized during the first year of life. IQ measures at 1 year are generally in the mildly retarded range, while by age 4 they have dropped to the moderately retarded range, and by age 13 the average IQ is within the range of severe retardation (Melyn & White, 1973). This decline in IQ scores appears to reflect the increasingly verbal nature of IQ test items at higher ages rather than actual mental deterioration. Higher IQs are generally seen in children reared at home rather than in institutions (Melyn & White, 1973). Female Down syndrome children exceed males by about five IQ points on the average (Clements, Bates, & Hafer, 1976).

The developmental delays associated with Down syndrome are apparent in virtually all behaviors. Gross-motor skills are among the least affected, and generally Down syndrome children are able to achieve such milestones as sitting and walking not long after unaffected children. By contrast, such fine-motor skills as tying knots and buttoning buttons are often significantly impaired. Self-help skills are also commonly deficient, with Down syndrome children usually 1 to 2 years behind unaffected children in the acquisition of such self-help skills as feeding, dressing, and toileting. Speech and language comprehension represent the areas of greatest deficit for Down syndrome children. Their articulation is commonly poor, and often, speech complexity is also impaired. The speech of many Down syndrome children at age 5 or 6 consists primarily of 1- or 2-word utterances, such as those characterisitic of 1- or 2-year-old unaffected children.

Generally, Down syndrome individuals demonstrate good adjustment in both institutional and community settings. The most common problems noted are short attention span, hyperactivity, low frustration tolerance, and emotional distress in response to changes in the environment.

Another set of mental retardation syndromes results from chromosomal replication errors involving the sex chromosomes rather than the autosomes. Among these is Klinefelter syndrome, in which an individual who is biologically male has an additional X chromosome. This disorder occurs once in every 600 live male births. Children with Klinefelter syndrome typically present with slim body proportions, long legs, and small testes. Behavior problems are common with this disorder, and intellectual functioning is usually in the low average to mildly retarded range (Nielson, 1970). Often, testosterone replacement therapy is necessary in early adolescence in order for individuals with Klinefelter syndrome to maintain their secondary sex characteristics.

Females can also be born with excess X chromosomes. As many as three extra X chromosomes (XXXXX) have been found. These abnormalities occur in approximately 1 out of every 850 births. The presence of a single extra X chromosome may not result in any retardation or physical stigmata; however, with increasing numbers of extra chromosomes there is increased risk of retardation. With two extra chromosomes (XXXX), the usual IQ range is from 30 to 80 with a mean of 55 (Howard-Peebles & Markiton, 1979).

Another abnormality of the sex chromosomes that may result in mental retardation is called the "Fragile X" syndrome (Turner, Daniel, & Frost, 1980). In this disorder, the X chromosome is constricted near the end of the long arm, making it vulnerable to breakage and faulty replication. Males with this disorder commonly demonstrate mental retardation, usually at least moderate in severity, and enlarged testes. Females with Fragile X syndrome usually demonstrate no physical abnormalities, and only one-third demonstrate mild retardation. Fragile X syndrome represents approximately 2% of the retarded population. In one study of mildly retarded girls without physical abnormalities, 7% had Fragile X syndrome (Turner, Daniel, & Frost, 1980). Fragile X syndrome ranks second only to Down syndrome in chromosomal disorders causing retardation.

Phenylketonuria (PKU) is an example of a heritable genetic condition, rather than a condition resulting from errors in chromosome replication. PKU is a recessive disorder and thus requires that both parents transmit the gene for the trait before the disorder expresses itself. The condition is relatively rare, occurring in 1 out of every 10,000 newborns. This suggests that the recessive gene for the disorder is present in 1 of every 54 individuals in the general population. Individuals who carry one gene for PKU (carriers) are perfectly normal. If two such individuals bear children, there is a 1 in 4 risk that each child will have PKU, and a 1 in 2 risk that each child will be a carrier of the trait. It occurs equally in males and females. PKU causes a deficiency of an enzyme that converts an amino acid called phenylalanine into another substance called tyrosine. If untreated, PKU usually results in severe to profound retardation, although some cases of individuals with normal intelligence have been reported. PKU children often demonstrate stereotypic behaviors, including rocking and hand flapping, and they have been reported to be more aggressive and hyperactive than other children of equivalent mental age (Johnson, 1969). There are no obvious physical stigmata associated with PKU, although affected children usually are somewhat microcephalic and have very light coloring and eyes. A musty odor in the urine is also usually present, as a result of excessive excretion of phenylalanine.

PKU is rare among mental retardation syndromes because of its preventability. Elevated levels of phenylalanine can be detected in the blood or urine of newborns, and it is now possible to detect the disorder prenatally. Placement of the child on a low-phenylalanine diet prevents the buildup of excessive amounts of the substance and the resulting central nervous system damage. The quickness with which the diet is implemented appears to be critical in the eventual level of cognitive functioning. Children who are placed on the diet within the first 13 weeks of life later have an average IQ score of 89, while those who are placed on the diet at an age of 27 to 156 weeks later have an average IQ score of 50, and those who are placed on the diet after 3 years of age later have an average IQ score of 26 (Baumeister, 1967).

Maintenance of children on the low-phenylalanine diet is extremely difficult. It has been traditionally assumed that the diet could be terminated at age 5 or 6 without any negative effects; however, research has indicated that children experience 9- to 12-point IQ declines following removal from the diet at that age (Berry, O'Grady, Perlmutter, & Bofinger, 1979). As a result of these findings, current practice recommends keeping a PKU child on the low-phenylalanine diet until the age of 12.

Retardation Associated with Prenatal Factors

A number of variables in the prenatal environment can affect later cognitive capabilities. Maternal diabetes, for example, can result in neurological deficits in the child, depending on the severity of the mother's diabetic condition, how well controlled it is by medication or diet, the child's gestational age when born, and the presence of other complications during pregnancy and delivery. Similarly, hyperbilirubinemia can result from both Rh and ABO incompatibility between mother and fetus, as well as other causes such as prematurity, and, if untreated, can result in neurological damage and retardation.

Several maternal infections, including rubella, toxoplasmosis, syphilis, and cytomegalovirus can also result in later retardation for the child. Approximately half of all children whose mothers have rubella during their pregnancy demonstrate some degree of mental retardation, varying from borderline to profound (Chess, Korn, & Fernandez, 1971). The period of greatest fetal vulnerability for both rubella and toxoplasmosis is the first trimester of pregnancy, while for syphilis the period of greatest vulnerability is the last trimester.

Drug and alcohol use during pregnancy are among the most common causes for later retardation in the child. Fetal alcohol syndrome (FAS) occurs in approximately 2 of every 1,000 births, an incidence roughly comparable to that of Down syndrome. Symptoms of FAS include craniofacial abnormalities, neurological deficits, short attention span, and mild mental retardation. In one study of heavy drinkers during pregnancy (average daily consumption of 5 ounces of alcohol), 32% of children born were found to have such congenital abnormalities (Ovellette, Rosett, Rosman, & Weiner, 1977). Babies born to these women were smaller than controls and 12% suffered from microcephaly. Among moderate drinkers (average daily consumption of 1 ounce of alcohol) in the same study, 14% of children born had congenital abnormalities, while only 8% of children born to nondrinkers had such abnormalities. Fetal vulnerability to excessive alcohol ingestion appears to be greatest during the first 6 weeks of pregnancy, a time when many women are not even aware that they are pregnant.

Maternal smoking has also been associated with fetal growth retardation and increased risk of prematurity, and some studies have also reported increased risk for school learning problems (Butler & Goldstein, 1973) and behavior problems (Dunn, McBurney, Ingram, & Hunter, 1977) in children born to heavy smokers.

Children born to heroin- and cocaine-using mothers have also been found to be at increased risk for lower birth weight, neurological deficits, short attention span, and behavioral problems (Blinick, Wallach, Jerez, & Ackerman, 1976). By contrast, however, there is little evidence of substantial and lasting negative effects on the fetus of smoking marijuana during pregnancy.

Retardation Associated with Perinatal Factors

By far the most significant perinatal factor associated with later mental retardation is premature birth and related low birth weight. Generally, infants are classified as premature if they are born before the 38th week of gestation or weigh less than 2,500 grams (about 5½ pounds). About 7 to 10% of all births are premature, with the risk much higher for nonwhite mothers, mothers who have received little or no prenatal care, mothers who are heavy cigarette smokers, and mothers younger than 20 or older than 35 (Creasy, 1990). Approximately 98% of all infants born after a gestational age of 32 weeks survive; however, the chances of survival and good health diminish with lower birth weight and gestational age. As a result, premature infants account for 75% of all neonatal deaths and have three times the risk of suffering neurological damage as full-term infants (Niswander & Gordon, 1972). Low birth weight also puts an infant at risk for later intellectual impairment. One study (Drillien, 1967) found that 58% of children with a birth weight less than 1,300 grams (about 3 pounds) had IQs of less than 80.

Mechanical injury and anoxia during the birth process have been greatly reduced by advances in obstetrics in recent years but can still occur in cases of abnormal positioning of the baby (breech, posterior, or transverse presentation), cephalopelvic disproportion, prolonged labor, or pinching of the umbilical cord. These perinatal injuries can result in a variety of motor and cognitive deficits that are collectively termed cerebral palsy. Cerebral palsy is estimated to occur in 6 of every 1,000 births in the United States. Only about half of all children diagnosed as cerebral palsied are mentally retarded, with the rest functioning within the average or above-average ranges of intelligence (Stephen & Hawks, 1974).

LEARNING DISABILITIES

Definition

Until the 1960s, children whose school performance was significantly below their perceived ability were generally described as "underachievers," with poor motivation for school work or emotional problems often accepted as causal explanations. In the 1960s, however, it became increasingly recognized that there existed a group of children with specific learning problems for whom motivational or emotional causal explanations were not adequate and who could be termed "learning disabled." The Children with Specific Learning Disabilities Act (1969) defined children with specific learning disabilities as exhibiting a disorder in a basic psychological process involved in processing or using spoken or written language. This included disorders of listening, thinking, talking, reading, writing, spelling, and arithmetic, but excluded learning problems primarily attributable to visual, hearing or motor handicaps, mental retardation, emotional disturbance, or environmental disadvantage. Since that time, this definition or a similar variant has prevailed in the United States.

Prevalence

It has been estimated that from 5% to 15% of American schoolchildren have some form of learning disability (Taylor, 1989). Boys are diagnosed with this disorder two to five times as often as girls. One reason that prevalence figures vary so widely for learning disabilities is that there is disagreement concerning specific criteria for diagnosing the presence of the disorder. There are two widely used methods for making such a diagnosis. The first of these requires a certain level of discrepancy between IQ test scores and academic achievement test scores. This approach excludes many lower IQ youngsters from consideration as learning disabled and fails to appreciate that learning disabilities affect IQ test performance as well as achievement test performance. A second approach to diagnosing learning disabilities is through the specification of a certain level of educational deficit, usually measured with academic achievement tests. This approach, however, often fails to differentiate learning disabled children from mentally retarded children.

Characteristics

A number of areas of specific deficit have been described in learning disabled children. They often demonstrate impulsivity, hyperactivity, and attentional problems and are also frequently described as experiencing deficits in auditory or visual processing, perceptual-motor coordination, and other "soft" neurological signs (Hynd & Willis, 1988). Slow or uneven development of language abilities is also frequently noted in children later diagnosed as learning disabled. Specific learning disabilities in such areas as reading, spelling, or arithmetic usually are not diagnosed until the child begins school.

Classification

The revised third edition of the *Diagnostic and Statistical Manual* of the American Psychiatric Association (DSM-III-R; APA, 1987) includes seven specific learning disabilities. These are:

1. Developmental arithmetic disorder
2. Developmental expressive writing disorder

3. Developmental reading disorder
4. Developmental articulation disorder
5. Developmental expressive language disorder
6. Developmental receptive language disorder
7. Developmental coordination disorder

The first three of these formal diagnostic categories constitute deficits in academic skills, and as mentioned earlier, are usually not diagnosed until the school years. Therefore, we will focus our attention on the latter four categories, which are often identified in the preschool child.

Developmental articulation disorder is often recognized in severe cases by age 3, although mild deficits may go unrecognized until formal speech evaluation in school. It is estimated (DSM-III-R) that at least 10% of all children below age 8 meet the formal criteria for this disorder, which include the failure to properly articulate the p, b, and t sounds for a 3-year-old and the failure to properly articulate the r, sh, th, f, z, and l sounds for a 6-year-old. A delay in age of initial speech is only slightly correlated with the occurence of this disorder, and there appears to be a familial pattern of association. The vast majority of children with developmental articulation disorder eventually develop nonimpaired speech and show no identifiable sequelae of this disorder. Many of them do not require intervention, while more severe cases need speech therapy, often for several years, to develop optimal communication abilities.

Developmental expressive language disorder is characterized by deficits in the development of vocabulary, grammar, and pragmatic language that are not attributable to mental retardation, hearing problems, or specific neurological conditions. Severe forms of this disorder are usually diagnosed by age 3. The DSM-III-R estimates that 3% to 10% of school-age children have developmental expressive language disorder. This disorder often occurs in conjunction with developmental articulation disorder and developmental coordination disorder and also has a familial pattern of association. Approximately 50% of children with this disorder catch up with their age peers in expressive language abilities by the time they start school, even without specialized help (DSM-III-R). The remaining 50% may require specialized therapy, but in most cases the children achieve normal expressive language abilities by late adolescence (DSM-III-R).

Developmental receptive language disorder is characterized by significant impairment in comprehension of language that is not attributable to mental retardation, hearing deficits, or inadequate education. This disorder is usually diagnosed by age 4 and may be associated with developmental articulation, expressive language, and coordination disorders, attention-deficit disorder, electroencephalogram (EEG) abnormalities, and enuresis (DSM-III-R). Prevalence estimates range from 3% to 10% of all school-age children. A familial pattern of association has not been identified for developmental receptive language disorder. Significant numbers of children with more severe deficits in receptive language abilities continue to demonstrate these deficits throughout their academic careers. Language disorders are discussed at greater length in Chapter 6.

Developmental coordination disorder is not properly a learning disability but rather is characterized by significant impairment in the development of motor coordination that is not attributable to mental retardation or a physical disorder. This condition is diagnosed only if the impairment is serious and pervasive enough to interfere with activities of daily living or academic achievement. In preschoolers, this condition is commonly manifested by delay in mastery of such developmental motor milestones as learning to tie shoelaces, button shirts, zip pants, and throw and catch a ball. During school years, common manifestations include difficulty cutting with scissors and poor printing and handwriting. This disorder is commonly diagnosed by age 4 and prevalence has been estimated to be as high as 6% of children aged 5 to 11 (DSM-III-R). A familial pattern of association has not been established for this disorder, although it is noted to occur commonly in conjuction with other nonmotor developmental disorders. Many of the children diagnosed with this condition continue to have coordination difficulties throughout their lives.

Etiology

Many current etiological theories concerning learning disabilities emphasize the importance of maturational delays in neurological development or mild neurological dysfunction and the impact of these factors on information-processing capabilities (e.g., Shapiro, Palmer, Watchel, & Capute, 1983). Evidence in support of these biological hypotheses includes the documentation of a correlation between events known to cause neurological damage (e.g., maternal alcohol use, fetal distress, or anoxia during birth) and later learning disabilities (Taylor, 1989). In addition, learning disabled children have been shown to differ from nonlearning disabled children on evoked brain potentials (Byring & Jarvilehto, 1985), and some researchers have found computed tomography (CT) scan asymmetries (Denckla, LeMay, & Chapman, 1985).

There also appears to be suggestive evidence that genetic variables may mediate the presence of learning disabilities (DeFries, Fulker, & La-Buda, 1987), although research has failed to discover a consistent chromosomal abnormality. Other theorists have emphasized the importance of early perceptual-motor learning experiences and have specified perceptual-motor exercises to remediate learning disabilities (Delacato, 1966), although there is little evidence for the effectiveness of these interventions. Early sensory deprivation, emotional problems, and cultural factors have also been suggested as significant in the development of learning disabilities.

ASSESSMENT

The assessment of cognitive abilities through the use of standardized psychometric instruments can be done with children as young as 2 weeks of age. The Denver Developmental Screening Test-Revised (DDST-R; Frankenburg, Dodds, Fandal, Kazuk, & Cohrs, 1975) was designed as a screening instrument to be used by pediatricians and other clinicians with children from 2 weeks to 6 years of age. The DDST-R assesses children's development in four areas: (1) personal–social functioning, (2) fine-motor coordination, (3) language development, and (4) gross-motor coordination. The test requires only 20 minutes to administer and score, with approximately half the items being scored based on parent report and half requiring testing and observation of the child in an examination or waiting room setting. The DDST-R can be supplemented with information from the Revised Denver Prescreening Developmental Questionnaire (R-DPDQ; Frankenburg, 1986) which relies completely on parent report. Developmental tasks in the four domains listed above are presented in chronological order based on the age at which 90% of the children in the standardization sample were able to perform them successfully. Only items that are passed by observation or parent report are scored, and the total number of items passed for the four domains are classified as abnormal, questionable, normal, or untestable. Subscores for the four domains are not interpreted. Scores on the DDST-R and the R-DPDQ are highly correlated with each other, despite concerns about the reliability of parent reports.

Classifications based on the DDST (predecessor of the DDST-R) are reported to correlate reasonably well with those based on other cognitive assessment instruments used with preschoolers. Frankenburg, Dodds, and Fandal (1970) report that 73% of the children who were classified as abnormal with the DDST also obtained Stanford-Binet IQs or Bayley infant scale developmental quotients (DQ) below 70. However, other research has found that correlation coefficients ranging from .25 to .52 were obtained between DDST and Bayley infant scale scores for a sample of children under 30 months of age (Appelbaum, 1978).

The Bayley Scales of Infant Development (BSID) (Bayley, 1969) is a comprehensive measure of infant cognitive functioning that has been normalized for infants from 2 months to 2½ years of age. The Bayley yields two standard scores: a Mental Developmental Index (MDI) and a Psychomotor Developmental Index (PDI). The MDI is derived from 163 items indexing manipulation of objects, sustained attention, imitation, comprehension, shape discrimination, vocalization, problem solving, memory, and expressive vocabulary. The PDI is derived from 81 items indexing gross- and fine-motor coordination. Items in both scales are arranged in order of normative chronological accomplishment.

The Bayley was well standardized on children from 2 to 30 months of age, and reliability coefficients appear to be adequate. The MDI of the Bayley is reported to correlate .57 with a Stanford-Binet: Form L-M IQ score for children in the 24- to 30-month age range (Bayley, 1969).

A revised version of the Bayley, the BSID-II, was published in 1993 and offers updated stimulus materials, more current normative data, and an upward extension of the age range to 42 months (Bayley, 1993). Correlations between the MDI and PDI from the BSID-II and the previous version of the Bayley are reported to be .62 and .63, respectively, with the mean MDI and PDI standard scores from the BSID-II being 12 and 7 points lower than the corresponding scores from the older Bayley (Bayley, 1993).

The MDI from the BSID-II correlates .79 with the General Cognitive Index (GCI) from the McCarthy Scales and .73 with both the Verbal and Full-Scale IQ scores from the Wechsler Preschool and Primary Scale of Intelligence-Revised (WPPSI-R) (Bayley, 1993).

The Bayley takes about 1 hour to administer and requires considerable training and experience of the clinician. Although it is probably the best available instrument for the assessment of cognition in very young children, it is important to note that reliability of scores is fairly modest for children in the lower age ranges and that situational variables can significantly affect such scores. It is also necessary to emphasize that scores obtained on the Bayley do not correlate highly with later IQ scores.

The McCarthy Scales of Children's Abilities (MSCA; McCarthy, 1972) is another adequately standardized assessment instrument for preschool children. It is designed for use with children from 2½ to 8½ years of age and takes about 1 hour to administer. The MSCA yields measures of verbal abilities, nonverbal reasoning, numerical ability, short-term memory, and motor coordination. In addition, a general measure of cognitive functioning, the General Cognitive Index (GCI) is produced.

The MSCA was standardized on approximately 1,000 children, and reliability was found to be adequate. The correlation between the GCI and the Stanford-Binet: Form L-M IQ averaged .82 in nine studies with normal children (Kaufman, 1982), with somewhat lower correlations for retarded and gifted children. The GCI also correlates fairly strongly with Full-Scale IQ scores derived from the WPPSI and the Wechsler Intelligence Scale for Children-Revised (WISC-R) (Kaufman, 1982) and with the Mental Processing Composite (MPC) from the Kaufman Assessment Battery for Children (K-ABC) (Zucker & Copeland, 1988). However, researchers (e.g., Lidz & Ballester, 1986) have noted that the MSCA yields GCIs that are significantly lower than Wechsler and Binet IQs for younger children and children with lower IQs, and have, therefore, cautioned against its use for individual classification.

The MSCA appears to have moderate to good predictive validity when scores are compared to academic achievement tests and teacher ratings of academic performance. For example, the correlation between preschool MSCA scores and Wide Range Achievement Test (WRAT) reading scores and teacher ratings of reading ability obtained 2 years later were .72 and .74, respectively (Reilly, Drudge, Rosen, Loew, & Fischer, 1985).

The WPPSI-R (Wechsler, 1989b) is a recently updated version of the Wechsler Preschool and Primary Scale of Intelligence (WPPSI) and is one of the most widely used cognitive assessment instruments with preschool children. It is designed for use with children from 3 years of age through 7 years, 3 months of age. The WPPSI-R has a total of 12 subtests and takes about 1 hour to administer. The test yields subtest standard scores and Verbal, Performance, and Full-Scale IQ scores.

The WPPSI-R was well standardized on 1,700 children and has good reliability. It correlates highly with the WISC-R and the MSCA, while correlations with the Stanford-Binet (Fourth Edition) are somewhat lower and are quite low between the WPPSI-R and the K-ABC (Gyurke, 1991). Predictive validity studies (Yule, Gold, & Bush, 1982) done on the earlier WPPSI have been rather impressive, with a high correlation ($r = .86$) found between WPPSI Full-Scale IQ scores obtained at age 5½ and WISC-R Full-Scale IQ scores obtained at age 16½.

The Stanford-Binet Intelligence Scale: Fourth Edition (SB: FE; Thorndike, Hagan, & Sattler, 1986) replaced the Stanford-Binet: Form L-M in 1986. It is organized differently from its predecessor in that, like the Wechsler scales, subtests are given from start to finish, rather than dissimilar items being assigned to age ranges. Like the Wechsler tests, subtests are combined into more global scales. The test is designed for use from age 2 to adulthood, however, only 8 of 15 subtests are administered to preschoolers.

The standardization sample for the SB: FE consisted of over 5,000 individuals from age 2 to age 23. The sample was balanced for geographic region, gender, ethnic group, and socioeconomic status. Reliabilities for the SB: FE Composite score are good for all age groups.

It appears that the SB: FE yields somewhat lower global scores than the WPPSI and the WISC-R (Thorndike et al., 1986). One study (Delaney & Hopkins, 1987) also demonstrated fairly low correlations between the performance of 5-year-olds on the SB:FE and on the WRAT-R given several months later and only moderate correlations between the performance of five-year-olds on the SB: FE and on the Woodcock-Johnson Achievement Test given several months later.

The K-ABC was specifically designed with the assessment needs of preschoolers in mind (Kaufman & Kaufman, 1983). The test is designed for use with children from 2½ to 12½ years of age. The K-ABC yields several global scores that can be viewed as roughly equivalent to IQ scores. One of these is the Sequential Scale score, which is considered as an index of linear, serial problem solving. Another is the Simultaneous Scale score, which is viewed as an index of spatial or wholistic organizational abilities. The MPC score is computed from both the Sequential and Simultaneous Scale scores. In addition, the Achievement Scale score indexes the ability to apply cognitive abilities to the acquisition of knowledge from the environment.

Standardization was good for the K-ABC, and reliability is reported to be acceptable (Kaufman & Kaufman, 1983). The K-ABC correlates moderately well with other cognitive assessment instruments used with this age group. Lyon and Smith (1986) found with a group of 4- to 6-year-old "at-risk" children that the K-ABC MPC correlated .59 with the MSCA GCI and .45 with the Stanford-Binet: Form L-M IQ score. The correlation between the K-ABC Achievement Scale and the Binet IQ was .71, however. Kamphaus and Reynolds (1987) found the K-ABC MPC norms to be approximately two standard score points lower than WISC-R and Stanford-Binet: Form L-M IQ norms and equivalent to IQ norms for the newer Stanford-Binet: FE. Lampley and Rust (1986), however, found that when they administered both the K-ABC and the Slosson Intelligence Test (SIT) to a group of normal preschoolers aged 2½ to 4 that the mean K-ABC MPC was 15 points lower than the mean SIT IQ score. This tendency for the K-ABC to yield lower global scores than earlier IQ measures may not be present, however, with ethnic groups or linguistically challenged children, and some research (Bing & Bing, 1985) has shown that children from minority racial groups perform comparatively better on the K-ABC than on other cognitive assessment instruments. Predictive validity studies have shown that the K-ABC Achievement Scale is a moderately good predictor of later school achievement (Kamphaus & Reynolds, 1987).

INTERVENTIONS

Interventions with mentally retarded and learning disabled pre-schoolers take three primary forms. First are therapies (primarily behavioral and pharmacological) that are designed to ameliorate specific problem behaviors, which may or may not be causally related to the child's cognitive deficiencies. Second are remediation procedures (primarily educational) that address these cognitive deficiencies directly. Finally, there are prevention programs designed to reduce the probability of cognitive deficiencies and maladaptive behaviors in "at-risk" children.

Behavior therapy techniques have long been used to reduce problem behaviors in cognitively impaired preschoolers. For example, Wolf, Risley, and Mees (1964) reported that they were able to reduce the frequency of tantrums and self-injurious behavior in a 3½-year-old boy through the use of behavior therapy procedures. Mulick, Hoyt, Rojahn, and Schroeder (1978) successfully rewarded toy play in a profoundly retarded individual in order to reduce the frequency of nail biting and finger picking. When the subject played with the toy, he was unable to bite his nails and pick at his fingers at the same time, so an increase in the frequency of toy play resulted in a decrease in the self-abusive behaviors.

Punishment or aversive stimulus approaches to behavior modification with cognitively impaired preschoolers can be very effective but, for both ethical and practical reasons, are usually considered only after positive reinforcement approaches have been attempted or when rapid suppression of a behavior is necessary for the welfare of the child or others (e.g., severe self-mutilative or assaultive behaviors). Matson and DiLorenzo (1984) present a number of reasons for not using punishment approaches with mentally retarded clients, including the emotional arousal and consequent aggression that often occur in response to punishment, the detrimental effects on rapport between client and therapist, the lack of permanence and generalizability of behavioral suppression gained through the use of punishment, the potential for suppressing desirable behaviors as well as undesirable ones, and the potential for abuse.

Response cost procedures involve punishment through the contingent withdrawal of a preexisting positive reinforcer and are often used in conjunction with token or point systems, with tokens or points being removed on demonstration of a prespecified undesirable behavior. For example, Shapiro, Kazdin, and McGonigle (1982) found that removal of previously awarded tokens on demonstration of "off-task" behavior was effective in improving classroom attentiveness in mentally retarded children. Similarly, the withdrawal of sensory stimulation can function as a response cost punisher. Zegiob, Jenkins, Becker, and Bristow (1976) used a cloth placed over a mentally retarded client's head to withdraw stimulation on demonstration of disruptive behavior and found that it was effective in reducing such behavior.

Extinction procedures involve the withholding of positive reinforcers (rather than the removal of preexisting reinforcers as in response cost) on demonstration of undesirable behaviors. Extinction procedures are fairly noninvasive and have been demonstrated to be effective in managing a wide range of maladaptive behaviors in retarded children. For example, Lovaas and Simmons (1969) found that withholding attention was effective in reducing self-injurious behavior in three retarded girls. The primary disadvantage of extinction procedures is that they can be quite slow in producing effects and, therefore, are probably not appropriate for use with severely disruptive and/or dangerous behaviors.

One procedure that combines elements of response cost, mild punishment, and extinction is time-out. Initially, time-out was viewed as purely an extinction procedure. More recently, however, it has become apparent that there are also components of punishment in time-out as usually implemented. Time-out procedures can vary in their invasiveness, from extremely mild to very extreme. The most mild form of time-out consists of merely withdrawing or withholding attention or other maintaining reinforcers while inappropriate behavior is being demonstrated. For example, Foxx and Shapiro (1978) found that contingent withdrawal of teacher attention and the opportunity to participate in reinforcing activities was effective in reducing disruptive behavior in a mentally retarded child. Similarly, Mansdorf (1977) found that the contingent withdrawal of the opportunity to watch TV or listen to music reduced tantrums in a retarded girl. More extreme forms of time-out usually involve a more complete removal from ongoing reinforcers as well as mild punishment through placement in a corner, isolated area, or special seclusion room. This procedure has proven to be effective in reducing a wide variety of more extreme disruptive behaviors in retarded children.

Physical restraint has been used as a mild form of punishment both independently and in conjunction with time-out. Bitgood, Crowe, Suarez, and Peters (1977) found that holding a mentally retarded client's arms to his side for 15 seconds was effective in reducing self-stimulatory behavior, and Rolider and Van Houton (1985) used physical restraint in conjuction with time-out in a corner to reduce the occurrence of self-abusive behaviors in a mentally retarded client.

Other punishing agents that have been used to reduce seriously maladaptive behaviors in retarded children include wrist slaps in conjunction with verbal scolding, water squirted in the face, and mild electric shock. The clinician must carefully consider the potential risks and benefits of punishment procedures before recommending their use.

Overcorrection (Foxx & Azrin, 1972) is a procedure that involves both mild punishment and training in appropriate alternative behaviors. When a maladaptive behavior is demonstrated, overcorrection procedures require that any negative effects of the behavior be corrected (restitution) and then that appropriate alternatives to the maladaptive behavior be practiced (positive practice). For instance, if a child kicked a chair over when walking by it, an overcorrection procedure might entail requiring the child to set the chair back up and then walk by it appropriately 10 times. It is sometimes necessary to physically assist compliance with overcorrection procedures in addition to providing verbal instructions. Overcorrection has been successfully used to reduce stereotypic behaviors (Rollings & Baumeister, 1981), self-injurious behaviors (Harris & Romanczyk, 1976), and social inappropriateness (Foxx, 1976).

Cognitive behavioral strategies have relatively little applicability to mentally retarded preschoolers because of the cognitive deficits they commonly present with. However, with older retarded children, such procedures as self-monitoring (Litrownik & Freitas, 1980) and self-reinforcement (Shapiro, McGonigle, & Ollendick, 1980) may be useful. Behaviors that have been addressed through these techniques include self-help skills, aggressive and disruptive behaviors, and cognitive performance (Mahoney & Mahoney, 1976).

Parents have been trained to effectively implement behavior therapy procedures with retarded preschoolers (Mash & Terdal, 1973), and group behavioral training for parents of retarded children has been shown to be more effective than reflective parent group interventions (Tavormina, 1975). Rinn (1985) described a parent behavioral training group in which parents were successfully taught the processes of problem behavior identification and implementation of behavior therapy interventions.

Psychotropic medications are often used in an attempt to reduce maladaptive behaviors in mentally retarded children. Rapoport and Kruesi (1985) specifically identify haloperidol (Haldol) as useful in reducing self-stimulatory and aggressive behaviors in such children. Some studies, however, have shown behavior therapy approaches to be superior to medication in controlling such behavior (Sandford & Nettlebeck, 1982). Some research (Durand, 1982) has shown that the use of haloperidol in conjunction with behavior therapy procedures produces reductions in disruptive behaviors superior to that achieved by either treatment alone. Practically speaking, few psychotropic medications are authorized for use with preschoolers, and most physicians would consider using such medi-

cations only when all other intervention strategies had proven ineffica-
cious.

Psychotherapy approaches, including group and individual verbal
psychotherapy (Selan, 1979), and play therapy (Moustakas, 1966) have long
been used with mentally retarded and learning disabled individuals. However, there continues to be little evidence for the efficacy of these techniques
with these populations, and some authorities (Christ, 1981) have specifically criticized their use. There does appear to be a role, however, for
parental therapy focusing on conflicts and expectations concerning the
cognitively impaired child (Abrams & Kaslow, 1977).

Educational remediations for cognitively impaired preschoolers have
focused primarily on the areas of self-help skills, cognitive development,
language abilities, motor skills, and social skills. Such programs have been
implemented with children as young as 3 months of age, with the primary
emphasis for infants being on sensory and language stimulation and motor
exercise (Johnson & Werner, 1975). Many intervention programs for young
infants rely primarily on parents' efforts and seek to improve the quality
of the parent–child relationship as well as provide specific educational
remediation (Kearsley & Sigel, 1979). Outcome data on remediation programs for children below the age of 2 are rather limited; however, there are
indications that sensory stimulation and motor rehearsal programs can
result in improved motor skills and sensorimotor cognitive processes
(Kahn, 1978) in cognitively impaired infants. There are conflicting results
concerning the long-term benefits of stimulation programs enacted during
the first 2 years of life, with some researchers reporting no later benefits
(Dunst, 1976), while others (Kahn, 1979) do document such effects.

Educational remediation programs for cognitively impaired preschoolers above the age of 2 have focused on the same areas as infant
programs, although with increased emphasis on cognitive and language
abilities. Common cognitive training approaches include such activities as
helping the child learn the names and attributes of objects in his or her
environment and learning to distinguish between unlike objects. Lan-
guage-training approaches range from those for children with no speech
(Guess, Sailor, & Baer, 1976) to those that attempt to expand existing speech
beyond the single-word level (Miller & Yoder, 1974). Often, use of reinforcement procedures can be effective in producing verbal responses, with
a common approach being allowing a child to have a desired object only
when it is correctly named (Ruder & Smith, 1974). In addition to imitation,
language training programs use conversational formats to elicit relevant
responses, with correction and verbal praise used to shape the correctness
of responses (MacDonald, 1974). The use of auxiliary communication
modes such as sign language, communication boards, and gestural codes

has also proven useful in language training with cognitively impaired preschoolers (Grinnel, Detamore, & Lippke, 1976).

Social skills training with cognitively impaired preschoolers involves primarily instruction in and modeling of play and interactional skills and the reduction of undesirable behaviors through instruction in appropriate competing responses and the application of behavior modification techniques as discussed previously. Group play offers an opportunity for cognitively impaired preschoolers to learn appropriate social behaviors through observation and imitation of other children.

Several studies have documented the effect of preschool educational remediation programs on later development. Hayden and Haring (1977) found that a group of mentally retarded 9-year-olds who had been enrolled in a comprehensive preschool remediation program were functioning at 95% of normal cognitive and social performance levels, compared to 61% for a comparable group who had not been enrolled in a preschool program. Similarily, Rynders, Spiker, and Horrobin (1978) found that a group of 35 Down syndrome children who had been enrolled in a structured preschool program from 6 months to 5 years of age performed significantly better on an IQ test than an unselected group of Down syndrome children.

In addition to remedial programs for children who are formally diagnosed as being cognitively impaired, a number of preschool educational programs have been established with the intention of preventing later cognitive deficits in children who are identified as being "at risk" for such deficits because of such societal factors as poverty, poor living conditions, and minority ethnic group membership. The best known of these programs is Head Start, established in the United States in the 1960s as a national, federally funded, preschool program for economically disadvantaged, largely minority, 3- to 5-year-olds. Unfortunately, early, methodologically flawed outcome research on the Head Start program failed to show any lasting benefits to enrollment in terms of later school performance, and enthusiasm for such programs waned. However, in 1983, a 15-year follow-up study of over 1,000 subjects from 14 preschool educational programs (Consortium for Longitudinal Studies, 1983) concluded that children enrolled in preschool educational programs outperformed comparable nonenrollees up to 4 years later on standardized achievement tests. After sixth grade, differences between enrollees and nonenrollees disappeared, however, and in the final follow-up enrollees' scores on standardized achievement tests only averaged in the 25th to 30th percentile range. The results also indicated that preschool program enrollees (particularly girls) had a more positive attitude toward school and that children who had been enrolled in a preschool program were less likely to be placed in special education and more likely to graduate from high school.

Ramey and Campbell (1984) published another evaluation of a preschool educational program for high-risk children. Their program, based at the University of North Carolina, enrolled children at 6 weeks of age, with educational interventions based on learning games for infants and on a communication skills curriculum for older preschoolers. Results indicated that program enrollees outperformed controls by approximately one standard deviation on IQ tests from age 1½ through age 4½.

The Brookline Early Educational Project (Pierson, Walker, & Tivnan, 1984) provided play groups beginning at age 2 for "at-risk" children, with a cognitive and language enrichment curriculum for 3- and 4-year-olds. Follow-up evaluation 3 years after the children had completed the program indicated that program participants were having significantly less difficulty than controls with classroom behavior and academic work.

In summary, it appears that learning problems can be accurately assessed and diagnosed early in a child's life and that effective interventions are available during the preschool years to, at least partially, remediate behavioral and cognitive deficits. There appears to be little justification for waiting until a child begins school before evaluating and treating learning problems.

3

Toileting Problems

Learning appropriate and socially acceptable toileting practices is one of the major tasks of the preschool years, and problems with toileting are among the most common causes of concern to parents. Chamberlain (1974) surveyed 200 parents of preschoolers about their concerns regarding their children and found that toilet training was the most commonly reported worry. Pediatric psychologists report that between 5% and 10% of their referrals from parents concern problems with toileting and toilet training (Roberts, 1986).

In evaluating toileting problems, it is critically important to have an accurate understanding of physiological maturation and normative data in this area. To achieve bowel and bladder control, it is necessary that the child have reflex sphincter control, which usually occurs between 9 and 12 months of age, and that myelinization of the nerve tracts to the lower body be completed, which usually occurs between 12 and 18 months of age (Brazelton, 1962). In addition, Brazelton (1962) believes that it is necessary that a child have the ability to sit and walk, understand some verbal content, relate to adults and be able to imitate their behavior, and be able to control impulses. Brazelton (1962) believes that most children achieve physiological and psychological readiness between 18 and 30 months of age. Azrin and Foxx (1974) have proposed a similar set of readiness criteria and believe that most children over 20 months of age meet these criteria. Christophersen (1988) suggested that parents wait until 3 months after their child met the Azrin and Foxx criteria before beginning toilet training. This would imply commonly waiting until approximately 2 years of age before beginning toilet training, which Brazelton (1962) reports is the average age at which parents begin such training.

Parental style and timing of toilet training have been suggested anecdotally as significant variables in the development of toileting problems, with some authorities reporting that children exposed to coercive toilet training are more likely to have later toileting problems (Brazelton, 1962). One study found that 35 of 41 enuretic children had experienced "early" toilet training, and the parents of 29 of these children described the training as "rigidly strict" (Bindelglas, Dee, & Enos, 1968).

Research suggests that substantial numbers of children below the age of 5 experience bowel or bladder incontinence and that formal diagnosis of a clinical problem probably should not occur before the age of 5. This is consistent with the diagnostic criteria established by the DSM-III-R (APA, 1987), although some authorities would consider such a diagnosis for children as young as 4 years of age (Shaffer, 1985).

Clinical problems with bladder (enuresis) and bowel (encopresis) control can be classified as primary or secondary. Primary enuresis and encopresis are diagnosed when the child reaches the age of 4 or 5 and has never achieved adequate bowel or bladder control, while secondary conditions are diagnosed when control is achieved and later lost.

ENURESIS

As mentioned previously, DSM-III-R (APA, 1987) requires that a child be 5 or older before a formal diagnosis of enuresis can be made. Although this requirement excludes the majority of preschoolers from such a diagnosis, the literature on enuresis still has considerable relevance to older preschoolers. Additional diagnostic criteria in the DSM-III-R include the requirement that involuntary urination occur at least twice a month for children between the ages of 5 and 6, and at least once a month for older children. Children with such physical disorders as seizure disorders are excluded from these criteria.

Estimates of the number of school-age children in the United States suffering from enuresis range from 3 to 7 million, with percentage estimates ranging from 2.2% to 25% (Schaefer, 1979). Boys are affected approximately twice as often as girls. Enuresis can involve either nighttime (nocturnal) or daytime (diurnal) wetting or both. Diurnal enuresis without accompanying nighttime wetting is unusual, but approximately 30% of children who demonstrate nocturnal enuresis also display diurnal enuresis (Forsythe & Redmond, 1974). Primary enuretics make up 85% of all cases of enuresis (DeJonge, 1973).

Spontaneous remission without treatment is a significant factor in enuresis. Forsythe and Redmond (1974) found that spontaneous remission rates averaged 14% per year between the ages of 5 and 9 and 16% per year between the ages of 10 and 19. Only 1% of 18-year-old males and virtually no females are enuretic (DSM-III: APA, 1980).

Historical Perspective

Enuresis was identified as a medical problem by the Egyptians as early as 1550 B.C. Over the centuries, such folk remedies as raising the foot of the bed, restricting fluid intake, administering herbal potions, and performing circumcision were implemented (Mowrer & Mowrer, 1938). These approaches had varying degrees of success, in many cases benefiting greatly from spontaneous remission.

More recently, emotional factors have been considered to be a primary cause of enuresis. Freud (1916) viewed enuresis as an ejaculation analogue and, therefore, as a way of expressing repressed sexual feelings. Imhof (1956) regarded it as a symbolic expression of an unmet need for love ("weeping through the bladder"). Robertiello (1956) also viewed enuresis as symbolic, representing a "cooling off" of the genitals, and thus a diminishment of sexual drive.

Current Etiological Conceptions

It now appears that enuresis is a condition with a number of possible causes, and that more than one causal mechanism can be operating in an individual case. Although the literature suggests that enuresis is largely a functional disorder, with no more than 10% of cases caused by physical factors (Pierce, 1972), the possibility of physiological causality dictates the need for comprehensive, multidisciplinary assessment and treatment strategies.

Physical Factors

Urogenital Tract Obstructions and Dysfunctions

A number of anatomical and structural problems in the urogenital tract may cause enuresis, including congenital weakness of the external sphincter muscle, urethral fistulas, obstruction of the urethral valves, or an abnormally short urethra (Brock & Kaplan, 1980). Often the presence of these conditions is indicated by other symptoms in addition to enuresis, including painful or frequent urination and irregular urine stream. Medical assessment and diagnosis are necessary to establish the presence of these conditions. Surgical procedures are available for the correction of many of

these conditions, although frequently remedial bladder training is necessary even after surgery.

Urinary Tract Infection

A high percentage of enuretic children, particularly girls, have urinary tract infections. However, the direction of causality is not entirely
clear, as enuresis can both be caused by urinary tract infections and
predispose a child to such infections. Forsythe and Redmond (1974) found
that less than 6% of enuretic children with urinary tract infections were
cured of enuresis after successful treatment of the infection. Symptoms of
urinary tract infections include fever; painful, difficult, or frequent urination; and dribbling. Antibiotics are often effective in treating these infections.

Nervous System Disorders

EEG abnormalities are more commonly found in enuretics than in
nonenuretics, with abnormal patterns found in 22% of enuretics and only
2% of nonenuretics (Pierce, Lipcan, McLary, & Noble, 1956). Grand mal
seizures may often be accompanied by involuntary voiding, and if such
seizures occur exclusively at night, as is sometimes the case, the cause for
the nocturnal enuresis will not be readily apparent. Petit mal seizures are
not usually associated with incontinence. Standard EEG recordings may
be ineffectual in diagnosing a subtle seizure disorder, and sleep or extended recordings may be necessary. Treatment for a documented seizure
disorder usually consists of administration of one or more antiseizure
medications and varies widely in effectiveness. It is important to note that
only a small minority of enuretic children need such medications and that
they can have significant detrimental side effects. Spinal cord lesions,
demyelinating diseases, and peripheral neuropathy due to such causes as
diabetes can also cause urinary incontinence and indicate the need for a
comprehensive medical assessment prior to psychological intervention.

Bladder Capacity

Some research has shown that enuretic children have smaller functional bladder capacity (FBC) than nonenuretics (Zaleski, Gerrard, &
Shokier, 1973), although other studies (Rutter, 1973) have demonstrated
considerable overlap in the FBCs of age-matched enuretics and nonenuretics. There is conflict in the literature concerning the effectiveness of retention-control or bladder-stretching exercises as a treatment for enuresis,

with some authorities proposing them as an effective treatment (Paschalis, Kimmel, & Kimmel, 1972), and others finding little value in the procedure (Doleys, Ciminero, Tollison, Williams, & Wells, 1977). Retention-control training will be discussed at length later in this chapter.

Sleep Arousal Disorders

Anecdotal evidence from parents and clinicians suggests that enuretics may be more difficult to arouse from sleep than nonenuretics. However, research has been contradictory in its findings with regard to enuretics' arousability. Similarly, there does not appear to be a clear relationship between enuresis and specific stages of sleep (Mikkelsen et al., 1980).

Heredity

Researchers have found that there is a higher incidence of enuresis in the relatives of enuretic children than in those of nonenuretics, with approximately 50% of parents and close relatives having experienced this problem as children (Baller, 1975). Bakwin (1973) noted higher enuresis concordance rates for monozygotic (68%) than for dizygotic (36%) twins, and a higher incidence of enuresis in children of two parents who were enuretic as children (77%) than in children of one enuretic parent (44%) and those of no enuretic parents (15%).

Psychological Factors

Intelligence

Although enuresis is more common among severely mentally retarded children than among children with average intelligence, there does not appear to be any relationship between intelligence and enuresis within the average range. In most cases, even severely mentally retarded individuals can learn bladder control with sufficient remedial training (Azrin, Sneed, & Foxx, 1973). Intellectual ability, therefore, does not appear to be a primary causal factor in enuresis.

Emotional Disturbance

Approximately 20% of enuretic children show indications of emotional disturbance (Rutter, Yule, & Graham, 1973), although it is possible that such emotional disturbances may be a product of enuresis rather than a cause. Some studies have found no significant relationship between childhood enuresis and emotional disturbance (Cullen, 1966), although other researchers have found that stress and anxiety are associated with enuresis, particularly secondary enuresis (Jehu, Morgan, Turner, & Jones, 1977). It appears, therefore, that emotional disturbance is not a primary cause of enuresis, and although stress and anxiety may be associated with secondary enuresis, the direction of causality in this relationship is unclear.

Interventions

In addition to the folk remedies mentioned earlier, there is a time-honored tradition of parental punitiveness toward enuresis that continues even today. Such measures as spanking, public humiliation, and withdrawal of privileges appear to be predicated on the assumption that the behavior is under the child's volitional control and have proved to be largely ineffective in treating the condition. Parents also commonly try environmental manipulations such as restricting fluids and periodically wakening and toileting the child throughout the night. The first of these procedures has only limited effectiveness, but random wakening (rather than at fixed times) has been demonstrated to have some treatment efficacy (Creer & Davis, 1975). Simply having a child record the occurrence of enuresis, and conversely "dry nights," has also been demonstrated to result in improvement (Doleys, 1977), as has wakening the child on finding the bed wet (Catalina, 1976). Such commonsense interventions result in improvement in approximately one-third of all enuretics (McGregor, 1937), although spontaneous remission may be responsible for a significant portion of this figure.

Psychotherapy

Even though there is little evidence that emotional disturbance is a primary cause of enuresis, verbal psychotherapy, play therapy, and family therapy have been among the most often implemented courses of treatment. There is little evidence, however, to support the superiority of psychotherapy to spontaneous remission in the treatment of enuresis (Friedman, 1968). However, hypnotherapy has been reported to be effective in treating enuresis (Kohen, Olness, Cornwell, & Heimel, 1984).

Medication

The most commonly prescribed medication for enuresis is imipramine hydrochloride (Tofranil), a tricyclic antidepressant, given in the afternoon or before bed. Its mechanism of action appears to be related to anticholinergic effects on the bladder. Of children treated with imipramine, 10% to 40% show a significant reduction in bed-wetting (Forsythe & Redmond, 1974), but relapses occur at a rate of over 50% when the drug is withdrawn, and complete dryness is uncommon (Ack, Norman, & Schmitt, 1985). The resulting "cure rate" of no higher than 25% is not particularly compelling when compared with the 15% per year spontaneous remission rate. In addition, imipramine overdoses can be fatal, and the drug has a number of potentially harmful side effects (Lake, Mikkelson, Rapoport, Zavadil, & Kopin, 1979). For these reasons, it has been recommended to physicians that imipramine be used only as "temporary adjunctive therapy" in the treatment of enuresis and that its use be restricted to children 6 years of age and older (Physicians' Desk Reference, 1993).

Recently, desmopressin (DDAVP), a hormonal nasal spray originally developed for use in the treatment of diabetes, has been used in the treatment of enuresis. Research indicates improvement in 10% to 60% of patients, although, like imipramine, there is significant relapse on discontinuation of the medication and potentially serious side effects (Klauber, 1989).

Stimulant medications (methylphenidate or dextroamphetamine sulfate) are also commonly prescribed for enuresis, with the presumed goal of lessening the child's depth of sleep. The efficacy and relapse rates roughly parallel those of imipramine, and there are also significant negative side effects with prolonged use (Schaefer, 1979). Oxybutinin (Ditropan) has been reported to have considerable effectiveness with enuretics who do not respond to imipramine (Schmitt, 1982), but its long-term efficacy remains unproven.

In summary, medication may result in some short-term improvement in enuresis but has proven largely ineffectual over extended periods of time. In addition, the potential for serious side effects with most medications used to treat enuresis makes it a less preferred treatment, particularly with preschoolers, than other alternatives.

Behavior Therapy

Bach and Moylan (1975) used modest monetary rewards (10 to 25 cents) for appropriate toileting and dry nights to reduce enuresis and encopresis in a 6-year-old boy. Benjamin, Serdahely, and Geppert (1971) found that such social reinforcers as hugging, kissing, and praise were more effective than social punishment (shaming, spanking, and name calling) in initially training nocturnal continence in children. Allgeier (1976) found that, along with self-monitoring, making access to liquids after dinner contingent on dry nights was effective in eliminating enuresis in two sisters. The mild punishment of having to change their own wet sheets also appears to decrease enuresis in some children The mechanism by which these procedures affect enuresis is unclear, although it may be that they inspire self-imposed limits on evening fluid intake and more conscientious pre-bed toileting.

Retention-Control Training

The theory behind retention-control training is that having a child refrain from urinating for progressively longer periods of time after feeling the urge to do so will result in increased FBC and improved sphincter control. As mentioned earlier, there is considerable controversy in the literature concerning the value of this procedure in the treatment of enuresis. Muellner (1960) found that implementing such a procedure did result in increased FBC (as measured by urine output) and that when children were able to retain 10 to 12 ounces of urine during the daytime, their nocturnal enuresis disappeared. Starfield and Mellits (1968) asked 83 enuretic children to refrain once a day from urinating for as long as possible (to a maximum of 40 minutes) after feeling the need to do so. These authors found that the enuresis of 85% of the children decreased, although it was eliminated in only 20% of cases.

Kimmel and Kimmel (1970) used retention-control training in conjunction with reinforcement procedures. This procedure resulted in a decrease in both diurnal and nocturnal enuresis in many cases, often within 2 weeks. Paschalis et al. (1972) replicated the above procedure and found that 3 months after the 20-day training program, 48% of the children were no longer enuretic, and 74% were significantly improved.

Stedman (1972) combined self-monitoring and retention-control training to treat a girl who was a primary enuretic. She was asked to record bladder distention sensations, frequency of daytime urination, and incidents of nocturnal enuresis. She was also asked to refrain from urination for 30 minutes after she felt a strong need to. Frequency of daytime urination and incidents of nocturnal enuresis both decreased significantly, and within 12 weeks, the girl was no longer enuretic. A 3-month follow-up found only a few isolated incidents of enuresis. The self-monitoring and retention-control requirements of many of these interventions are too demanding for preschoolers, but most children above the age of 3 can be expected to report wet or dry beds and pants, and most can delay urination for at least brief periods of time when given direct encouragement and meaningful reinforcement.

Other researchers have reported less positive results with retention-control training. Rocklin and Tilker (1973) also used the Kimmel and Kimmel procedure but found only a 30% "cure" rate. Doleys and Wells (1975) implemented a 21-day retention-control training program with a 3-year-old girl and found no decrease in nocturnal enuresis, despite an increase in FBC. They then initiated a program of nighttime waking and toileting, which did result in a decrease in enuresis. Harris and Purohit (1977) also found that retention-control training resulted in increases in functional bladder capacity but no decrease in frequency of enuresis.

In addition to retention-control training, some researchers have implemented sphincter-control training. Such training involves having the child practice starting and stopping the flow of urine once urination has begun. This procedure is applicable only to older preschoolers. Walker, Miller, and Bonner (1988) have reported some success in using this procedure in conjunction with retention-control training.

In summary, the research suggests that there is some value in the use of retention-control training in the treatment of enuresis, although the relationship between FBC and enuresis is unclear. It appears that the children most likely to benefit from retention-control training are those with demonstrated small FBC, as indicated by reduced urinary output and frequent daytime urination.

Enuresis Alarms

In the early 1900s, Pflaunder (1904) used electrical alarms that rang a bell when children hospitalized on a pediatric ward wet the bed. Although the intention of these alarms was merely to alert nursing staff that the child's bed needed changing, Pflaunder noted a decrease in incidents of enuresis. Later, Mowrer and Mowrer (1938) demonstrated the efficacy of a similar device in treating enuretic children. Since that time, numerous studies have been done documenting the effectiveness of such enuresis alarms. Young (1969) found that in 19 studies using enuresis alarms, the success rates ranged from 68% to 100%, with a mean of 71%. Doleys (1977) reviewed the literature on enuresis alarms between 1960 and 1975 and found that 75% of all cases were treated successfully in 5 to 12 weeks. However, he did note a 41% relapse rate, with two-thirds of the relapsed enuretics being successfully reconditioned. Other researchers have also noted high relapse rates. DeLeon and Sacks (1972) reported a 20% relapse rate 4 years after successful treatment, and Young and Morgan (1972) reported an initial relapse rate of 35%, which was later reduced to 13% through the use of overcorrection procedures.

There are a number of different types of enuresis alarms in current use. All of them function to turn on an alarm (buzzer or light) when urine completes an electrical circuit. The most commonly used model consists of two metal sheets (the top one with holes in it) separated by a fiber insulating sheet. When urine wets this middle sheet, it becomes conductive, and a buzzer and/or light is turned on. Unfortunately, this device requires approximately 10 milliliters (ml) of urine to activate it and, therefore, response time is slow. The apparatus is also difficult to dry sufficiently so that it may be reset for children who wet more than once a night. False alarms are fairly common because of inadvertent touching of the two metal sheets. Newer versions of the enuresis alarm consist of small sensors that attach to the front of the child's underpants or pajama pants and a buzzer unit that is attached to the wrist or top of the shoulder on an undershirt or pajama top. These alarms are sensitive to a few drops of urine and, therefore, have much quicker response times than the older models. In addition, the sensors can be more easily dried and are much less prone to false alarms.

There is considerable debate concerning the theoretical rationale by which enuresis alarms produce therapeutic effects. Originally (Mowrer & Mowrer, 1938), it was suggested that a classical conditioning paradigm was in operation, with the conditioned stimulus (bladder distention cues) gradually gaining the ability to produce wakefulness (the conditioned response) through pairing with the unconditioned stimulus (the buzzer or light). More recently, however, this interpretation has been criticized as representing backward conditioning, which has been shown to be an ineffective conditioning model. In addition, this interpretation fails to explain why children treated with enuresis alarms usually do not learn to get up and urinate at night as you would expect if they were associating bladder distention cues with wakefulness. Instead, they begin to sleep through the night without wetting (White, 1971). More recent interpretations (Azrin, Sneed, & Foxx, 1974) have emphasized the operant conditioning aspects of enuresis alarms, with the sound of the buzzer and subsequent abrupt awakening functioning as a negative consequence that can be prevented by learning not to urinate during sleep.

Effective use of the enuresis alarm usually requires professional guidance (Schaefer, 1979). Usually, there is a baseline period of 2 weeks or more, during which data are gathered but no interventions are initiated. When the enuresis alarm is put into operation, parents are commonly told to take the child into the bathroom when the alarm sounds, make sure he or she is awake (splashing cold water in the child's face, if necessary), and have him or her attempt to urinate, even if the bed is already wet. It is also important that the child be given age-appropriate responsibility for remaking the bed with dry sheets and that the alarm be reset. Criteria for discontinuing use of the alarm must also be established with parents. Schaefer (1979) recommends that it be used until there have been 28 consecutive nights with only one enuretic incident. Forsythe and Redmond (1974) found that keeping the child on the alarm 2 to 4 weeks after achieving dryness reduces the chance of relapses.

A number of modifications in the standard enuresis alarm procedure have been developed in an attempt to improve its effectiveness. An over-correction procedure, consisting of having the child drink large quantities of liquids immediately before bedtime after the enuresis has been initially controlled through use of the alarm, has been found to be effective in reducing relapse rates (Jehu et al., 1977). Using a modified enuresis alarm, which activates on an intermittent rather than a continuous schedule, has also been shown to be effective in reducing relapse rates (Finley & Besserman, 1973).

The use of cold baths as an aversive stimulus following alarms does not appear to be any more effective than the standard enuresis alarm protocol (Tough, Hawkins, McArthur, & Van Ravensway, 1971). The delivery of electric shock on urination also does not produce results superior to those obtained with the alarm alone (McKendry, Stewart, Jeffs, & Mozes, 1972). McConaghy (1969) found that the use of the enuresis alarm in conjunction with imipramine was more effective initially than use of the alarm alone and resulted in lower relapse rates than use of the medication alone.

In summary, the use of the enuresis alarm appears to be more effective than psychotherapy (DeLeon & Mandel, 1966), retention-control training (Fielding, 1980), and medication (Wagner, Johnson, Walker, Carter, & Wittner, 1982). The problem of high relapse rates appears at least partially solvable through the use of overcorrection and intermittent reinforcement procedures, and the technique has none of the potentially dangerous side effects of medication. The use of the enuresis alarm does require a considerable time commitment and disruption of sleep for the parents and child, however, and it does not offer an immediate cure, generally requiring 3 months or longer to achieve optimal effects. It is important to note that use of the enuresis alarm also requires a fairly high level of comprehension and cooperation on the part of the child; therefore, its use should be restricted to children old enough to meet these requirements.

Dry Bed Training

Azrin et al. (1974) combined the use of the enuresis alarm with several reinforcement and training procedures in a highly structured program that they called "dry bed training." They found that this procedure eliminated enuresis in all 24 children in their initial experimental group, with no relapses after 6 months. This success was achieved with an average of only two enuretic incidents per child after the first night of training. Doleys, McWhorter, Williams, and Gentry (1977), however, reported only a 62% success rate after a 6-week training period, with a 37% relapse rate. Bollard and Woodroffe (1977) reported that parent-implemented dry bed training eliminated enuresis in all 14 of their subjects within an average of 12 days, with only two relapses (14%) after 6 months. Griffiths, Medrum, and McWilliam (1982) were also able to eliminate enuresis in 100% of their subjects, although it took as long as 20 weeks and there was a 27% relapse rate after 9 months.

Dry bed training consists of an intensive initial training session during which parents and child preview the entire procedure (with a therapist or by themselves). The child is then encouraged to drink fluids and, whenever she or he feels the need to urinate, to delay urination as long as possible. One hour before bedtime, 20 practice trials are conducted, during which the child gets up from bed, goes into the bathroom, and attempts to urinate. At bedtime, the child drinks more fluids and reviews the procedure. Each hour during the night, the parents wake the child and ask if he or she can delay urination for another hour. If the reply is yes, the child is allowed to return to sleep. If the reply is no, the child is taken to the bathroom and praised for appropriate toileting. More fluids are given, and the child is returned to bed. If the enuresis alarm sounds, the child is mildly reprimanded and taken to the bathroom to finish urinating. The child must then change pajamas, remake the bed with dry sheets, and practice going to the bathroom 20 times.

After this initial training session, the child is asked to practice correct toileting 20 times at bedtime if she or he has been enuretic the previous night. The parents waken and toilet the child at their bedtime each night, with the time of this toileting advancing by 30 minutes following dry nights until it occurs only 1 hour after the child's bedtime, at which time it is discontinued. Enuresis alarms result in the same procedure as during the initial training night. Dry nights result in praise and other reinforcement. After 7 consecutive dry nights, the enuresis alarm and parental wakenings are discontinued, and the child's bed is inspected for wetness each morning. A wet bed results in the child being required to remake it with dry sheets and having 20 practice trials of correct toileting at bedtime that night. A dry bed results in praise and reinforcement from parents. Two enuretic incidents within 1 week result in reinstitution of the enuresis alarm and parental wakenings until 7 consecutive dry nights are achieved again.

Azrin and Thienes (1978) modified dry bed training to make it less invasive by eliminating the enuresis alarm and stopping parental wakenings after 1:00 A.M. on the initial training night. They reported that this modified procedure was more effective than use of the enuresis alarm alone and yielded results comparable to the original procedure. However, Nettelbeck and Langeluddecke (1979) found that dry bed training with the enuresis alarm was significantly more effective than the same procedure without the alarm. Bollard and Nettelbeck (1981) even found that use of the enuresis alarm alone was superior to dry bed training without the alarm, which produced no better results than the no-treatment control condition. Bollard (1982) found no differences between dry bed training with the enuresis alarm and use of the alarm alone in treatment effectiveness, although Bollard and Nettelbeck (1982) found that dry bed training did add to the enuresis alarm's effectiveness.

In summary, the dry bed training procedure appears to add to the effectiveness of the enuresis alarm but to have limited usefulness when used without the alarm. It is extremely important to note, however, that this is a very invasive procedure that can be aversive to both children and parents. It is also important to repeat the caution expressed earlier regarding the high demands this procedure places on children for comprehension and cooperation, and the resulting inappropriateness of these procedures for young preschoolers.

ENCOPRESIS

There has been widespread disagreement historically over whether encopresis, or fecal incontinence, is primarily a medical or psychogenic disorder. There has also been a great deal of disagreement and inconsistency concerning the age at which bowel incontinence is classifiable as a disorder, the frequency of soiling necessary for diagnosis, the inclusion of organically based bowel dysfunctions in the diagnostic category, and the patterns of toileting behavior and stool characteristics that differentiate enuresis from normal toilet training and other elimination disorders.

The DSM-III-R (APA, 1987) requires the following characteristics for a diagnosis of functional encopresis: (1) repeated, voluntary or involuntary passage of feces into places not appropriate for that purpose (e.g., floor, clothing); (2) at least one inappropriate passage of feces per month for 6 months; (3) chronological and mental age of at least 4; and (4) ruling out physical disorders. By the use of these criteria, incidence rates ranging from 0.3% to 8% of children have been reported (Bellman, 1966; Doleys, Schwartz, & Ciminero, 1981). The frequency of encopresis declines with age, with 8.1% of 3-year-olds, 2.8% of 4-year-olds, and 2.2% of five-year-olds still soiling their pants regularly (Bellman, 1966). Males are three to four times as likely as females to suffer from encopresis, and approximately half of all encopretic children have been successfully toilet trained before relapsing into encopresis.

Historical Perspective

Encopresis has been recognized as a clinical condition since ancient times, however, the first use of the term "encopresis" was by Potosky in 1925 (Wright, Schaefer, & Solomons, 1979). Encopresis was initially viewed as analogous to enuresis, with similar etiological conceptualizations and attempts at treatment. During the first half of the 20th century, the favored etiological framework was psychodynamic, with such factors as a mother–child power struggle (Hilburn, 1968) and symbolic expression of hostility toward parents (Hushka, 1942) being viewed as causal. Intrapsychic explanations for encopresis remain very prevalent today, among both parents and mental health professionals who do not specialize in this area. As a result, some form of psychotherapy is one of the most common recommendations made when a child presents with encopresis.

Physical Causes

The most common medical cause for encopresis is probably aganglionic megacolon or Hirschsprung disease (Vaughan, McKay, & Behrman, 1979). This is a congenital neurological defect in which a portion of the colon lacks sufficient neuronal innervation to perform adequate peristalsis. As a result, fecal material accumulates and becomes impacted at this point, resulting in an enlarged colon (megacolon). In most cases of Hirschsprung disease, symptoms are present in infancy, with constipation, anemia, and failure to thrive commonly reported (Levine, 1981). Hirschsprung disease is diagnosable through anal manometry and biopsy (Levine, 1981) and can be treated surgically through removal of the dysfunctional area of the colon and reconnection of the adjoining functional sections. It should be noted, however, that functional encopresis occurs approximately 400 times as frequently as Hirschsprung disease (Levine, 1981). Other medical causes for encopresis include peripheral neuropathology, including demyelinating diseases, seizure disorders, malabsorption syndromes, structural anomolies of the digestive tract, and meningomyelocele. Again, however, it is worth noting that over 90% of cases of encopresis do not involve any detectable medical condition.

Psychological Causes

For the vast majority of cases for which no specific medical causality has been discovered, two primary causal mechanisms have been postulated, one intrapsychic and the other behavioral.

Intrapsychic Conceptions

Within the psychodynamic literature, encopresis is invariably interpreted as an indication of emotional disturbance, with the primary component often identified as conflict with parental figures during toilet training (Bemporad, Pfiefer, Gibbs, Cortner, & Bloom, 1971). Unfortunately, most of this research is based on anecdotal and correlational data, with few testable hypotheses. More recent, behaviorally oriented research suggests that, although children with encopresis demonstrate emotional disturbance at a somewhat higher rate than nonencopretic children, there is little support for the notion that emotional disturbance is generally causative of encopresis (Friman, Mathews, Finney, Christophersen, & Leibowitz, 1988). It has also been demonstrated that successful behavioral treatment of encopretic children does not result in "symptom substitution," as one might expect if the disorder were the product of underlying emotional disturbance that was not addressed by the treatment (Levine, Mazonson, & Bakow, 1980).

Behavioral Conceptions

From the behavioral perspective, encopresis arises out of failures in environmental learning experiences. Primary encopresis, or a failure to become initially bowel trained, can result from inadequate teaching of such prerequisite skills as undressing or sphincter contraction when the urge to defecate is felt, or the child's failure to learn such discriminative internal cues as rectal distention in time to reach the toilet (Doleys et al., 1981). Secondary encopresis, or a relapse into fecal incontinence after the child has been successfully bowel trained, can be related to inadequate reinforcement for appropriate toileting, conscious negativism or manipulativeness, or avoidance conditioning (Doleys et al., 1981). This avoidance conditioning results when defecating in the toilet becomes paired with aversive events, which can range from being frightened by being in the bathroom alone, to parental punishment or scolding during toilet training, to painful defecation because of constipation. The avoidence of toileting can, in turn, result in voluntary fecal retention and chronic constipation.

Fecal Retention

The literature suggests that voluntary or involuntary fecal retention related to chronic constipation is a primary causal factor in 80% to 95% of all cases of encopresis (Christophersen & Rapoff, 1983). The constipation may result from a diet with insufficient roughage or bulk, inadequate water intake, sedentary habits, genetic predisposition, or stress, or it may develop when the child voluntarily retains feces because of painful defecation, fear of the bathroom, or other factors. Once constipation begins, it tends to become chronic and may develop into fecal impaction, in which fecal material becomes compressed and dehydrated in the colon. This mass of fecal material cannot be evacuated by normal peristalsis and gradually increases in size due to the accretion of additional fecal material. As a result of this large fecal mass, the colon becomes distended (psychogenic megacolon) and loses its muscle tone. Additional fluid fecal material pools behind this impacted mass and occasionally seeps past, causing a watery discharge similar to diarrhea. As a result of the distended colon and the watery nature of the discharge, the child is often unaware that she or he has soiled.

Assessment

As mentioned previously, it is critical that a comprehensive medical examination be conducted on children who are referred for encopresis. The two primary issues to be addressed are whether a specific medical condition (e.g., Hirschsprung disease) is responsible for the encopresis and whether significant fecal impaction (megacolon) is present.

After the physical examination, a thorough history is necessary, covering both physical and psychosocial aspects of the child's life. The principal value of this aspect of the assessment centers on the concept of specific subtypes of encopresis. There are a number of ways of classifying encopretics, with the concept of primary versus secondary encopresis particularly widespread in the literature. Another dimension by which encopretics are categorized is according to the degree of conscious awareness and control they experience regarding their soiling. There is obviously something very different about the child whose soiling incidents represent "true" accidents in spite of sincere efforts to overcome the problem and children who either deliberately defecate in their clothing as an expression of anger or simply do not care enough about the social ramifications of soiling to interrupt ongoing activities for a trip to the bathroom.

Probably the single most useful dimension for classifying encopretic subtypes is the presence or absence of constipation as a major component of the symptom picture (Kohlenberg, 1973). Particularly where the constipation is chronic, resulting in significant fecal impaction, this factor has a major bearing on the likelihood of success of the various treatment approaches. Specifically, any approach failing to provide for medical evacuation (by enema, suppository, or surgical procedures) of the impacted colon will be doomed to failure, especially if the condition has progressed to the point of functional megacolon and normal functioning of the colon has been compromised. Research has shown stool impaction to be present in from 80% to 95% of encopretic cases (Christophersen & Rapoff, 1983).

Anxiety-related considerations also provide a useful basis for categorizing cases of encopresis. The two most common subtypes are young children who are fearful of the bathroom or toileting process and therefore must either soil their clothing or retain feces, and the chronically anxious child whose anxiety results in loose stools and frequent diarrhea. The pattern of frequent minor accidents exhibited by this latter child is often referred to in the literature as irritable bowel syndrome.

Research comparing "treatment-resistant" to more successfully treated cases of encopresis has identified several significant variables that need to be explored during the assessment process (Levine & Bakow, 1976). Symptom severity, in terms of both the frequency and magnitude of the soiling and the degree of underlying constipation, is highly predictive of treatment outcome, with children who soil while in school or after getting ready for bed having particularly poor outcomes. Paradoxically, children who soil despite little fecal retention also have poor treatment outcomes, possibly because of different etiologies to their encopresis. Children who have other behavioral, developmental, or academic problems in addition to their encopresis also have a poorer treatment outcome than children who have no such concomitant difficulties. Parents' ability to implement encopresis treatment programs in a conscientious and consistent fashion is also highly related to the success of the treatment, with poorer outcome for parents who believe that the encopresis is willful and attribute it to emotional rather than physiological causation. Finally, poor outcome in the treatment of encopresis is related to difficulty in early bowel training, with a high proportion of treatment-resistant cases never being successfully trained.

Treatment

Psychotherapy

Verbal psychotherapy and play therapy were the primary treatment approaches used for encopresis until the 1970s. Since that time, the use of psychotherapy for the treatment of soiling has declined greatly, as more behavioral and medical approaches have gained currency. The few experimental studies of the effectiveness of this approach have yielded unimpressive results. Berg and Jones (1964) followed up 70 children who had been treated for encopresis with psychotherapy and found no difference in rates of remission between those who had been treated and those who had not. Lifshitz and Chovers (1972) studied the effects of psychodynamic therapy on encopresis and found that the untreated control group showed greater improvement than the group that received therapy. McTaggert and Scott (1979), however, reported that 7 of 12 encopretics were "cured" through the use of play therapy, and 3 others showed significant improvement. Again, the possible role of spontaneous remission or therapeutic variables occurring in the natural environment was not discussed. There have also been some reports in the literature of effective treatment of encopresis through the use of hypnosis (Kohen et al., 1984).

Medical Intervention

The standard pediatric approach (Davidson, 1980) to encopresis relies heavily on various combinations of enemas and laxatives for initial evacuation of the colon, followed by use of mineral oil and stool softeners (e.g., Dulcolax, Metamucil, or Colace) to facilitate continuing bowel functioning. Physicians also commonly recommend to parents that the child's diet be modified to provide more fruit, fluids, and roughage to prevent constipation (Nisley, 1976). This approach also calls for increased encouragement and reminders from parents regarding appropriate toileting. The pediatric approach is reported to have limited and inconsistent effectiveness, and it has been suggested that this is due to insufficient attention to the behavioral aspects of encopresis (Schaefer, 1979). In response to this criticism, Levine (1982) developed a modified version of the standard pediatric protocol that has been shown to be more effective. He delineated the specific procedures guiding the use of enemas, laxatives, mineral oil, and dietary modification, with suggestions as to the timing of each intervention. He also stressed the value of such behavioral interventions as self-monitoring and reinforcement and emphasized the need for family and individual counseling to handle psychosocial complications. Levine's (1982) approach also has a strong educational emphasis, demonstrating to the child (and parents), with diagrams and pictures, what biological factors are responsible for the encopresis. The treatment program is presented to the child as a (bowel) muscle-building program. In addition, much reassurance is provided to the child by the physician concerning the frequency and normality of the problem. In contrast to many behavioral programs,

Levine recommends against requiring the child to wash out soiled clothing, although he does suggest that the child should clean his or her body after a soiling incident.

Behavioral Intervention

Behavioral techniques have been shown to be highly effective in addressing encopretic symptomatology (Johnson & Van Bourgondien, 1977). Positive reinforcement for appropriate toileting behavior is the most frequently reported behavioral approach to encopresis. Though sometimes effective by itself, this approach usually needs to be combined with such other interventions as enemas, dietary change, or family therapy to be maximally therapeutic. The usual positive reinforcement approach is to award primary (toys, candy) or secondary (stars, stickers, tokens) reinforcement to the child contingent on appropriate defecation in the toilet. Reinforcers must be appropriate to the child's age and developmental level, and the interval between awarding of a secondary reinforcer and its redemption for a primary reinforcer must not be overly long. Young and Goldsmith (1972) successfully treated an 8-year-old boy with soiling of 1 year's duration by rewarding him with a toy car at the end of each day with no soiling and at least one bowel movement in the toilet. Ayllon, Simon, and Wildman (1975) reported the successful treatment of a 7-year-old boy with chronic encopresis through the use of positive reinforcement. The boy was awarded a star for each day without soiling. When seven stars were earned, the child was allowed to go on an outing with the therapist. In addition to the positive reinforcer, the boy was required to wash his own clothing on occasions when he did soil. The authors report that the encopresis was eliminated within 4 weeks, at which point praise from the mother was gradually substituted for stars, and she began taking the child on outings less formally linked to bowel behavior.

Plachetta (1976) used parental praise and monetary reward as reinforcers in eliminating a 6-year-old boy's encopresis. The boy had soiled twice a day for several months prior to treatment. He was instructed to sit on the toilet on four scheduled occasions each day, with a penny earned for each 10-minute period he remained on the toilet, and a nickel earned for each bowel movement while he was on the toilet. Parents were instructed to generally ignore any soiling that occurred and to discontinue spankings for soiling incidents. The child was required to wash his own clothes after soiling and to chart his progress by placing stars on a wall chart for appropriate toileting.

One caution that needs to be raised concerning the use of positive reinforcement approaches is the need not to make the absence of soiling the sole criterion for reward. If this is the case, the child may obtain reinforcement by simply withholding feces rather than demonstrating appropriate toileting, thus compounding the initial problem.

Punishment procedures are sometimes used separately and sometimes combined with reward approaches to increase the effectiveness of the intervention. Time-out contingent on soiling incidents has been reported to decrease the frequency of such incidents (Edelman, 1971). Ferinden and Van Handel (1970) effectively used the aversive consequence of washing soiled clothes in cold water with an abrasive soap, along with other interventions, including counseling. Crowley and Armstrong (1977) used an overcorrection procedure in which children washed other clothing in addition to their soiled ones as one component of a comprehensive treatment package. The other elements of the package were positive reinforcement (praise) for appropriate toileting, role-playing excusing oneself from ongoing social activities to go to the toilet, positive practice sitting on the toilet attempting to defecate, and "habit-training" sessions in which children practiced "squeezing" and "pushing" as components of bowel control and defecation. This approach led to a complete cure in three severely encopretic boys in 5 to 9 weeks. Follow-up at 18 months indicated no relapses.

Another combination of these two procedures, with a strong emphasis on punishment, is Doleys's full cleanliness training (Doleys, McWhorter, Williams, & Gentry, 1977). Adapted from the dry bed training approach to enuresis (Azrin et al., 1974), full cleanliness training calls for frequent parental prompting to attempt toileting in the initial phase, along with use of positive reinforcement for attempts at defecation on the toilet and frequent "pants checks" to detect soiling that has occurred. Soiling incidents result in the child being required to scrub his or her underwear and pants for 20 minutes each, and then take a bath in cool water for another 20 minutes. Doleys believes that these aversive consequences are responsible for much of the success of the technique (Doleys, McWhorter, Williams, & Gentry, 1977). He reports a high success rate, with the typical time required for the elimination of soiling being between 9 and 16 weeks.

One of the most widely used and most documented treatment approaches is that developed by Wright (Wright & Walker, 1977). This approach calls for the initial evacuation of the child's colon via enema (under a physician's supervision). A behavioral contract is then established between parents and child, specifying expectations for appropriate toileting and criteria for earning rewards. Subsequently, at an agreed-on time each day, the child attempts to defecate on the toilet. If this attempt is successful, he or she is given a small reward. If the attempt is not successful, no reward is given and a glycerine suppository is inserted to aid the child in defecating. A short time later, the child attempts to defecate in the toilet again. If the child is successful this time with the aid of the suppository, a smaller reward is given. If the child is unsuccessful, an enema is given and no reward is provided. Strict limitations are imposed on the frequency of enemas to prevent physiological hazards. Wright suggests 10 consecutive daily enemas as a limit, beyond which their use should be limited to one every 2 or 3 days.

An additional opportunity for reward is provided at the end of the day, at which point the child's clothing is examined for evidence of soiling. If no soiling has occurred, a reward is given. If at this time (or any other time during the day) soiling is detected, a mild punishment, such as 15 minutes of time-out or denial of TV privileges for the evening, is administered. Wright also emphasizes the use of charting and other visual indicators of progress to maintain child and parent motivation.

One of the key principles of the Wright treatment approach to encopresis is the highly standardized, step-by-step procedure that is applied in fairly rigid fashion. However, one area in which the program is highly individualized is in the selection of reinforcers that are motivating to the child and both financially and logistically feasible. Wright suggests that activity reinforcers are particularly appropriate for this purpose and that the use of such rewards as special activities or play time with a parent offers the additional advantage of potentially improving the parent–child relationship. Over the course of the treatment process, the criteria for earning rewards are gradually raised and the frequency of reward delivery is gradually decreased. Verbal praise and social reinforcement are continued for every demonstration of appropriate toileting and nonsoiling, however.

Following 2 consecutive weeks of no soiling, the use of suppositories and enemas is gradually cut back to no more than 1 day per week, even if the child does not have a bowel movement every day. Incidents of soiling result in "backing up" the process by making cathartics available for an additional day per week. Wright and Walker (1977) also suggest administering an enema the morning following a soiling relapse.

Wright and Walker (1977) reported a 100% success rate for this treatment program in encopresis cases for which parents were capable of carrying out the treatment protocol. Although the time necessary to effect a "cure" ranges from 10 to 38 weeks, dramatic improvement was usually noted within the first few weeks of the program. Wright and Walker (1977) note that 10% to 15% of parents are unable to satisfactorily implement the program, and that response is highly variable in those cases.

Several approaches similar to Wright's program have been reported in the literature. Ashkenazi (1975) used glycerine suppositories and positive reinforcement, but not enemas, to successfully treat 16 out of 18 encopretic children. Several of Ashkenazi's subjects had toilet phobias that were treated with positive reinforcement for successive approximations to appropriate toileting. Young (1973) successfully used an approach consisting of required toileting efforts after meals, positive reinforcement for appropriate toileting, and administration of the drug Senekot before bedtime to facilitate defecation. Christophersen and Rainey (1976) used enemas and suppositories combined with positive reinforcement and hygiene training to successfully treat a series of encopretic children.

4

Eating Problems

Problems involving quantity and quality of food intake and eating patterns are a frequent cause of concern for parents of young children. It has been estimated that almost half of all preschoolers have eating problems at some point (Bentovim, 1970). These problems range from selective refusal to eat certain food items to life-threatening ingestion of nonfood items and health-threatening obesity. In this chapter, we will review normal developmental patterns of food choice, appetite, and eating skills, as well as discussing both medical and psychological disorders involving eating behavior. In addition, the related topics of colic, bruxism, and thumb-sucking and pacifier use will be addressed. Behavioral, medical, and mental health interventions with documented efficacy in treating these disorders will also be presented.

As mentioned in Chapter 1, infants are born with a rooting reflex, which facilitates finding the mother's nipple, and a rudimentary sucking reflex. This sucking reflex matures over the first 3 or 4 months of life into a more complex and efficient behavior using negative pressure to obtain milk. During these first months of life, infants also typically demonstrate an extrusion reflex, by which unwanted (nonmilk) food items are pushed out of the mouth by tongue thrusts. This reflex usually disappears around 4 months of age. Around 4 to 6 months of age, the infant's digestive system has matured to the point that semisolid foods such as cereal can be introduced. When the infant is 6 to 8 months of age, pureed fruits and vegetables are appropriate for introduction into the diet, with meats, beans, and eggs following soon after. It is important to note that the child's stomach capacity expands from 10 to 20 ml at birth to approximately 200 ml by 1 year of age, so quantities of food necessary to achieve satiety increase correspondingly.

Motor skills related to eating also develop rapidly during the first few years of life. At 4 to 6 months of age, infants begin to shift food in their mouths and to demonstrate chewing-like movements. They also, at this time, first engage in intentional hand-to-mouth movements and generalized reaching toward the bottle or breast. At around 7 months of age, with the arrival of their first teeth, infants begin to engage in biting behaviors. If spoon-fed, they will begin to reach for the spoon and attempt to draw it toward their mouths. At 9 to 10 months of age, infants demonstrate adequate pincer grasp control to pick up small food items and the ability to self-direct spoons into their mouths, even though frequently the food is lost on the way. Children this age are also typically able to begin drinking from a spouted cup and demonstrate the ability to lick food from their lower lip and engage in lateral chewing movements. By 15 months of age, most children can feed themselves with a spoon, although messiness is a continuing parental concern. They are also capable of eating foods with more solid consistency, although it should be cut into small enough pieces for safe consumption.

It should be noted that approximately 25% of American women are still breast feeding their infants at 6 months of age (Martinez & Nalezienski, 1981), and a number of them continue this practice into the child's second year of life or even longer. There appear to be no significant psychological or health dangers from such extended breast feeding, although children who do not receive adequate quantities of solid foods after 1 year of age are at increased risk for anemia and vitamin deficiencies (Krause & Mahan, 1984).

It is normal for preschoolers to have variable appetites with strong food preferences that change abruptly. Even infants demonstrate wide variability in the type and amount of food they will consume when allowed the freedom to choose. Encouragingly, however, even after extended periods of such free choice, most infants remain well nourished and healthy.

Psychodynamic theory (Freud, 1965) emphasized the importance of early feeding experiences for later personality development. Despite this emphasis on such issues as breast feeding versus bottle feeding and age of weaning, later research has failed to show any reliable specific relationship between feeding events and adult personality (Kessler, 1966). What is evident, however, is that difficulties with feeding may serve as an indication of broader parent–child or developmental problems.

COLIC

Colic is a common condition of infancy that is not actually a disorder of feeding but is often associated by parents with hunger and/or food intake. Wessel, Cobb, Jackson, Harris, and Detwiler (1954) defined colic as episodes of fussing, crying, and irritability that last 3 or more hours per day, and that occur on more than 3 days per week in otherwise healthy and well-fed infants. Typically, colic first occurs during the first few weeks of the infant's life and lasts for 3 to 5 months. The child often grimaces with pain and demonstrates abdominal distention and leg flexion. Diarrhea and vomiting are not associated with colic, although there is a tendency to flatus. The incidence of colic is between 5% and 15% of healthy infants (Wessel et al., 1954). Parental feeding techniques, quantity of food intake, and mother's diet have not been found to be associated with the disorder (Illingworth, 1954). A number of researchers and practitioners have attributed the disorder to either parental anxiety or innate infant temperament (Spock, 1963), although the etiology has not been definitively established. Most researchers agree that colic is a self-limiting condition without long-term detrimental effects.

Treatment for colic consists largely of coping with the infant's distress until he or she outgrows the condition. Parents have anecdotally reported for years that a variety of movement, noises, and tactile stimuli appear to quiet their children, and recent formal research has corroborated these claims (Loadman, Arnold, Volmer, Petrella, & Cooper, 1987). Such actions as taking the child for a ride in the car (or even just sitting in the car with the engine running), placing the child's baby seat on top of an operating washing machine, or walking while holding the child appear to be effective for individual children. It is not known whether these interventions function primarily as distractors and relaxers or whether more central treatment mechanisms are in operation. Research has shown that the common pharmacological agents homatropine, phenobarbital, and alcohol are ineffective, individually and in combination, in treating colic (O'Donavan & Bradstock, 1979).

THUMB-SUCKING

Another concern of parents of preschoolers that does not actually involve feeding but that will be considered here is thumb-sucking. There are several theories as to the cause of excessive or prolonged thumb-sucking in children. Freud (1965) viewed thumb-sucking as a response to inadequate early oral gratification and/or the result of fixation during the oral stage of personality development. Thumb-sucking has also been associated in the past with anxiety and insecurity in infants and young children (Kessler, 1966). More recent theories, however, have emphasized that thumb-sucking is a natural and logical extension of the adaptive, innate sucking reflex (Brazelton, 1967). Approximately 45% of all children engage in thumb-sucking at some point during childhood (Klackenberg, 1949). Most children, however, stop sucking their thumbs by age 4 or 5, with only 2% continuing beyond age 13 (Block & Rash, 1981).

Extensive thumb-sucking after the age of 4 or 5 does involve both medical and psychological hazards, although these are relatively mild. Frequent thumb-sucking beyond this age can contribute to dental malocclusion, involving protrusion of the upper teeth and retroclination of the lower teeth (Curzon, 1974). Deficient swallowing reflex, the presence of abnormal tongue thrust, and speech deficits have also been associated with prolonged, extensive thumb-sucking (Block & Rash, 1981). The psychological hazards of extensive thumb-sucking during the elementary school years include the dangers of ridicule by peers and/or adults and the possibility of the habit interfering with both social and cognitive developmental opportunities.

Probably the best approach to treating thumb-sucking in preschoolers is a conservative one. In infants and young toddlers, providing a pacifier designed to minimize dental problems may prevent thumb-sucking from becoming a high-frequency behavior. Subsequently, it may prove much easier to remove the pacifier or control its use than to eliminate thumb-sucking (McReynolds, 1972). Pediatric dentists sometimes recommend the use of a palatal bar or crib with sharp spurs, which make insertion of the thumb into the mouth painful. These devices are reasonably effective if used for several months but potentially have negative effects on eating and speech and may engender negative emotional reactions (Hargett, Hansen, & Davidson, 1970). There are also reports in the research literature that thumb-sucking can be reduced by removing objects associated with the practice. For example, Friman (1988) reported that thumb-sucking was successfully decreased in a preschool girl by taking away a doll that the girl always held in her other hand when she was sucking her thumb. Friman and Leibowitz (1990) successfully used a positive reinforcement program in conjunction with coating the thumbs with a bad-tasting substance to reduce thumb-sucking in 22 children between the ages of 4 and 11. Children's thumbs were coated with the substance (available from a pharmacist) on wakening, at bedtime, and whenever the child was observed sucking his or her thumb. The positive reinforcement program consisted of random selection from a menu of tangible and activity reinforcers for reduction in thumb-sucking. Friman and Leibowitz (1990) reported that 12 of the 22 children ceased sucking their thumbs within 3 months of initiation of treatment and that 20 of the 22 children had stopped sucking their thumbs within 1 year after treatment was initiated. Previous work by Friman and associates (Friman & Hove, 1987) demonstrated that use of a bad-tasting substance applied to the thumb could be effective even in the absence of a positive reinforcement program.

MEDICAL DISORDERS AFFECTING FEEDING

A number of physical disorders are known to result in feeding problems in young children, including food allergies, thyroid dysfunction, other endocrine abnormalities, and neuromuscular problems affecting sucking and swallowing responses. An example of a congenital obstruction of the gastrointestinal tract that affects food intake is the occurrence of pyloric stenosis (Thompson, 1987). In this disorder, the infant is born with overdevelopment of the muscles surrounding the passage from the stomach to the duodenum and intestines. This overdevelopment restricts the passage of food and resulting digestion. Usually when the child is 2 to 3 weeks old, he or she begins demonstrating projectile vomiting, constant hunger, and absent bowel movements. Palpation, x-rays, and ultrasonography can establish the diagnosis, and surgical enlargement of the pyloric passage (pyloromytomy) usually offers a complete cure. Failure to treat the condition can result in dehydration, malnutrition, and even death.

Vomiting is a common occurrence in preschoolers and can result from a number of medical conditions and nonmedical occurences, including ingestion of spoiled food or nonfood items; excess stomach gas; ingestion of excessive quantities of food or drink; too rapid feeding; ear, nose, and throat infections; many common communicable diseases; Reye's syndrome; peptic ulcer disease; and increased intracranial pressure (Thompson, 1987). A high percentage of cases of vomiting in preschoolers is idiopathic, or of unknown cause. The dangers of vomiting in young children include the possibility of aspiration of the vomitus into the child's air passages, causing suffocation or aspiration pneumonia. Therefore, infants who are at risk for vomiting should be placed on their stomach or side following feeding. Long-term effects of persistent vomiting can include dehydration, electrolyte imbalance, and malnutrition.

FEEDING PROBLEMS NOT RELATED TO MEDICAL DISORDERS

Failure to Thrive

Two disorders that appear to be at least partially caused by emotional factors are failure to thrive and psychosocial dwarfism. Failure to thrive is a disorder in which children up to the age of 4 show weight loss or a failure to gain adequate weight despite receiving adequate nutrition. These children often demonstrate food refusal, vomiting, and diarrhea. Three to 5% of infants under 1 year of age admitted to pediatric teaching hospitals are diagnosed with failure to thrive, with organic causes found in fewer than 30% of cases (Mitchell & Greenberg, 1980). The mechanisms most often considered to be operative in cases of nonorganic failure to thrive are disturbed parent–child interactions and analogues of childhood depression (Bakwin & Bakwin, 1972). Lack of nutritional knowledge on the part of parents, improper feeding techniques, and parental stress also appear to be contributing factors (Kotelchuck, 1980).

Historically, nonorganic failure to thrive was first described by Spitz's (1945) use of the term "hospitalism" to describe the failure to grow and the developmental retardation that commonly occurred with institutionalized infants. Spitz attributed this disorder to a lack of maternal love and nurturance. Subsequent research has focused on dysfunction in the relationship between infants and their mothers, with Talbot, Sobel, Burke, Lindemann, and Kaufman (1947) reporting mothers of failure-to-thrive infants as being frequently clinically depressed, Pollitt and Thompson (1977) finding them to have high rates of alcoholism, and Fischoff, Whitten, and Pettit (1971) suggesting the frequent occurrence of character disorders. Pollitt and Eichler (1976) described mothers of failure-to-thrive infants as being colder and demonstrating less positive affect than mothers of other infants and as providing less vocal stimulation to their children. However, other research (Pollitt, Eichler, & Chan, 1975) has failed to find increased psychopathology in mothers of failure-to-thrive infants. Some researchers have focused on child characteristics as causal in failure to thrive. Kotelchuck (1977) found that failure-to-thrive infants were perceived by parents as being fussier, more reactive, and slower than other infants. Failure to thrive has been found to be highly correlated with prematurity, and both groups of infants demonstrate a less vigorous sucking response than normal infants (Gryboski, 1969). Infants identified as at risk for failure to thrive also have a higher pain threshold before crying and a longer latency of response to pain (Lester & Zeskind, 1978). One difficulty with interpreting these data is that the direction of causality is not entirely clear; did failure to thrive and consequent malnutrition cause these behavioral deficits, or did these innate behavioral patterns affect the child's psychosocial environment and result in failure to thrive? It appears that both organismic and environmental variables are significant in the interaction that produces the failure-to-thrive syndrome.

Several research studies have documented later cognitive deficits in failure-to-thrive children, although again the direction of causality is uncertain. For example, Glaser, Heagarty, Bullard, and Pivchik (1968) found lower than average mean IQ scores for children who had been identified with failure to thrive as infants when they were evaluated from 8 months to 8 years later. Similarly, Fitch et al. (1976) found lower developmental quotients for children who had been hospitalized for failure to thrive than for controls 6 months after hospitalization.

A number of demographic and other variables have been identified as associated with failure to thrive. Failure-to-thrive children tend to come from low socio-economic status families and are frequently the youngest of many children (Hufton & Oates, 1977). From 25% to 40% of failure-to-thrive children are born prematurely (Newberger, Reed, Daniel, Hyde, & Kotelchuck, 1977). Alcohol abuse has been cited as frequent in the families of failure-to-thrive children (Pollitt & Thompson, 1977), and fetal alcohol syndrome may be a significant causal factor.

Treatment for failure to thrive children is usually focused on parent–child interactions, particularly those surrounding feeding. Mira and Cairns (1981) were able to substantially increase a 1-year-old boy's weight and social responsiveness by instructing his mother in such interactional skills as modeling, imitation, verbal feedback, and verbal praise. Moore (1982) was successful in developing a program to prevent rehospitalization and stabilize weight gain in failure-to-thrive children. This program focused on education and role modeling for parents in child care and nurturing skills, along with supportive counseling and environmental intervention to reduce parental stress.

A common intervention used with failure-to-thrive children is hospitalization, and researchers report that over 40% of cases demonstrate significant weight gain during hospital treatment (Kotelchuck, 1977). More consistent and positive attention from nursing staff and the lack of parental conflicts surrounding feeding appear to be significant factors in this improvement.

Psychosocial Dwarfism

A condition that has been historically linked to failure to thrive in children is psychosocial dwarfism (PSD). This disorder is characterized by growth disturbance, such that the child is below the third percentile in stature for age. In addition, children with this disorder frequently demonstrate endocrine dysfunction and behavioral disturbances, including hoarding of food and water, gorging and vomiting, and eating garbage and drinking from the toilet. All of the children in the initial report identifying PSD as a separate syndrome (Powell, Brasel, & Blizzard, 1967) had developmental delays and IQ scores below 80, and subsequent research has corroborated that the majority of PSD children function cognitively within the mildly retarded range (Drash, Greenberg, & Money, 1968; Ferholt et al., 1985; Hopwood & Becker, 1979). Diagnosis of PSD also requires evidence of a severely disturbed relationship between the primary caretaker and the child. The onset of the disorder is usually between the ages of 2 and 4 years and is not attributable to other physical and mental disorders or simple malnutrition.

When PSD was first clearly identified in 1967 (Powell et al., 1967), one of the factors that caused it to be differentiated from other cases of suspected idiopathic hypopituitarism was the fact that these children showed a clear acceleration in growth rate and improvement in endocrine status when removed from their homes, before any other treatment was initiated. In addition, only 1 of the original 13 children identified by Powell and associates (1967) demonstrated clinical malnutrition. These factors caused the researchers to conclude that psychosocial factors, particularly those involved in the caretaker–child relationship, were primary in the etiology of the disorder.

It appears that the psychosocial factors involved in PSD are similar to those implicated in nonorganic failure to thrive. Bowden and Hopwood (1982) reviewed 10 cases of PSD and found a definitive history of failure to thrive during infancy in four children and suspected failure to thrive in four others. Powell et al. (1967) found that marital discord was evident in 82% of families of PSD children, with 63% of the parents separated or divorced. Drash et al. (1968) reported that in approximately two-thirds of their sample of PSD children, one or both parents had subjected the PSD child to extreme emotional rejection. Fifteen percent of the children had been physically abused. Ferholt et al. (1985) also reported severe parent–child relationship problems in most of their sample of PSD children. They also reported that in most cases the children's severe behavioral problems occurred while the children were with the parents and disappeared while the children were at school, in the hospital, or visiting friends.

The consistent endocrine findings in PSD have included lowered somatomedin levels suggestive of hypopituitarism, abnormally low fasting growth hormone levels, and decreased pituitary production of corticotropin (Campbell, Green, Caplan, & David, 1982). As noted above, most endocrine abnormalities disappear without specific medical treatment when the child's psychosocial environment is improved through out-of-home placement or other intervention.

Most of the extreme behavioral abnormalities demonstrated by PSD children involve feeding behaviors. In the sample by Drash et al. (1968), over 50% of the children engaged in overeating, many to the point of vomiting. Thirty percent ate from garbage pails, and 2 out of 14 ate feces or drank water from the toilet. Over one-third of the children roamed the house at night looking for food. Over 60% of the children demonstrated disruptive and/or aggressive behavior patterns, and many exhibited short attention span and learning problems. Hopwood and Becker (1979) reported similar findings, and additionally reported that one-third of the PSD children over 4 years of age in their sample were encopretic, and over 50% were enuretic. The study by Ferholt et al. (1985) of 10 PSD children offers further corroboration of the high frequency of occurrence of these symptoms. Seventy percent of these children ate or drank inappropriate materials, including garbage, pet food, and toilet water. Ninety percent of the children had severe temper tantrums, 60% had sleep disturbances, and 50% had attentional problems. Ferholt et al. (1985) reported that all 10 children demonstrated depressive symptomotology.

The treatment of choice for psychosocial dwarfism is removal of the child from the home to a hospital, foster home, or other setting offering a more therapeutic psychosocial milieu. Researchers (Hopwood & Becker, 1979) note that seldom is it possible to effect enough change in family relationships to allow the child to remain at home during treatment. Almost all authorities report that dramatic changes in growth rate, endocrine status, and behavior occur almost immediately on removal from the home and placement in a therapeutic environment (Ferholt et al., 1985; Powell et al., 1967). Ferholt et al. (1985) further report that children with PSD who had demonstrated substantial improvement in their condition showed significant recurrence of their symptomatology when returned home after extended placement (up to a year) in foster care. Money and Annecillo (1976) reported that the IQs of 75% of PSD children removed from their homes increased significantly over a period of 2 to 8 years. Some IQs increased as much as 55 points. The largest IQ increases were associated with the most therapeutic placements and the longest period out of the natural home, and were accompanied by the greatest reduction in behavioral symptoms of PSD. The children who demonstrated no change in IQs received relatively nontherapeutic placements (such as a state psychiatric hospital) and showed little reduction in PSD symptomatology.

Rumination

Rumination is a feeding disorder of infancy characterized by the voluntary regurgitation of food or liquid. It is fairly rare among nonretarded infants, although among mentally retarded children the incidence of rumination has been reported at approximately 9% (Ball, Hendrickson, & Clayton, 1974). The disorder is potentially fatal, with Kanner (1972) reporting that 20% of a sample of cases had died as a result of malnutrition or other complications. Children frequently appear to derive pleasure from rumination (Bakwin & Bakwin, 1972) and have been observed to cause the onset of regurgitation by putting their fingers down their throats or chewing on objects.

Several etiological explanations have been offered regarding rumination. Psychoanalytic explanations interpret the behavior as an infant's attempt to provide oral stimulation that is missing in cases of "faulty" mothering (Richmond, Eddy, & Green, 1958). Behavioral explanations have focused on the innate pleasure of the self-stimulation provided and the attention that the behavior elicits from others (Linscheid, 1978). It is worth noting that rumination occurs occasionally in almost all infants and that it escalates to the level of a clinical problem in very few cases.

Treatments that have been reported to be efficacious in eliminating rumination have included increasing parental attention and affection along with thickening the food that the child eats (Bakwin & Bakwin, 1972; Kanner, 1972). Psychoanalytic practitioners have reported success following extended psychotherapy with the parents (Berline, McCullough, Lisha, & Szurek, 1957). Behavioral practitioners have reported success with a variety of approaches. Lang and Melamed (1969) used electric shock as an aversive stimulus contingent on rumination in a 9-month-old boy and were successful in eliminating the behavior within 5 days of the initiation of treatment. Follow-up assessments at 1 month, 5 months, and 1 year after treatment found no recurrence of the rumination. Sajwaj, Libet, and Agras (1974) reported that squirting lemon juice into a 6-month-old infant's mouth contingent on rumination was also an effective treatment. The question has been raised as to whether the effectiveness of these treatments is due to the aversive nature of the stimuli or whether the stimuli simply distract the infant from the act of rumination.

Pica

Pica is a disorder characterized by the frequent ingestion of inedible substances. The name for the disorder is derived from the Latin word for magpie, a bird known for the wide variety of objects it ingests (Block & Rash, 1981). Most children below a year of age put many of the objects they handle into their mouths. If this behavior persists past 18 months of age, however, and is characterized by actual eating of nonnutritive substances rather than merely tasting or chewing them, a diagnosis of pica may be made. The disorder is more commonly found in mentally retarded children and those from lower socioeconomic status families. It also appears that the ingestion of some inedible substances may be actively promoted by certain subcultures in the United States. For example, rural residents in the southern United States have historically been taught to eat certain clays and soils as children or adolescents (Millican & Lourie, 1970). There appears to be little support for the hypothesis that pica is related to specific nutritional deficiencies in children's diets (Millican & Lourie, 1970). Lack of parental supervision and/or attention, however, does appear to be a significant correlate (Kanner, 1972).

There are a number of negative effects from pica, the most serious of which are accidental poisoning, intestinal obstruction, and lead poisoning. In one study (Millican & Lourie, 1970) 55% of the children hospitalized for accidental poisoning exhibited pica. In the past, a significant danger has existed for children with pica because of the presence of lead in paints. Children would ingest paint flakes by chewing on window sills, stair rails, and baby furniture. Although lead is now banned from use in most commercially available paints, lead-containing paint is still available for ingestion by children with pica who live in older, substandard housing that has not been repainted recently or by children who are using older cribs or other furniture that has not been repainted. As recently as the late 1970s, 400,000 cases of lead poisoning by paint were reported annually (Wright, Schaefer, & Solomons, 1979). There are several other sources of lead poisoning for children who do not exhibit pica. Acidic drinks (such as fruit juice) consumed from pottery containers with improperly applied lead glazes, folk medicines (such as azarcon, used in the Mexican-American subculture), and airborne lead from car exhausts are significant sources of lead poisoning. The symptoms of lead poisoning occur gradually and include weakness, anorexia, vomiting, abdominal pain, and in the later stages, muscular incoordination, convulsions, and possible death. About half of affected infants and young children show signs of encephalitis, and the mortality rate in these cases is approximately 25%. Long-term effects of lead poisoning include neurological damage and mental retardation (Thompson, 1987).

Treatment approaches with pica are rather varied. The disorder tends to disappear by age 4 or 5 in most children of normal intelligence. Millican and Lourie (1970) suggested educational intervention in which mothers of children with pica were advised of the health hazards inherent in the disorder and encouraged to spend more time with their children and to discourage their ingestion of nonfood items. They also reported that the lessening of social and environmental deprivation in the lives of children with pica resulted in a diminishment of symptomatology, and they suggested psychotherapy for older children with persistent pica. Madden, Russo, and Cataldo (1980) successfully used behavior therapy approaches in treating pica in three 2-year-old girls. These approaches included training in discriminating edible from nonedible substances, positive reinforcement for not ingesting nonedible substances, and overcorrection procedures when ingestion of nonedible substances occurred. Finney, Russo, and Cataldo (1982) similarly reported the successful behavioral treatment of pica in four preschoolers hospitalized for lead poisoning. They reduced pica behaviors to practically zero after 60 treatment sessions through the use of differential reinforcement of other behaviors (DRO) and overcorrection procedures. The reinforcer used during the DRO phase was food treats, and the overcorrection intervention consisted of brushing the child's mouth with mouthwash.

Bruxism

Another common behavior among preschoolers, which will be discussed in this chapter, is bruxism, or excessive toothgrinding. Although all children occasionally grind their teeth, the incidence of bruxism in the general population is estimated at 5% (Reding, Rulbright, & Zimmerman, 1966). The negative effects of extensive bruxism include abnormal and uneven wear to the teeth, damage to the gums and other periodontal structures, and resorption of the alveolar bone (Scandrett & Ervin, 1973). In addition, bruxism has been implicated in temporomandibular joint (TMJ) problems (Scandrett & Ervin, 1973), facial pain, and headache (Schwartz & Chayes, 1968).

A number of etiological factors that have been linked to bruxism are listed in Table 4-1.

Children demonstrating more than occasional toothgrinding should be seen by a dentist to rule out malocclusion as a cause and to assess the degree of abnormal tooth wear. They should also be seen by a pediatrician to assess the possible presence of the physical factors listed below. If the bruxism occurs solely during sleep, as in a high percentage of cases, and

Table 4-1. Etiological Considerations in Bruxism[a]

1. Malocclusion	8. Hyperthyroidism
2. Anxiety	9. Epilepsy
3. A positive family history	10. Acute hemiplegia
4. Mental retardation	11. Meningitis
5. Organic brain damage	12. Side effects of fenfluramine
6. Allergy	13. Normal sleep activity
7. Sinusitis	

[a]From Block, R. W., & Rash, F. C. (1981). *Handbook of behavioral pediatrics.* Chicago: Year Book Medical Publications.

no other causal factors are identified, then it will most likely resolve over time, even without treatment. The child can be fitted with a tooth-protecting mouthguard to prevent damage while waiting for this remission to occur. Diazepam therapy has also been reported to have been helpful in severe cases (Ferber & Rivinus, 1979).

Bruxism has long been linked with emotional distress and mental illness. Lindqvist (1972) found that bruxistic children displayed significantly more stress symptoms and nervous disorders than children who did not demonstrate bruxism. Other researchers, however, have failed to find a clear relationship between emotional factors and bruxism (Reding, Zepelin, & Monroe, 1968), and it appears likely that bruxism is the product of multiple causes, of which emotional distress is only one.

As mentioned above, the use of protective mouthguards and anxiolytic medication have been found to be effective in the treatment of nocturnal bruxism. Other treatment approaches for bruxism with documented efficacy include dental treatment to remedy malocclusion (Scandrett & Ervin, 1973) and psychological/behavioral interventions. Although psychotherapy has often been recommended for older children, there is little but anecdotal evidence of its effectiveness (Nadler, 1973). Heller and Strang (1973) used a loud blast of sound contingent on audible toothgrinding to greatly reduce the rate of a subject's nocturnal bruxism. Biofeedback approaches have also been shown to be effective in treating bruxism in older children and adults. Solberg and Rugh (1972) reported significant improvement in two-thirds of the subjects who wore an electromyogram (EMG) biofeedback unit for 2 to 7 days. Rugh and Solberg (1975) also reported that contingent awakening based on EMG feedback was successful in reducing the frequency of nocturnal bruxism, although the frequency increased again when the contingency was discontinued. There are no published reports of the implementation of these procedures with preschoolers.

FOOD REFUSAL

As many as 45% of all preschool children demonstrate some problems with their eating behavior (Bentovim, 1970), with one of the most common of these problems being food refusal. Food refusal is defined as a child's insistence on eating only a small number of foods, eating only foods with a particular texture, or not eating a sufficient quantity of food to ensure adequate nutrition (Williamson, Kelley, Cavell, & Prather, 1988). Often food refusal becomes evident when a child is first begun on solid foods or after the resolution of medical problems that have interfered with the normal feeding process. Food refusal often occurs in conjunction with a variety of behavioral problems, which may include gagging and vomiting food, spitting food out, leaving the table, temper tantrums, whining and complaining, playing with food, and dawdling (Williamson et al., 1988). Although food refusal usually does not result in severe medical consequences, its negative effects can include malnutrition, growth retardation, parent–child conflict, and social skills deficits (Williamson et al, 1988). For most children, the problem is time-limited, even without treatment.

The assessment of food refusal problems is complex and requires recognition of the interaction between environmental, biological, and behavioral variables. The possibility of medical problems contributing to the food refusal problem dictates the need for a comprehensive pediatric evaluation as part of the assessment process. In addition to the medical evaluation, a complete developmental history, with the emphasis on feeding behaviors, is necessary. Standardized interview formats are available to assist the practitioner in gathering this information (Krieger, 1982). Some practitioners recommend observational assessment of current parent–child interactions surrounding feeding, although it may be possible to gather equivalent information through interviews with the parents or videotaping. The most effective intervention in cases of food refusal is the prevention of problems through introduction of new food types and textures at the appropriate age and education of parents in preventing the emergence of such related behavioral problems as picking, dawdling, and throwing tantrums. Christophersen and Hall (1978) suggest that parents use contingency management procedures to control inappropriate behavior and to shape food choice. They recommend the use of such behavioral techniques as star charts and parental attention and praise to reinforce trying new foods and time-out or the removal of preferred foods to extinguish problem behaviors.

More severe cases of food refusal can also be treated through the use of behavioral interventions. For example, Bernal (1972) used a combination of behavioral techniques to treat food refusal in a 5-year-old girl. The food refusal problems began when the girl choked on a piece of solid food and the mother went back to feeding her only strained baby foods. When the mother later tried to reintroduce solid foods, the girl refused to eat them. The mother attempted to withhold baby foods, hoping that the child would become hungry enough to eat solid food, but this attempt was unsuccessful. Observation suggested that the mother was reinforcing the food refusal with attention contingent on the problem behaviors. Intervention consisted of instructing the mother to reinforce the child with attention and praise only when she was eating solid food and implementing a shaping procedure in which access to preferred foods was made contingent on eating solid foods. Television watching was also used as a reinforcer for eating solid foods. Implementation of these procedures resulted in the child adding 50 solid foods to her diet over the 4-month treatment period.

Hatcher (1979) used similar interventions to treat food refusal in a 2-year-old girl. In this case, the behavioral interventions were implemented in the hospital, because the child's malnourished condition had placed her in medical jeopardy. Over 13 weeks of treatment, the child gained substantial weight and was eating a significantly wider variety of foods. A 2-year follow-up revealed no reemergence of the food refusal problem.

Siegel (1982) used a combination of classical and operant conditioning approaches to treat food refusal in a 6-year-old boy. This boy was earlier placed on a diet of soft foods because of a gastrointestinal illness. Later, when his medical condition had resolved, he refused to eat solid foods when his parents tried to reinstate them. He gagged and vomited if solid foods were placed in his mouth. Contingency management procedures that provided reinforcement for eating solid foods were ineffective because the boy continued to gag and vomit when he took solid foods into his mouth. Therefore, a gradual progression of exposure to solid foods was initiated, beginning with only smelling the foods, then touching the food with his tongue, then chewing the food and spitting it out, and finally chewing and swallowing the food. The act of chewing solid foods was also paired with the pleasurable act of watching television in a counterconditioning paradigm. This program resulted in a tremendous increase in the number of foods the child would eat and in the child being able to eat a complete meal of solid foods with his family after 20 weeks of treatment.

Palmer, Thompson, and Linscheid (1981) also used behavioral techniques to treat food refusal in a 6-year-old paraplegic boy with borderline intelligence. This child never progressed beyond eating pureed foods and responded to his parent's attempts to force-feed him solid foods by gagging and developing a strong fear of eating such foods. It was determined through videotape observation that the boy used asking his mother questions as a way to avoid eating the solid foods she presented. Therefore, in feeding sessions with therapists, withdrawal of attention was made contingent on irrelevant conversation as well as refusal to eat solid foods. In addition, praise, attention, and the opportunity to eat preferred foods was made contingent on eating solid foods. Over 13 treatment sessions during a 3-week period, the child significantly increased the amount of food he ate and began eating a wide variety of solid foods. A 12-month follow-up assessment of his diet at home indicated a maintenance of treatment progress.

OBESITY

The idea that obesity can be a problem in early childhood is a new and fairly controversial one. We are used to chubbiness in babies and traditionally interpret it as a sign of good health. Research, however, indicates that there may be a correlation between obesity in early childhood and later in life. For example, Charney, Chamblee, McBride, Lyon, and Pratt (1976) found that 36% of infants who were obese were later reported to be overweight as adults. This was in contrast to the 14% of infants who were average or below in weight who were later reported to be overweight as adults. Similarly, Miller, Barrett, Hampe, and Noble (1972) reported that there was a significant correlation between weight-for-height ratios at age 5 and at age 22, and Abraham and Nordsieck (1960) reported that 80% of overweight 10- to 13-year-olds were still overweight 13 to 25 years later.

Coates and Thoresen (1978) suggest that because of this correlation between early childhood weight problems and obesity later in life, along with the increased medical risks and social and psychological problems that accompany obesity, early childhood obesity should be a focus of concern for parents and clinicians. Research suggests that from 5% to 10% of preschool children are obese, depending on the definition used (Maloney & Klykylo, 1983). Further, it appears that obesity has increased by 54% in 6- to 11-year-old children in the past 20 years (Dietz, 1988). Obesity in children appears to be strongly linked to socioeconomic status (SES), occurring nine times more frequently in girls of lower SES than in girls of higher SES (Stunkard, d'Aquill, Fox, & Filion, 1972).

Obesity in young children has multiple causes. There are a number of specific medical and genetic conditions that can result in childhood obesity. However, these disorders only occur rarely and can often be differentiated from obesity related to food intake by the fact that children with these conditions are usually below the 25th percentile in height and have delayed bone age (Woolston & Forsyth, 1989). The possibility of medical causes and/or complications in cases of childhood obesity, however, necessitates pediatric consultation before treatment is initiated.

There is certainly a strong correlation between the weight status of children and that of their parents. If one parent is obese, a child has a 40% to 50% chance of being obese, and if both parents are obese, this percentage increases to over 70% (Linscheid, 1992). Before we too rapidly assume, however, that this relationship is solely due to genetic factors, it is worth noting that similar results have been found for adoptive children (Garn, Cole, & Baily, 1976). It appears that the strong relationship between parent and child weight status may be as much or more a function of family eating and activity patterns as of genetics.

Hartz, Giefer, and Rimm (1977) determined heritability to account for only 11% of the variability in weight status, while family environment was responsible for 39% of the variability.

Over the years, childhood obesity has also been attributed to psychogenic factors. Bruch (1957) described two groups of children whose obesity was related to psychopathology. In one group, the onset of obesity was in reaction to upsetting or traumatic events, such as school failure or the death of a friend. In the other group, the obesity was the result of family dysfunction and disorganization, with mothers overfeeding their children as a result of ambivalence and guilt. Christoffel and Forsyth (1985) studied 17 children with infantile obesity and found that all of the children were from disorganized and dysfunctional homes. None of the parents were able to set limits adequately, and 59% of the mothers were overweight or obese themselves. None of the children had abnormal medical findings suggestive of medical or genetic reasons for their obesity. A number of these children lost weight after being placed in foster homes, while all of the children who remained with their families continued to be obese.

Most commonly, however, early childhood obesity occurs in the absence of such apparent family pathology and is the result of simple excessive caloric intake in comparison to caloric expenditure on the part of the child because of a lack of concern/supervision by parents or maladaptive cultural practices and/or misinformation. Genetic heritability may increase the child's vulnerability for weight problems but is usually not the dominant variable.

Treatment for early childhood obesity has largely focused on effecting dietary changes, often through the use of behavioral interventions. The major behavioral treatment components that have been used in the treatment of childhood obesity include self-monitoring, stimulus control techniques, regulation of eating behaviors, family interventions, reinforcement procedures, cognitive restructuring, exercise programs, and nutritional education (Linscheid, Tarnowski, & Richmond, 1988).

Self-monitoring of dietary input and activity may involve only parents of obese children (Israel, Stolmaker, Sharp, Silverman, & Simon, 1984), or for older preschoolers, it may also involve the child (Coates & Thoresen, 1981). A number of techniques exist to assist children (and parents) in monitoring their eating and exercise behaviors. These include food and activity checklists, point charts, token systems, and a variety of other feedback and information-organizing strategies (Coates & Thoresen, 1981). Cohen, Gelfand, Dodd, Jensen, and Turner (1980) found that children who maintained weight loss over an extended period of time reported engaging in more self-monitoring than children who did not maintain their weight loss.

Stimulus control techniques involve the identification of situations or environments that may trigger inappropriate or excessive eating. These "eating signals" may then be avoided or changed to promote healthier eating habits. An example of a stimulus control intervention appropriate for preschoolers is the "traffic light diet" developed by Epstein, Marshall, and Masek (1978), in which foods are classified as "green," or low in calories and high in nutrition and thus recommended for unlimited consumption by the child; "yellow," or foods that are high in calories but have nutritional benefits and must, therefore, be consumed in moderation; and "red," or foods that are high in calories and low in nutritional benefits and thus have little place in a healthy diet. The color signals are initially externally presented to the children with the hope that, over time, they will internalize the stimulus control message. Other approaches have included the restriction of eating to certain times and places and the elimination of eating in conjunction with activities (such as TV) with which it has been linked in the past. Weiss (1977) found that obese children using stimulus control techniques lost more weight and maintained their weight loss better than those using diet and self-reinforcement.

Approaches to regulation of eating behavior include helping children to slow their rate of eating to allow satiety signals to inhibit overeating. Specific techniques that have helped children slow their rate of eating have included instructions to put the fork or spoon down between bites, requirements to chew food a certain number of times before swallowing, and structured delays during the course of a meal. Epstein, Parker, McCoy, and McGee (1976) reported that instructions in and praise for decreasing eating rate resulted in a significant decrease in food consumption by three obese 7-year-olds.

Family interventions appear to be particularly important in the treatment of obesity in young children, most of whom have only limited control over the type and quantity of food available to them. One of the most important roles parents can occupy in their child's treatment for obesity is that of model. Israel et al (1984) found that when parents of 8- to 12-year-olds served as either role models by losing weight themselves, or as helpers in their child's weight-loss program, both groups of children lost weight and kept it off, but the parent role model group had better results for younger children. Epstein, Wing, Koeska, and Valoski (1986) found that parents and obese children as young as 14 months of age could benefit from instruction in diet, exercise, and behavioral principles. Children involved in these groups decreased their percentage of overweight from 42% to 27% in the first 2 months of the program.

Reinforcement approaches to weight loss have used a variety of positive reinforcers to effect change in such obesity-related behaviors as activity level (Epstein, Woodall, Goreczny, Wing, & Robertson, 1984), and food choice, and quantity of food eaten (Wheeler & Hess, 1976). In most cases, parents have been instructed in the delivery of reinforcers. Some practitioners have incorporated response cost techniques (Aragona, Cassady, & Drabman, 1975) and contingency contracting approaches (Dinoff, Rickard, & Colwick, 1974) into their reinforcement programs.

Cognitive restructuring treatment approaches involve the identification of maladaptive beliefs and attitudes that may contribute to the child's obesity and the elimination of these factors through teaching or reinforcing counterbalancing cognitions. Coates and Thoresen (1981) suggest that cognitive restructuring is a vital part of the treatment package for childhood obesity, particularly for older children. An example of a cognitive restructuring intervention would be the verbal reinforcement of a child's focus on short-term attainable goals rather than becoming discouraged by the seeming impossibility of losing 50 pounds or more.

Exercise is increasingly seen as an important component of all treatment for childhood obesity. Exercise has a number of benefits, including increasing caloric utilization, mitigating health risks associated with obesity, suppressing appetite, increasing basal metabolism rate, and lessening the loss of muscle resulting from dieting (Brownell, 1982). Epstein et al. (1984) found that diet plus exercise resulted in significantly greater weight loss for obese children than diet alone. Epstein, Wing, Koeske, Ossip, and Beck (1982) developed an exercise program for children, incorporating naturalistic exercise as part of the child's daily life (e.g., using stairs instead of elevators). This program was found to be effective in promoting weight loss, even if it was not accompanied by dietary regulation. In addition, the naturalistic exercise approach was more effective than a traditionally structured aerobic exercise program in long-term maintenance of weight loss and fitness.

Nutritional education approaches are generally less appropriate for use with preschoolers than with older children. The most useful approach with preschoolers seems to be to provide nutrition information to parents, particularly if the child's obesity is thought to result, even partially, from parental misinformation about diet and nutrition. An approach mentioned earlier as a stimulus control technique also qualifies as an effort to conduct nutrition education appropriate to older preschoolers. This is the "traffic light diet," by Epstein et al. (1978), in which foods are divided into "red," "yellow," and "green" food groups.

In summary, concerns about eating and related issues are common among parents of preschoolers. Most eating problems are not related to specific medical conditions but are instead the result of family environment and interaction variables. The most severe eating disorders—failure to thrive, psychosocial dwarfism, rumination, and obesity—can have major long-term detrimental effects on child development and health. It is important that every mental health professional working with preschool children be familiar with the indicators of these disorders.

5

Sleep Problems

Few preschoolers are referred to mental health practitioners with a primary complaint of sleep problems. More commonly, friends, relatives, popular media, or pediatricians advise parents concerning children's sleep problems. In a recent community survey, parents of young children were asked where they would seek help if their child had a sleep problem: 91% indicated they would ask family or relatives, 87% said they would seek advice from friends, 87% said they would seek information from books or magazines, 71% indicated they would talk to a nurse or physician, and only 47% said they would seek help from a psychologist or mental health professional (Johnson, 1991).

However, mental health professionals working with preschoolers frequently consult on sleep problems while treating children with other primary complaints. Approximately one-third of children's sleep problems occur in the context of wider behavioral problems (Richman, 1981). In a longitudinal study, Zuckerman, Stevenson, and Bailey (1987) found that 18% of 8-month-olds and 29% of 3-year-olds had sleep problems, and sleep problems were associated with behavior management difficulties and maternal depression. Sleep problems are particularly prevalent in preschool-age children with developmental disorders (Stores, 1992). Often, sleep problems in infants and preschoolers are initiated by a transient problem such as colic, otitis media, or travel, and are exacerbated or maintained by patterns of parent–child interaction at bedtime, naptime, or during nighttime awakenings. In other children, good sleep habits may never have been learned because of a chaotic family environment precluding the establishment of sleep routines. Although physicians and friends frequently advise parents that young children will outgrow their sleep problems, severe problems are likely to persist. Butler and Golding (1986) found that 46% of children who had sleep problems in infancy still had them at age 5. Infancy and the preschool years are particularly fruitful times for intervention because younger children are more adaptable in their habits and routines, and their sleep environment is more under the control of parents (Ferber, 1989a).

In this chapter, we will briefly describe what is known about normal sleep patterns in young children from infancy through the preschool years. Within this developmental framework, we will consider a variety of sleep problems that arise in preschoolers, including difficulty falling asleep, nighttime awakenings, refusal to go to bed at night, nighttime fears and anxieties, nightmare disorder, confusional partial arousals, sleep terror disorder, and rhythmic body movements.

NORMAL DEVELOPMENT OF SLEEP PATTERNS IN PRESCHOOLERS

During the first few days of life, a newborn sleeps an average of 16 to 17 hours each day, broken into periods less than 4 hours long (Parmelee, Schulz, & Disbrow, 1961). "Sleeping through the night" or "settling" refers to consistently sleeping without awakening between 12:00 A.M. and 5:00 A.M., and most infants are considered to be "settling-ready" if they are steadily gaining weight and are approximately 6 to 9 weeks old. Soon after birth, infants begin to establish a "circadian rhythm," a biological cycle that repeats itself every 24 to 25 hours that includes patterns of sleeping, hunger, and body temperature. Once the circadian rhythm becomes established, sleep becomes more consolidated, with most 3- to 6-month-old infants settling for a 5-hour stretch at night (Ware & Orr, 1992). The average amount of daytime and nighttime sleep required by children from the age of 1-week to 6-years is displayed in Figure 5-1. As can be seen from the figure, the average amount of sleep required decreases steadily during the preschool years, while the proportion of sleep that occurs during the night rather than the day increases.

During sleep periods, infants cycle through stages of rapid-eye-movement (REM) and non-rapid-eye-movement (NREM) sleep in 50- to 60-minute cycles, rather than the 90-minute cycle typical of adults. While most adults spend only 20% of their sleep period in REM, infants up to age 8 or 9 months spend 50% of their sleep time in REM (Schaefer & Petronko, 1987). It is easier to be awakened from REM than from deeper NREM sleep, and this may account for why infants seem to be more readily awakened by noises than are adults (Schaefer & Petronko, 1987). Children usually fall asleep in 10 to 15 minutes, are in deep

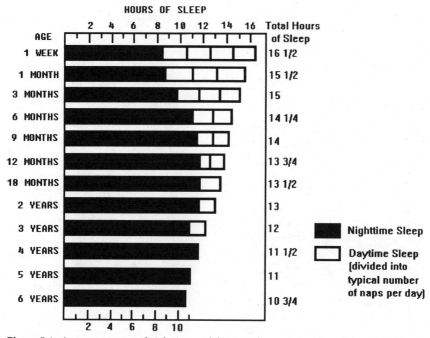

Figure 5-1. Average amount of nighttime and daytime sleep required by children from 1 week to 6 years of age.

NREM sleep 5- to 20-minutes later, and have the first REM period 1 to 2 hours after sleep onset (Ware & Orr, 1992). Deep sleep (NREM stages 3 and 4) is most prominent during the first third of the night (or daytime sleep period), and night terrors usually occur during this time. In contrast, REM sleep is most prominent during the last third of the sleep period and is when children are most likely to experience nightmares (Schroeder & Gordon, 1991). Infants, children, and adults awaken several times during the night, typically at the end of each sleep cycle (Ferber, 1985). As adults, we usually have no memory of these awakenings because we fall rapidly back to sleep for the next cycle. However, transitioning back to sleep on one's own is a learned behavior that infants must acquire, and there is considerable individual variability in how well both infants and toddlers soothe themselves back to sleep.

DIFFICULTY FALLING ASLEEP, BEDTIME STRUGGLES, AND
NIGHTTIME AWAKENINGS

Parents who seek help for their preschooler's problems going to sleep and staying asleep are typically suffering from sleep deprivation themselves. Long-term lack of sleep may be interfering with the parents' daytime parenting, work productivity, interpersonal relationships, and mood (Douglas, 1989). Difficulty falling asleep at bedtime, refusing to go to bed and stay in bed, and frequent nighttime awakenings will be considered together here because they often co-occur in young children, often share similar causes, and may be treated using similar methods.

Prevalence

Sleep problems are extremely common in infants, toddlers, and preschool-age children, and are usually more troubling to parents than to their children. In her survey, Johnson (1991) found that 42% of infants and toddlers were reported by their parents to have difficulty settling for sleep at night. In another community survey, Richman (1981) found that 24% of 1- to 2-year-old children awakened 2 to 4 nights per week and an additional 20% awakened 5 to 7 nights per week. Similarly, Johnson (1991) found that 35% of children under the age of 3 persistently awakened and cried during the night. Bedtime struggles and refusals also appear to be common, with 42% of parents participating in a community survey indicating that their children resisted going to bed (Johnson, 1991).

Etiology

Like adults, infants and preschoolers form associations with drowsiness and falling asleep, and they experience difficulty sleeping in the absence of familiar sleep stimuli (Ferber, 1985). For most children with healthy sleeping patterns, relaxation and then drowsiness are associated with a series of bedtime preparation activities occurring about 20 to 30 minutes prior to a preset bedtime. These bedtime rituals vary among families but typically include bathing, putting on pajamas, brushing teeth, saying goodnight to siblings, having a last sip of water and trip to the bathroom, and being tucked into bed after a story, soothing music, or quiet conversation. Caffeine beverages are typically avoided near bedtime, as they may contribute to difficulties falling and staying asleep (Edelstein, Keaton-Brasted, & Burg, 1984). Just as the steps leading up to being tucked into bed signal the onset of relaxation and drowsiness, the characteristics of the setting in which the child is accustomed to falling asleep signal sleep onset. In children with healthy sleep patterns, onset of nighttime sleep is often associated with dimming of the lights (typically not complete darkness), comforting objects such as stuffed animals or favorite blankets, and lying in the crib or child's bed.

Problems with falling asleep are common when there has been a change in prebedtime rituals or in the specific stimuli associated with sleep onset. Transient sleep problems occur in most children when families travel or have overnight guests. These problems resolve quickly once nighttime rituals and familiar sleep stimuli are reinstated. However, long-lasting sleep-onset problems may arise when children are allowed to form and maintain sleep-onset associations that are "dysfunctional." A dysfunctional sleep stimulus would be one that is not always available at the time and place the child should fall asleep. For example, parents may allow their child (who has no prior history of problems falling asleep) to sleep in their bed while guests are visiting, and then fail to enforce the reinstatement of the child's normal sleep routine once the guests are gone. Similarly, the 3-year-old who is transitioning from sleeping in the crib to sleeping in a regular child's bed may be allowed to sleep with the parents on a temporary basis while "getting used" to the new bed. The longer the child is allowed to continue sleeping with the parents, the stronger the associations will become between sleep and the presence of the parents and the parents' bed, and the harder it will be for the child to fall asleep in his or her own bed.

Some preschoolers with sleep-onset problems have never achieved healthy sleep associations and are experiencing the continuation of a sleep problem that began during infancy. Parents may inadvertently prevent their infant from learning to fall asleep independently when the baby is taught to associate the onset of sleep with rocking, patting on the back, and being fed by the parent. Thus, the infant's sleep will be disrupted whenever the parent is unavailable to serve as the sleep stimulus, such as when the infant is with a babysitter, the parent is ill, or the parent is busy or asleep. Paret (1983) found that 9-month-olds who were good sleepers were able to soothe themselves back to sleep after waking up during the night, but nightwakers required the presence of the mother to return to sleep.

Nighttime awakening is sometimes due to uncomfortable medical conditions such as fever, middle ear infections, gastroesophageal reflux, allergy to cow's milk or other food, respiratory difficulties caused by enlarged tonsils or adenoids, teething pain, diaper rash, colic, or urinary tract infection (Ferber, 1989a). Sleep problems may also occur as a side effect of a variety of medications. For example, mild insomnia occurs in about 65% and severe insomnia occurs in about 18% of children treated with low to moderate doses of stimulant medication (Barkley, McMurray, Edelbrock, & Robbins, 1990). However, the relationship between stimulant medication and sleep problems is difficult to assess because there may be a higher than normal base rate of sleep-onset problems in children with attention-deficit disorder, even in the absence of stimulant medication treatment (Cashman & McCann, 1988). Difficulties with sleep onset and nighttime awakening have also been reported to be side effects of antiasthma bronchodilator agents such as aminophylline (Cashman & McCann, 1988).

Nighttime awakening during infancy and toddlerhood can be associated with particular feeding patterns. Mothers who use La Leche League style breast feeding (nurse frequently, tend not to separate from the child at night, and nurse late into toddlerhood) have been shown to have infants and toddlers up to age 2 with fragmented sleep patterns typical of most babies early in infancy (Elias, Nicolson, Bora, & Johnston, 1986). After 6 months of age, consuming large amounts of milk before going to sleep and periodically throughout the night should be avoided because it can result in more frequent awakening due to wet, uncomfortable diapers and conditioning of infants to be hungry at night rather than during the day (Schaefer & Petronko, 1987).

Persistent problems with nighttime awakening are most often behaviorally based and are similar to those described for the onset of nighttime sleep. As noted earlier in this chapter, children awaken briefly a number of times during the night as part of their normal sleep cycle. To have lengthy periods of relatively uninterrupted sleep, young children must learn to make a transition from wakefulness to sleep on their own, without parental intervention. Over two-thirds of infants and toddlers who sleep through the night are self-soothers and are not nursed, rocked, or comforted to sleep (Johnson, 1991). Learning to sleep through the night is preempted by parents who have immediate and prolonged interactions (e.g., rocking, playing, feeding) with their infants whenever they awaken during the night. This habit often forms in families with colicky babies and continues even after the colic has resolved (Weissbluth, 1987). Infants who have been taught to fall asleep at bedtime only in the presence of a parent will typically be unable to fall back asleep after a nighttime awakening without a repeat of the bedtime routine of rocking, patting on the back, or feeding.

Assessment

A comprehensive evaluation for sleep problems should begin with a thorough medical evaluation to rule out the various physical conditions that could precipitate nighttime awakening. Douglas (1989) recommends that the medical evaluation be supplemented with a detailed interview in which information is gathered on (1) bedtime and settling to sleep patterns (e.g., extent that a prebedtime routine is used, elements of the routine, duration of the routine), (2) waking at night patterns (e.g., number of times per night and number of nights per week), (3) daytime sleep patterns (e.g., number, length, and timing of naps), (4) previous advice and therapy, (5) the child's daytime behavior (e.g., co-existing behavior problems), and (6) family relationships and social life (e.g., quality of the parent–child and marital relationships, social support network). During the interview, information about parental expectations concerning optimal sleep/wake patterns should be collected to assess for inappropriate developmental expectations (Cashman & McCann, 1988). If the child attends day care or preschool, information may be collected from the teacher concerning daytime sleep patterns.

Because parents may not relate all relevant information in the interview, a "sleep diary" is often helpful in understanding the nature of sleep problems (see Schroeder and Gordon, 1991, for a sample sleep diary). For the initial evaluation, it is recommended that parents complete the diary for a 2-week period to obtain a sufficient sample of sleep behavior. Critics of sleep diaries have noted that some parents have difficulty completing the measure during the nighttime, there may be confusion concerning which parent will make the entries, and parents often underestimate the number of times their children soothe themselves back to sleep after awakening during the night. However, research generally supports the accuracy of sleep diaries. Studies have found that parent-completed diaries largely agree with videotapes made of sleep behavior (Keener, Zeanah, & Anders, 1988), and interview and diary data correlate at approximately .70 (Elias et al., 1986).

Because approximately one-third of children with sleep problems also have significant behavior problems, the medical evaluation, interview, and sleep diary should be supplemented with behavior rating scales normed for preschoolers such as the Child Behavior Checklist (CBCL; Achenbach, 1991, 1992) and the Eyberg Child Behavior Inventory (ECBI; Eyberg & Ross, 1978). The CBCL form for 2- to 3-year-olds also includes a seven-item sleep problem scale that is useful as a screening device for initial problem identification. Patterns of coerciveness in the parent–child relationship may also be assessed through observational methods. The Parenting Stress Index (PSI; Abidin, 1990) can provide information on the degree and types of stressors the parents are experiencing and their attitudes toward parenting.

Treatment

If any medical condition appears to be contributing to nighttime awakenings (e.g., milk allergy, otitis media), it should be addressed by the physician prior to implementing a behaviorally based program. However, improvement of a medical condition that may have been the initial cause of sleep difficulties will not always cause sleep problems to resolve. Both children and parents may need help relearning appropriate sleep habits to replace the poor habits that formed in response to the medical condition.

For preschoolers who have difficulty falling asleep and have no well-established bedtime routine, the first intervention should be to educate parents about the importance of having consistent bedtime rituals that will serve as cues for relaxation and drowsiness. Parents should be encouraged to plan a sequence of steps for bedtime lasting no more than 20 to 30 minutes and including some special one-on-one time with a parent (e.g., listening to a tape of a calming lullaby or reading a book). The sequence of steps must have a clearly set endpoint (e.g., story has been read so the lights are dimmed and the parent leaves). Initially, the bedtime routine should begin at about the time the sleep diary suggests that the child is currently falling asleep, even if it is considerably later than the parent would like. As the child starts to learn the routine and to associate it with feeling sleepy, the bedtime can be moved up gradually, in increments of 30 minutes, without the preschooler recognizing that a change in bedtime has occurred (Douglas, 1989). Unfortunately, some families with chaotic lifestyles who have not established consistent bedtime rituals have difficulty doing so even with the encouragement and support of a therapist.

If the results of the evaluation suggest that the parent's presence is necessary for the child to fall asleep either at bedtime or after a nighttime awakening, the intervention should include education concerning the importance of teaching children to self-soothe to sleep. One of the most commonly suggested techniques is rapid extinction or "crying it out." The parents are advised to tell the child that they will not return to the room after saying good-night, to put the infant or young child to bed while still awake, and to leave the room, paying no further attention when the child cries or calls out. Schroeder and Gordon (1991) describe the use of a child's bedtime book entitled *We Will See You in the Morning* (Spitznagel, 1976) to help children understand what will happen and to help their caregivers be consistent. Parents are warned to expect postextinction bursts in which the child cries more frequently, more intensely, and for longer periods than at baseline. Initially, some infants and young children persist in crying for as long as 1 to 2 hours before they exhaust themselves and fall asleep. Ferber (1985) recommends returning to briefly check on the crying child according to a preset schedule of increasing time intervals. Most parents find this approach more acceptable than letting the child cry it out without periodic checks (Johnson, 1991). If the older preschooler will not stay in bed, Ferber (1985) recommends closing the child's door (and holding it closed) for progressively longer periods of time until the child finally stays in bed. Both procedures described by Ferber are designed to be implemented over a 7-day period. Several empirical studies evaluating the effectiveness of extinction programs (often in combination with modifications of bedtime routine) have demonstrated that most children learn to sleep through the night with 1 to 4 weeks of treatment (e.g., Sanders, Bor, & Dadds, 1984).

Many parents find the use of rapid extinction both stressful and distasteful (Johnson, 1991). Some authors have suggested that extinction may produce negative side effects such as fearfulness, feelings of rejection, and an impaired sense of security (Elizabeth, 1988). However, empirical studies have documented no negative side effects from the use of extinction, and several researchers have found behavioral and emotional improvements in the adjustment of infants and toddlers successfully treated using extinction (e.g., France, 1992). Others have criticized this method on the grounds that many parents attempt to use extinction but are unable to keep from comforting the child after prolonged crying, in effect making the problem worse (e.g., Rickert & Johnson, 1988). However, use of the highly structured step-by-step procedure described by Ferber (1985) appears to be effective in discouraging parents from reinforcing prolonged crying.

Because some parents find rapid extinction undesirable or difficult to implement, graduated extinction programs have been developed. Lawton, France, and Blampied (1991) described the use of a program in which parents gradually reduced attention to bedtime disturbance and night waking from average baseline levels to zero over a 28-day period. Parents were instructed to reduce their time attending to the child's bedtime or nighttime disruption by approximately one-seventh every 4 days in order to reach zero by 28 days. The authors noted that although graduated extinction was largely successful, there were some difficulties with the program. It was still stressful for parents, postextinction response bursts still occurred, and it was considerably more complex to implement than regular rapid extinction (Lawton et al., 1991).

With older preschoolers who have difficulty going to bed and staying in bed throughout the night, contingency management procedures can be effective (Cashman & McCann, 1988). Parents are instructed in the use of a next-morning star chart for recording the child's successes with going to bed and staying in bed. The particular behaviors that are selected as targets should be determined based on the information obtained during the evaluation; but in general, the first goals should be easily achieved so that children will experience initial success. Very young children appear to benefit from verbal reminders throughout the day about behavioral targets and contingencies. The targets may then be made gradually more challenging to shape the child into better sleep behavior. For most preschoolers, brightly colored stickers and enthusiastic parental praise are sufficient reinforcers, and more complex contingency management systems relying on delayed exchange of tokens for privileges or prizes are rarely needed. When the assessment reveals that bedtime struggles are a part of a larger picture of oppositional behavior, the treatment focus should begin with a parent-training intervention targeting noncompliance and improvement of the parent–child relationship. In most cases, improvements in daytime behavior and consistency in parental limit setting will generalize to bedtime behavior, and additional therapeutic interventions for bedtime are rarely needed (see Chapter 8 for a discussion of parent-training programs appropriate for use with preschoolers with conduct problems). Many caregivers rely on parenting books to provide them with information on managing their children's sleep problems. Although several good books are available, we particularly recommend the book by Ferber (1985) entitled *Solve Your Child's Sleep Problems*. Medication is sometimes used to treat children who have persistent problems falling asleep or who awaken during the night. However, sedatives suppress REM sleep and deep sleep, and they may actually increase sleep problems. Occasionally, parents report medicating their infant or young child with small amounts of alcohol mixed into milk or with a liquid antihistamine before bedtime (Schaefer & Petronko, 1987). Although these methods may assist children in falling asleep more quickly, their sleep is more likely to be disrupted and fragmented, with more frequent nighttime awakenings. In general, medication is rarely effective as a long-term solution to young children's sleep problems (Schaefer & Petronko, 1987). In her community survey, Johnson (1991) noted that most parents expressed strong disapproval of the use of medication to promote sleep onset and maintenance, and only 6% of parents reported having used medication to get their children to sleep.

NIGHTTIME FEARS AND ANXIETIES

Most children show occasional anxiety and fears at nighttime. The specific content of the fears varies among children and tends to change over the course of development. Toddlers and older preschoolers may experience anxiety over separation from the parents at bedtime, fear of the dark or of monsters lurking in the shadows, anxiety about the possibility of nighttime wetting or soiling, fear of being abducted from their bedroom by a stranger, or fear of falling asleep and never waking up. For most children, these fears are unpleasant but transitory developmental phenomena and do not cause terror or panic. However, some preschoolers develop persistent and intense nighttime fears that lead to significant sleep problems for the whole family or that may be part of a larger pattern of problems (Douglas, 1989).

Prevalence

As mentioned earlier, most normally developing preschoolers experience some anxiety and fears at bedtime. In a study of 100 children between 1½ and 3 years old, Crowell, Keener, Ginsburg, and Anders (1987) found that 24% expressed fear of the dark, all used a nightlight, and most slept with a transitional object. Beltramini and Hertzig (1983) reported that 47% of their sample of 1- to 5-year-old children insisted on having a nightlight on in their bedroom at some point.

Etiology

Some children may be more vulnerable than others to both daytime and nighttime fears because of a family history of anxiety disorders. However, nighttime anxiety is most often due to a combination of daytime stress and bedtime circumstances that set the stage for children to focus on their worries. Sometimes nighttime fears arise or are exacerbated when children are put to bed at an unrealistically early hour before becoming relaxed and drowsy. It is not unusual for children lying in bed wide awake in a darkened room to become increasingly anxious and fearful as they think about daytime worries and notice how the shadows resemble frightening, imaginary creatures. Children who are struggling to master important developmental milestones (such as separation, toileting, independence) or those whose families are subjected to significant stress are most likely to experience problems with nighttime fears. Identifiable stressors may include marital discord, separation or divorce, financial or professional difficulties, parental affective illness, medical disorder or death, family move, start of school, toilet training, and birth of a sibling (Ferber, 1989a). The content of the nighttime fear may not be thematically related to specific daytime stressors, but may be a fear commonly reported by children of the same developmental level.

Assessment

In evaluating a child whose parents are concerned about nighttime fears, the most important information is usually obtained from interviews with the child's major caregivers. Information about the child's affect and bedtime behavior is useful for assessing the degree to which the fear or anxiety is genuine versus primarily a strategy for delaying bedtime or gaining permission to sleep with parents. Parents should also be asked to provide information about the child's bedtime routine and use of aids to reduce fear, such as transitional objects and nightlights. Because some young children with nighttime fears may experience other internalizing problems, the interview should also address indicators of problems such as separation anxiety, generalized anxiety, other specific fears and worries, somatic complaints, and sad affect (see Chapter 10 for a more complete discussion of the assessment of young children's fears). Information should be obtained about developmental milestones the child may be struggling to master (e.g., toilet training), any familial stressors (e.g., parental loss of employment) that may have precipitated bedtime anxiety, and strategies the parents have used to minimize the impact of these stressors.

Treatment

For most children, nighttime fears resolve in the absence of intervention (Ferber, 1985). For those with problems persisting more than 1 month or who are experiencing significant levels of distress, brief parent counseling is usually sufficient for helping parents to alleviate their children's nighttime anxieties, and individual child therapy is rarely needed (Ferber, 1985). Parent counseling should address the way in which parents respond to the child at bedtime as well as strategies for decreasing daytime stressors. As much as possible, the child's bedtime routine should be maintained with adjustments made in bedtime if it has been set unreasonably early. Parents should offer reassurance about nighttime fears and may choose to lie down with the child briefly to provide comfort. Taking the child into the parent's bed is typically not recommended because it can lead to further sleep disruption and dysfunctional sleep associations. "Co-sleeping" has been reported to be a highly persistent behavior across childhood and has been shown to co-vary with children's fear of the dark (Klackenberg, 1982).

Ferber (1985) advises parents not to engage in lengthy, detailed rituals of chasing monsters from the room and shining lights in all corners of the bedroom and closet. Such activities do not help young children to understand that monsters are not real. Physical comfort and brief reassurance are more useful for helping children develop a sense of mastery over their fears. Parents should be advised to allow their children to sleep in a partially lighted room rather than insist on complete darkness, to provide comforting transitional objects, to remove items that may be eliciting or exacerbating fears, and to allow the bedroom door to remain ajar so that the child does not feel isolated from the rest of the family. Several books addressing nighttime fears are available for toddlers and preschool-age children (e.g., Morris, 1980; Showers, 1961; Viorst, 1978), and reading such a book as part of the bedtime routine can provide additional reassurance and comfort.

With older preschoolers and school-age children, rehearsal of positive self-statements such as "I can take care of myself when I am in the dark" or "I am a brave girl and I can handle the dark," accompanied by awards of "bravery tokens" for use of coping statements, may decrease nighttime fears (Graziano & Mooney, 1980). However, cognitive interventions alone are not as effective as cognitive strategies combined with behavioral components such as graduated exposure (Ollendick, Hagopian, & Hutzinger, 1991). For example, Sheslow, Bondy, and Nelson (1982) found that *in vivo* exposure to the dark was a key component of successful treatment of fear of the dark in kindergarten students. Because toddlers and older preschoolers may not be able to learn the relatively sophisticated relaxation procedures commonly used in desensitization (see discussion by Ollendick and Cerny, 1981), some studies have paired exposure to the dark with other behaviors thought to be incompatible with fear, such as playing or having a snack (e.g., Kelly, 1976).

Interventions focusing on daytime stressors are at least as important as bedtime interventions. Depending on the nature of the stress identified during the assessment, parents may need to relax their developmental expectations, arrange for more individual time with the child who has a new sibling, curtail discussions of adult concerns and worries in the presence of the child, avoid exposing the child to overt marital conflict, arrange a visit or two to the new preschool or day care the child is anticipating attending, discuss the concept of death with a child who has misconceptions, or gradually shape successful separation in a child who is afraid to be alone in his or her room. More intensive individual therapy may be warranted when children's nighttime fears are secondary to traumatic stressors such as the terminal illness of a parent, separation from family due to placement in foster care, kidnapping, or abuse.

NIGHTMARE DISORDER

Nightmare disorder, referred to as dream anxiety disorder in DSM-III-R, involves "repeated awakenings from the major sleep period or naps with detailed recall of extended and extremely frightening dreams, usually involving threats to survival, security, or self-esteem" (APA, 1993, p. Q:4). These awakenings usually occur during the second half of the sleep period, and the child becomes quickly oriented and alert. Although many people confuse nightmares with sleep terrors or confusional partial arousals, they can be clearly differentiated by the detailed dream recall, the lack of physical activity during the nightmare, and the time of occurrence during the sleep period (Schroeder & Gordon, 1991). It is unclear whether infants have sufficiently mature sleep patterns to experience nightmares, but on awakening from a nightmare, young toddlers in their second year of life are often able to name what frightened them (Ferber, 1985). From toddlerhood to the age of 7, children gradually develop an understanding of dreams as internal events that are not real but produce very real emotions. Occasional nightmares are not associated with any major emotional or behavioral problem. However, persistent nightmares may reflect greater than normal levels of daytime anxiety (Ferber, 1985).

Prevalence

Almost all children have an occasional nightmare, but 11% of non-referred children have been reported to experience them at least once a week (Fisher & Wilson, 1987). Nightmares occur most frequently in preschool-age children and adolescents (Ferber, 1985). Depending on study criteria and populations served, approximately 7% to 30% of children referred to pediatricians and clinical psychologists experience nightmares (Dollinger, 1986; Salzarulo & Chevalier, 1983). Nightmares appear to be particularly prevalent in children being treated for anxiety and affective disorders (Simonds & Parraga, 1984).

Etiology

Although illnesses and particular medications may occasionally precipitate nightmares, like nighttime fears they typically occur in response to stress experienced during the day. Stressors that may increase a preschooler's risk for experiencing nightmares include exposure to marital discord, parent–child conflict associated with developmental milestones such as toilet training, coping with the birth of a new sibling, beginning preschool or day care, general familial stress associated with financial problems, an accident, or illness of a parent or sibling (Ferber, 1985). The content of the nightmare appears to be related to developmental changes in common childhood fears and concerns (see Chapter 10 for a discussion of normative fears in young children). As with nighttime fears, children who have family histories of nightmare problems are somewhat more likely to experience nightmares themselves (Cashman & McCann, 1988).

Assessment and Treatment

Sufficiently detailed information should be gathered in the parent interview to rule out sleep terror disorder and the degree to which nightmare complaints are reinforced through granting of co-sleeping privileges, late-night snacks, or extra television time. For young children with nightmares, a careful assessment including caregiver interviews and parent report measures (e.g., the Louisville Fear Survey, the CBLC) should be conducted to evaluate whether the child is experiencing other internalizing or anxiety-related symptoms (Greening & Dollinger, 1989). Through careful parental interviewing and a measure of parenting stress (e.g., Parenting Stress Index), daytime stressors can be identified that may contribute to the nightmares.

When nightmares occur, parents should be counseled to go to the child and provide comfort and reassurance in the child's room. Ferber (1985) explains that the types of reassurance that are most effective will depend on the child's level of understanding of nightmares. One-year-olds and most 2-year-olds do not understand that nightmares are not real, and attempts to explain this in the middle of the night when the child is distressed will probably only result in confusion. Physical comforting is probably the most helpful until the child is calm and ready to fall back asleep. Three-year-olds are comforted by both physical contact and verbal reassurance that they are safe and the parent will protect them. Four- and 5-year-olds are beginning to understand the nature of dreams and nightmares, but even though they understand that nightmares are not real, they are still quite frightened. They benefit from being reminded it was only a dream, having the light on to reinforce that they are awake and the dream is over, and having an opportunity to talk about the nightmare with a sympathetic listener (Ferber, 1985). If the child needs prolonged comforting, it is better to stay with the child until he or she falls back asleep than to encourage co-sleeping by taking the child into the parent's bed.

If the occurrence of nightmares is linked to stress within the family, treatment often involves parent counseling about how familial stressors may influence the child's behavior. Parents are encouraged to limit their expression of anxiety in the child's presence, to limit sharing of nonessential details of financial concerns or interpersonal conflicts, and to find an alternative and appropriate adult source of support. Many parents, particularly single parents who are struggling financially, reinforce their young children for accepting levels of responsibility that are more appropriate for older children, not realizing that this may generate considerable anxiety and fear of failure.

In addition to parent counseling, behavior therapy conducted directly with the child can be useful for reducing both daytime and nighttime anxiety. Contingency management, relaxation therapy, and systematic desensitization have all been reported to be successful in case studies of children with nightmare disorders (Greening & Dollinger, 1989). For a detailed discussion of these treatment approaches, the reader is referred to Chapter 10.

CONFUSIONAL AROUSALS AND SLEEP TERROR DISORDER

Sleep terror disorder involves recurrent episodes of abrupt awakening from sleep, usually occurring during the first third of the major sleep period and beginning with the child sitting bolt upright with eyes open and screaming in panic (APA, 1993). During each episode, there is intense anxiety and signs of autonomic arousal such as tachycardia, rapid breathing, and sweating, and the child is not responsive to comforting. Sometimes, the child will try to flee blindly and may injure himself or herself in the process. The episodes usually end within a few minutes. In contrast to nightmare disorder, the child does not remember a detailed dream and has no memory of the episode.

Confusional arousals are often mistaken for sleep terror disorder (Ferber, 1989b). Confusional arousals are partial arousals usually occurring during stage 4 of non-REM sleep. Instead of beginning abruptly with the panicky scream characteristic of sleep terror disorder, an episode typically begins with some movement or moaning and progresses to crying, calling out, and often thrashing about in the bed or crib. The child usually perspires heavily, and his or her eyes may be open or closed. Rather than looking terrified, the child is likely to appear confused and agitated. The confusional arousal episode usually lasts longer than an episode of sleep terror, ranging from 2 to 40 minutes, with a typical episode lasting 5 to 15 minutes (Ferber, 1989b). As in sleep terror disorder, the child is not responsive to parental attempts at awakening or comforting.

Prevalence

The true incidence of confusional arousals in young children is unknown; however, it is believed that almost all children under the age of 5 have at least a mild form of this from time to time (Ferber, 1989b). In contrast, sleep terror disorder is much less common and occurs in about 7% of children (APA, 1987). Sleep terrors occur more frequently in preschoolers than in older children, and they typically disappear as the central nervous system matures (Schroeder & Gordon, 1991).

Etiology

The partial arousal that characterizes sleep terrors may be an exaggeration of the developmentally normative partial arousal that occurs at the end of all delta sleep cycles. According to Ferber (1989b, p. 641), "Instead of making a brief but more complete arousal before descent into the next sleep cycle, the child seems caught, as if both deep sleep and arousal systems were functioning simultaneously." Partial arousal can be triggered by an external event as well as an internal one. For example, moving a child or making a loud noise near the end of stage 4 sleep can precipitate a confusional event or screaming (Ferber, 1989b). Partial arousal episodes are more frequent in children with a history of febrile seizures or obstructive sleep apnea, and in those with chaotic sleep schedules. These episodes are more likely to occur on nights when the child is particularly fatigued.

Treatment

Treatment typically involves only brief parent consultation (Ferber, 1989b). Parents are given information concerning the developmental nature of partial arousals, are reassured that they do not represent any significant psychological or physical abnormality, and are told that partial arousals are typically much more bothersome to the parent than to the preschool child. Parents should be advised to allow the episodes to run their course, intervening as little as possible and only when necessary to protect the child's safety. Attempts at restraining the child or providing comfort can sometimes exacerbate the episode, increasing its intensity and duration. Parents should also be counseled concerning the amount of sleep their preschooler requires as well as the importance of maintaining a consistent sleep schedule (Ferber, 1989b).

RHYTHMIC BODY MOVEMENTS

Some infants and preschool-age children appear to derive comfort or pleasure from engaging in rhythmic body movements during times of rest, drowsiness, or sleep. Depending on the type of body movement, three variants have been identified as "head banging," "body rocking," and "head rolling" (Thorpy & Glovinsky, 1989). In head banging, the child is lying down and repeatedly bangs his or her head into the pillow or sometimes a solid object like a wall or crib railing. In body rocking, the child gets on hands and knees and the whole body moves from anterior to posterior, often with the child ramming his or her head into a pillow. In head rolling, the child is lying down and moves his or her head rhythmically from side to side. Most of these episodes of rhythmic body movements occur nightly at the onset of sleep, but they can occur during sleep, during nighttime awakenings, and on awakening in the morning (Thorpy & Glovinsky, 1989). The infants or young children usually appear to enjoy the activity and rarely cry. Individual episodes vary widely in duration but typically last 15 minutes or less, and once asleep, most children sleep without any further disturbance (Klackenberg, 1971). The average age of onset for rhythmic body movements is 6 to 8 months, and virtually all children who develop such behavior do so before 18 months of age (Thorpy & Glovinsky, 1989).

Prevalence and Etiology

Klackenberg (1971) found that 66% of healthy 9-month-old children exhibited some form of rhythmic activity. Body rocking is most prevalent, occurring in 19% to 21% of normal children, whereas head banging and head rolling each occur in between 3% and 6% of otherwise normal children. Rhythmic body movements are more common in boys than in girls, with approximately two-thirds of identified children being male (Thorpy & Glovinsky, 1989). Head banging and body rocking are more prevalent in mentally retarded children, but it is widely recognized that such behavior frequently occurs in healthy children without evidence of developmental disability or psychopathology. Very little is known about the cause of rhythmic movements in otherwise normal young children, but it may be a form of vestibular self-stimulation that is particularly pleasurable during periods of early motor development (Sallustro & Atwell, 1978).

Treatment

In most children who are not developmentally disabled, rhythmic body movements spontaneously disappear by the time the child is 4, and treatment is rarely indicated beyond parental education and reassurance (Thorpy & Glovinsky, 1989). Head banging in otherwise normal children usually does not lead to injury, but parents should be advised to ensure that the child's sleeping area is adequately padded. In contrast, head banging in developmentally disabled children may persist for years in the absence of intervention and is more likely to result in injury if the sleep area is not sufficiently padded or the child does not wear a protective helmet. Case studies have reported success using a variety of behavioral techniques for eliminating rhythmic body movements such as overpracticing a competing response (e.g., arm exercises), differential reinforcement of desired responses (e.g., praise for keeping his or her head on the pillow), and reinforcement of the nonoccurrence of the self-injurious behavior (e.g., remaining in the room contingent on nonoccurrence of head banging). Others have successfully and rapidly eliminated rhythmic body movements by using a mild punishment (e.g., turning on the bedroom light, activating an alarm that the child has to turn off) contingent on head banging or body rocking (studies reviewed by Thorpy & Glovinsky, 1989).

6

Communication and Language Problems

With the recent reauthorization of the Individuals with Disabilities Education Act (IDEA), public schools are now required to serve 3- to 5-year-old children with communication handicaps and will likely be providing language services to the 0 to 3 population in the near future. This new focus on early intervention will also affect mental health practitioners who frequently collaborate with school speech and language pathologists in providing services to preschoolers. Because approximately 50% of very young children with expressive and receptive language problems also have significant emotional and behavioral disturbances (Beitchman, Nair, Clegg, Ferguson, & Patel, 1986), it is not unusual for speech therapists to refer these children for psychological evaluation and behavior management services prior to or concurrent with speech and language interventions. Conversely, mental health professionals are often in the position of being the first professionals to identify emerging language problems in their preschool-age clients and must be prepared to provide appropriate referrals for speech and language evaluations and therapy.

In this chapter, we will provide an overview of normal speech articulation and language acquisition in very young children and provide cues for identifying those who are not following the expected developmental trajectory. We will present assessment and treatment information on speech and language disorders typically identified during the preschool years, including expressive and mixed receptive/expressive language disorders, phonologic disorder, stuttering, and elective mutism. Some of the assessment and intervention procedures described in this chapter are employed primarily by speech and language pathologists, rather than mental health practitioners. However, it is important that mental health clinicians working with preschool-age children be familiar with these procedures in order to make appropriate referrals, formulate comprehensive treatment plans, interpret the results of speech and language evaluations, and advocate for the young children they serve.

NORMAL DEVELOPMENT OF SPEECH AND LANGUAGE

The development of normal speech articulation follows an orderly progression of stages. When we use the term "speech articulation," we are referring to the movement and placement during speech of the lips, tongue, jaw, and vocal cords (Bloodstein, 1984). Although there is considerable age variation, most normally developing children pass through the five speech articulation stages described by Cantwell and Baker (1987). The "Early Vocalization Stage" occurs between 1 and 4 months of age and is characterized by crying during the first month, followed by gurgling and cooing from the second to the fourth months. From the ages of 3 to 15 months, the "Babbling and Playing with Sounds Stage" occurs. At about 3 to 4 months of age, the infant begins to produce a mix of consonants and vowels, and intonation develops such that the voice rises and falls in an imitation of speech. Toward the end of this stage, babies may alternate vocalizing with parents and seem to recognize their own names. In the "First Speech Sounds Stage" (11 to 18 months), there is a decrease in the number of speech sounds, and babies produce their first words. These are typically a consonant and vowel combination such as "ma," "ba," and "da" or repeated syllables such as "mama" or "dada." Next comes the "Systematic Acquisition of Speech Sounds Stage" (18 to 50 months), in which there is rapid growth in children's ability to articulate and make their speech comprehensible. According to Cantwell and Baker (1987), mothers report that 25% of their two-year-olds' speech is intelligible, whereas nearly 100% of what is said by their four-year-olds is understandable. The phonological process errors made by preschoolers are not random but follow systematic rules. Cantwell and Baker (1987) enumerated the following normal errors commonly made by children under 3:

1. Omitting the last consonant sound or sounds of a word (e.g., saying "ka" for "cat," "ba" for "ball").
2. "Devoicing" consonants (substituting /p/ for /b/, /t/ for /d/, /k/ for /g/, or /f/ for /v/).
3. "Stopping" consonants (substituting /b/ for /v/, /p/ for /f/, /t/ for /th/, /d/ for /th/).
4. "Gliding" consonants (substituting /w/ or /y/ for /l/ or /r/).

5. "Reducing" consonant clusters (substituting a single consonant for a group of consonants; e.g., saying "top" for "stop," "mall" for "small," "mik" for "milk," "tet" for "tent," "bu" for "blue").

6. Omitting unstressed syllables in words of two or more syllables (e.g., saying "raf" for "giraffe," "fant" for "elephant") (p. 22).

Although these phonological process errors are normative in very young children, they may persist in older speech-disordered children. The "Stabilization of Articulation Skills Stage" occurs between 50 and 80 months. By the age of 5, approximately 90% of children's speech is understood by unfamiliar adults, and the only articulation errors remaining in normal children are "lisping" (errors involving the sounds /s/, /sh/, /z/, /ch/, or /dg/) and "lalling" (distortions of the sounds /l/ or /r/; Cantwell & Baker, 1987).

Just as normal development of articulation skills follows a systematic pattern with some individual variability, so does the development of language. Language as considered here is the system of vocal, written, gestural, or other symbols used to represent meanings. Cantwell and Baker (1987) describe six stages in the development of language. In the "Prelinguistic Stage," babies up to 1 year old demonstrate communication in the form of eye contact, smiling, vocalizing in response to particular sounds, and pointing. Commonly, the first recognized words are the baby's name, "no," and "hot." The "Single-Word Utterance Stage" occurs between 12 and 18 months of age. First words usually refer to familiar objects, foods, and activities, and may be accompanied by gestures. On average, the first word is spoken at 11 months, but the range of 8 to 18 months is considered to be within normal limits. Although early talkers tend to remain verbally advanced throughout the preschool years, recent research indicates that they are not more likely to be early readers (Crain-Thoreson & Dale, 1992). Errors that are common during the single-word stage include "underextension" (using a word to convey only part of the word's meaning) and "overextension" (using a word to refer to something more general than the word's true meaning). During this stage, "egocentric speech" is observed in which children frequently talk aloud to themselves in single words or in long strings of unintelligible jargon. These children can understand many more words than they produce; the names of body parts, household objects, toys, and family members are usually understood by 18 months (Cantwell & Baker, 1987).

In the "Two-Word Utterance Stage" (18 to 24 months), the child builds a single-word vocabulary of approximately 50 words and then begins combining words into two-word messages. The average vocabulary of a normal 13-month-old is 12 words but increases to 142 words by the age of 20 months (Bates, Bretherton, & Snyder, 1988). Although gender differences in vocabulary growth favoring girls are consistently found in young toddlers, those differences disappear at about the second birthday (Huttenlocher, Haight, Bryk, Seltzer, & Lyons, 1991). At the beginning of this stage, children understand simple commands, but by the end, they are able to understand complex three- or four-part commands and begin to understand pronouns. True conversations are rare, as conversational turn taking has not been mastered, and children often speak repetitively on a single topic. Echolalia has been observed in normal children of this age, but it typically disappears by the age of 27 months (Cantwell & Baker, 1987). Between the ages of 14 and 36 months comes the "Beyond Two Words: The Simplified-Sentences Stage." In this stage, children combine words in ways that leave out prepositions, articles, and auxiliary verbs (e.g., Go bed Daddy). Morphemes are typically acquired in the following order: "ing," "on," "in," and "-s." Morphemes are commonly overgeneralized, resulting in errors such as "eated," "runned," and "leafs." Real conversations occur, and the failure to make oneself understood may elicit frustration and periodic tantrums. The next stage is "Grammar Development," which occurs between the ages of 36 and 55 months. This is the most rapid period of language development, and wide individual differences have been noted. Sentences become longer and more grammatically complex, and vocabulary increases dramatically; approximately 1,000 new words are gained between the ages of 3 and 4 (Cantwell & Baker, 1987). In this stage, children master spatial (e.g., under, over, above) and temporal (e.g., first, last, before, after) words, and use language to describe both present and past events. The final stage we will consider is "Subtle Refinement of Language Abilities." Children 55 months of age and older display much slower and more subtle gains in language. Fewer grammar errors are present, but those that may persist include agreement of nouns and verbs for singular versus plural (She have five fingers) and past-tense irregular verbs (They had aten).

LANGUAGE DISORDERS

Acquisition of language represents the fundamental building block for most other cognitive and social development of preschoolers. Language disorders have been associated with a variety of negative outcomes including mental retardation, peer rejection, externalizing and internalizing disorders, academic failure, and even abuse. However, early identification and intensive intervention during the preschool years may partially or completely remediate language disorders.

Subtypes and Prevalence

DSM-IV (APA, 1993) separates language disorders into two types: expressive language disorder (called developmental expressive language disorder in DSM-III-R) and mixed receptive/expressive language disorder (called receptive language disorder in DSM-III-R). In expressive language disorder, scores obtained from standardized measures of expressive language development are substantially below those obtained from standardized measures of both nonverbal intellectual capacity and receptive language development. According to DSM-IV, the disorder is characterized by limited vocabulary, errors in tenses, or difficulty remembering or using sentences with developmentally appropriate length or complexity (APA, 1993). Expressive language disorder is evident by 24 months of age. According to a conservative estimate, 2.2% of 3-year-olds have an expressive language disorder, and the percentage is likely to be higher in younger toddlers (Silva, 1980). However, at least one-third to one-half of preschoolers with expressive language disorders develop normal language skills by the time they are 5 (Bishop & Edmundston, 1987). Most preschoolers with expressive language disorder are boys (Whitehurst, Fischel, Caulfield, DeBaryshe, & Valdez-Menchaca, 1989), and a large percentage of them display behavior problems such as defiance and overactivity (Caulfield, Fischel, DeBaryshe, & Whitehurst, 1989).

In mixed receptive/expressive language disorder, children are unable to understand words or sentences, and scores on measures of both receptive and expressive language development are substantially below the child's measured nonverbal intelligence (APA, 1993). The severity of the disorder varies from mild cases, in which only particular types of words or statements are not understood, to severe cases, in which basic vocabulary and simple sentences are not understood. Between 3% and 10% of school-age children have a mixed receptive/expressive language disorder, with the age of onset typically before the fourth birthday (APA, 1993). The prognosis for children with mixed receptive/expressive language disorders is less favorable than for children whose receptive language is developing normally.

Etiology

Both biological and environmental variables contribute to the risk for language disorders. In particular, the role of middle ear inflammation, or otitis media, in language disorders has recently received considerable research, clinical, and media attention. In this condition, middle ear infection is accompanied by the accumulation of fluid (effusion) or wax, frequently resulting in reversible conductive hearing loss. Initial treatment typically involves antibiotics, followed by the surgical insertion of tympanostomy tubes if the infection recurs as many as four to six times in a year (Roland & Brown, 1990). According to Teele, Klein, and Rosner (1984) approximately 40% of preschoolers' visits to pediatricians are for otitis media. By age 3, approximately two-thirds of children have experienced at least one episode, and one-third of children have experienced three or more episodes (Howie, 1980; Teele et al., 1984).

It has been suggested that preschoolers who experience frequent, prolonged episodes of conductive hearing loss secondary to otitis media during critical periods of language development may be at risk for language disorders. Early studies of children whose language was within the normal range revealed an association between history of otitis media and relatively lower scores on measures of speech and language (e.g., Teele et al., 1984). Furthermore, parent reports of otitis media were found to be three times more likely in children with expressive language disorders than in normal children (Whitehurst et al., 1989). However, not all children with expressive language disorders have a history of otitis media, and there are many non-language-disordered children who have a history of middle ear disease. Recent longitudinal research suggests that the timing of the occurrence of otitis media is particularly important in predicting language improvement following restoration of normal hearing. According to Lonigan, Fischel, Whitehurst, Arnold, and Valdez-Menchaca (1992), expressive language delays that are influenced primarily by ear infections occurring between 12 and 18 months of age usually dissipate when the transient hearing loss is resolved. Degree and pattern of parental verbal stimulation over time may mediate the effects of otitis media on language development (Freeark et al., 1992).

Several other biological variables have been examined as possible contributors to the etiology of language disorders. A small percentage of children with expressive language disorders has been shown to have oromotor deficiencies causing them to drool and choke on food more often than children without language disorders. Other studies have found no association between expressive language disorders and prematurity, birth weight, birth complications, and brain laterality (Whitehurst, Fischel, Arnold, & Lonigan, 1992).

Environmental variables such as amount and type of early language exposure have also been implicated in the etiology of language disorders. Language disorders have been shown to be more prevalent in lower- than middle-income children. Many lower-income families display deficiencies in adult–child conversation, parental responsiveness, parental use of labels and complex language structures, availability of books and play materials, and consistency of caregiving (Simon, Larson, & Lehrer, 1988). For example, McCormick and Mason (1986) found that 47% of parents on public aid reported having no alphabet books in their home for their preschool-age children, compared to 3% of professional parents. Some have suggested that it is the type more than the amount of verbal stimulation that may account for young children's language delays. In studies of parent–child verbal interaction with language-delayed preschoolers, parents are found to interact with their children in much the same way as parents of younger children with normal language acquisition. However, it may be the child's language delay that causes parents to speak differently, not vice versa (Whitehurst et al., 1992).

In an attempt to integrate biological and environmental findings, Whitehurst and colleagues (1992) suggest that children initially have difficulty learning to talk for biological reasons, and thus develop an extensive repertoire of gestures and vocalizations for communication. Parents are eager to communicate with the child and respond in ways that reinforce gestures and vocalizations, which decreases the need for the child to learn to use words for communication. Because pointing and grunting are not as informative as words, children with expressive language disorders act out their communicative frustration through whining, crying, and other misbehavior, which motivates parents to discover what the child wants and to provide it. This reinforces disruptive behaviors, and some parents may be less likely to consistently discipline these children because of their language delays. Finally, because parents tailor their language based on the child's level of expressive language, children with expressive language delays usually generate a language environment that is more appropriate for younger children.

Assessment

The evaluation should begin with a thorough developmental interview with the child's parents. Accuracy of parent report of linguistic milestones is better for expressive than receptive language and can be enhanced though review of developmental records such as baby books and home videos (Cantwell & Baker, 1987). A hearing screen should be conducted to rule out problems in hearing acuity. Informal samples of expressive and receptive language may be obtained through observations of parent–child verbal interactions in the waiting area and through examiner–child interactions in a playroom setting. It is also useful to collect information about the level of language and cognitive stimulation the child receives at home. When possible, we recommend a home visit with formal evaluation using the Home Observation for Measurement of the

Environment (HOME; Caldwell & Bradley, 1984). As stated earlier, the diagnosis of expressive language disorder is not made unless the child scores significantly lower on a standardized test of expressive language development than on standardized measures of both nonverbal intelligence and receptive language development. Whitehurst and colleagues (1992) recommend that for clinical purposes, the diagnosis should be made when the expressive language score is at least 2.33 standard deviations below the mean, with the corresponding receptive score and cognitive score within 1 standard deviation of the mean for the normative sample. To diagnose mixed receptive/expressive language disorder, scores on measures of both receptive and expressive language must be significantly lower than those obtained on a standardized measure of nonverbal intelligence (APA, 1993).

A widely used measure of expressive and receptive language is the Sequenced Inventory of Communication Development-Revised Edition (Hedrick, Prather, & Tobin, 1984). This standardized test is appropriate for children younger than 5 and evaluates behavioral responses to objects and pictures. Expressive language may also be assessed by using "cloze" procedures in which a child completes a phrase or sentence begun by the examiner and by asking children to name simple pictures. Spontaneous language samples may be analyzed by speech and language pathologists according to a variety of complex systems (see van Kleek & Richardson, 1990). Receptive language assessment should include a measure of vocabulary comprehension such as the Peabody Picture Vocabulary Test-Revised (Dunn & Dunn, 1981; ages 2 to adult) and a measure of grammatical comprehension such as the Test of Auditory Comprehension of Language-Revised (Carrow-Woolfolk, 1985; ages 3 to 9).

The results of language evaluation should be compared with the child's performance on a nonverbal measure of intelligence. Appropriate nonverbal IQ measures for preschoolers include the Bayley Scales of Infant Development-II (ages 2 to 20 months), the nonverbal scale of the Kaufman Assessment Battery for Children (ages 2 years, 6 months to 12 years, 6 months), and the Performance Scale of the Wechsler Preschool and Primary Scale of Intelligence-Revised (ages 3 to 7). Because of the high rate of concurrent externalizing and internalizing problems in language-delayed children, formal language evaluation should be supplemented with screening measures of behavioral and emotional functioning such as the Child Behavior Checklist (Achenbach, 1991, 1992). For more complete information about language evaluation in preschoolers, the reader is referred to van Kleek and Richardson (1990).

Treatment

The treatment of language disorders in preschoolers ranges from naturalistic approaches for whole language learning, to highly structured, discrete learning-trial approaches. The settings in which language interventions are employed include speech and language clinics, psychology clinics, elementary schools, preschools, and the home. Some language intervention models use a one-on-one or small group approach with a speech and language pathologist, while others teach the child's major caregivers to employ language stimulation strategies. Although children generally demonstrate significant gains in language structure within the speech clinic, a lack of cross-setting generalization has been a persistent problem in the speech and language pathology literature. Recognition of the need to enhance generalization of treatment effects has prompted a movement toward more naturalistic approaches that employ the child's primary caregivers as change agents and take advantage of naturally occurring contingencies in the child's environment.

Speech and language pathologists conducting naturalistic interventions within the clinic setting usually follow a three-step process in which they (1) set up a developmentally appropriate play context; (2) use scaffolding strategies (e.g., "You are pushing the...[pause for child to fill in the blank]," "We need the...[point to object for child to name]") to assist the child in initiating communication; and (3) provide positive consequences for communication attempts by confirming, expanding, or extending the child's message and provide assistance in improving or "repairing" ineffective communication attempts (Norris & Hoffman, 1990). Although much clinical lore supports the efficacy of these strategies for eliciting communication in young children, the model of one-on-one instruction during two to three 30-minute sessions each week has not been systematically studied, and some suggest that it may not be optimal for promoting generalization of skill use (Whitehurst et al., 1992).

Perhaps the people who are in the best position to provide naturalistic language stimulation are parents. Unfortunately, research on parent–child interactions shows that parents of children with developmental language disorders tend to ask questions unrelated to the child's current focus, talk at levels that are too complex, talk too long and too fast, fail to promote turn taking, interrupt, and control conversational topics (Goodman, Greenberg, & Pollak, 1993). Because of the undeniably important role that effective parental verbal stimulation plays in the development of language skills, interventions that target enhancement of parent–child verbal interaction focusing on activities of central interest to the child are potentially powerful (e.g., Fitzgerald & Karnes, 1987). Parent-training programs based on the work of Hanf (1969) include a dyadic child-centered play component that has been found useful for enhancing verbal stimulation in developmentally delayed preschoolers (McElreath & Eisenstadt, 1994). Speech and language pathologists have developed a similar, widely used parent–child interactional model for remediating language delays in preschoolers. Treatment programs based on this "interactive model" involve coaching parents in the use of child-oriented, interaction-promoting, and language-modeling techniques, without direct teaching of linguistic structures. Based on their review of treatment outcome studies, Tannock and Girolametto (1992) concluded that this model of intervention enables parents to motivate and enhance children's use of existing communicative and linguistic abilities, but there is little evidence that parental use of these skills leads children to acquire new linguistic structures. However, Whitehurst et al. (1992) reported substantial increases in expressive language skills immediately after parent training compared to a no-treatment control group. A notable difference between their intervention and the interactive model was the inclusion of specific language teaching assignments.

Whitehurst and colleagues (1988) also have described a brief program that teaches parents to use picture-book reading to enhance children's expressive language skills. This method is referred to as "dialogic reading" and was designed to alter roles during picture-book reading so that the child gradually becomes the teller of the story while the mother becomes an active listener, prompting, rewarding, and expanding her child's efforts to talk (Valdez-Menchaca & Whitehurst, 1992). Mothers are instructed to begin with simple questions about the actors, objects, and actions shown in the pictures and slowly move into open-ended questions such as "What's happening on this page?" In two 30-minute sessions, parents were taught how to use the books to evoke expressive language from the children rather than simply reading them aloud. After three to four practice sessions per week for 4 weeks, expressive language development was significantly enhanced for treatment participants compared to control children who were read to in their parents' regular reading style, and the gains were maintained at 9-month follow-up (Whitehurst et al., 1988). Although this program was initially evaluated for children with normal language development, the effects have been largely replicated in a sample of language-delayed, low SES Mexican children in a day care setting (Valdez-Menchaca & Whitehurst, 1992). Although more empirical evaluation is clearly warranted, this intervention holds promise for preschoolers with developmental language disorders. Valdez-Menchaca and Whitehurst (1992) caution that the dialogic reading intervention will likely need to be longer and more intensive for low SES children with language disorders.

Because a large percentage (43% to 59%) of children with developmental language disorders experience significant behavioral problems
(Cunningham, 1989), treatment approaches that address both language
and behavior difficulties are particularly appealing. Cunningham (1989)
has developed a 15-session parent-training program (based in part on the
work of Hanf, 1969) with conjoint group sessions for the language-delayed
preschooler and siblings. This approach is designed to (1) equip parents
with a repertoire of child management skills so that they can respond
flexibly to their child's conduct problems, (2) help families develop effective problem-solving skills and more balanced distribution of child management responsibilities, and (3) increase supportive communication
among all family members. Although the principal focus of treatment is on
the amelioration of behavior problems, modules are included for teaching
parents strategies for enhancing language-delayed preschoolers' conversational skills. Parents are taught to respond attentively to the child's
speech or play, adjust the complexity of their speech to match their child's
level of language comprehension, provide an adequate variety of developmentally appropriate language input, and encourage sustained conversational interactions (Cunningham, 1989). The conjoint group for
preschoolers involves play activities designed to encourage the development of language and social skills. Although most of the elements of this
program have received empirical support in separate investigations, information on the efficacy of the full package is not yet available.

Mental health professionals working with preschoolers with developmental language disorders should routinely consult with classroom
teachers and day care staff. Research examining the way in which preschool teachers interact with their students suggests that many ask convergent or closed-ended questions (e.g., "Do you like this color?") rather than
expansive or open-ended questions (e.g., "What do you like about this
picture?") (Wittmer & Honig, 1989). Children's responses to preschool
teachers' questions are often either repeated verbatim or not responded to
at all (Weber & Shake, 1988). In a recent analysis of the interactions of
preschool teachers and language-delayed children, teachers only occasionally responded to the children's efforts at initiating communication, and
when teachers did respond contingently, they frequently responded in
ways that led to termination rather than maintenance of the interaction
(Rhyner, Lehr, & Pudlas, 1990). Most individual education plans (IEPs) for
language-delayed preschoolers include specific language objectives for
which teachers are accountable, influencing teachers to adopt a directive,
didactic instructional approach (Goodman et al., 1993). However, the
language abilities of children with mild to moderate developmental language disorders as well as those of children with normally developing

language are better enhanced through use of expansive questions, reflections that build on previous child verbalizations, child-centered activities, alteration of language complexity to enhance comprehension, and more use of sustained conversation. Mental health professionals consulting in this context can assist teachers in balancing didactic language instruction with more naturalistic or "milieu" instruction (Warren & Kaiser, 1988). An example of a simple naturalistic technique for stimulating language use is the brief time-delay method in which the teacher (or parent) uses a 5- to 15-second delay in responding to a child's nonverbal cues in order to allow the child sufficient opportunity and motivation to attempt verbal communication. In addition, children with suspected intermittent conductive hearing loss secondary to otitis media should be treated much as if they were hearing impaired, with modifications made in the preschool learning environment to improve linguistic input. Simon and colleagues (1988, p. 119) suggest "(a) preferential seating, (b) signalling the child by name or touch when the child is required to listen, and (c) increasing face-to-face verbal interactions and decreasing speaking to the child's back or speaking to the child at a distance."

Another promising therapeutic approach for preschool-age children with language disorders is computer-aided instruction. A variety of generic and designer software programs (working in conjunction with a speech synthesizer) targeting a variety of linguistic skills are now available for use in preschool classrooms with children as young as 2. These programs may be directed toward recognition of cause and effect, picture recognition, understanding of word meanings, drill and practice work, vocabulary building, and reading readiness skills such as visual discrimination, letter naming, and beginning word recognition. Software programs that are particularly suitable for preschool-age children include *Exploratory Play* (Meyers & Fogel, 1985), *First Words* (Wilson & Fox, 1982), and *The Stickybear ABC* (Hefter, Worthington, Worthington, & Howe, 1982). Empirical information about the efficacy of computer-aided instruction is only beginning to emerge and is generally mixed (Steiner & Larson, 1991).

Because preschoolers with language disorders are at increased risk for reading-based learning disabilities (Scarborough & Dobrich, 1990), early intervention in reading readiness skills is recommended. In addition to pairing letters with letter names and being able to construct the alphabet, a prerequisite for reading is the development of "phonological awareness." Phonological awareness is the awareness of the sound structure of language. It includes "the awareness that words are composed of syllables and phonemes, and that words can rhyme or begin/end with the same sound segment" (Catts, 1991, p. 196). Language-impaired children's deficits in phonological awareness are directly related to their early reading difficulties (Magnusson & Naucler, 1990). Preschool teachers, speech pathologists, and parents can all assist young children in developing phonological awareness through a variety of techniques such as sound play activities (e.g., reciting nursery rhymes, making up alliterative or nonsense-word sequences, deciding if pairs of words rhyme, deciding which word sounds longer), segmentation and blending exercises (e.g., tapping out syllables in a word, separately pronouncing each syllable in words, combining separate words into compound words such as railroad), and sound manipulation tasks (e.g., substituting the /f/ in "fan" with /m/) (Catts, 1991).

PHONOLOGIC DISORDER

Phonologic disorder (formerly called developmental articulation disorder in DSM-III-R) involves a failure to use developmentally expected speech sounds and may include errors in sound production, substitutions of one sound for another, or omissions of sounds such as final consonants (APA, 1993). To receive a DSM-IV diagnosis, phonologic disorder must interfere with academic achievement or social communication. In children with mental retardation, speech-motor or sensory deficits, or environmental deprivation, the language difficulties must be in excess of that which is usually associated with the problem (APA, 1993). The speech pattern in phonologic disorder often sounds like "baby talk" and ranges in severity from multiple articulation errors resulting in unintelligible speech, to a single error in which speech is completely intelligible. The phonological process errors often reflect the child's need to reduce a complex adult language model to a simpler level with fewer rules (Hodson & Paden, 1983). Although most children with this disorder reach language milestones on time, some also exhibit expressive or mixed receptive/expressive language disorders, especially in the areas of syntax and morphology (APA, 1987).

Prevalence and Etiology

Approximately 10% of children below the age of 8 have phonologic (developmental articulation) disorders (APA, 1987). However, very little is known about the etiology of this condition. The first-degree relatives of children with phonologic disorder are more likely than the general population to have had a phonologic disorder and hearing problems (APA, 1987), implicating a possible etiological role for genetics.

Assessment

In evaluating children with suspected phonologic disorders, it is important to rule out hearing impairment and malformations of the speech apparatus as causes for phonological process errors. Mouth-motor control for nonspeech activities such as feeding should be observed and any history of feeding problems explored (van Kleek & Richardson, 1990). Van Kleek and Richardson (1990) described the following features of children's speech that should be assessed: (1) the child's repertoire of speech sounds or "phonetic inventory," (2) the word and syllable shapes the child produces, (3) the accuracy of speech sound production, (4) the sequential constraints on which sounds may occur together, (5) the simplification patterns or phonological processes the child uses, (6) the suprasegmental aspects of speech, and (7) the intelligibility of the child's speech. Readers who are interested in the specific techniques available for assessing each of these features are referred to van Kleek and Richardson (1990). Formal measures of phonological processes (e.g., Assessment of Phonological Processes-Revised; Hodson, 1986) should be supplemented with measures of intellectual functioning (to rule out mental retardation) as well as receptive and expressive language (to assess for comorbid language disorders).

Treatment

Most children with phonologic disorder achieve normal speech without intervention by about age 5 (Whitehurst et al., 1991). However, 20% to 30% of preschoolers with specific articulation difficulties require special education services once they reach school, even after their phonological process difficulties appear to be resolved (Shriberg & Kwiatkowski, 1988). Paul (1991) argues that early phonologic disorder, even after resolution, is a major risk factor for long-term problems with complex language use and associated problems in academic functioning.

Preschoolers with multiple phonological process errors and unintelligible speech are clearly in need of articulation intervention to enhance the effectiveness of their attempts at communication and reduce associated frustration with communication failures. Frequently, they are provided with 20- to 30-minute individual speech therapy sessions twice per week, directed toward the production and mastery of specific phonemes. Recognition and production tasks are used for training speech targets at increasingly more complex linguistic levels. Strategies used for articulation training with young children are described in detail by Hodson and Paden (1983). Because of the risk for later academic problems, Paul (1991) argues that these children should be involved in phonological awareness activities as a preventive measure to reduce early reading delays.

STUTTERING

Stuttering is a disturbance in the normal fluency and time patterning of speech that is inappropriate for the child's age, interferes with academic achievement or social communication, and is not due to a nonpsychiatric medical condition (APA, 1987). Stuttering usually first becomes evident between ages 2 and 7, and gradually develops over several months. It is most problematic in situations in which the child feels pressure to communicate. Other problems commonly associated with stuttering include anxiety, overactivity and attentional problems, phonologic disorder, and expressive language disorder. When children become aware that they have a stuttering problem, they often develop motor components to help exert control over the stuttering. For example, children may stamp their feet, tap their fingers, hit their hands against their bodies, or exhibit facial grimaces in an attempt to reinitiate normal speech.

Prevalence

The male-to-female ratio in preschool children who stutter is considerably lower than in adults (Yairi & Ambrose, 1992), but is estimated to be approximately 3:1 (APA, 1987; Fiedler & Standop, 1983). According to the DSM-III-R, 10% of elementary school children stutter, and the prevalence rate is thought to be higher in younger children (APA, 1987).

Etiology

Considerable evidence implicates both genetics and cognitive factors in the etiology of stuttering. According to a recent study, more than two-thirds of preschoolers who stutter have a positive family history for stuttering, with approximately 45% of preschool stutterers having an immediate family member who stutters (Ambrose, Yairi, & Cox, 1993). Stuttering may be elicited by anticipatory anxiety or by certain situations (e.g., show and tell at preschool) or people (e.g., a particular teacher), may be due to rapid speech, may be the result of overcompensation for slow speech, or may be controlled by self-defeating thoughts about personal performance (e.g., I won't be able to talk correctly in front of the other kids and they'll laugh).

Assessment

Assessment of stuttering should include observation of the child's speech in a variety of contexts representative of those that elicit anxiety and stress. Relaxed conversation, situations requiring shorter utterances, more pressured situations, and interaction with various people are observed, and the type and frequency of dysfluencies are counted (van Kleek & Richardson, 1990). Observations are made concerning the rate of speech, breath stream, voice production, tensing of the musculature during speech, and sequencing of speech movements. Expressive language function is frequently assessed to determine whether a deficit in this area may have precipitated or maintained the stuttering. An oromotor examination can rule out problems such as deformities of the speech mechanism and poor oromotor coordination (Cantwell & Baker, 1987).

Treatment

There is controversy concerning the frequency with which stuttering spontaneously remits without intervention. According to some reports, at least two-thirds of stutterers spontaneously recover within the first 1½ years after onset, and females appear to have a stronger tendency toward recovery than males (Yairi & Ambrose, 1992). However, Ramig (1993) found that 90% of young children (ages 3 to 8) still had significant stuttering problems 5 to 8 years after initial diagnosis. Most clinicians now advocate early intervention before school age, as soon as a dysfluency is evident (Ham, 1990).

Treatment of stuttering in preschool-age children has involved direct teaching of alternative patterns of speaking, differential reinforcement of speech patterns, and anxiety reduction associated with speaking. In the direct teaching approach, young children are taught to slow speech by prolonging syllables, substituting prolonged vowels, developing an easy onset of speech, and changing breath control, volume, and pitch (Ham, 1990). In the differential reinforcement approach, parents and preschool teachers are taught to provide increased attention to nonstuttering verbalizations while minimizing attention to stuttering. While this may reduce the effects of reinforcement for stuttering, it does not offer children instruction in alternative speech patterns. In the anxiety reduction approach, systematic desensitization is used to reduce anxiety associated with speaking in public (DiLorenzo & Matson, 1987). This may involve training in simple relaxation skills (e.g., deep breathing, visual imagery) as well as *in vivo* desensitization in situations that are most likely to elicit stuttering (often the preschool classroom). All of these interventions are supported by case studies and small sample descriptive reports. Most structured programs for speech fluency developed by speech and language pathologists (e.g., Cooper & Cooper, 1985) target the cognitive, affective, and behavioral components of stuttering.

ELECTIVE MUTISM

Elective mutism is a persistent refusal to talk in one or more major social situations (such as school) in children with demonstrated ability to speak (APA, 1993). To receive a DSM-IV diagnosis, the mutism must persist for at least 1 month and interfere with educational achievement or social communication, and it may not be due to embarrassment associated with having a speech or language disorder such as stuttering (APA, 1993). Children with "reluctant speech" (i.e., will speak in all settings if sufficiently motivated or coaxed) have a much more favorable outcome and should be differentiated from those with mutism. By definition, elective mutism is a motivational disorder, and no significant abnormality of language comprehension or production can account for the mutism (Tancer, 1992). Children who are electively mute are also frequently described as negativistic, shy, controlling or manipulative, oppositional, socially isolated, and tending to perform poorly in academic settings (Kolvin & Fundudis, 1982). In most cases, the onset is before age 5, but the problem is usually diagnosed after school entry, at an average age of 6 years, 10 months (Kolvin & Fundudis, 1982). Tancer (1992) recommends that a minimum symptom duration of 6 months be used in making the diagnosis of elective mutism in order to exclude children going through a period of adjustment and immigrant children learning a new language.

Prevalence

Brown and Lloyd (1975) found that 7.2 per 1,000 5-year-olds did not speak 8 weeks after school entry, but at 12-month follow-up only 0.66 per 1,000 remained mute. Consistent with the latter estimate, an epidemiological study found that 0.8 per 1,000 7-year-old children were electively mute (Kolvin & Fundudis, 1982). Elective mutism is slightly more prevalent in females than in males, with male-to-female ratios of between 1:1.2 and 1:1.7 (Tancer, 1992).

Etiology

In very young children adjusting to their first school experience, transient mutism probably represents normal separation anxiety or an adjustment syndrome that diminishes with familiarity and should be distinguished from protracted elective mutism (Tancer, 1992). Reed (1963) first proposed that elective mutism might be a learned pattern of behavior with two subtypes: (1) those who are immature and manipulative, with their mutism being reinforced by attention from parents and teachers, and (2) those who are tense and anxious, with refusal to speak best viewed as a speech phobia in which mutism is reinforced through avoidance of the anxiety associated with speaking. Based on her recent review of the literature, Tancer (1992) concludes that for persistent problems, an association has been found between elective mutism and maternal overprotectiveness, language and speech disorders, mental retardation, and hospitalization or trauma before age 3. However, causal connections between elective mutism and these factors have not been established.

Treatment

Most interventions for electively mute children are behaviorally based and include social and tangible reinforcement, shaping and fading techniques, and response cost. The few psychodynamic treatment approaches described in the literature have typically reported poor outcomes (Barnett & Carey, 1992). Although several case studies and small sample reports of behavioral treatment for elective mutism generally report success, no controlled outcome studies are available. Based on their review of the literature, Labbe and Williamson (1984) indicated that a combination of response initiation, stimulus fading, contingency management, reinforcer fading, and maintenance of speech via natural reinforcers may be effective in the treatment of electively mute young children (see Labbe and Williamson, 1984, for recommendations on selection of treatment strategies for individual cases). For those who find bibliotherapy a useful adjunctive approach, a children's book called *Cat's Got Your Tongue? A Story for Children Afraid to Speak* (Schaefer, 1992) has recently been published on elective mutism.

7

Psychosomatic Problems

In recent years, there has been increased recognition of the importance of the relationship between physical and psychological illness and health in children. Wright (1977) has recommended that the term "psychosomatic" be expanded to include not only physical problems caused by emotional disturbance, as it was previously defined, but also the physical effects of difficulties in learning, development, and personality, as well as the psychological effects of physical illness and disability. Using this expanded definition, over 100 psychosomatic disorders have been identified that affect a large percentage of preschool children. Although all of these conditions cannot be discussed in this chapter, it is hoped that this discussion will highlight methods of assessment and treatment that are generalizable to conditions not discussed.

ASTHMA

Asthma is a respiratory disorder that is characterized by intermittent, variable, and reversible obstruction of the airway due to bronchial edema, mucous secretion, and bronchiospasm (Scadding, 1966). It is estimated that between 5% and 15% of all children below the age of 12 experience asthma symptoms at some time (American Lung Association, 1975). The onset of asthma most often occurs between the ages of 3 and 8. Asthma tends to improve with age. Approximately 70% of asthmatics report themselves to be significantly improved or free of asthma attacks 20 years after the onset of symptoms (Bronheim, 1978).

The characteristic presentation of asthma in children is as a series of intermittent attacks. The frequency of these attacks may vary from daily to less than once a year and may fluctuate over time for a particular child.

Thus, a child may experience a series of asthma attacks over a 1-week interval and then may experience no further problems for weeks, months, or years. The severity of asthmatic attacks may also vary considerably. Some children experience no more than a sensation of tightness in the chest or slight difficulty catching their breath after exertion. Others (less than 1%) die from the respiratory insufficiency secondary to an asthma attack (Purcell, 1975). The severity of asthma attacks can also vary considerably within the same child, often with little predictability (Creer, Harm, & Marion, 1988).

The intermittent and reversible nature of the respiratory obstruction that characterizes asthma is what distinguishes the disorder from such chronic respiratory disorders as emphysema (McFaden, 1980). Some researchers and clinicians distinguish between "extrinsic" asthma, which is triggered by specific external allergens (e.g., pollen) and irritants (e.g., cigarette smoke) and may cause no difficulty if those stimuli are avoided, and "intrinsic" asthma, which lacks clear precipitating stimuli (Creer & Winder, 1986). This differentiation, however, may only reflect the failure to identify a discrete precipitant rather than its absence.

There is considerable controversy concerning the role of emotional and personality variables in the etiology of childhood asthma. Although early psychoanalytic theorists (French & Alexander, 1941) believed that asthma was the product of a child's unresolved dependency on her or his mother, most clinicians and researchers currently believe that although emotional stress can act as a precipitating factor in causing attacks in an asthmatic child, emotional/personality factors are not an actual root cause of the disorder itself (Chong, 1977). Tal and Miklich (1976) had children with severe asthma visualize the most frightening and angriest experiences of their lives and found that in 38% of the children a significant reduction in airway flow occurred. The effect was most pronounced for visualization of angry experiences. Similarly, Hahn (1966) found a decrease in respiratory flow in asthmatics exposed to criticism or unsolvable problems.

The relationship between asthmatic children and their families has also been the focus of experimental attention as a critical variable in precipitating attacks. Purcell et al. (1969) studied asthmatic children during periods when they were being cared for by their own parents and during times when they were being taken care of in their own homes by substitute parents. Some children had improved respiratory function while their parents were absent. Neisworth and Moore (1972) found that the frequency of asthma attacks was reduced if parental attention was withdrawn contingent on wheezing. Other authors have also found disturbed relationships between mothers and their asthmatic children (Travis, 1976), with maternal overprotectiveness and dependency in the child frequently evident. The direction of causality of these findings appears unclear, however. Travis (1976) also reports that asthmatic children (by their own reports in psychotherapy) use their asthmatic condition and the occurrence of asthma attacks to avoid punishment, express their anger at perceived parental mistreatment or neglect, and evade school responsibilities.

Assessment in cases of asthma has two elements: one medical and the other behavioral/emotional. The purposes of the medical assessment are to confirm the diagnosis of asthma, to attempt to determine any precipitating allergens or irritants, and to assess the effectiveness of medications for the treatment of both acute and chronic symptoms. The purposes of the behavioral assessment are to assess the emotional/behavioral consequences of the disorder for the child, determine the role of psychological factors in the precipitation of asthma attacks, ascertain the presence of any family interaction patterns that may contribute to maintenance of the disorder, and make recommendations concerning any psychological treatment that may be warrented. This behavioral/emotional assessment may rely on several sources of information, including behavioral checklists such as the Asthma Problem Behavior Checklist (Creer, Marion, & Creer, 1983), structured interviews with the parents and child (Purcell & Weiss, 1970), asthma diaries kept by children and/or parents (Creer & Winder, 1986), and direct observation (Renne & Creer, 1985).

Although the use of medication is the dominant treatment for childhood asthma there appears to be a significant role for psychological treatments. There is little current support for such treatment through the modality of verbal psychotherapy or psychoanalysis; however, research suggests that more focused behavioral (and verbal) interventions may offer significant benefits in such areas as reducing the frequency of attacks due to psychological stressors, increasing compliance with medical treatment regimens, and diminishing the negative psychosocial effects of the disorder.

A number of studies have demonstrated the effectiveness of behavior therapy based interventions in accomplishing these goals. For example, Renne and Creer (1976) used positive reinforcement to shape appropriate use of an intermittent positive-pressure breathing (IPPB) apparatus, and Marion, Creer, and Burns (1983) used modeling and reinforcement to shape behaviors necessary for the effective use of nebulized medications.

Coughing spells in asthmatic children can often trigger asthma attacks and are disruptive to school and home adjustment. This problem has been addressed with several behavioral interventions. Neisworth and Moore (1972) used the withdrawal of parental attention and found that this procedure eliminated those behaviors over 40 evening sessions. Alexander et al. (1973) used a negative reinforcement approach involving mild electric shocks to eliminate coughing spells in an asthmatic boy. The child could avoid the shocks by refraining from coughing for progressively longer periods of time when presented with asthma-provoking stimuli. A 5-year follow-up study (Creer, 1977) demonstrated that the coughing problem had not reappeared.

Several behavioral procedures have proven useful in reducing the amount of time that asthmatic youngsters are hospitalized. Creer (1970) reduced the reinforcing aspects of a hospital stay by denying hospitalized children access to television and comic books and keeping them isolated from other children. There was a significant reduction in the amount of time these children were hospitalized. Creer (1977) also found that a satiation procedure was effective in reducing hospitalization time for an asthmatic child. In this intervention, the child was required to stay in the hospital for a minimum of 3 days whenever he stated the need for hospital care, even if the symptoms requiring hospitalization were not severe or even apparent. During the 8 months following implementation of this procedure, the child was hospitalized for only 12 days, whereas he had been hospitalized for 33 days during the previous 8 months. Systematic desensitization and relaxation training procedures have also proven effective in reducing the anxiety and panic responses that are responsible for triggering or maintaining asthma attacks in so many children (Alexander, Miklich, & Hershkoff, 1972).

A number of studies have investigated the use of biofeedback approaches to treat asthmatic symptomatology in children. Scherr, Crawford, Sergent, and Scherr (1975) investigated the effectiveness of EMG biofeedback plus relaxation training in 22 asthmatic children and found that the procedure resulted in improved air flow and reductions in the number of asthma attacks and medications used. Kahn, Staerk, and Bonk (1973) used direct biofeedback of bronchial dilation to train asthmatic children to improve their respiratory function. Following 15 training sessions, respiratory function was significantly improved in the treatment group compared to no-treatment controls, and follow-up evaluation after 8 to 10 months showed significantly fewer asthma attacks, emergency room visits, and medications used by those who had received the treatment.

A major issue in the treatment of asthmatic children is medication compliance. Overall medication compliance for children with asthma is estimated to be at approximately 10% (Creer et al., 1988). Baum (1983) has demonstrated that the teaching of self-management skills to children with asthma can result in better medication compliance. Creer et al. (1988) used a comprehensive self-management program to teach decision-making and attack management skills to asthmatic children and their parents. Acquisition of these skills, which included medication compliance, resulted in improved respiratory function, more positive attitudes toward asthma, decreased school absenteeism, and greatly reduced health care costs.

CYSTIC FIBROSIS

Cystic fibrosis is another respiratory ailment that affects preschoolers and for which behavioral/mental health interventions can be useful. Cystic fibrosis is a recessive genetic disorder that occurs in 1 out of 2,000 live Caucasian births (Nader & Ben-Yoseph, 1984). The result of the genetic abnormality is the production of abnormally thick and viscous mucus in the gastrointestinal tract, lungs, and pancreas. In the lungs, this mucus obstructs the bronchi and bronchioles, causing respiratory insufficiency. Chronic pulmonary disease is the cause of death in over 90% of cystic fibrosis patients (Wood, Boat, & Doershuck, 1976). In the pancreas, essential enzymes are blocked by the mucus, resulting in chronic malnutrition (Allan & Phelan, 1980). Symptoms of cystic fibrosis may appear weeks, months, or years after birth. Generally, the earlier the onset of symptoms, the more severe the disease. Early symptoms include chronic coughing, dyspnea, wheezing, and cyanosis. Stools in infants are often large, loose, fatty, and light in color. Babies do not gain weight in spite of having a good appetite and appear malnourished.

In recent years, advances in the diagnosis and treatment of cystic fibrosis have resulted in significant improvement in life expectancy for individuals diagnosed with the disorder. In 1966, the median survival age was 11 years, while by 1989 it had increased to 28 years (Fitzsimmons, 1990). Although this improvement in life expectancy is certainly good news, it means that the children affected with cystic fibrosis and their families are subjected to years of daily respiratory therapy treatments, complicated medication regimens, and frequent hospitalizations for diagnostic and treatment purposes. It also means that they have years to consider the early mortality that is still characteristic of this disease.

Behavioral and mental health interventions have been found to have applicability to several aspects of treatment of cystic fibrosis, including compliance with treatment regimens. One of the most important treatment components in the care of cystic fibrosis patients is postural drainage, which involves the patient being repeatedly clapped on various areas of the chest by a parent or therapist to dislodge secretions there. It is recommended that these treatments be administered from two to six times per day, depending on disease severity. Bellisari (1985) has shown that compliance with postural drainage regimens is low, probably as a result of its interference with normal life activities and a lack of appreciation for its value as an intervention. Stark, Miller, Plienis, and Drabman (1987) reported that the use of a behavioral contracting approach was effective in increasing an 11-year-old girl's compliance with a postural drainage regimen. A written contract was negotiated between the girl and her mother (with a psychologist's assistance), which specified that postural drainage would be performed at four times during the day, and that the girl and her mother would engage in a joint pleasurable activity following each treatment. There was also a weekly reward specified for completing 75% of the treatments. The girl quickly increased her compliance to 100%, and at 2-month follow-up, continued to comply at almost that level. Although younger preschoolers probably will not be able to fully participate in the process of negotiating a behavioral contract, the idea of using immediate activity reinforcers to reward adherence to a treatment regimen has validity for almost any age.

Diet and exercise are other areas in which compliance to treatment recommendations can be vitally important for preschoolers with cystic fibrosis. Typically, it is recommended that children with cystic fibrosis consume 150% of the recommended daily amount of calories (Hodges et al., 1984). Stark and Passero (1987) have developed a behavioral treatment program intended to effect weight gain in children with cystic fibrosis. The program focuses on identification of appropriate foods, setting caloric goals, establishing rewards for goal attainment, and behavioral contracting with parents. Similarly, engaging in exercise is important for cystic fibrosis patients and may be more effective than postural drainage in loosening mucus in the lungs (Orenstein, Henke, & Cherny, 1983). At least one study has found that participation in an exercise program (swimming) resulted in improvement in global ratings of disease status (Edlund et al., 1986). One program has used behavioral interventions to increase home exercise compliance in children with cystic fibrosis (Hobbs, Stratton, Geiss, Kramer, & Ozturk, 1987). This program included such behavioral elements as self-monitoring of exercise frequency and duration, and awarding reinforcers specified in behavioral contracts if contract criteria were met.

DIABETES

Diabetes is the most common endocrine disorder of childhood, affecting 1.9 per 1,000 school-age children, or as many as 150,000 children in the United States. The rate of occurrence of new cases is highest among 5- and 6-year-olds. The most common presenting symptoms include excessive thirst (polydipsia); frequent and excessive urination (polyuria), even when dehydrated; weight loss; and constant hunger (polyphagia). The preschooler who is toilet trained may begin wetting the bed again or may have frequent daytime accidents. Often the onset of symptoms is rapid, occurring within a period of a week or less. These symptoms may go unrecognized, in which case a ketoacidotic coma or death may result. In contrast to adult-onset diabetes, which can often be managed through careful attention to diet, juvenile-onset diabetes (or insulin-dependent diabetes mellitus, IDDM) invariably requires insulin treatment (Thompson, 1987).

Although there is some individual variability, the common requirements for diabetic maintenance include (1) blood-glucose monitoring via urine or blood sampling from one to four times a day; (2) insulin administration, usually by injection, once or twice a day; (3) adherence to a prescribed diet; and (4) exercise (Wing, Epstein, Nowalk, & Lamparski, 1986). In addition, children with diabetes must engage in conscientious foot and skin care because of the increased risks of infection and ulceration that accompany the disease.

Obviously, the diabetic monitoring and treatment regimen is a difficult one for young children to adjust to, and research has shown that their compliance to it is generally poor (Simonds, 1979). A number of behavioral interventions have been shown to be effective at increasing compliance. For example, Lowe and Lutzker (1979) improved a 9-year-old girl's compliance to a medical regimen through a program using prompts and token reinforcement. Similarly, Epstein et al. (1981) implemented a training program that used verbal praise and token reinforcement to increase diabetic children's adherence to a demanding monitoring and treatment regimen. Carney, Schechter, and Davis (1983) were able to increase the frequency of self-monitoring of blood glucose in three youngsters through the use of contingent parental praise and a point system. Gross, Magalnick, and Richardson (1985) used a family-based behavioral self-training format to try to increase treatment regimen adherence and decrease family conflict. The children and their parents met separately in weekly groups to work on specific behavior change projects. After 8 weeks, improved regimen adherence and reduced diabetes-related family conflict was reported in comparison to control subjects.

Behavioral interventions have also proven effective in treating frequently seen symptoms of diabetes. For example, Boggs, Geffken, Johnson, and Silverstein (1992) used the bell and pad urine alarm procedure (Mowrer & Mowrer, 1938) to treat nocturnal enuresis in five diabetic children. The procedure was effective in stopping the enuresis in all five of the children, with treatment gains maintained for the four subjects available at a 2-month follow-up. Enuresis is reported as a symptom in approximately 40% of all newly diagnosed children above the age of 5 (Hamilton, Mundier, & Lister, 1976).

The use of stress management procedures is another area in which mental health interventions can be useful with the diabetic child. Research has shown a significant relationship between stress and metabolic control in youngsters with diabetes (Delamater, Smith, Lankester, & Santiago, 1988). Rose, Firestone, Heick, and Faught (1983) reported that anxiety management training had a beneficial effect on glucose levels in five diabetic girls, and Kaplan, Chadwick, and Schimmel (1985) reported positive effects of coping skills training with diabetic youngsters on treatment regimen adherence and metabolic control. EMG biofeedback has been used with adults in conjunction with relaxation training (Seeburg & DeBoer, 1980) and has resulted in improved metabolic control; however, these results have not been replicated with older children, much less preschoolers.

Social skills training has been identified as a useful intervention in helping diabetic children reduce social stress and avoid nonadherent behaviors (e.g., eating ice cream at a birthday party). Gross and Johnson (1981) developed a training format that used child-identified stressful social situations and had a therapist model appropriate responses to those situations and then critique the child's role-playing efforts. Gross, Johnson, Wildman, and Mullett (1981) and Gross, Heimann, Shapiro, and Schultz (1983) report that such social skills training programs result in significant improvement in children's adjustment to their disease.

Overall, it appears that, although psychosocial factors are not significant in a causal sense in diabetes, they are critically important in the areas of treatment adherence, overall adjustment to the disease, and stress reduction. For preschool children, explanations of dietary limitations and the need for monitoring and treatment procedures should be attempted at their level of understandability, and parental supervision and enforcement should be implemented as necessary.

CANCER

Pediatric cancer is another area in which, although psychosocial factors are unimportant in an etiological sense, mental health interventions can be important in reducing symptomatic complaints, increasing treatment compliance, and improving patients' adjustment and quality of life. Childhood cancer has an annual incidence of approximately 12 cases per 100,000 children in the United States. Although this incidence rate is relatively low, 6,000 to 7,000 new cases are diagnosed each year, and cancer leads all other diseases as a cause of death in children (Pratt, 1985). The diagnosis of pediatric cancer is most often made between birth and 4 years of age, with 40% of initial malignancies occurring during this period (Altman & Schwartz, 1983). Leukemia is by far the most common form of cancer seen in children and accounts for approximately 35% of all cases. Eighty percent of cases of childhood leukemia are classified as acute lymphocytic (or lymphoblastic) leukemia (ALL). This form of leukemia is characterized by the formation of malignant cells in the bone marrow which then make their way into the bloodstream, suppressing the number of normal red blood cells. The cause of ALL is not known, although genetic factors appear to be significant, as the incidence is much higher for children who suffer from Down syndrome and the concordance rate is high for twins (Thompson, 1987).

Common symptoms during the early stages of ALL include listlessness and fatigue, enlargement of the lymph nodes, low-grade fever, and leg and joint pain. The skin may take on a yellow tint. As the disease progresses, the liver and spleen become enlarged, causing discomfort, and skin hemorrhages and lesions of the mouth may occur. Dyspnea, anorexia, vomiting, and weight loss are also commonly seen. Blood may be evident in the urine (Thompson, 1987).

Treatment for ALL usually proceeds in stages and consists of initial chemotherapy to induce remission, central nervous system (CNS) prophylaxis (intended to prevent the spread of the disease to the brain or spinal cord), and maintenance chemotherapy. Chemotherapy is conducted with a variety of toxic agents, while CNS prophylaxis usually consists of a combination of chemotherapy and radiation treatment (Hynd & Willis, 1988). Bone marrow transplantation has increasingly become a treatment option in recent years (Johnson, 1984).

The prognosis for children with ALL has improved greatly in recent years. In 1967, the 5-year-event-free survival rate for children with the disease was only 18%. By 1981, this figure had increased to 60% (Young, Ries, Silverberg, Horm, & Miller, 1986), and it is currently much higher than that.

The second most common type of cancer found in young children is brain tumors, which account for 20% of all childhood cancers (Menkes, 1985). It is estimated that the annual incidence of such tumors is between two and five cases for every 100,000 children (Farwell, Dohrmann, & Flannery, 1977). The most common sites for such tumors in young children are the cerebellum, fourth ventricle, and brain stem, with almost half occurring in the cerebellum (Farwell, Dohrmann, & Flannery, 1977). As with ALL, the etiology of brain tumors in children is largely unknown.

Common early symptoms of brain tumor in young children are headache, irritability, lethargy, nausea and vomiting, and specific cerebellar signs including gait difficulties, postural changes, incoordination, loss of speech intonation, and in the older child, changes in printing or writing (Hynd & Willis, 1988).

Treatment for brain tumors in children usually consists of a combination of surgery (if feasible), chemotherapy, and radiation treatment. All of these interventions have been shown to potentially have significant negative effects on children's long-term cognitive and psychological functioning (Duffner, Cohen, Thomas, & Lansky, 1985).

The prognosis in cases of childhood brain tumors varies considerably depending on the site and size of the tumor and its histologic characteristics. The prognosis for children with brain tumors is generally poorer than for children with leukemia, and the prognosis for brain-stem tumors is much poorer than for tumors in other areas of the brain. This is, in part, because of the inaccessibility of brain-stem tumors to surgical excision (Farwell, Dohrmann, & Flannery, 1977).

Mental health interventions used with children with cancer range from family and individual psychotherapy to address issues of mortality, depression, anxiety, and family conflict, to hypnotherapy and behavioral interventions designed to help children cope with the pain of medical treatments.

Even fairly young preschool children have been shown to be aware of the seriousness of their condition and the possibility of impending death. Often this awareness derives from the reactions of family members and others around them and authorities in the area suggest psychotherapeutic treatment for the entire family in cases of emotional difficulties secondary to terminal-stage illness or poor prognosis (Spinetta & Deasy-Spinetta, 1981). There is considerable controversy surrounding the question of what to tell the young child with cancer about his or her condition, treatment, and prognosis. Naiman, Rolsky, and Sherman (1976) suggest that most children over the age of 8 can be told about their illness, even if they are not given specific prognostic information, and Koocher (1980) has suggested that the child be at least told the name of his or her disease and the types of medical treatment that will be required. According to Nitsche et al. (1982), many health professionals recommend that children be informed of their status when it is apparent that their illness is terminal. Chesler, Paris, and Barbarin (1986) interviewed parents of 42 children with cancer and found that 19% of the parents told their child nothing about his or her illness; 29% of parents talked with their child only about superficial and procedural aspects of his or her illness; 22% gave their child some information about the nature of his or her illness and the need for medical procedures, but did not mention cancer or provide prognostic information; 16% told their child everything about his or her disease (including naming it) except exact prognosis; and 14% of parents told their child everything about his or her illness, including the prognosis. Twenty-nine percent of this sample was below the age of 4 when the diagnosis was made and, the child's age was the single most important variable in determining how much parents told their child about his or her illness. Spinetta, Swarner, and Sheposh (1981) interviewed parents of children who had died of cancer and found that those who had best adjusted to the child's death were those who had given their child information about the illness consistent with his or her age, level of development, and inquisitiveness, and who could view the death from the context of religious beliefs.

Several researchers have investigated the incidence of depression, anxiety, and marital distress in childhood cancer patients and their families. Mulhern, Fairclough, Smith, and Douglas (1992) found that 7% of pediatric cancer patients demonstrated depressive symptomatology falling within the clinical range. Dahlquist et al. (1993) found that 13% of mothers of newly diagnosed pediatric cancer patients had clinically elevated anxiety and depression ratings. Approximately one-fourth of the parents reported significant marital distress.

Mental health professionals should be available to provide supportive treatment for the child with cancer and parents and other family members, or to refer them to one of the self-help groups that have emerged in this area, such as the Candlelighters (Stehbens, 1988). Mental health interventions also have an important role in helping pediatric cancer patients deal with the pain and discomfort of necessary medical treatments and the disease itself. The pain involved with such medical procedures as spinal taps and bone marrow aspirations is relatively short lasting and is strongly related to the fear and anxiety surrounding the child's approach to the procedure. Such interventions as prior exposure to the equipment involved, role-playing procedures with dolls, and play therapy that also provides information about treatment procedures have proven effective in reducing children's discomfort (Jay, Elliot, Katz, & Seigel, 1987). Olness (1981) found that pediatric cancer patients as young as 3 years of age could be taught self-hypnotic techniques that were effective in reducing pain and discomfort associated with bone marrow aspiration, chemotherapy, and radiation treatment. For children, including many young preschoolers, who will not cooperate with hypnotic procedures, Zeltzer, LeBaron, and Zeltzer (1984) reported that simple distraction techniques, such as playing games, counting things in the room, and talking with a parent can reduce the discomfort of medical procedures, as can deep breathing and other relaxation-inducing techniques.

Hypnosis has also been shown to be effective in reducing the nausea and vomiting associated with chemotherapy in pediatric cancer patients (Zeltzer et al., 1984). Kolko and Rickard-Figuero (1985) allowed adolescent cancer patients to play video games during chemotherapy administration and found that this procedure significantly reduced both anticipatory and postchemotherapy side effects.

In summary, it appears that mental health interventions with pediatric cancer patients are extremely varied and address issues of treatment compliance and adjustment to side effects as well as issues of mortality. All modalities of treatment, from play therapy to school consultation, appear to have a place in the comprehensive treatment of the child who has, or has had, cancer.

AIDS

Research has estimated that from 1,700 to 5,000 HIV-infected children are born in the United States every year, with 1 out of every 476 births in one state (Massachusetts), for example, being to an HIV-positive mother (Hoff et al., 1988). There are currently over 3,000 cases of pediatric AIDS in the United States and an additional 10,000 to 15,000 children who are HIV positive. Approximately 72% of the cases of pediatric AIDS are the result of perinatal transmission from infected mothers, with another 20% resulting from contaminated blood transfusions (Centers for Disease Control, 1988).

Olson, Huszti, Mason, and Seibert (1989) have identified several areas of useful involvement for psychologists and other mental health professionals in cases of pediatric AIDS. They indicate that, given the high percentage of children who are infected perinatally, one of the potentially most effective areas of involvement is in prevention of the disease in women of childbearing age. Several studies have shown that such high-risk behaviors as sharing intravenous (IV) needles and unprotected sexual intercourse can be reduced through the use of peer counselors who provide support and protective information (e.g., McAuliffe et al., 1987).

Psychotherapy with pediatric AIDS patients can focus on several important issues. As mentioned above in the section on pediatric cancer, there is considerable controversy around the issue of telling the young child about his or her illness and the prognosis. However, many young children with AIDS understand the severity of their condition and the fact that their prognosis is poor. Individual and family psychotherapy should certainly focus on issues of death and dying when they are apparent. A complication of mental health work with children with AIDS is the fact that many of their parents have died from, or are sick with, the disease. Children who have witnessed their parents die are greatly concerned when they find out that they have the same illness, and this anxiety must be addressed.

Other issues that commonly emerge in psychotherapy with pediatric AIDS patients and their families are parental guilt and anger concerning transmission of the virus and children's anger at parental behaviors that may have infected them. These issues usually are more evident with older children than with preschoolers.

Mental health professionals can also be usefully involved, according to Olson et al. (1989), in designing public education programs to change attitudes toward AIDS and its victims. Several studies have shown relationships between knowledge about AIDS and positive attitudes toward AIDS patients (Huszti, 1987).

PAIN

Pain in children is a very complex and variable phenomenon that results from a wide variety of medical conditions and is mediated by a multitude of psychosocial factors. We have already discussed the issue of pain management with regard to several specific medical conditions and will attempt in this section to broaden that discussion and extend it into previously uncovered areas.

The treatment of pain in children is made more difficult by the fact that the subjective experience of pain is so different in children of different ages, and the clinical assessment of pain is influenced both by this developmental process and by the difficulty young children have in communicating complex experiences such as pain. To aid in this assessment process, a number of clinical instruments and procedures have been developed. One of the more widely used pediatric pain assessment instruments is the Varni/Thompson Pediatric Pain Questionnaire (PPQ; Varni, Thompson, & Hanson, 1987). The PPQ consists of child and parent forms. The child form uses a visual analogue scale (VAS), a verbal descriptor selection task, and a body outline to quantify severity and identify location, and it assesses a number of aspects of subjective pain experience. The parent form provides for objective corroboration of the child's self-report. The PPQ has been used with children as young as 5 years old (Walco & Dampier, 1990) and reportedly has reasonable psychometric properties and clinical utility (Varni et al., 1987).

The VAS also been used independently of the PPQ. This instrument consists of a horizontal line with an anchor descriptor of "no pain" on one end and "severe pain" on the other end. Happy and sad faces are added in the appropriate places to young children's forms. Fairly young children have demonstrated the ability to discriminate between levels of pain on this instrument. Other variations on this instrument include the "pain thermometer," which uses a numerical scale, and "happy face–sad face" rating formats, as well as the use of colors to indicate pain intensity (Dolgin & Jay, 1989).

Lollar, Smits, and Patterson (1982) developed a projective instrument, the Pediatric Pain Inventory (PPI) for the assessment of pain in children. Use of this instrument involves the presentation to the child of pictures depicting pain in different situations and the solicitation of the child's judgment of the pain's severity, duration, and so on.

Another approach to the assessment of pediatric pain has been the use of behavioral observation formats and rating scales. Behavioral observation scales use well-defined categories of behavioral responses that have been shown to correlate with subjective pain experience. These scales ask parents, medical personnel, or mental health practitioners to indicate the presence or absence of these behaviors during either live or videotaped observation. Widely used and reliable observation scales include the Observation Scale of Behavioral Distress (OSBD; Elliot, Jay, & Woody, 1989) and the Child–Adult Medical Procedure Interaction Scale-Revised (CAMPIS-R; Blount, Powers, & Sturges, 1988). Rating scales that use global ratings of a child's distress have also been shown to correlate highly with information gathered from observational scales (Blount et al., 1988). Physiological measures of pediatric pain have not been widely used by researchers or clinicians because of the complexity and unreliability of the equipment involved and the poor correlation sometimes seen between these measures and the subjective pain experience (Jay & Elliot, 1988). It is interesting to note, however, that at least one study has found physiological arousal to correlate highly with observed distress for children under 7 years of age, an age group for which self-report measures are not particularly reliable (Jay & Elliot, 1988).

Varni (1983) has classified pediatric pain into four types: (1) pain accompanying a specific disease state; (2) pain accompanying physical trauma; (3) pain accompanying medical or dental procedures; and (4) pain occurring in the absence of a specific disease state or injury (idiopathic pain). Dolgin and Jay (1989) have summarized the mental health interventions in pediatric pain management according to this classification.

Examples of the use of mental health interventions that have been demonstrated to be effective with pain resulting from disease states include a self-hypnotic intervention that was used with sickle-cell disease, a blood disorder affecting one out of 400 African-American children born in the United States (Charache, Lubin, & Reid, 1989). Zeltzer, Dash, and Holland (1979) taught self-hypnosis to two youngsters with sickle-cell disease and found that, by using the technique to increase vasodilation, the youngsters were able to significantly reduce the frequency and severity of painful episodes. Although it may appear that self-hypnotic interventions have little utility with a preschool population, Crasilneck and Hall (1973) and La Baw, Holton, Tewell, and Eccles (1975) were able to use similar interventions effectively with patients as young as 4 years old. Varni (1981) used relaxation training, breathing exercises, and guided imagery to reduce arthritic pain in five children with hemophilia.

Many of the same mental health interventions described above have also been effectively implemented to reduce pain associated with injury or trauma. Elliot and Olson (1983) used relaxation, imagery, reinforcement, and distraction techniques to reduce burned children's distress during debridement and hydrotherapy. Their subjects were as young as 6 years old. Andolsek and Novik (1980) used hypnotic techniques to reduce distress in children being treated in an emergency room for non-life threatening lacerations and injuries. Varni, Bessman, Russo, and Cataldo (1980) demonstrated operant conditioning techniques to reduce pain behaviors and increase splint wearing and mobility in a 3-year-old with scarring and contractures secondary to severe burns.

Similar mental health interventions have been used to control pain and distress behaviors associated with painful medical procedures. Jay, Elliott, and Varni (1987) used a comprehensive behavioral treatment package consisting of modeling, positive reinforcement, breathing exercises, imagery/distraction training, and behavioral rehearsal to reduce the pain/distress behaviors of leukemia patients as young as 3 years of age undergoing bone marrow aspiration. Implementation of this package substantially reduced distress behaviors compared to controls and a group that received a pharmacological intervention (Valium).

Modeling and information interventions alone have also proven effective with pediatric patients undergoing painful procedures. Melamed and Siegel (1975) had children as young as 4 who were scheduled for minor surgery view a film in which a child undergoes an operative procedure and discusses his fears and how he copes with them. Children who saw this film rather than one unrelated to surgery demonstrated fewer pre- and postoperative distress behaviors. Dash (1981) used a participant modeling procedure and hypnosis to eliminate a needle phobia in a 5-year-old cardiac patient. Peterson, Schultheis, Ridley-Johnson, Miller, and Tracy (1984) found that either filmed or live modeling procedures were superior to a traditional informational presentation in reducing fear and distress behaviors in children as young as 2 years old. Peterson and Shigetomi (1981) found that modeling interventions could be made even more effective by combining them with instruction in active coping skills. It also appears that information and modeling interventions can be effective as a general preventive intervention for children not imminently facing painful medical procedures. Elkins and Roberts (1984) demonstrated that an experiential and information program called "Let's Pretend Hospital" could reduce medical fears in unselected first graders.

Hypnosis interventions alone have also been found to have considerable efficacy in reducing pain and distress behaviors in children undergoing painful medical procedures, although very little research has used hypnosis with children under the age of 6. A study by Kuttner (1984) did use preschoolers. This study assessed the effectiveness of a hypnotic procedure called imaginative involvement, in which hypnotic suggestions for pain reduction were woven into the telling of a favorite story. A distraction intervention aimed at reducing pain during bone marrow aspiration in children as young as 3 years old was also assessed. Results indicated that imaginative involvement was most effective in reducing anxiety and pain behaviors in children below the age of 7, while the distraction intervention was more effective with children from 7 to 10 years of age. Both interventions were more effective than an attention placebo intervention in reducing anxiety and pain behaviors. Zeltzer and LeBaron (1982) used a similar storytelling technique combined with imagery and deep breathing to reduce pain in cancer patients as young as 6 years old undergoing bone marrow aspirations and spinal taps. This technique was found to be generally more effective than supportive counseling. The hypnotic storytelling technique appears to be more appropriate for preschoolers than traditional hypnotic induction techniques. A similar fantasy facilitation technique (De Mille, 1973) has been found to be effective in reducing anxiety in chronically ill children as young as 5 years old (Johnson, Whitt, & Martin, 1987).

Other mental health interventions that have been used to reduce anxiety, pain behaviors, or self-reports of pain secondary to medical procedures in young children include desensitization (Poster & Betz, 1983), thought stopping (Ross, 1984), emotive imagery (Ayer, 1973), symbolic imagery (Keane, 1980), and preparation through doll or puppet play (Cassell, 1965).

Idiopathic pain syndromes, or pain for which no physical cause has been identified, most closely coincide with the lay definition of "psychosomatic" pain. One of the most common forms of idiopathic pain is headache, which occurs in 40% of children by age 7, with 5% experiencing it on a recurring basis (Sillanpaa, 1983). Headache is a significant cause of social and educational disruption for children, with 70% of children who miss 4 or more school days in a year suffering from recurrent headaches (Egermark-Eriksson, 1982). Most pediatric headaches are migraine in nature, which means that their proximal cause is changes in cerebral blood flow. The other major type of children's headaches is tension headaches, which are due to tightness of the shoulder, neck, and skeletal muscles. The pain that accompanies migraine headaches can be severe enough to be debilitating and is sometimes accompanied by nausea, vomiting, and visual disturbances. Migraine attacks may occur daily and often last for several hours. Usually between attacks, migraine sufferers are pain free. Tension headaches may be severe but often present with chronic, less intense pain that does not occur in discrete attacks.

There are multiple causal factors for both types of headaches. There is an identified familial component to migraine headaches (Barlow, 1984), and a number of environmental events have been isolated that can precipitate attacks, including stress, fatigue, sun, certain patterns of light, exertion, blood sugar level, hormone levels, and specific food sensitivities (Barlow, 1984). There appears to be no evidence for an emotional basis to migraines beyond the stress relationship cited above. Stress, both chronic and acute, has also been implicated as a causal factor in tension headaches (Bakal, 1982).

The pharmacological treatment of headaches in children has consisted mainly of the use of aspirin and acetaminophen for symptomatic relief, although aspirin is not currently recommended for use with preschoolers because of concern over Reye's syndrome (Thompson, 1987). Several prophylactic medications that are widely used to prevent migraines in older children, amitriptyline and propranolol, have not been researched in younger children, and have not been shown to be reliably effective in treating older children (Forsythe, Gillies, & Sills, 1984).

The shortcomings in pharmacological treatment of pediatric headache have led to an increasing reliance on behavioral and mental health interventions. The first step in implementing such treatments is to see that the child has had a complete physical examination by a medical practitioner familiar with pediatric headaches. A cursory physical examination by a family doctor is likely to miss such causal factors as hypoglycemia. The second step is the collection of data from the patient and his or her parents concerning the characteristics of the headaches and precipitating or ameliorating events, both internal and external. Through this questioning, precipitants such as food allergies can be identified, and the treatment may be as simple as avoiding those foods. The consequences of the headaches (parental attention, missing school) should also be investigated in order to determine if secondary gain is a significant maintaining factor.

Psychological interventions for headache can generally be classified as self-regulatory procedures such as imagery, relaxation, hypnosis, and cognitive restructuring or as manipulations of socioenvironmental contingencies (Varni, Jay, Masek, & Thompson, 1986). Children generally respond to these procedures at least as well as adults (Holroyd, 1986). Most of the research documenting the efficacy of these treatment procedures does not involve preschool children, but there appear to be no reasons that many of these procedures could not be applied to that age group, as have many of the psychological treatments used to treat other types of pain.

Olness and MacDonald (1981) reported that three children whose migraines were unresponsive to medication improved when treated with self-hypnosis training and thermal biofeedback. Similarly, Houts (1982) reported that an 11-year-old showed significant decrease in headache frequency after 10 sessions of relaxation training and thermal biofeedback. Labbe and Williamson (1983) used thermal biofeedback and autogenic training to reduce headache activity in three children, and Fentress, Masek, Mehegan, and Benson (1986) demonstrated improvement in elementary school children's headaches after treatment with relaxation training alone or in conjunction with EMG biofeedback.

Ramsden, Friedman, and Williamson (1983) were able to eliminate headaches in a 6-year-old girl by allowing her to engage in a preferred activity at school at the end of each headache-free day and penalizing her for an excessive number of headaches with forfeiture of recess. Masek (1982) used parental contingency management of praise and attention, in conjunction with EMG biofeedback and breathing exercises, to decrease headache frequency by 50% over a period of several months in 20 children with migraines. Masek and Hoag (1990) present a case illustration in which a 6-year-old boy was treated with meditational relaxation, imagery, and EMG biofeedback for five sessions with no improvement. At this point, the above approaches were discontinued and treatment with progressive muscle relaxation and thermal biofeedback was begun. He demonstrated significant improvement over the next four sessions, which was maintained at a 6-month follow-up. The lesson here seems to be that the response to different treatment approaches is unpredictable and that seemingly equivalent techniques may each need to be implemented in an effort to find one that works.

Another idiopathic pain syndrome that has received research attention is recurrent abdominal pain (RAP), which affects approximately 10% of all children. An organic cause for the pain is found in only about 8% of cases (Apley, 1975). Familial factors appear to be significant in RAP, although it is not known if this reflects genetics or modeling (Christensen & Mortensen, 1975). As many as one-third of children with RAP continue to have frequent stomach pains as adults (Apley, 1975).

Again, mental health interventions with children with RAP need to be preceeded by a complete physical examination by a physician who is experienced with the syndrome. Although only a small percentage of children with RAP will have organic causes identified, it is important to diagnose such conditions as lactose intolerance, which may be solely responsible for the pain (Lebenthal, Rossi, Nord, & Branski, 1981).

Following the physical examination, a complete psychosocial evaluation needs to be conducted. Such factors as child personality characteristics (hypersensitive, anxious, depressed, and compulsive), parenting style (overprotective and anxious), and marital discord have all been identified as possible causal factors and should be addressed in this evaluation (Barr & Feuerstein, 1983). In addition, possible maintaining reinforcers and sources of secondary gain in the home or school environment should be identified.

A number of mental health treatments have been found to have efficacy in the treatment of RAP. Again, relatively little of the research has been done with preschool children, but the extension of many of these treatment approaches to that age group appears valid. White (1979) found that verbal family therapy combined with behavioral approaches was very effective in treating RAP. Sank and Biglan (1974) found that the problem diminished dramatically with use of the intuitive behavioral approach of requiring a 10-year-old boy to stay in bed when he missed school with RAP, along with positive reinforcement (tokens redeemable for money) for school attendance and decreased pain reports. Miller and Kratochwill (1979) also used a time-out procedure to eliminate RAP in a 10-year-old girl. In addition to these approaches, Feuerstein and Dobkin (1990) recommend that verbal psychotherapy and cognitive behavioral therapy be used to treat depression and anxiety that may have a causal role in the occurrence of RAP.

In summary, there are a wide variety of mental health interventions that have demonstrated efficacy in the area of preschool psychosomatic problems. However, for these interventions to be implemented with maximal effectiveness, assessment and treatment must take place within the context of a collaborative working relationship between mental health and medical practitioners. Such a relationship will allow for careful consideration of the biological, behavioral, and psychosocial factors involved in each case and will encourage the development of treatment strategies that address all of these elements. Such comprehensive treatment strategies offer the best hope for improving the lot of young children with psychosomatic problems.

8

Conduct and Attentional Problems

One of the most frequent concerns expressed by parents of preschool-age children referred to mental health clinics is conduct problem behavior (Gordon, Schroeder, & Hawk, 1992). Conduct problems in young children include noncompliance, destructive behavior, overactivity, physical and verbal aggression, and deliberate cruelty toward animals. Preschoolers appear to progress from less serious to more serious behavior problems more rapidly than do older children (Loeber, Green, Lahey, Christ, & Frick, 1992), and their problems are accompanied by significant familial stress. In fact, parents of conduct problem preschoolers report parenting stress levels comparable to those found in parents of children with pervasive developmental disorders such as autism (Donenberg & Baker, 1993). Difficult child behavior and inadequate parental coping resources place these families at risk for developing abusive parenting practices (Abidin, 1990).

The stress of managing the behavior of conduct problem children is shared by day-care and preschool staff. Few children are harder to maintain in a group care situation than highly active and aggressive preschoolers. Some require constant one-on-one supervision so that they do not injure themselves through reckless behavior (e.g., running into the street) or harm other children in aggressive episodes (e.g., biting).

It has been widely believed that young children with conduct problems are negotiating a difficult developmental phase, such as the "terrible twos," and will outgrow their externalizing behaviors (Crowther, Bond, & Rolf, 1981). Although this is largely true for children whose acting-out behavior falls within normal limits compared to same-age peers, it is not true for young children with severe conduct problems (Egeland, Kalkoske,

Gottesman, & Erickson, 1990). Unfortunately, there is mounting evidence that serious disruptive behaviors persist, placing these preschoolers at risk for behavior disorders in elementary school and substance abuse and legal offenses in middle school and high school (e.g., Campbell, Breaux, Ewing, & Szumowski, 1986; Hinshaw, 1992; Campbell & Ewing, 1990; McGee, Partridge, Williams, & Silva, 1991).

Recent evidence suggests that the development of conduct problems in young children follows a predictable sequence. The earliest problems noted by parents are hyperactive motor behavior emerging by 1 to 2 years of age, then stubbornness at about age 3 to 4, followed by attentional problems at age 4 to 5, cruelty toward animals at about age 5, and serious oppositional behavior and conduct problems including lying, theft, and fire setting at about age 6 (Loeber et al., 1992). This is not to say that all preschoolers with conduct problems progress through each of these problem behaviors. A complex array of factors including child, family, and environmental characteristics interact in ways that lead to either amelioration of behavioral disturbance or progression along the identified sequence of conduct problems (Loeber et al., 1992).

Within the context of normal development, we will discuss the prevalence, etiology, assessment, and treatment of preschool conduct problems in the domains of oppositional and aggressive behavior, inattention and overactivity, and antisocial behavioral symptoms that have been identified as emerging during this developmental period, including lying, stealing, and fire setting. Although we provide a separate section for each of these domains, we recognize that there is considerable overlap in behavioral presentation; research on school-age children has demonstrated high rates of comorbidity among antisocial, attention, and learning problems. Furthermore, although DSM disruptive behavior disorder diagnoses are often applied to acting-out preschoolers, they will not be emphasized in this chapter. We share the concern of many of our colleagues that in this area, DSM has not incorporated a sufficient developmental framework, nor has it been empirically validated for preschool-age children (Campbell, 1990; Ott, Eisenstadt, Eugrin, & Frick, in press).

NORMAL BEHAVIORAL DEVELOPMENT

Many studies have examined the frequency with which normal preschoolers display problem behaviors. For example, Campbell and Breaux (1983) found that at least 50% of mothers of normal preschoolers reported that their children were sometimes restless or disobedient, cried easily, got in fights, and didn't share. Seventeen of 22 items suggesting heightened activity level were rated as "pretty much" characteristic of 30% or more of these nonreferred preschoolers. Child management problems appear to peak at age 3, and both parent and teacher reports of specific problems decline thereafter. As several authors have noted (e.g., Campbell, 1990; Forehand & Wierson, 1993), the nature of behavioral problems that nonreferred preschoolers display is strongly related to the particular developmental hurdles facing the child. At the age of 2 to 3, young children begin seeking independence and autonomy, and as they work on these developmental issues, they are likely to be noncompliant with parents and to have temper tantrums. Rates of compliance with parental commands vary as a function of the method used to assess them, but normal preschoolers obey 50% to 75% of parental commands (Schroeder & Gordon, 1991). As verbal competency develops, the nature of noncompliance changes from simple direct defiance to more complex negotiation to avoid or defer compliance (Kinzynski, Kochanska, Radke-Yarrow, & Girnius-Brown, 1987). At the age of 4 to 5, preschoolers are expected to begin learning to play cooperatively with other children, and normative behavior problems include aggression, difficulty sharing, and difficulty taking turns. Aggression in the context of peer interactions declines as children acquire more sophisticated verbal means of negotiating with one another and learn to regulate their own emotions. Thus, as they are confronted with the challenges of early childhood, most preschoolers demonstrate transient behavioral problems that are substantially reduced with the successful mastery of developmental milestones.

Although a wide variety of oppositional and aggressive behaviors occur during the course of normal development, very few preschoolers display these behaviors at extreme levels. When conduct problem behaviors occur across caregivers and with extreme frequency or intensity, they are unlikely to be transient and are indicative of serious and persistent conduct problems. Similarly, there are some conduct problems (e.g., stealing) that preschoolers rarely exhibit and that are clearly indicative of a serious conduct problem.

PROBLEMS WITH OPPOSITIONAL AND AGGRESSIVE BEHAVIOR

Oppositional and aggressive behaviors in preschoolers include disobeying parental requests, talking back, whining, taunting and teasing, throwing temper tantrums, being destructive, hitting, kicking, biting, and cursing. Parent–child interactions in these families often are characterized by a high level of parental directiveness and low levels of child compliance with escalating negativity. Aggressive and disruptive preschoolers tend to be disliked by their preschool classmates (Olson & Brodfeld, 1991) and are at risk for peer rejection when they enter kindergarten (Ladd & Price, 1987). Noncompliance has been described as the keystone to the development of conduct disorder behaviors (Loeber & Schmalling, 1985).

Prevalence

Across age groups, noncompliance is the most frequent presenting problem in child psychology clinics (Schroeder & Gordon, 1991). Epidemiological studies with preschoolers have found prevalence rates of serious oppositional conduct problems similar to the 4% to 9% reported for school-age children (Cohen, Velez, Kohn, Schwab-Stone, & Johnson, 1987; Earls, 1982). Although substantial evidence with older children indicates that boys are more likely than girls to be described as aggressive, overactive, inattentive, and disobedient, the evidence for gender differences in preschool-age children is equivocal (Campbell, 1990).

Etiology

The etiology of oppositional and aggressive conduct problems in preschoolers is best understood as the complex interaction of an array of child, parent, family, and social variables. In her excellent review of developmental processes in the etiology of child behavior problems, Campbell (1990) suggests that some combination of child characteristics and parenting behaviors are primary determinants of enduring problems, while family and social context variables may exacerbate or maintain problems. In contrast, transient problems may occur as a response to family factors or social context but are unlikely to cause long-term problems in the absence of vulnerabilities in the child or problems in the parent–child relationship.

Assessment

The assessment of preschoolers with oppositional and disruptive behavior may have several goals. Most commonly, the mental health practitioner is asked to evaluate whether the child's behavior is outside of normal limits and to formulate treatment recommendations for the home and preschool settings. Evaluations are also conducted before and after parent-training interventions to monitor the family's treatment progress. The evaluation should involve multiple informants and modalities, particularly because both parent and teacher reports are subject to biases associated with stress level and depression (McMahon & Forehand, 1988).

The evaluation should begin with a thorough developmental and behavioral interview. Current developmental status may be assessed with a structured interview such as the Vineland Adaptive Behavior Scales (Sparrow, Balla, & Cicchetti, 1984). The child's behavioral history should include information about the age of onset and nature of the behavior problems, settings in which oppositional and disruptive behaviors occur, the child's behavior with all significant caregivers, the quality of the child's peer interactions, and detailed information about the discipline strategies parents have tried. If the child is in a day-care or preschool setting, the clinical interview with the parents should be supplemented with a teacher interview conducted over the phone or in conjunction with a classroom observation.

Much information can be gathered through direct observation of parent–child interactions. We recommend combining both informal and structured observations. Parent–child interactions may be observed informally when the parents complete paper and pencil forms while the child is expected to play independently. Notes can be made on the strategies parents use to enlist cooperation and independent play, as well as on the child's responsiveness to parental commands and limit setting. A number of formal coding systems are available for recording behaviors during structured parent–child interactions. We particularly recommend the system developed by Eyberg (Eyberg & Robinson, 1983) called the Dyadic Parent–Child Interaction Coding System (DPICS). The DPICS records a variety of parent and child behaviors relevant to assessing both cooperative and coercive parent–child interactions. The parent and child are observed interacting for 5 minutes in each of three standard situations: child-directed interaction (CDI) in which the parent is to follow the child's lead, parent-directed interaction (PDI) in which the parent is instructed to get the child to follow the parent's lead; and cleanup, in which the parent is instructed to get the child to clean up all of the toys in the playroom without the parent's assistance. Because the three situations vary in the degree of parental control required, the DPICS is efficient in eliciting a wide range of behaviors in a brief clinic-based observation period, and is especially useful for evaluating session-by-session progress and pre- to posttreatment changes following parent training interventions.

Parent and teacher interviews and direct observations should be supplemented with norm-referenced parent- and teacher-report measures of child conduct. The extensively validated parent report form of the Child Behavior Checklist (CBCL; Achenbach, 1991, 1992) is useful for assessing a wide range of both externalizing and internalizing problems, and has recently become more useful for preschoolers with the addition of a version for 2- to 3-year-old children. Another brief parent-report measure with excellent psychometric properties that is frequently used with preschoolers is the Eyberg Child Behavior Inventory (ECBI; Eyberg, 1974, 1992). The ECBI produces an intensity score that gives an estimate of the frequency of behaviors in the home setting and a problem score that allows parents to indicate whether they perceive each of the behaviors to be a problem, independent of its frequency of occurrence. Parent report of social skills and behavior problems may be obtained via the preschool form of the Social Skills Rating System (Gresham & Elliott, 1990). Parent report information should be supplemented with teacher report measures, including the Sutter-Eyberg Student Behavior Inventory (SESBI; Funderburk & Eyberg, 1989) and the Social Skills Rating System (Gresham & Elliott, 1990).

Parent factors that have been implicated as predictors of poor outcome in parent training include depression, severe psychopathology, and substance abuse (Webster-Stratton, 1985). To screen for these factors, a broad measure of parent personality functioning such as the Minnesota Multiphasic Personality Inventory-2 (MMPI-2) or more focused measures such as the Beck Depression Inventory may be administered. The Parenting Stress Index (PSI; Abidin, 1990) measures stress associated with having to parent a difficult child, as well as other sources of stress in the parent's life including health and marital problems. In the context of a full assessment, this measure can help to identify parent–child dyads who are at risk for developing abusive parenting practices.

Treatment

Probably the most extensively researched and validated mental health intervention for preschool-age children is parent training based on the Hanf-model approach. Hanf (1969) developed a two-stage treatment model for working with families with noncompliant young children based on direct coaching of parents in differential attention skills and time-out. Several well-known Hanf-model parent-training programs have been developed for use with young children with oppositional and aggressive behavior (e.g., Barkley, 1987; Forehand & McMahon, 1981). A treatment program that we find particularly useful is Eyberg's Parent–Child Interaction Therapy (PCIT; Eyberg & Boggs, 1989; Hembree-Kigin & McNeil, in press). PCIT differs from other Hanf-model approaches in its emphasis on teaching parents a set of traditional play therapy skills to improve the parent–child relationship.

PCIT is conducted in the context of dyadic play situations and includes two stages, child-directed interaction (CDI) and parent-directed interaction (PDI). Although the traditional sequencing of stages has CDI preceding PDI, a recent study demonstrated that many families preferred the reverse order and reported more favorable treatment outcome when PDI was taught before CDI (Eisenstadt, Eyberg, McNeil, Newcomb, & Funderburk, 1993). Each stage of treatment begins with a didactic session in which parents are instructed in a set of parenting skills via instruction, modeling, and role-playing. Parents spend additional sessions practicing the skills with their child in a clinic playroom while they are coached by the therapists from an observation room using a bug-in-ear microphone device (available from Farrall Instruments, Inc., P.O. Box 1037, Grand Island, Nebraska 68802–1037). In-session data are used to guide the training and home practice assignments. In each stage, treatment continues until a set of skill mastery and child behavior criteria are met. The major goal of CDI is to create or strengthen a positive and mutually rewarding parent–child relationship. In CDI, parents are taught to allow their child to lead the play activity via a set of specific communication skills. Parents are instructed to describe, imitate, and praise the child's appropriate behavior, reflect appropriate child speech, and ignore inappropriate behavior. Parents are taught not to criticize the child and not to use commands and questions that make it difficult for the child to lead the play. CDI is conducted at home in daily 5- to 10-minute play sessions using a set of constructional toys (e.g., Duplos, Legos, Mr. Potato Head).

The major goal of PDI is to decrease problematic behavior while increasing low-rate prosocial behaviors. In this second stage, parents are taught how to direct their child's activity. Parents are asked to use clear, positively stated, direct commands and consistent consequences for behavior. When the child obeys a parental command, the child receives a specific or "labeled" praise for compliance. Parents are taught to implement a structured time-out procedure in response to child noncompliance. In PDI, parents also learn to establish and enforce "house rules" and to manage their child's behavior both at home and in public places. To enhance cross-setting generalization, some behavior management sessions may be conducted in the home or in public settings in which child behavior is particularly difficult, such as a grocery store, shopping mall, or restaurant.

In programmatic work examining the effectiveness of PCIT, Eyberg and colleagues have demonstrated statistically and clinically significant improvements in child disruptive behavior and noncompliance (Eyberg & Robinson, 1982). Using only in-clinic training, treatment effects have been found to generalize to the home (Boggs, 1990), to the preschool and grade school setting (McNeil, Eyberg, Eisenstadt, Newcomb, & Funderburk, 1991), and to untreated siblings (Eyberg & Robinson, 1982). In addition, PCIT with individual families has been shown to be more effective than parent group didactic training (Eyberg & Matarazzo, 1980). In a sample of families with a high proportion on welfare (35%) and many single mothers

(55%), improvements were demonstrated not only on oppositional child behaviors, but on parent report of activity level, parenting stress, child internalizing problems, and child self-esteem (Eisenstadt et al., 1993). A full description of PCIT treatment procedures is available in Hembree-Kigin and McNeil (in press).

PROBLEMS WITH OVERACTIVITY AND INATTENTION

Preschoolers with overactivity and attentional problems are often described as being constantly on the go, daredevils, and escape artists. Parents may complain about their child's irritability and moodiness; poor sleeping and eating patterns; tendency to engage in dangerous, destructive, and impulsive behaviors; and aggression toward peers. These are challenging children to parent who require intensive supervision.

Prevalence and Diagnostic Issues

The mean age of symptom onset is between 3 and 4, ranging between infancy and age 7 (Barkley, 1990). Inattentive behaviors tend to appear later than hyperactive behaviors, and early onset of these problems is predictive of poorer outcome in adolescence (McGee, Williams, & Feehan, 1992). Because most normally developing preschoolers are overly active by adult standards, it is difficult for mental health professionals to discriminate between those displaying developmentally appropriate levels of activity and those whose hyperactivity and distractibility pose a serious problem. Some researchers in this area question the appropriateness of using the DSM-III-R attention-deficit/hyperactivity disorder (ADHD) diagnosis in its current form with preschoolers because it may needlessly stigmatize very young children whose high level of activity is within developmental norms (Campbell, 1990).

A recent study lends support to concerns about overidentifying ADHD in preschoolers. In a community sample of 82 preschoolers, 15% were found to meet DSM-III-R criteria for ADHD (Ott, Eisenstadt, Eugrin, & Frick, in press), approximately three times the prevalence rate expected based on studies of older children. However, increasing the number of symptoms required to make the diagnosis to 2 standard deviations (SD) above the preschool sample mean (in this case, to 11 symptoms) resulted in a diagnostic rate of 5%, which is more consistent with prevalence rates for older children. Schroeder and Gordon (1991), among others, advocate using a classification system that provides descriptive categories for behavior problems rather than psychiatric diagnoses.

Etiology

It is now widely accepted that children with attention-deficit disorders have a largely hereditary biological predisposition to these problems. According to Barkley (1990), what is inherited may be a tendency toward dopamine depletion in, or at least underactivity of, the prefrontal–striatal–limbic regions and their interconnections. Other factors can exacerbate this condition, such as pregnancy complications, exposure to toxins or neurological disease, family conflict, economic stress, and dysfunctional child-rearing practices. However, there is currently little evidence to suggest that persistent, clinically significant levels of inattention and overactivity can be caused by purely environmental factors such as poverty, family chaos, diet, or poor child management (Barkley, 1990). Specifically, environmental toxins such as food additives, refined sugar, and allergens have been proposed as possible causes of attentional problems in young children, but have garnered little empirical support (Barkley, 1989). According to Barkley (1990):

> The following factors would appear to be useful as potential predictors of the early emergence and persistence of ADHD in children: (1) family history of ADHD; (2) maternal smoking and alcohol consumption and poor maternal health during pregnancy; (3) single parenthood and low educational attainment; (4) poor infant health and developmental delays; (5) the early emergence of high activity level and demandingness in infancy; and (6) critical/directive maternal behavior in early childhood. (p. 109)

Assessment

The clinical assessment of preschoolers suspected to have attentional problems or overactivity should include a variety of informants and assessment modalities, assess behavior in multiple settings, and elicit information about child, parent, and family functioning. Barkley (1990, pp. 261–277) provides a useful format for interviewing parents of children referred for attentional problems and overactivity. Clinical interviews conducted with all significant caregivers (including day-care or preschool teachers) should be supplemented with norm-referenced measures appropriate for use with preschoolers. We recommend that parents be asked to complete the CBCL as a broad screening measure, the ECBI to specifically assess oppositional conduct problems, and the Conners Parent Rating Scale-Revised (CPRS-R; Conners, 1989; Goyette, Conners, & Ulrich, 1978). The CPRS-R has norms for children as young as 3, is brief, and assesses five content areas: Impulsive–Hyperactive, Conduct Problems, Learning Problems, Psychosomatic, and Anxiety. It is recommended that teachers be asked to complete the 28-item Conners Teacher Rating Scale-Revised

(CTRS-R; Goyette et al., 1978). It provides norms for children age 3 and above, and assesses content areas of central interest: Conduct Problem, Hyperactive, and Inattentive–Passive. Teachers may also be asked to complete the SESBI and the Social Skills Questionnaire (Gresham & Elliott, 1990). On parent and teacher report measures, it is recommended that a criterion of 2 SD above the population mean (97th percentile) be used as a cutoff for identifying children whose overactivity and inattention symptoms are serious, likely to persist, and predictive of later academic problems (Barkley, 1990).

Because of the biases that may influence parent and teacher reports, the development of objective laboratory measures of activity level and attention is appealing. Unfortunately, most laboratory measures (e.g., actometers, continuous-performance tests) are limited in their clinical usefulness by a lack of normative comparison data, a lack of sensitivity to behavioral context (antecedents and consequences), and questionable external validity (Barkley, 1990).

Interviews and parent- and teacher-report measures should be supplemented with direct observations in natural or clinic analogue situations. A preschooler in a one-on-one situation with an examiner is often much calmer, more attentive, and more compliant than is typical in the home or classroom setting, and these interactions should not unduly influence diagnostic, placement, or treatment decisions. Preschool classroom observations are highly recommended because they provide the best picture of the child's deficits, place teacher observations in context, and yield invaluable information for forming treatment recommendations. The best information is obtained when children are observed at different times of day, on multiple days, and during a variety of activities that vary in their demand for rule-governed behavior. We have found it useful to ask the teacher to point out three children to observe: the target child, a child who has average behavior for the classroom (not a model of excellent behavior), and the child whose behavior most closely approximates that of the target child (see McNeil et al., 1991). Observing the average child provides a marker for what is normative behavior in that classroom, and observation of the child whose behavior most closely approximates that of the target child allows the examiner to determine how much more disruptive the referred child is than the next most difficult to manage child. To maximize the chances that children will be compared while engaging in tasks with similar demands, each is observed for very brief periods (10 seconds) in rotation, with intermittent brief rest periods for marking child behavior and making notes. This method may be used to produce information about the percentage of the observation period in which the target and comparison children were on-task and compliant and did not engage in disruptive behavior. Barkley (1990, p. 338) describes a similar procedure.

Although there is no good substitute for a preschool observation, it is not always feasible to conduct one, and a clinic analogue observation can produce useful information. To assess the quality of the parent–child relationship, a formal coding system with standard situations may be used, such as the DPICS. To obtain a sample of task persistence, less formal observations can be made in which the parent completes forms or reads magazines while the child sits at a table and independently engages in activities typical of preschool-level work (e.g., coloring, puzzles). This situation provides a sample of the child's ability to attend to work, the strategies parents employ to encourage independent work, and the degree of oppositionality.

To formulate the best intervention plan, it is important to assess family functioning. We recommend a set of procedures similar to that described for the families of oppositional and aggressive children, including the PSI, a measure of marital functioning, the MMPI-2, and perhaps the Beck Depression Inventory. To minimize parents' resistance to testing, assessment of family functioning should be predicated on strong rapport and prefaced with a sensitive explanation of the importance of screening for areas of family functioning that may influence the preschooler's behavioral adjustment and treatment efficacy.

Treatment

The treatment plan for young children with attentional problems and overactivity should be developed in response to information gathered in the evaluation. If inattention and overactivity are mild and are not accompanied by serious aggression and oppositional behavior, and if the parents have good coping resources, parent counseling and brief parent training may be sufficient. If the child's overactivity appears to have been exacerbated by a situational stressor such as marital conflict, birth of a new sibling, or a recent move, those issues should be addressed in parent counseling. However, when a preschooler presents with extreme overactivity accompanied by other behavioral or developmental problems and significant familial stress, the intervention plan should be multimodal and is likely to include counseling on accident prevention in the home, consideration of the appropriateness of a trial of stimulant medication (see discussion below), individual or marital counseling for the parents, parent training, preschool consultation, and referral to a parent support group.

Enhancing safety through child-proofing the home should be addressed early in treatment because highly active young children are particularly prone toward being hurt in household accidents (Hartsough & Lambert, 1985). A number of products are commercially available to limit children's access to hazardous materials and areas such as drawer and cabinet safety latches, doorknob covers, electrical outlet covers, and stair guard gates. It is not unusual for parents to complain that their highly active 2- or 3-year-old finds ways to escape from the house if not under continuous supervision. This is both a dangerous and frightening behavior that may be prevented through installation of locks inside the home that the child is unable to manipulate or doorknob covers that small hands cannot turn. Until the young child is consistently obeying household rules, some parents choose to put a U-bolt lock on the refrigerator doors to prevent messes and food spoilage. Parents should be advised to keep pot handles turned inward while cooking to prevent scalding accidents. Child-proofing should also be done to prevent destruction of valuables, moving them to "off-limits" areas to which the child has access only under close supervision. It is important that age-appropriate, highly durable toys be available within the child's reach so that parents can redirect children when they play with "off-limits" objects. Although many parents are able to implement these child-proofing recommendations on their own, others need assistance in problem solving and are best helped through a home visit. For a recent review of pediatric accident prevention issues, the interested reader is referred to Finney and colleagues (1993).

Nearly all parents have heard that stimulant medications are effective for treating hyperactivity; however, few know that there are limits on the age at which these medications should be prescribed. According to Barkley (1990), in most cases, children under the age of 4 should not be given stimulant medications. First, relatively few empirical studies of stimulant medication with this age range have been conducted, and it is not fully understood how these medications affect the preschooler's rapidly developing nervous system. Those studies that are available show a significantly lower probability of effectiveness with children younger than age 5 (especially children age 3 or younger) than with children age 5 and older (30% versus 75% respond positively; Barkley, Swanson, Gadow, Gittelman, Sprague, Conners, & Barclay, 1990). According to Barkley and his colleagues (1990):

> It is hypothesized that this pattern occurs because of the maturation of the prefrontal cortex and its rich connections to the limbic system between 4 and 5 years of age and that these brain areas are the major sites of action of the stimulants. Prior to age 3 this substrate may not be sufficiently mature for the stimulants to achieve a positive behavioral response. (p. 8)

Second, there is a higher incidence of side effects in children under 4. Stimulants can produce temporary symptoms of psychosis in children younger than 3 or 4, even with moderate doses. In very young children, the peripheral organ systems that are responsible for the breakdown and excretion of stimulants and their by-products are less mature, and this may increase the risk for negative side effects (Barkley, McMurray, Edelbrock, & Robbins, 1990). Third, a major justification for the use of stimulants with older children is the need to maximize their chances of benefiting from their school placement so that they do not fall behind academically. Such an argument with preschoolers is less compelling. The primary use of stimulants with preschoolers is behavioral control; however, there is evidence that parent-training interventions for young children are particularly effective in establishing behavioral control without relying on chemical use.

These arguments notwithstanding, there may be some exceptional circumstances in which stimulant use with severely hyperactive preschoolers may be warranted. For example, stimulants may be prescribed in situations where the child's behavior places him or her at risk for abusive parenting and rapid behavioral change is necessary to enhance the child's safety. It is strongly recommended that the medication be carefully titrated with frequent monitoring for side effects. Galvin (1988) has written a useful book for helping parents explain stimulant medication to young children. In nearly all cases, pharmacotherapy should be accompanied by a parent-training intervention to teach parents how to manage the child's behavior while the child is not on stimulants. It is important to note that some parent-training studies have found improvements in compliance and oppositional behavior but little change in attention and activity (e.g., Pisterman et al., 1992).

A widely recognized intervention for children with overactivity and attentional problems is Barkley's (1990) 10-step program. Barkley supplements his parenting skills training with didactic material specifically on attention deficit disorders and teaches parents to use a home token system. The objectives of Barkley's program are to increase parental knowledge and understanding of attention-deficit disorders, to provide parents with ongoing supervision in the use of contingency management techniques, and to facilitate parental adjustment to having a child with attentional problems (Barkley, 1990). The program can be conducted with individual families or in groups and requires between 8 and 12 sessions. Step 1 (Program Orientation and Review of ADHD) is designed to acquaint parents with the mechanics of the treatment program, to increase parental knowledge about attentional problems and overactivity, and to address faulty perceptions parents may hold about themselves or their child. Parents are taught that "for most children, ADHD is a biologically based, inborn temperamental style that predisposes them to be inattentive, impulsive, and physically restless, as well as deficient in their capacity for rule-governed behavior" (Barkley, 1990, p. 416). It is emphasized that attentional problems and overactivity are, for many children, lifelong problems to be managed and compensated for, but not "cured." Parents are encouraged to ask questions, to share their emotional reactions to what they have learned, and to discuss their expectations for treatment. In step 2 (Understanding Parent–Child Relations and Principles of Behavior Management), the parents are presented with a framework for understanding disruptive child behavior that includes child characteristics, parent characteristics, familial stressors, and situational consequences. General principles of behavior management are also presented. Step 3 (Enhancing Parental Attending Skills) involves teaching parents to set aside 15 to 20 minutes a day to practice attending to positive child behaviors and ignoring mildly inappropriate behaviors, while allowing the child to lead the interaction. These attending skills are extended to reinforcing appropriate independent play and compliance with effective parental commands in step 4 (Paying Positive Attention to Appropriate Independent Play and Compliance; Giving Commands More Effectively).

Parents are taught how to implement a token economy system within the home to enforce house rules and encourage children to complete chores during step 5 (Establishing a Home Token System) and step 6 (Review of Home Token System; Using Response Cost). For young children, poker chips are used as reinforcers for obeying commands and spontaneous displays of appropriate behavior, and are later exchanged for predetermined privileges. When the response cost procedures are implemented, parents may take back chips for noncompliance or violation of household rules. The reader should be cautioned that the home token program may not be effective for very young preschoolers who do not have the cognitive maturity to comprehend symbolic reinforcers (Barkley, 1987). In steps 7 (Using Time-Out from Reinforcement) and 8 (Extending Time-Out to Other Misbehavior; Managing Children's Behavior in Public Places), parents are taught to implement a time-out chair procedure for particularly difficult behavior that has not been effectively addressed by the token economy. Step 9 (Handling Future Behavior Problems) includes a review of previously covered topics, fine-tuning, anticipation of backsliding, and school behavior management suggestions. The final step is to conduct a booster session approximately 1 month after completing step 9 in which pretreatment assessment instruments are readministered to assess progress and future periodic booster sessions may be scheduled.

Classroom consultation is critical in the treatment of overly active and inattentive preschoolers. They are often described as unable to follow group rules, aggressive with other children, unsuccessful in bids for social interaction, prone toward temper tantrums, unable to stay seated, and disobedient to teachers. Because of these problems, they miss out on important opportunities to learn preacademic skills and to have positive peer socialization experiences, and they may develop negative attitudes toward their own abilities and toward school in general. Not surprisingly, behaviors these children display place them at risk for expulsion from preschool, adding an additional stressor to already stressed caregivers. Classroom behavioral interventions for preschoolers with attentional problems and overactivity usually include both teacher-administered behavioral strategies and classroom modifications. The peer-administered reinforcement programs that are available for use with older children are typically not appropriate for this age range, nor are the delayed-reinforcement programs that are home-based, because they cannot provide very young children with the immediate consequences they need (Forehand & Wierson, 1993).

Any preschool classroom behavioral intervention should begin with both a teacher interview and a classroom observation. If the parent is hoping to keep the child in the school, it is important to facilitate a positive parent–teacher relationship and to serve as an ambassador of goodwill between the family and the school. Many preschool teachers are not knowledgeable about the nature, causes, and appropriate management of attentional problems and overactivity in young children, and the initial intervention should focus on imparting this information in a respectful and collegial fashion. An effective way to begin this consultative interaction is by providing supportive feedback to the teacher about how difficult this type of behavior is to manage and commenting on the many positive strategies the teacher used during the classroom observation.

Pfiffner and Barkley (1990) present several principles for classroom management that should be shared with the teacher. First, rules and instructions should be clear and brief, and the child should be asked to repeat back the direction given by the teacher. Visual reminders of rules should be prominently posted throughout the room. Second, consequences should be given more quickly and more frequently. Third, consequences should be more powerful than those needed to manage the behavior of most young children. Occasional praise or reprimands are ineffective, whereas more success is obtained with frequent, enthusiastic praise and tangible reinforcers. Fourth, punishment should be balanced by larger and more salient rewards or it is likely to be ineffective. Positive reinforcement programs should begin well ahead (1 to 2 weeks) of the introduction of negative consequences. Fifth, because these children habituate rapidly to reinforcers, the menu of reinforcers should be rotated more frequently than is necessary for other children. And sixth, children should be prepared

ahead of time for transitions to remind them of changing rules and consequences.

Preschoolers with attentional problems and overactivity are responsive to both teacher social reinforcement and tangible reinforcers. Ignoring
disruptive behaviors in the classroom setting is typically ineffective. The
attention-seeking behavior is likely to escalate past an acceptable point,
and many of the behaviors these children display are being reinforced by
attention from other children or are innately pleasurable. A more effective
strategy is to redirect the child to a behavior that is incompatible with the
problem behavior or to praise the specific behavior of children who are not
disruptive, while waiting for the disruptive child to imitate the children
being praised. Tangible tokens (e.g., poker chips) can be effective with
older preschoolers if the rules for earning them are made clear and they are
awarded in such a way as not to serve as a distractor. Pfiffner and Barkley
(1990) recommend placing chips in small fabric pockets that are safety
pinned to the back of the child's shirt. The children should have the
opportunity to exchange their chips for rewards or classroom privileges
several times throughout the school day. Time-out from attention (usually
in a time-out chair) is a powerful punishment for preschoolers and should
be part of an overall contingency program with many more opportunities
for rewards than punishment. Preacademic exercises should be brief, interactive, and delivered with enthusiasm to maintain interest. Children
with attentional problems tend to stay on task better in the morning hours,
and more demanding activities (e.g., learning colors, circle time) should be
placed early in the child's daily school routine, saving less demanding
activities (e.g., free play, snack time) for later in the day.

Overly active and distractible young children seem to benefit from
particular structural features of preschool classrooms (Children with Attention Deficit Disorders, 1988). They tend to function best in rooms with
four walls, rather than open classrooms where they are tempted to climb
over dividers and intrude on the activities of other groups of children. For
individual activities, they work best in an individual seat or desk rather
than at a group table where they can more easily disrupt the activities of
other children. Quiet classrooms seem to be best, and teachers should avoid
seating the distractible child in noisy areas, such as near the air conditioner,
near the heater, or in high-traffic areas. Visual distractors should be mini-
mized as well, with seating placed well away from windows and door-
ways. In addition, visual reminders enhance compliance with classroom
rules (e.g., circles drawn on the floor to sit on during circle time, lines drawn
on the floor where children are to line up).

Referral to a support group for parents of children with attention
deficit disorders can be beneficial in battling social isolation, boosting a

parent's sense of competence through feedback from peers, and assisting the parent in "learning the ropes" in becoming a good advocate for the child's therapeutic and educational needs. Support groups are run by local chapters of two national organizations for parents of children with attentional problems: Children with Attention Deficit Disorders (CHADD), National Headquarters, Suite 185, 1859 North Pine Island Road, Plantation, FL 33322, and Attention Deficit Disorders Association (ADDA), 4300 West Park Boulevard, Plano, TX 75093.

ANTISOCIAL CONDUCT PROBLEMS

Serious antisocial behavior problems are rare in preschoolers but may begin to emerge at about age 6. Notable among these early antisocial behaviors are persistent and intentional lying, stealing outside of the home, and intentional fire setting. When they occur in combination with other behavior problems and familial stressors, these problems may serve as early indicators of a developing pattern of serious conduct disturbance, similar to the conduct disorder symptoms described in older children. As with older children, there may be a history of parental antisocial behavior (e.g., criminality, substance abuse, family violence, failure to maintain employment), and insufficient parental supervision may play a role in the development and maintenance of these problems.

Lying

Most young children tell fanciful "tall tales," and at times, it may be difficult to get a playful child to sort out fact from fiction. Developmental research indicates that children as young as 4 years old know the difference between the truth and telling a lie, and by age 4, they also know that it is wrong to lie (Steward, Bussey, Goodman, & Saywitz, 1993). According to Lewis, Stanger, and Sullivan (1989), young children's first lies are usually technically false statements because they are not made with the intention of trying to deceive. Most studies show that children come to understand the concept of "false belief" sometime between the ages of 4 to 4½ and are not capable of purposeful deception at younger ages (Bussey, 1992). Children are more apt to lie through omission of information than commission, and they are much more likely to lie to keep themselves out of trouble than to get someone else into trouble (Steward et al., 1993). Telling an occasional lie to try to avoid parental disapproval is developmentally normative for 4- to 6-year-olds and does not constitute a clinically meaningful problem. However, lying does become a problem warranting intervention when it is frequent and persistent, and occurs in the context of other antisocial behaviors such as aggression, stealing, fire setting, and other destructive acts. Lying may develop through a common sequence of events. Initially, the child may misbehave and tell the parent the truth about the misbehavior. The parental response is likely to be punishment for the misbehavior, so the next time the child lies to avoid punishment and is rewarded when the lie is successful. Getting caught in a lie often causes children who are otherwise oppositional to work very hard to be better liars so that they won't be caught the next time (Blechman, 1985).

It is easier to prevent the development of lying than it is to eliminate it once it is a well-established pattern. Lying may be prevented though rewarding and praising honesty while continuing to administer an appropriate consequence for the misbehavior that was lied about. Very little empirical information is available on methods for treating lying in young children, and few clinical strategies have been described. According to Blechman (1985), it should be made very clear to the child that the consequences for misbehavior will be much more severe if the child has not been truthful about the misbehavior. Of course, it is also helpful for parents to model honesty and verbalize their own feelings about the importance of telling the truth even when they would rather not. In severe cases, we have had success using a parent-training program (Parent–Child Interaction Therapy) to treat lying in the context of other conduct problems (Eisenstadt et al., 1993).

Stealing

Taking the belongings of others is not considered stealing until the child has sufficient cognitive ability to understand that the action is wrong, and the child attempts to conceal the item or behavior from others. Stealing outside the home is usually precipitated by a climate within the home that is tolerant of taking the belongings of parents or siblings (Patterson, 1982). Such behavior may not be considered a serious transgression and may be tolerated without punishment.

As is the case with lying, little empirical information is available on effective treatment for very young children. Stealing is usually reinforced by the pleasure of having the desired object, and an effective consequence is requiring the child to return the stolen item and apologize to its owner (Blechman, 1985). However, if a persistent pattern of stealing emerges, it is usually accompanied by lying to cover up the theft. As with lying, we have had success treating repeated stealing within the context of a parent-training program for other conduct problems. It should be noted that some parents with a well-established pattern of failure to track and punish antisocial behaviors in their children may not be sufficiently motivated to follow through with the intensive monitoring required to eliminate stealing (Patterson, 1982).

Fire Setting

The term "fire play" has been used to describe involvement with fire that is motivated by curiosity and exploration, whereas "fire setting" has been used to signify a deliberate attempt to damage or destroy property or life (Grolnick, Cole, Laurenitis, & Schwartzman, 1990). Such a motivation-based distinction appears to be particularly relevant for mental health professionals working with very young children who are involved with fire. Preschoolers who engage in fire setting as opposed to fire play may display concomitant externalizing problems such as overactivity, oppositionality, and aggression. Kolko and Kazdin (1990) found less structure and rule enforcement and greater psychological distress, marital maladjustment, and exposure to stressful life events in families of fire setters than in families of children who did not set fires. Very little information is available about the prevalence of fire involvement in preschool-age children; however, Jacobson (1985) found that first incidents of fire setting occurred at an average age of 6.

Intervention must begin with limiting access to fire-making materials. Given that 90% of fires started by children are ignited by lighters or matches (Grolnick et al., 1990), these should be removed from the home or placed in a locked cabinet. Discussion of danger alone has been shown to have little impact on young children's safety behavior and is not recommended as a primary means of preventing future fire play or fire setting (Bergman, 1982). Children who are involved with fire are less likely than other children to anticipate parental punishment for fire play (Grolnick et al., 1990), indicating that efforts to deter fire play may be aided by emphasis on the immediate punishment that the child will incur. Given the relationship between deliberate fire setting and other serious behavior problems, interventions for young children should target not only the fire setting, but other conduct problems that co-occur with fire setting using one of the parent-training programs described earlier in this chapter (Forehand, Wierson, Frame, Kemptom, & Armistead, 1991).

9

Fears and Anxiety

Internalizing problems are among the most understudied areas in preschool mental health. The lack of research attention devoted to young children's fears parallels the tendency of parents to place low priority on treatment of internalizing problems. Fears and phobias in young children have been reported to account for only 5% of all referrals for intervention (Ollendick & Francis, 1988). According to Campbell (1990, p. 66), "Internalizing behaviors are often ignored or not recognized by adults in the child's environment because they are usually less dramatic and less irritating to others than externalizing symptoms." Fears are common in very young children, with mothers reporting an average of four to five fears for 2- to 6-year-old children (Jersild & Holmes, 1935).

Preschoolers' fears and anxieties have been considered low-priority targets for intervention because they are thought to be transient. Research on the stability of fears and anxiety in young children has produced inconsistent findings. Although numerous early studies reported that young children's fears and anxieties were short-lived, more recent studies have found evidence for stability.

The low priority placed on young children's fears and anxieties is clearly compounded by the difficulties associated with studying a largely internal event in children who may be too young to provide valid self-report information. However, even in older age groups, the basic nature and classification of childhood anxiety disorders remain understudied. At present, no satisfactory classification system has been developed for childhood anxiety and fears because basic empirical research is sorely lacking. Despite general concerns that DSM needs to incorporate a stronger developmental framework, diagnostic criteria for the adult anxiety disorders continue to be applied without modification for children. Little research addresses the validity of these disorders in school-age children, and virtually no information is available on their validity in preschoolers.

On a more positive note, despite deficits in basic research on the nature and classification of childhood anxiety, there is growing research and clinical interest in this area. In this chapter, we will present information on the normative development of fears and anxiety and discuss our current understanding of the manifestation and treatment of specific fears, generalized anxiety, and separation anxiety in preschoolers.

NORMATIVE FEARS IN PRESCHOOLERS

Specific fears are quite common in preschoolers. According to Miller (1983), children between the ages of 2 and 6 have an average of three fears. The particular events that elicit fear and the behavioral expression of fear and anxiety follow a clear developmental progression. Research on the normal development of fears has been well summarized by several authors (e.g., Campbell, 1986; Marks, 1987; Ollendick & King, 1991), and the following description is based largely on their accounts. Fears in the newborn appear to be innate reactions to the sudden loss of physical support or to intense and unpredictable sensory stimuli such as loud noises. The adaptive behavioral expression of fear in a newborn consists principally of crying, which serves to alert the caregiver that the infant may be in danger. By about 6 months, the infant shows fear responses in reaction to novel and strange stimuli such as masks, dogs, and certain toys such as a jack-in-the-box. Because of an increasing capacity for purposeful movement of the head and gaze direction, infants are able to respond to the feared stimulus not only by crying but by turning their heads or averting their eyes, thus summoning a caregiver as well as decreasing anxiety by decreasing visual exposure to the feared object. When infants begin to crawl, their fear of heights becomes apparent, and with newly acquired mobility, they are able to move away from an anxiety-provoking stimulus, such as a stairway. Fearfulness of strangers emerges at about 8 months, when infants have developed object permanence and have a strongly developed preference for primary caregivers. Fear of strangers is typically expressed through gaze aversion, turning away, crying, and attempts at escape or regaining proximity to a parent. The presence and degree of fearfulness depends on a variety of historical and contextual factors such as the proximity of familiar people, familiarity of the setting, past experience with unfamiliar people, the infant's characteristic reactions to arousal, and the way in which the infant is approached by the stranger (Rheingold & Eckerman, 1973).

Between the ages of 12 and 30 months, most toddlers experience anxiety associated with being separated from their caregivers, particularly their mothers. This anxiety may be expressed through separation protest, crying, clinging, and tantrums. However, separation fears dissipate for most securely attached children who learn what to do in their parent's absence and experience success with predictable separation and reunification. When toilet training begins at about age 2, fears and anxiety associated with toileting become common. Depending on the child's level of expressive language development, fears or anxiety associated with toileting may be expressed verbally or through somatic complaints such as stomachaches or headaches. It is not unusual for toddlers who are fearful of the toilet to burst into tears when "the potty" is mentioned or struggle to get away as they are led to the bathroom. Fears of dogs and other large animals are common for 3-year-olds who find the animals' behavior unpredictable and threatening.

The development of imaginative capabilities precedes the understanding of the difference between reality and fantasy. This sets the stage for 2- to 4-year-olds to experience intense fears of imaginary creatures and monsters. The specific content of the fears and the attributes of the imagined creatures become more detailed with greater cognitive development. This fear of monsters may manifest itself in reluctance to be alone, fears about being in particular parts of the house such as the basement, and nighttime fears. Fear of the dark is common for 4-year-olds, perhaps because the decrease in visual input at night facilitates imagination of frightening creatures or threatening people such as robbers. For more information on nighttime fears and anxieties, the reader is referred to Chapter 5.

Between ages 2 and 4, fears associated with separation may reemerge, particularly in children beginning preschool or day care with no prior experiences with successful separation and reunification. For children of this age, separation anxiety may be translated into specific fears of abandonment, kidnapping, or death of a parent. Children who have not successfully mastered their separation anxiety by age 5 may experience intense anticipatory anxiety and somatic discomfort prior to beginning kindergarten, and not uncommonly, they may fear getting lost at the large school. Separation anxiety may be expressed through somatic complaints when separation is anticipated (e.g., on school mornings), and school refusal may occur. By the age of 6 or 7, fears of imaginary threats and separation are usually replaced by fears related to bodily injury, death, crime, natural disasters, school performance, and peer relationships.

Children who use transitional objects such as blankets and stuffed animals have been popularly characterized as anxious and insecure. In reality, a large proportion of children in the United States and other countries use transitional objects, and there have been no convincing data linking the practice with current or future psychopathology, including anxiety (Passman, 1987).

SPECIFIC FEARS

"Fear" is defined as "a pattern of three types of reactions to a stimulus of perceived threat: (1) motor reactions, such as avoidance, escape, and tentative approach; (2) subjective reactions, such as verbal reports of discomfort, distress, and terror; and (3) physiological reactions, such as heart palpitations, profuse sweating, and rapid breathing" (Barrios & O'Dell, 1989, p. 168). A "phobia" is a highly intense and persistent reaction to a stimulus posing little objective danger (Marks, 1969). Phobias are commonly subdivided into social phobias (fear of public scrutiny or social embarrassment) and simple phobias (fear of a circumscribed stimulus) (APA, 1987). Preschool-age children are much more likely to exhibit simple than social phobias (Strauss, 1993). Barrios and O'Dell (1989) point out that it is important to assume a developmental perspective when considering what represents "objective danger" to a preschooler. Some relatively innocuous stimuli from an adult perspective may represent real threats to very young children who are more physically vulnerable. Some of the more common early childhood phobias include those of animals, blood, water, darkness, closed places, thunderstorms, and medical procedures (King, 1993).

Prevalence

Little is known about the prevalence of excessive fears or phobias in preschoolers. In school-age children, estimates of the rate of phobic disorders have ranged from less than 1% (Rutter, Tizzard, & Whitemore, 1970) to 2.4% (Anderson, Williams, McGee, & Silva, 1987). Most studies indicate that girls report greater numbers of fears and anxieties than boys, irrespective of age (Barrios & O'Dell, 1989).

Etiology

Several behavioral theories for the etiology of fears have been described including the two-factor theory (Mowrer, 1960), revised respondent conditioning theories (e.g., Seligman, 1971), approach–withdrawal theory (Delprato & McGlynn, 1984), self-efficacy theory (Bandura, 1977), and bioinformational theory (Lang, 1979). For a review of the merits and criticisms of each, the reader is referred to Barrios and O'Dell (1989). Although several researchers have found a tendency for fearfulness to run in families, it is unclear whether this is due to environmental or genetic factors (Rutter et al., 1990).

Assessment

The assessment of fears in a preschooler should yield hypotheses about the source of the fears; evaluate the degree to which the fears interfere with the child's cognitive and emotional development and/or negatively affect the family; identify other co-existing internalizing and externalizing problems; identify factors that may amplify or reduce the fears; provide baseline information about the intensity, extent, and behavioral expression of the fears against which treatment effects can be gauged; and result in the formulation of specific intervention recommendations. King (1993) recommends that the evaluation begin with a detailed parent interview. Information to be collected in the clinical interview includes (1) the development and history of the fear, (2) any accompanying anxieties, (3) the current family context, (4) factors that appear to exacerbate or ameliorate the fears, (5) how family members have responded to the fears (e.g., reinforced them by chasing imaginary monsters or by removing a feared but friendly dog), (6) familial history of anxiety disorders, (7) current levels and sources of parental anxiety, and (8) how the child's and family's usual activities are affected by the child's fearfulness.

Parents are not always the most accurate reporters of their own behavior or of their children's level of distress; thus, direct observation in the environment in which the child is fearful can provide important information (King, 1993). When it is not possible to observe in the natural environment, a Behavioral Avoidance Test may be conducted in which the feared situation is simulated in the clinic and the child's level of avoidant behavior is measured (e.g., amount of time spent in the presence of the fear-provoking stimulus, distance from the stimulus) (King, 1993). When trained observers are available, formal observation of more generalized anxiety may be conducted using an observational coding system such as the Preschool Observation Scale of Anxiety (Glennon & Weisz, 1978).

The evaluation should also include a measure of parenting stress, such as the Parenting Stress Index (PSI; Abidin, 1990), and a broad-based standardized measure of child functioning, such as the Child Behavior Checklist (CBCL; Achenbach, 1991, 1992). The CBCL is useful for evaluating anxiety and affect problems in preschoolers as well as screening for accompanying problems that parents may not have mentioned during the clinical interview. Unfortunately, most child- and parent-report instruments for measuring childhood fears and anxiety are not normed for preschoolers. Even in the absence of age-appropriate norms, use of one of the parent-report checklists with items appropriate for very young children (e.g., the Louisville Fear Survey; Miller et al., 1972) may help parents to identify additional fears that they failed to report during the clinical interview. Similarly, although age-appropriate norms are not available, older preschoolers may be able to provide some self-report information using Ollendick's (1983) simplified version of the Fear Survey Schedule for Children Revised (FSSC-R), which uses a three-point scale (none, some, a lot).

Self-report of emotions is generally considered unreliable in very young children who are just acquiring affective labels and an awareness of internal states. However, some researchers and clinicians have attempted to elicit preschoolers' self-reports using simple pictorial methods such as the "fear thermometer" in which the bottom of the thermometer represents no fear and the top signifies extreme fear and anxiety. In considering the advantages and disadvantages of such methods, Schroeder and Gordon (1991, p. 330) state that:

> Fear thermometers are not very reliable, but asking the child to rate the intensity of his or her fears does allow the clinician to establish a fear hierarchy and enables the child to distinguish among different levels of fear. A drawing of the thermometer is helpful for younger children. The clinician can also give young children a concrete way to describe fear or anxiety (e.g., "it feels a lot or just a little like bees or butterflies"), or can have them draw themselves and indicate how different parts of the body feel, as well as give colors to their feelings.

The "faces" scale is another pictorial method that has been used with preschool-age children in which they select which of a short series of faces depicting varying degrees of distress looks most like them when they see, touch, or think about the feared stimulus (Jay, 1988).

Treatment

In deciding whether to treat a fearful preschooler, it is also important to consider from a developmental perspective the degree of mismatch between the preschooler's perception of danger and the actual hazards presented by the feared stimulus (Barrios & O'Dell, 1989). Adaptive fears to real threats should generally not be eliminated. For example, it may be quite adaptive for a toddler who cannot swim to be fearful of bodies of water, and for a young child with limited capacities for escape or self-defense to be fearful of unfamiliar large animals. Treatment may also be unnecessary when the child is unlikely to encounter the feared stimulus in the future. According to Barrios and O'Dell (1989), treatment typically is warranted when the fears significantly affect the current or future normal functioning of the child; anytime a child experiences strong, recurrent subjective distress; and whenever an unusually high number of even moderate fears are present.

Behavioral techniques appear to be the most successful in treating intense fear in preschoolers (Gordon et al., 1992). Successful interventions have involved some variant on the widely researched techniques of systematic desensitization, modeling, and contingency management. In systematic desensitization, a fear hierarchy is constructed in which situations are rank-ordered from least to most fearful (Ollendick & Cerny, 1981). With preschoolers, this can be based on behavioral observations and on children's self-report of fear via a pictorial measure such as the fear thermometer. The child imagines engaging in each of the steps on the hierarchy while engaging in a response that is incompatible with fear (Wolpe, 1958). With older children, relaxation training and pleasant imagery are typically used. Recognizing the difficulties often encountered in maintaining the interest and attention of young children during relaxation training, Ollendick and Cerny (1981) presented progressive muscle relaxation protocols that are more appealing to young children. Other anxiety-antagonistic responses in which preschoolers may be instructed to engage include eating a snack, playing with a desirable toy, singing along with a favorite song, and sitting on the mother's lap. Because many preschoolers lack the cognitive development to engage in sophisticated imaginal interventions, live exposure to the feared stimulus may produce superior effects (Ollendick & Cerny, 1981).

In modeling interventions, the child watches a model (often the parent or another child) interact appropriately with the feared stimulus and then practices duplicating those actions with the guidance and praise of the parents and therapist. Numerous procedural variations on modeling exist, but it has generally been found that better outcomes are obtained with models that most closely match the age, gender, and fear level of the child (Perry & Furukawa, 1980). In contingency management, the child is rewarded for interacting with the feared stimulus using either social or tangible reinforcers, and any secondary reinforcement (e.g., extra nurturance from the parent) of fearful behavior is eliminated (Schroeder & Gordon, 1991).

Effective treatment of specific fears almost always involves forcing the child to confront the feared stimulus (Reed, Carter, & Miller, 1992). Particularly with preschoolers, parents may feel guilty and ambivalent about requiring their young child to face the source of his or her fear. The therapist should anticipate these reservations for the parents, warn them about the possible intensity of the child's reaction, and discuss with them the negative ramifications of supporting the child's avoidance rather than supporting confrontation of the feared stimulus (Reed et al., 1992). Some authors (e.g., Mansdorf & Lukens, 1987) recommend teaching the parents to use coping self-statements to assist them in adhering to the treatment procedures. For example, parents might be taught to replace the inhibiting cognition "My child is sick, so I shouldn't push" with the more positive coping cognition "This is the way to help."

For less intense or normative levels of fears, symbolic modeling through stories may be helpful (Gordon et al., 1992). Children can be taught how story characters cope with their fears and then be prompted and rewarded for use of positive coping statements. However, it should be noted that cognitive interventions have not consistently been shown to benefit preschool-age children, perhaps because the language-based self-control required for self-instructional training does not fully appear in most children prior to age 6 (Braswell & Kendall, 1988). Thus, symbolic modeling may be most likely to benefit children of at least kindergarten age and older preschoolers of relatively advanced cognitive development.

GENERALIZED ANXIETY

"Anxiety" is the diffuse and moderate fear reactions that occur in the absence of an immediately discernible threat (Barrios & O'Dell, 1989). Young children with generalized anxiety may express persistent and unrealistic worry about future events (e.g., being expelled from preschool for not getting their toys cleaned up fast enough), unrealistic worry about their past behavior (e.g., believing that the parent won't love them anymore because they made a sloppy picture), unrealistic worry about their competence (e.g., worrying that they will never be smart enough to learn to read), somatic complaints (e.g., stomachaches, headaches), excessive needs for reassurance (e.g., repeatedly checking on parents' or siblings' well-being), self-consciousness (e.g., being afraid to speak in a group of children and say the wrong thing), and physical tension (e.g., excessive motor movement, hunched shoulders, hair twirling or pulling, nail-biting). We have also noted that anxious preschoolers and kindergartners are often hypervigilant about the behavior and well-being of other children, becoming noticeably upset when a classroom rule is broken or needing to check repeatedly on the well-being of classmates. In anticipation of novel situations, children may ask numerous questions about imagined hazards. Strauss, Lease, Last, and Francis (1988) have observed that overly anxious young children are less likely than older children to worry about their past behavior, perhaps because their level of cognitive development is more consistent with a present or future orientation. In school-age children, there is some indication that those who are overly anxious are likely to come from higher SES households with relatively high achievement expectations (e.g., Last, Francis, Hersen, Kazdin, & Strauss, 1987).

Preschoolers who persistently experience anxiety across a variety of situations and not exclusively in reaction to the threat of separation from a caretaker might be assigned a DSM-III-R diagnosis of overanxious disorder. However, in DSM-IV, these problems have been subsumed within the adult category of generalized anxiety disorder. The applicability of the adult criteria to children has been contested with a recent study showing that none of 104 children referred to a child and adolescent anxiety disorder clinic met DSM-III-R criteria for generalized anxiety disorder (Last, Perrin, Hersen, & Kazdin, 1991).

It is questionable whether anxiety problems and mood disorders are distinct dimensions in young children (Campbell, 1990). According to Achenbach's (1992) work with toddlers, internalizing problems appear to cluster into two factors in children under age 4: anxious/depressed and withdrawn. Although somatic problems form a third factor contributing to the internalizing dimension in children age 4 and older, they contribute to neither the internalizing nor externalizing dimension in 2- to 3-year-olds (Achenbach, 1991, 1992). Indicators of anxiety and sad affect are not well differentiated in preschoolers and are commonly reported by parents of both clinic-referred and nonreferred children.

Etiology

The behavioral theories of the etiology of specific fears mentioned earlier in this chapter may be applied to generalized anxiety as well and will not be reiterated here. As is the case with specific fears, there is evidence that anxiety disorders tend to run in families, but it is not yet clear whether the intergenerational transmission is genetic, environmental, or a combination of the two (Rutter et al., 1990). The finding that generalized anxiety is more common in children of parents with high achievement expectations suggests that parents may transmit their perfectionist tendencies to their offspring. In addition, a variety of medical conditions or medication reactions can cause young children to experience symptoms of anxiety. These include reactions to caffeine and stimulant medications, central nervous system problems, metabolic disorders (e.g., hypoglycemia), endocrine disorders (e.g., hyperthyroidism), and cardiac problems (e.g., mitral valve prolapse; Behar & Stewart, 1981).

Assessment

Not surprisingly, it is rare for a parent to bring a preschool-age child in for assessment of generalized anxiety, and in our experience, when such an event occurs, the child's level of discomfort and that of the family is usually extreme. The assessment recommendations offered in the specific fears section in this chapter are appropriate for nonspecific anxiety as well. In addition, a medical evaluation should be conducted to rule out the various medical conditions or medication reactions that may cause anxiety symptoms (Schroeder & Gordon, 1991). For an excellent review of developmental issues in the assessment of anxiety, the reader is referred to Beidel and Stanley (1993).

Treatment

Little information is available on treatment methods for generalized anxiety in young children. Francis (1989) and Last (1992) note that there are no outcome studies in the research literature on the behavioral treatment of overanxious disorder in children. In the absence of empirical work evaluating interventions for generalized anxiety in young children, we will offer observations based on our own clinical experience. It should be noted that our clinical recommendations integrate a variety of techniques developed by others, and the efficacy of their combined use in preschoolers has not been empirically evaluated.

With overly anxious 4- and 5-year-olds, we have had success using a combination of parent counseling, parent–child relationship enhancement, and parent training for teaching children coping skills. We begin treatment with parent counseling in which we share current knowledge about the tendency for anxiety and perfectionism to run in families. The parents are encouraged to explore their expectations for their child and to identify cross-generational patterns of anxiety. They are taught how to use daily routines and preparation just before transitions (avoiding the extremes of no preparation and preparation too far in advance) to decrease anticipatory anxiety. In some families with overly anxious preschoolers, parents share their adult worries (e.g., financial concerns, work stress, conflicts with spouse and extended family) with the young child and reinforce the child for assuming responsibilities that are inappropriate for their developmental level. Parents are counseled to establish clear boundaries, filter adult worries and concerns, seek support from another adult rather than their child, and discourage the child from assuming inappropriate levels of responsibility. Finally, parents are instructed to encourage their child to engage in competing responses (e.g., watch a cartoon, play with a favorite toy, have a snack) in situations that appear to exacerbate the anxiety.

Following this initial counseling, parents are instructed in a set of child-directed interaction (CDI) play therapy skills designed to strengthen the parent–child relationship (see the description of CDI skills presented in Chapter 8 of this volume). Once parents demonstrate mastery of these skills, an additional didactic session is held in which parents are instructed in ways to teach their child positive coping during the child-directed play sessions. For example, parents are taught to make errors during their own play (e.g., coloring outside of the lines, knocking over their own towers), model mild initial frustration followed by a positive coping statement such as "That's okay, it looks pretty anyway" or "I don't mind. I know I can build it again if I want." The parent looks for opportunities to model coping in response to the particular situations that frustrate the child, to prompt the child to make coping statements, and to shape coping behavior by praising successive approximations (e.g., "I'm proud of you. It fell down and you didn't cry. That's terrific!"). Parents complete 5- to 10-minute daily home practice sessions throughout treatment and are encouraged to prompt their children in positive coping skills any time they notice anxiety. As noted by Klesges, Malott, and Ugland (1984), in some cases, treatment of parental or sibling anxiety may be a prerequisite for enduring treatment effects with the preschooler.

Little empirical work has been conducted on pharmacotherapy with overly anxious children, and we advise caution in the use of any psychoactive medication with preschoolers. One small-sample clinical trial of alprazolam with 7- to 17-year-old children with overanxious disorder has been reported (Simeon & Ferguson, 1987). Although the authors indicated that 58% of children were improved after 4 weeks of treatment, the results are difficult to interpret in the absence of a placebo control group.

SEPARATION ANXIETY

Separation anxiety disorder (SAD) involves inappropriate and excessive anxiety associated with separation from a major caregiver, usually the mother (APA, 1987). Young children with SAD often worry excessively about the absent caregiver's safety, may be preoccupied with fears of kidnappers, often have recurrent nightmares with themes of separation, and may insist on bed sharing. Preschoolers may "shadow" the caregiver, following him or her around the house to maintain proximity.

The DSM-III-R criteria for SAD have been criticized on the grounds that insufficient information is provided to allow the clinician to discriminate between what is "excessive" separation anxiety warranting a psychiatric diagnosis versus the developmentally normal and adaptive separation anxiety characteristic of early childhood (Campbell, 1990). According to the DSM-III-R, SAD may be most likely to develop following a significant stressor such as a loss, an illness, or a move (APA, 1987). However Campbell (1990) cautions against making a diagnosis when the preschooler's response to a traumatic event might better be conceptualized as adaptive:

> Because young children may not be expected to cope easily with certain kinds of stressful events or to readjust quickly to major life change but instead may need the close support of an attachment figure to help them make the necessary transitions, the expression of anxiety through nightmares, physical symptoms, or separation protest may be adaptive rather than pathological. Thus, a 3-year-old who shows a major reaction to a loss or other major life change or upsetting event expressed as clinging and other signs of separation distress may be behaving in predictable ways that clearly do not warrant a diagnosis of a psychiatric disorder. However, in the absence of any identifiable event in the life of a young child who becomes virtually panic-stricken at the prospect of separation, such a diagnosis may be warranted (pp. 71–72).

Prevalence

Because of difficulties discriminating between normative anxiety associated with separation and SAD in preschoolers, prevalence data in very young children are largely unavailable. Kastrup (1976) found that parents of 13.7% (12% of boys and 16% of girls) of 5- to 6-year-old Danish children reported that their young children experienced fear of separation. However, this estimate is likely to be high, given that children were not required to meet SAD diagnostic criteria. Currently, it is unclear whether SAD affects equal numbers of boys and girls.

Etiology

Theories for how severe separation anxiety develops usually incorporate transgenerational and age-related vulnerability, an attachment-related stressful event, and reinforcement principles. Fifty percent or more of mothers of children with SAD have been reported to have a history of generalized anxiety disorder, and many also have a history of major depression (Last et al., 1987). Children of parents with histories of generalized anxiety disorder may be more vulnerable to developing separation anxiety through either genetic predisposition or environmental factors (Rutter et al., 1990). Children may be most vulnerable to developing severe separation anxiety during the developmental period in early childhood in which separation anxiety is normative and considered to be ontogeneti-cally programmed (Strauss, 1993). Gittelman-Klein and Klein (1980) found that 80% of children with SAD experienced its onset after an attachment-altering event such as an illness or death in the family or a move. As noted by Campbell (1990), the expression of anxiety in response to separation from a primary caregiver during such times is probably adaptive. How-ever, this adaptive anxiety that serves to keep the caregiver close at hand may not be transient under certain reinforcement conditions. For example, Stokes, Boggs, and Osnes (1989) noted that crying, clinging, and throwing tantrums are negatively reinforced when they bring about the cessation of separation, or return of the parent. The parent who does not allow the distressed child to experience separation followed by reliable and success-ful reunification prevents the child from learning that catastrophic conse-quences do not result from separation. Additionally, the behaviors associated with separation anxiety may be positively reinforced through increases in parental affection and attentiveness (Stokes et al., 1989).

Others have argued that problems with separation anxiety develop as the result of the quality of early experiences with attachment figures (Bowlby, 1973). In summarizing this viewpoint, Campbell (1986) states that

> Infants who have experienced responsive and available mothering develop a sense of security and trust. They have learned that when their mother leaves, she will return and that their signals of distress or discomfort will be acknow-ledged and responded to. Secure infants are less likely to become upset by typical brief separations than are insecure infants who have experienced a relationship with an unpredictable, unavailable, rejecting, or unresponsive attachment figure. The latter infants will be prone to more intense upset at separation and/or experience chronic anxiety about the whereabouts, respon-siveness, and eventual return of the attachment figure, who has failed to serve as an adequate protector or source of comfort (pp. 38–39).

Thus, preschoolers demonstrating extreme separation anxiety may be responding in a characteristic way based on early, and perhaps continu-ing, experiences with caregiving inconsistency.

Assessment

The evaluation should begin with an interview gathering information on the child's attachment experiences from early infancy through the time of evaluation. The course of separation anxiety may be recognized as chronic and developing out of a pattern of inconsistent and unresponsive caregiving, or the onset may have been more acute and in association with an attachment-altering event. The degree of impact the separation distress has had on the young child's development and on the family should be evaluated as well. Administration of a measure of parenting stress is helpful (e.g., PSI) in examining the caregiver's general stress level, stress associated with parenting the identified child, and additional stressors that are not specific to parenting. A broad-based parent-report measure of child behavioral and emotional functioning (e.g., CBCL) should also be given to assist in identifying any comorbid problems. Parent–child interaction observations can be particularly important in assessing specific aspects of separation distress and the general quality of the parent–child relationship. We recommend informal observations of the degree of separation the child can tolerate as well as more formal parent–child interaction observational methods such as the Dyadic Parent–Child Interaction Coding System (DPICS; Eyberg & Robinson, 1983) and the Preschool Observation Scale of Anxiety (Glennon & Weisz, 1978).

Treatment

Treatment of preschoolers who are experiencing severe separation anxiety should involve a combination of behavioral intervention, parent counseling, and parent–child relationship strengthening. If during the course of the evaluation a recent attachment-altering event is identified that likely precipitated the anxiety, the best course of treatment may be the provision of extra nurturance and support as the child adjusts to the recent event as well as minimization of separation from the primary caregiver (Campbell, 1990). However, if the separation anxiety has persisted for an extended time period or is significantly interfering with the child's development or family routines, a behavioral intervention should be initiated. The goal is for the avoidant child to gather experience with successful separation in which no calamitous event occurs. The child can be shaped into successful separation through a program of gradual exposure (Thyer, 1993) accompanied by activities incompatible with anxiety, such as watching a favorite cartoon, holding a special toy, or eating a snack. Depending on the child's initial level of tolerance for separation, the "separation" may begin with the parent sitting some distance away in a familiar setting and gradually progress to brief outings in which the child is left at home with a familiar caregiver.

In addition to graduated exposure, parents should be instructed in the most effective ways of preparing the child for separations (i.e., providing an age-appropriate explanation for the separation, estimation of when the parent will return, explicit instructions for what the child is to do in the parent's absence, and what special activity will happen when the parent returns). Abrupt departures without explanation are likely to result in greater distress (Weinraub & Lewis, 1977). Social and tangible reinforcers for good separation behavior should be implemented, and parents should be sensitized to the ways in which they may have inadvertently rewarded clinging and excessive dependency through protracted parting scenes. As noted for children with generalized anxiety, young children experiencing significant separation distress may benefit from a specific parent-training program targeting enhancement of the parent–child relationship, such as the child-directed interaction stage of Parent–Child Interaction Therapy (Eyberg & Boggs, 1989; Hembree-Kigin & McNeil, in press).

At present, pharmacotherapy for SAD in preschoolers has not been widely evaluated in well-controlled clinical trials. The effectiveness of the tricyclic antidepressant imipramine in older children has received some support. In their review of pharmacotherapy for childhood anxiety disorders, Gittelman and Koplewicz (1986) tentatively concluded that tricyclic antidepressants may be effective for severe, early SAD. Last and Francis (1988, p. 218) also reported that based on their clinical experience combining imipramine with behavior therapy, "the advantages of the drug are extraordinarily clear." However, both of these groups caution that the research in this area is subject to severe methodological limitations and that the relatively low-frequency, but potentially serious, side effects of imipramine (e.g., myocardial toxicity, poor frustration tolerance, temper outbursts) should not be overlooked.

SCHOOL REFUSAL

Attendance at preschool or day care is approaching the norm for children under age 5. Not surprisingly, the literature on school refusal and school phobia focuses almost exclusively on children of at least grade school age. However, we believe that educational and sociological trends coupled with greater sensitivity to preschoolers' needs will result in the recognition of a similar phenomenon in preschool children, perhaps more aptly called "preschool phobia."

Considerable confusion has occurred in the childhood anxiety literature concerning the proper use of terms such as "school refusal," "school phobia," and "separation anxiety." At present, most clinicians and researchers agree that the refusal to attend school (school refusal) may be precipitated by anxiety associated with separation problems (separation anxiety disorder) or from excessive fear about some aspect of school itself (specific phobia of school) (Last & Francis, 1988). In older children, school refusal (or truancy) may also occur as a part of a larger pattern of conduct problems, unrelated to fear or anxiety (Berg, 1993). Unfortunately, much of the research on school-related fear and anxiety has failed to distinguish between children with true school phobia and those with school refusal secondary to separation anxiety, making it difficult to interpret the results of prevalence and intervention studies.

Young children who experience true phobias of school may be fearful of an unfamiliar teacher who seems threatening (i.e., is very tall, has a loud voice), of being physically harmed by other children (e.g., being bitten or hit), of particular aspects of the classroom (e.g., a frightening picture on the wall, a classroom mascot such as a hamster or snake), or of being reprimanded by the teacher. These fears are specific to some aspect of the school environment, and fearfulness is not displayed in other settings requiring that the child part from the caregiver (Kleinknecht, 1991). In contrast, the child who refuses to attend preschool because of problems associated with separation anxiety will have difficulty parting with the caregiver in a variety of situations (e.g., staying with the babysitter, visiting at relatives' houses, attending a neighbor child's birthday party). Preschoolers who are school phobic and those who have school refusal secondary to separation anxiety frequently experience somatic discomfort such as stomachaches, headaches, and nausea on school mornings as they anticipate confronting the source of their fear. Children with true school phobia rarely display a pattern of conduct problems in situations that are not fear-provoking (Last, Strauss, & Francis, 1987). However, some preschoolers without either a significant separation anxiety or a specific school-related phobia protest about being left at school as part of a larger pattern of oppositional behavior. These children are likely to throw a tantrum and behave aggressively toward the parent at the time of parting, and often settle down and function better in the parent's absence.

Among school-age children and adolescents, estimates of the prevalence of school phobia have ranged from .4 to 1.5% (e.g., Granell de Aldaz, Vivas, Gelfand, & Feldman, 1984; Ollendick & Mayer, 1984) and have been found to be more prevalent in boys than in girls (Last et al., 1987). There is some evidence to suggest that younger children who refuse to attend school are more likely to exhibit separation anxiety symptoms, while older children and adolescent school refusers are more likely to be truly school phobic (Smith, 1970).

Evaluation of preschoolers with school refusal should focus on discrimination between the three potential causes for refusal. If separation anxiety is identified as the source of school refusal, interventions should be planned as discussed in the SAD section of this chapter. For children whose school refusal constitutes true school phobia, a behavior therapy intervention incorporating desensitization and exposure is recommended. However, in some cases a very real threat (e.g., abusive caregiving, large animals) may be present in the day-care setting, and this possibility should not be discounted without investigation. In some situations, the appropriate course of action is to alter particular fear-provoking aspects of the preschool or day-care environment, or to change to a new preschool. Finally, children who engage in coercive exchanges with their parents over school attendance as part of a pattern of externalizing behavior problems may best be helped through one of the parent-training interventions for conduct problems described in Chapter 8.

10

Autistic and Pervasive Developmental Disorders

Recently passed federal legislation has brought unprecedented attention to the educational needs of preschoolers with developmental disabilities. In 1986, the Education of the Handicapped Act (Public Law 99-457) greatly increased assistance to states for providing education services to 3- to 5-year-old children with developmental handicaps. In 1991, this act was reauthorized by Congress and renamed the Individuals with Disabilities Education Act (IDEA), or Public Law 102-119. Part B of IDEA required that participating states provide a free, appropriate public education in the least restrictive environment to all children and young adults (between the ages of 3 and 21) with disabilities by the 1991–92 school year. Schools are to provide specially designed instruction to meet the unique needs of children with disabilities, including classroom instruction, physical education, home instruction, instruction in hospitals and institutions, and related services such as transportation, speech pathology and audiology, psychological services, physical and occupational therapy, recreation, medical and counseling evaluation services, and early identification and assessment of disabilities (Thiele, 1993). Preschoolers are to be provided these services at no cost and as part of an individualized education plan (IEP) developed with parent collaboration and consent. Although these services were to be in place by the 1991–92 school year, many communities do not yet have sufficient educational and early childhood mental health resources to meet the needs of all eligible preschoolers. Mental health professionals with expertise in assessing and intervening with young developmentally disabled children will be increasingly in demand to provide services to these children as well as consultation to public school early intervention programs.

In DSM-III-R, children with pervasive developmental disorders either received a diagnosis of autistic disorder or were grouped together in a residual category of "pervasive developmental disorder not otherwise specified." In a movement toward greater diagnostic specificity, the Task Force on DSM-IV (APA, 1993) has expanded the range of pervasive developmental disorder categories to include autistic disorder, Rett's disorder, childhood disintegrative disorder, Asperger's disorder, and a residual category of pervasive developmental disorder not otherwise specified (to include atypical autism). In this chapter, we will review current knowledge concerning the nature, etiology, assessment, and treatment of pervasive developmental disorders during the preschool years.

AUTISTIC DISORDER

The key features of autistic disorder, first described in 1943 by Leo Kanner, included an inability to relate normally to people, language abnormalities, good cognitive potential based on excellent rote memory, repetitive and stereotyped play, and a desire for sameness in the environment (Kanner, 1943). The observation concerning good cognitive potential was later refuted, and it is currently recognized that between 70% and 80% of autistic children are also mentally retarded (Bryson, Clark, & Smith, 1988). In the 1960s, the myth of a psychogenic cause for autism was largely dispelled, and basic research efforts were redirected toward identifying biologically based causes for the syndrome.

Despite agreement on a general set of deficits that characterize autistic disorder, heterogeneity among autistic children and variability across domains of development within individuals is the rule. Some autism researchers assert that the core deficit is an impairment in the ability to relate to others (Volkmar, 1987). Although autistic children do form some degree of attachment to their caregivers, the quality and intensity of their relationships differ from those of normal children. They may show less distress than is normal when separated from a caregiver, are less likely to respond to reunion by sharing or showing their parent something, and may fail to seek comfort from a parent when hurt or frightened (Schreibman, Koegel, & Koegel, 1990). In infancy, some autistic children may not cuddle with caregivers, may avoid prolonged eye contact, may not raise arms in anticipation of being picked up, may be unusually content to be alone, or may be difficult to console. Although they may look at people just as frequently as normally developing children, the duration of their gazes may be shorter (Dawson, Hill, Spencer, Galpert, & Watson, 1990). Autistic preschoolers are less likely to follow another person's gaze or use facial expressions to communicate emotions during periods of eye contact (Baron-Cohen, 1989). As toddlers and preschoolers, many avoid interacting with other children, preferring solitary play. Autistic children engage in less functional, imaginative, and symbolic play than do nonautistic developmentally handicapped peers (e.g., Stone, Lemanek, Fishel, Fernandez, & Altemeier, 1990). Several studies have noted that children with autism exhibit deficits in joint attention such that they are less capable of coordinating their attention between an object and another involved person, a skill that normally develops by age 2 and provides a forum for language and emotional development (Lewy & Dawson, 1992). Deficits in verbal and motor imitation have been consistently noted in children with autistic disorder, and motor imitation may be the best discriminator between preschool autistic children and nonautistic mentally retarded peers (Stone et al., 1990).

Other researchers have stressed deficits in language and communication as the core feature of autism. Approximately half of children with autistic disorder do not develop meaningful speech, and in those who do, a variety of communication abnormalities have been identified (Prizant & Wetherby, 1993). Approximately 85% of those who develop speech display "echolalia" (the repetition of others' words or phrases without comprehending the content of the verbalization) early in their language development (Schuler & Prizant, 1985). The echolalia typically serves no communicative function and may be either an immediate or delayed repetition. Pronominal reversals have also been described in which the child may use the word "you" instead of "I" in making a request. In some children, speech appears to be used primarily as a means of self-stimulation, rather than communication. Even those with well-developed linguistic skills usually speak concretely about current activities and do not use expressions of emotion, imagination, or abstraction (Schreibman et al., 1990). Speech may sound mechanical with inaccuracies in pitch, rhythm, inflection, pace, intonation, or articulation. Some children with autistic disorder demonstrate extreme sensitivity to changes in the environment, and rigid insistence on sameness appears to increase with age (Marcus & Stone, 1993). The child may insist on a particular arrangement of objects on the table or on completing tasks or activities in a rigid order. Changes in the environment or routine may elicit intense tantrums that do not cease until the environment or routine is restored, or the child is exhausted.

Other children with autistic disorder (and nonautistic mentally retarded children) engage in self-stimulatory behavior in which they repeatedly perform an action that does not appear to serve any function other than to provide sensory or kinesthetic feedback. Self-stimulatory behaviors may include body rocking, flapping the arms or hands, gazing at lights, gazing at spinning objects, wiggling fingers in the visual periphery, repetitive vocalizations, toe walking, and listening to the same song repeatedly. Some children will engage in self-stimulatory behavior for most of their waking hours if not redirected. Such behavior may contribute to a "bizarre" appearance, alienate nonhandicapped children, and interfere with the acquisition of more functional skills. Some autistic children, particularly those of lower intellectual functioning display self-injurious behavior, which most commonly includes head banging, hand biting, hair pulling, scratching, and slapping of the face or sides (Schroeder, 1991). One of the major sources of stress identified by parents of autistic children is the visible, embarrassing, or dangerous behaviors their children engage in such as self-stimulation and self-injury (Konstantareas & Homatidis, 1989).

Although most children with autistic disorder are mentally retarded, a notable minority have IQs above 70. Higher functioning children with autistic disorder are less likely to avoid cuddling, exhibit gross deficits in social interaction, engage in self-injurious behavior, or exhibit finger and hand flicking, and they may be more likely to show pronominal reversal, sensitivity to noise, and complex ritualistic behavior (Yirmiya & Sigman, 1991). Long-term follow-up studies of low-functioning children with autism suggest that most require residential care in adolescence and adulthood (Rutter, 1970), while many higher functioning autistic children are able to reside at home or in group homes, may complete high school or some college, and may be able to maintain some type of employment (e.g., Venter, Lord, & Schopler, 1992). Researchers report that seizure disorders exist in as few as 5% to as many as 80% of autistic children, with the chance of developing seizures increasing with the onset of adolescence (Gillberg & Steffenburg, 1987).

At present, it is widely agreed that autistic disorder and childhood schizophrenia represent two distinct diagnoses with differences in age of onset, family history of schizophrenia, speech and language patterns, intellectual functioning, prevalence rates, presence of hallucinations and delusions, developmental course, and recommended interventions (Dawson & Castelloe, 1992). For example, schizophrenia is extremely rare before the age of 7 or 8 (Green et al., 1984), while autistic disorder is evident by 3 years of age. Childhood schizophrenia is more rare, occurring at approximately 0.7 the rate of autistic disorder (Dawson & Castelloe, 1992). Although children with schizophrenia may function at a lower intellectual level than unaffected peers, they are usually much higher functioning than autistic children and possess better developed linguistic skills (Kolvin, Humphrey, & McNay, 1971). Furthermore, the hallmarks of thought disorder in schizophrenia, hallucinations and delusions, are rare in autistic children, and the intensive treatment programs that show promise for enhancing the development of autistic children do not address the core thought disturbance that children with schizophrenia experience.

Inconsistencies have also occurred in the classification of higher functioning autistic-like children. Some researchers have noted distinctions between high-functioning autistic children and those diagnosed with Asperger's disorder (Ozonoff, Rogers, & Pennington, 1991). Children with Asperger's disorder display many of the same deficits in social relatedness as children with autistic disorder; however, they do not have significant impairments in language and cognitive functioning. Although children diagnosed with Asperger's disorder possess adequate linguistic skills, they often fail to adjust their communication for the social context, do not use effective nonverbal communication, and fail to establish friendships. As with children with autistic disorder, they may have a restricted repertoire of interests and may focus intensely on idiosyncratic pursuits (Tantam, 1988). An epidemiological survey conducted in Sweden (Gillberg & Gillberg, 1989) found that 2.6 to 3 per 1,000 children had Asperger's disorder, making it three to five times more common than autistic disorder. Because of the similarities to autistic disorder, some researchers have argued that Asperger's disorder is part of the autism spectrum and should not be classified as a separate disorder (Gillberg & Gillberg, 1989).

Prevalence

Recent studies have estimated the prevalence of autistic disorder at 11 to 15 of every 10,000 children (Bryson et al., 1988; Short & Marcus, 1986). It occurs more often in males than in females, with a ratio of about 3.5:1 (APA, 1987). It is now well established that the social class distribution of families with an autistic child closely resembles that of the general population (Schopler, Andrews, & Strupp, 1979). The incidence rate increases dramatically in siblings of autistic children (Ritvo et al., 1989).

Etiology

For the past 30 years, it has been widely accepted that autistic disorder is a biologically based disorder of development. Research efforts directed toward the identification of a single, specific etiology have been unsuccessful, and the consensus is that autistic disorder is a syndrome that represents the final common pathway of a number of different etiologies including biochemical, metabolic, genetic, electrophysiological, and structural abnormalities (Dawson & Castelloe, 1992).

Although abnormalities in levels of serotonin, dopamine, and brain opioids have been reported, no biochemical marker for autism has yet been identified. Autism has also been associated with metabolic disorders such as untreated phenylketonuria and genetic disorders such as Fragile X syndrome, and possibly tuberous sclerosis and neurofibromatosis (Taft, 1993). Electrophysiological abnormalities posited as playing an etiological role in autistic disorder have included infantile spasms (seizures that occur in infants up to about 19 months of age that are usually the result of brain injury at birth), increase in seizure disorders in adolescence, atypical lateralization of brain activity as indicated by EEG studies, and a reduced P3 component of the event-related potential (ERP) in response to auditory stimuli.

A variety of pre- and perinatal complications have been associated with autistic disorder. Prenatally, some children with autism have been the product of a pregnancy in which there was maternal bleeding after the first trimester, suboptimal obstetrical scores, gestational exposure to hormones, and various maternal viral infections. In a small subgroup of autistic children, perinatal complications have been noted, such as cesarean section, forceps delivery, fetal malposition, hemorrhage during delivery, and difficult and long labor. However, no single pre- or perinatal factor has been consistently implicated in autism, and most are also associated with mental retardation. It may be that a variety of early problems increase the chances of a nonspecific neurological injury, resulting in autistic disorder and mental retardation (Gillberg, Gillberg, & Steffenburg, 1990), or the "preautistic" fetus may be unusually liable to a wide range of obstetric and neonatal complications (Goodman, 1990).

Dawson and Lewy (1989) have postulated dysfunction of the cortical–limbic–reticular system, which is the basis of attention to novel, unpredictable stimuli (such as social stimulation) and arousal regulation. In support of this viewpoint, young autistic children have been reported to display abnormal physiological responses to novel stimuli, to be slower to habituate, and to attend more to a partner when that person's responses were highly contingent and predictable (Klinger & Dawson, 1992). These findings have formed the basis for child-directed interventions in which imitation is used to increase social and cognitive skills such as complexity of toy play, turn taking, joint attention, and symbolic play (Klinger & Dawson, 1992).

Assessment

Comprehensive evaluation of preschoolers suspected to have autistic disorder should establish an accurate developmental diagnosis and provide a thorough picture of the child's developmental strengths and weaknesses to assist in formulating intensive intervention plans and monitor treatment progress (Lord, 1993). For an in-depth review of assessment procedures in autistic disorder, the reader is referred to Schopler and Mesibov (1988) and Marcus and Stone (1993).

Conventional intelligence tests may be useful for assessing whether language impairments are below what would be expected as a function of mental retardation alone, and for providing the best estimates of future functioning. Intellectual assessment of normally developing infants and preschoolers has been shown to be a poor predictor of future academic functioning; however, intellectual assessment of developmentally handicapped preschoolers has better predictive validity (Maristo & German, 1986). Intellectual assessment is also an integral component in decision making concerning classroom placement for higher functioning autistic children. For most autistic preschoolers, nonverbal measures of intelligence are recommended (e.g., Leiter International Performance Scale, Bayley Scales of Infant Development-II). Autistic preschoolers are not usually motivated to perform on standardized test procedures, and it is common practice to reinforce cooperation with bites of food or brief access to a favorite toy. Frequent breaks are usually needed, and testing is often extended over multiple sessions for inattentive preschoolers with disruptive behaviors.

A thorough evaluation of adaptive behavior is important for establishing developmental objectives. There is wide inter- and intraindividual variability in the adaptive behavior of young autistic children. Some autistic children are self-reliant in many respects, learning early to open and close jars and to feed themselves rather than seek assistance from a caregiver. Other children appear to be unmotivated to learn self-help skills and demonstrate significant delays in dressing, eating, and toileting skills. An instrument that we have found helpful is the Vineland Adaptive Behavior Scales (Sparrow, Balla, & Cicchetti, 1984), which provides parent-report information on socialization, communication, self-help skills, and motor abilities. Although useful for treatment planning, Lord (1993) cautions that the Vineland seems to yield very low age equivalents and rather high standardized scores for autistic preschoolers.

A more detailed evaluation of communication is helpful in establishing specific language and communication treatment goals. Prizant and Wetherby (1993) recommend that the following major questions be addressed in the evaluation: (1) What gestures, sounds, and/or words does a child use that serve a communicative purpose, and are these used intentionally? (2) Does a child use words, and if so, do the words have referential meaning? (3) How many different words and word combinations does the child use referentially? and (4) For a child who is using word combinations, does the child use the individual words alone and in combination with other words, or is an utterance equivalent to a single word? This information may be collected via a combination of parent-report information, observation of parent–child interactions, informal assessment procedures conducted by the examiner, and more formal language testing.

Measures that have been developed specifically for use with children suspected to have autistic disorder include the Psychoeducational Profile-Revised (PEP-R; Schopler, Reichler, Bashford, Lansing, & Marcus, 1990) and the revised version of the Childhood Autism Rating Scale (CARS; Schopler, Reichler, & Renner, 1986). The PEP-R provides diagnostic, developmental, and educational information for children functioning between 9 months and 6 years of age, and evaluates beginning imitation, language, cognitive skills, relating and affect, use of materials, and sensory deficits (Marcus & Stone, 1993). The CARS assesses some of the core and associated features of autistic disorder using direct observation or interview information obtained from a caregiver. We have found both of these instruments to be useful components of a comprehensive assessment battery targeting both diagnosis and intervention planning.

Behavioral observations play an important role in assessing the social and communication deficits characteristic of children with autistic disorder. Although some clinicians expect to see no indicators of attachment between autistic children and their caregivers, 4- and 5-year-old children with autistic disorder do respond to separation from their mothers and seek physical proximity during clinic-based parent–child interaction observations. To minimize the chance that social deficits will be masked by the structure of the observation, Lord (1993) recommends that parent–child interaction observations be conducted in nonstructured situations rather than parent-dominated play or formal contexts such as the strange situation paradigm. She indicates that the focus of the observations should be on deficits in the child's attempts to elicit joint attention, on emotional expressiveness during shared activities, on reciprocal social smiling, and in the number of approaches to the mother during unstructured play, all factors that have discriminated young autistic children from other groups of children. Functional play skills may be assessed by observing the child's use of toys, such as a play telephone, musical instruments, a comb and brush, building blocks, and toy cars; and symbolic play skills can be assessed through observations of the child's use of dolls, puppets, and stuffed animals (Marcus & Stone, 1993). Joint attention, sharing of affect, and imitation with a stranger and with a parent may be observed informally or with a structured observation procedure such as the Prelinguistic Autism Diagnostic Observation Schedule (DiLavore, Lord, & Rutter, 1992). Observations of children with peers or siblings can also be informative. A marked lack of interest in other children can be observed in young autistic toddlers and preschoolers who have not had many previous opportunities for peer interaction (Cohen, Paul, & Volkmar, 1987). In those who have had repeated exposure to peers, the absence of pretend play with familiar children will be most evident (Lord, 1993).

Providing assessment feedback to parents requires both sensitivity and considerable clinical skill. Few experiences are more painful than learning that one's child has a serious disability, and parents deserve to receive this information in an honest, accurate, and supportive fashion. Shea (1984, 1993) has offered helpful guidelines for conducting the interpretive session. We strongly recommend that mental health professionals who provide testing feedback to parents of developmentally disabled young children read Shea's work in full. According to Shea (1993, pp. 186–187), the interpretive session should have the following three goals: "(1) to convey information; (2) to assist parents with their emotional reactions to news of their child's handicaps or special needs; (3) to make plans related to the next steps in providing for the child's needs." Parents should be told the name of the disorder (autistic disorder, mental retardation), and its nature should be explained in language that the parents can understand. It is important to encourage parents to express their ideas about what might have caused their child's disability. Parents need to be reassured that nothing they did caused the disorder and there was nothing they could have done to prevent it. Parents should not leave the interpretive session without a clear understanding of the next steps that will be taken to initiate services for their child.

Treatment

The importance of intensive early intervention for maximizing developmental outcomes in young autistic children is beyond dispute (Olley, Robbins, & Morelli-Robbins, 1993). There is evidence that pervasive developmental disorders can be reliably diagnosed in 1- and 2-year-olds (Gillberg et al., 1990) and that the best outcomes are obtained when children begin treatment before the age of 3 (Strain & Hoyson, 1988).

Although few autistic preschoolers with severe or profound mental retardation score in the average range of intellectual functioning later in life, many do achieve notable improvements in functioning as a result of intensive treatment efforts. Lower functioning children (e.g., those without any verbal communication and scoring in the severe to profound range of mental retardation) may be expected to require supervised care throughout their lives, even when provided with early intervention services. Treatment goals for severe to profoundly retarded autistic preschoolers commonly address basic self-care skills such as toileting, dressing, and feeding; reduction of aggressive and self-abusive behaviors; and development of some rudimentary communication skills. Higher functioning children (those with some early communicative language and scoring in the mild range of retardation or higher) have the potential to achieve near-normal functioning and independent living when provided intensive, high-quality early intervention services (Bristol & Schopler, 1993). For higher functioning autistic preschoolers, intensive efforts should be directed toward the development of language skills, social interaction, and preacademic skills (Lovaas & Smith, 1988) (Table 10-1).

At present, research does not support the placement of preschool-age children with autistic disorder in residential treatment programs. Equivalent or better outcomes have been obtained through home-based and outpatient clinic interventions (Sherman, Barker, Lorimer, Swinson, & Factor, 1988). Parent training has been shown to produce superior results when compared with individual outpatient treatment (Koegel, Schreibman, Britten, Burke, & O'Neill, 1982), and psychodynamic and family systems interventions have not been shown to be useful for addressing the core deficits in autistic disorder (Lord, 1993). In comprehensive intervention packages, home-based or clinic-based interventions (usually involving parents as therapeutic agents) are combined with preschool treatment programs.

Many treatment programs for autism have been described; however, a thorough review by Simeonsson, Olley, and Rosenthal (1987) indicated that only two programs for young autistic children have demonstrated clear success based on experimentally rigorous outcome research: the Young Autism Project (Lovaas, 1987) and the preschool program called "Learning Experiences...An Alternative Program for Preschoolers and Parents" (LEAP; Strain, Jamieson, & Hoyson, 1985). We will briefly describe these model programs as well as another widely disseminated model program, the Treatment and Education of Autistic and Related Communication Handicapped Children (TEACCH; Marcus & Schopler, 1989). A thorough review of treatment approaches for preschoolers with autistic disorder is beyond the scope of this chapter, and the interested reader is referred to *Preschool Issues in Autism*, an excellent recent book edited by Schopler, Van Bourgondien, and Bristol (1993).

The Young Autism Project directed by Lovaas in the Department of Psychology at the University of California, Los Angeles, is an intensive program designed primarily for children with autistic disorder who are under the age of 4. Children acquire skills "through reinforcement of successive approximations, promoting and fading procedures, and teaching subjects to imitate adults' behaviors as well as to learn through observation of other children" (Lovaas & Smith, 1988, p. 297). To achieve

Table 10-1. Social and Communication Goals for Young Autistic Child

Social goals
Spontaneous and comfortable maintenance of proximity
Imitation and social responsiveness
Functional and beginning symbolic play
Shared activities and cooperation at a simple level
Adaptive skills
Turn taking
Making initiations and asking for help and information
Negotiating for space and activities
Alertness to social contexts and appropriate behaviors
Understanding and appropriately expressing affect

Communication goals
Regulate another's behavior to request action, request object, protest
Engage in social interaction to request social routine, greet, call, request permission, show off
Reference joint attention to label or comment on objects or actions, request information, and provide or request clarification
Develop persistence and use of repair strategies
Replace aberrant communicative behavior with socially acceptable means
Improve readability of communicative means
Develop symbolic level of communicative means from contact to distal gestures, from depictive to symbolic gestures (including signs), and from presymbolic sounds to referential words
Develop ability to segment echolalic utterances into meaningful units and produce creative word combinations
Develop ability to consider what information the listener needs to understand the message and to revise the message as needed to clarify intentions or referent for listener
Develop ability to collaborate on topics in conversation

[a]Adapted from Lord, C. (1993). Early social development in autism. Prizant, B. M., & Wetherby, A. M. (1993). In E. Schopler, M. E. Van Bourgondien, & M. M. Bristol (Eds.), *Preschool issues in autism.* New York: Plenum.

maximum effectiveness, therapy is conducted at least 40 hours per week over a period of several months or years, and all caregivers in the child's natural environment are trained in the teaching principles. The training methods have been well documented in a treatment manual (Lovaas, 1981) and in a set of instructional videotapes. Step-by-step modules include learning readiness skills such as sitting and attending, imitation of actions and verbalizations, matching to sample, eating, toilet training, dressing, combing hair, brushing teeth, receptive and expressive labeling, stopping echolalia, use of prepositions and pronouns, size, color, shape, managing the child in community settings, and preparing the child for school (Lovaas, 1981).

In a somewhat controversial evaluation of the efficacy of the Young Autism Project, Lovaas (1987) reported that 9 of 19 (47%) preschool children achieved normal intellectual and educational functioning by the time they were in first grade as a result of receiving at least 2 years of 40 or more hours of treatment each week. Another 40% were mildly retarded and assigned to classes for language-delayed children, and only 10% were profoundly retarded and assigned to classes for autistic/retarded children. Control groups of autistic children receiving only 10 hours per week of the same intervention and those receiving no treatment from the Young Autism Project fared significantly worse. A follow-up study evaluating these children at an average age of 14 years indicated that the children classified as normal functioning by first grade were indistinguishable from normal control subjects on a battery of intellectual, personality, and adaptive behavior measures (Lovaas & Smith, 1988). Lovaas's research has been criticized on several grounds, including the adequacy of his outcome measures and control groups and the representativeness of his sample. However, Lovaas has responded to these criticisms, and a replication study with improved procedures is reportedly underway.

Another model program, LEAP (Strain et al., 1985), is an integrated preschool program that includes considerable parent participation. Although the best practices in special education now emphasize social integration of preschoolers with developmental disorders, segregation still remains the norm for most young children with autism. The movement toward social integration is based in part on research demonstrating that exposure to normal peers is more likely to promote the development of appropriate social, communication, and functional play skills than is exclusive exposure to developmentally handicapped peers. However, interaction does not automatically occur in integrated classrooms, but must be encouraged by including activities that may be enjoyed by children of various developmental levels, through strategic seating arrangements and through direct programming involving coaching and rewards for integrated peer interactions. The LEAP integrated preschool program (Strain et al., 1985) at the University of Pittsburgh uses peer-mediated instruction, group instruction, approximately 12 hours per week of conceptual and skill training for parents, and transition programming. In a study of six autistic and six autistic-like preschoolers who received approximately 2 years of treatment, the children showed significant improvements in eight developmental domains, were observed to engage in positive social interactions as frequently as their nonhandicapped peers, and were equivalent to normal peers on measures of language, on-task behavior, and deviant behavior (Strain et al., 1985). Strain and Hoyson (1988) have also reported a more favorable outcome with less program effort when children began participating before 3 years of age.

Another well-known model program is the University of North Carolina at Chapel Hill's project TEACCH, the only statewide system for the study and education of young autistic children. After undergoing a comprehensive developmental evaluation, children and their families are provided with a variety of treatment options that may include an "extended diagnostic" with several months of parent training and homework assignments, brief parenting consultation, attendance at a TEACCH preschool classroom, or attendance in a regular preschool with consultation from TEACCH program teachers (Lord, Bristol, & Schopler, 1993). After participating in the TEACCH program, parents have demonstrated significant improvements in their teaching skills (Marcus, Lansing, Andrews, & Schopler, 1978), have reported high rates of consumer satisfaction (Schopler, Mesibov, & Baker, 1982), and noted improvements in child compliance (Marcus et al., 1978) and appropriate behavior in the home (Short, 1984). Unfortunately, research on the TEACCH program has involved children across a wide age range, and results specific to preschool-age children are not yet available.

A number of psychopharmacological treatments for autism have been explored. Unfortunately, no medication has proven effective for long-term treatment of the core social and cognitive symptoms of autism. The neuroleptics have been the most widely studied, with reports indicating that haloperidol may improve problems of behavioral excess such as agitation, hyperactivity, aggression, stereotypic behaviors, and affective lability, but does little to address social withdrawal, abnormal interpersonal relationships, and cognitive deficits (Ornitz, 1985). Despite the improvements achieved in disruptive behavior, neuroleptics have serious side effects, including the risk for tardive dyskinesia with long-term treatment, and it is difficult to make a case for their use in preschoolers whose disruptive behavior can usually be managed through behavioral means. A drug treatment that generated considerable enthusiasm and controversy during the 1980s is fenfluramine. Improvements in social responsivity and communication were reported to be dramatic in some children, particularly those with relatively high baseline IQs (du Verglas, Banks, & Guyer, 1988). Much of the initial enthusiasm for fenfluramine dissipated with the recognition that habituation occurs, with most of the beneficial effects wearing off after only a few months of use (Campbell, Deutsch, Perry, Wolsky, & Palij, 1986). Although promising initial results have been obtained showing increases in social relatedness following administration of the opiate antagonist naltrexone (Campbell et al., 1988), much more research needs to be completed before conclusions can be made concerning the efficacy of opiate antagonist treatment. Little empirical support has been found for the efficacy of vitamin and dietary interventions (Holm & Varley, 1989).

Because of the high rate of seizure activity in children with autistic disorder, anticonvulsant medications are often prescribed. Anecdotal evidence suggests that in some children, Tegretol may decrease both seizures and aggressive outbursts (Holm & Varley, 1989). Approximately 70% of autistic children experience sleep problems (Konstantareas & Homatidis, 1989). Short courses (less than 2 weeks) of sedative-hypnotics, such as diphenhydramine (Benadryl), have been reported to be effective in decreasing the transient sleep problems reported in autistic children (Holm & Varley, 1989). Because overactivity and restlessness are reported in as many as 85% of autistic preschoolers (Volkmar, Cohen, & Paul, 1986), the use of stimulant medications has been evaluated. Findings have been generally negative, with several reports of significant increases in stereotypic and disruptive behaviors, accompanied by only mild improvements in attention. Thus, stimulant use in autism is not currently recommended (Holm & Varley, 1989).

All intervention packages should include a family support component. Numerous authors have written concerning the stresses associated with raising a handicapped child (Bristol, 1987). Some have suggested that children with autistic disorder are less gratifying to parent than are other mentally retarded children (e.g., those with Down syndrome) who do not display additional deficits in social relatedness (e.g., Hoppes & Harris, 1990). One study found that almost 40% of mothers of developmentally handicapped young children are at risk for depression (Bristol, Gallagher, & Schopler, 1988). Family support may take many forms, including family therapy, individual therapy for parents or siblings, marital therapy, group therapy, and assistance with obtaining respite care and transportation. Regardless of the particular intervention package used, an integral part of treatment with any family should be encouragement and support for their involvement in advocacy efforts on behalf of their children (Sullivan, 1984). Despite recent legislation guaranteeing an appropriate and free public education for autistic children ages 3 to 5, most communities have few truly appropriate services for these children, and access is often limited by lengthy waiting lists and residence outside of service areas.

RETT'S DISORDER

Rett's disorder is a progressive neurological condition with a pattern of apparently normal development over the first 6 to 18 months of life followed by developmental stagnation and then rapid deterioration in cognitive and motoric functioning (Van Acker, 1991). Most parents report normal prenatal and perinatal histories with normal physical and mental development until sometime between 7 and 18 months of age (Van Acker, 1991). At that point, there is a slowing or cessation in the acquisition of developmental milestones. Over a period of a year or less and before the third birthday, there is rapid deterioration of mental and motor capacity characterized by loss of acquired speech, voluntary grasping, and purposeful use of hands. The children show a lack of sustained interest in interpersonal interaction and have severe to profound mental retardation. Along with this developmental deterioration comes a deceleration in head growth, jerky movements of the torso and limbs, and a broad-based gait with short steps and swaying of the shoulders. A cardinal feature of the disorder is stereotypic hand clasping, hand washing, and hand-to-mouth movements (Van Acker, 1991). As these children become adolescents, their growth rates slow, they experience spasticity and loss of lower limb mobility, they may lose the ability to walk, and they may develop scoliosis. Some adults with Rett's disorder have been identified, but little is known about the course of the disorder in adulthood.

Prevalence

Epidemiological studies conducted in Sweden (Hagberg, 1985) and in Scotland (Kerr & Stephenson, 1986) have yielded prevalence rates for Rett's disorder of 1 per 15,000 and 1 per 12,000 to 13,000 live female births, respectively. Approximately 10,000 people in the United States are believed to have Rett's disorder; however, fewer than 11% (1,200 cases) have currently been identified. To date, only females have been confirmed as having this disorder, although researchers have described case studies of a few males with similar symptoms and developmental histories (Coleman, 1990). Hagberg (1985) noted that Rett's disorder is twice as common as phenylketonuria in girls and may be responsible for one-fourth to one-third of progressive developmental disabilities among girls.

Etiology

The cause of Rett's disorder has not yet been established, but the evidence for a genetic etiology is promising (Van Acker, 1991). The disorder has been confirmed only in females and has shown complete concordance in monozygotic twins (Zoghbi, 1988). Researchers hypothesize the presence of X-linked gene mutations that might cause the early abortion of affected male fetuses, explaining the presence of the disorder in females only.

Assessment

A primary assessment goal is the establishment of a clear diagnosis. In many cases, pediatricians are unfamiliar with the disorder, and it is believed that the majority of preschoolers with Rett's disorder have not yet been diagnosed. Because mental health professionals are often called on to conduct developmental evaluations for young children with autistic-like symptoms, they may be in the position to first recognize the cardinal features of Rett's disorder.

The presentation of Rett's disorder in preschoolers resembles autistic disorder in some aspects, and a few researchers (e.g., Gillberg, 1989) have argued that it might best be thought of as a subtype of autism. However, Rett's disorder is distinct from autistic disorder in developmental course, motoric involvement, and prognosis. Because of the rarity of autistic disorder in girls, Van Acker (1991) recommends that Rett's disorder be evaluated in all girls under the age of 2 presenting with severe autistic symptomatology. To aid in differential diagnosis, Table 10-2 presents a comparison of the features of Rett's disorder and autistic disorder.

The evaluation of a toddler or preschooler suspected to have Rett's disorder should include a thorough developmental interview, direct observations of motor functioning, and a detailed near-baseline evaluation of cognitive, social, and motor development. These children experience a variety of associated medical problems, and should be referred to a pediatric neurologist for medical evaluation. Because of the progressive nature of the disorder, the developmental evaluation may be repeated periodically to document maintenance or deterioration of functioning.

Treatment

Currently there is no cure for Rett's disorder, and treatment of preschoolers with this condition usually focuses on improvement or maintenance of mobility, preventing limb and spinal deformities, maintaining nutrition and growth, managing seizure activity, eliminating self-injurious behaviors, helping the child to maintain an awareness of others and the environment, and promoting recognition of contingencies between the child's actions and environmental responses (Van Acker, 1991). The inter-

Table 10-2. Comparison of Rett's Disorder and Autistic Disorder[a]

Rett's disorder

1. Normal development to 6 to 18 months
2. Progressive loss of speech (always absent) and hand function
3. Profound mental retardation in all functional areas
4. Acquired microcephaly, growth retardation, decreased weight gain
5. Stereotypic hand movements always present
6. Progressive gait difficulties, with gait and truncal apraxia and ataxia
7. Eye contact present, and sometimes very intense
8. Little interest in manipulating objects
9. Seizures in at least 70% in early childhood (various seizure types)
10. Bruxism, hyperventilation with air-swallowing and breath-holding common
11. Choreoathetoid movements and dystonia may be present

Autistic disorder

1. Onset from early infancy with no loss of previously acquired skills
2. More scatter of intellectual function. Visual-spatial and manipulative skills often better than apparent verbal skills
3. Physical development normal in the majority
4. Stereotypic behavior is more varied in manifestation and is always more complex; midline manifestations are rare
5. Gait and other gross-motor functions normal in first decade of life
6. Language sometimes absent; if present, peculiar speech patterns always present; markedly impaired nonverbal communication
7. Eye contact with others typically avoided or inappropriate
8. Stereotypic ritualistic behavior usually involves skillful but odd manipulation of objects or sensory self-stimulation
9. Seizures (usually temporal-limbic complex partial) in 25% in late adolescence and adulthood
10. Bruxism, hyperventilation, and breath-holding not typical
11. Dystonia and chorea not present

[a]From Trevathan & Naidu (1988). The clinical recognition and differential diagnosis of Rett syndrome. *Journal of Child Neurology, 3* (Suppl.), 6–16. Reprinted with permission.

vention program must be multidisciplinary and should be implemented by a team consisting of physical and occupational therapists, a pediatric neurologist, a nutritionist, an educational specialist skillful in work with severely handicapped young children, and a mental health professional to provide family support.

11

Child Abuse

According to the National Committee for the Prevention of Child Abuse
(NCPCA), 2.9 million children were reported to child protective services
agencies as alleged victims of abuse or neglect in 1992 (NCPCA, 1993),
almost twice the American Humane Association's estimate of 1.5 million
in 1983 (Russell & Trainor, 1984). Although staggering, these figures may
underestimate the true incidence of abuse. Both medical and mental health
practitioners have been found to comply inconsistently with abuse
reporting laws (Kalichman, 1993). Abuse of very young children may be
especially underreported because of their limited verbal ability and social
isolation.

The child welfare system has not been adequately prepared for handling the high volume of complaints and providing families with needed
social services. Only about 60% of families with substantiated complaints
during 1992 received some type of children's protective service, often
consisting only of removal of the child from the home during the investigation (NCPCA, 1993). Unfortunately, the demand for mental health services for child abuse survivors and their families has often outstripped our
collective professional knowledge and training. Descriptions of innovative
individual and group treatment programs have been widely distributed
and implemented prior to careful evaluation of their effectiveness (Friedrich, 1990). Many have called for a redoubling of effort toward primary
prevention (Willis, Holden, & Rosenberg, 1992). As has been the case with
intervention, programs for the prevention of child abuse have been widely
disseminated without documentation of their effectiveness. Indeed, some
have argued that these programs may be completely ineffective or even
harmful to young children (Melton, 1992).

In this chapter, we will review research documenting the prevalence
and correlates of both physical and sexual abuse of preschoolers. Etiologi-

cal theories and known risk and protective factors will be presented. Promising prevention and treatment programs for preschoolers will be described in the context of research evaluating their efficacy. It should be noted that this chapter does not separately address the issue of neglect. For an excellent recent review of issues in child neglect, the reader is referred to Paget, Philp, and Abramczyk (1993).

PHYSICAL ABUSE OF PRESCHOOLERS

Nature and Scope of the Problem

The National Center on Child Abuse and Neglect (NCCAN, 1988) defines physical abuse as acts of commission that involve either demonstrable harm or endangerment to the child. Although estimates vary depending on the definition of abuse and sampling methods used, a recent estimate is that at least 2.5% of all children in the United States are abused and neglected each year, and between 1,000 and 5,000 die each year as a result of abuse (NCCAN, 1988). Preschoolers are disproportionately represented among cases of severe and fatal physical abuse (Culbertson & Schellenbach, 1992). Walker, Bonner, and Kaufman (1988) reported data from the American Association for Protecting Children (AAPC) and the American Humane Association demonstrating that children under age 5 represent 64% of those receiving major injuries from physical abuse, and the mean age of children who have died as a result of abuse is 2.6 years. A curvilinear pattern in age of victimization has been reported, with physical abuse and neglect peaking between ages 3 and 8 (Egley, 1991). Belsky (1993) suggests that very young children may be more likely to be abused because physical force is more often used against them in discipline situations, they spend more time with their caregivers, they are more susceptible to injury because of their physical vulnerability, and their less well-developed emotional control may make them more likely to evoke hostile care from their parents. There is recent evidence that boys are more likely than girls to be victims of severe physical abuse (Bonner, Kaufman, Harbeck, & Brassard, 1992). Estimates are that 97% of children who are physically maltreated are abused by a parent, usually their natural parent (AAPC, 1985).

Physical abuse includes injuries such as bruises or broken bones resulting from spanking, slapping, shoving, or hitting with a fist or object, and neurological injury resulting from shaken baby syndrome. Definitions of physical abuse are widening to include other forms such as pre- and postnatal exposure to toxic substances including alcohol and cocaine. According to a 1989 national survey, as many as 375,000 drug-exposed children are born in the United States each year (Daro & Mitchell, 1990). A rarer form of abuse that differentially affects preschoolers is Munchausen syndrome by proxy (MSBP; Meadow, 1977). In MSBP, a caregiver, usually the mother, presents her child for medical care based on simulated symptoms (via altered laboratory specimens or falsified medical history) or real but induced symptoms (e.g., via poisoning). As a result, the child may experience unnecessary invasive medical procedures, hospitalization, and sometimes death. Reliable incidence rates are unavailable, but MSBP is frequently undetected by community medical practitioners and is grossly underreported (Kaufman, Coury, Pickrell, & McCleery, 1989).

Etiology, Risk, and Protective Factors

Physical abuse is the result of a complex interaction between environmental stress, parent characteristics, and child characteristics. Unfortunately, relatively little empirical information is available concerning protective factors and how they interact with risk factors. Holden, Willis, and Corcoran (1992) reviewed research identifying the following environmental and familial risk factors for abuse: low socioeconomic status, work-related stress or unemployment, single-parent status of the mother, marital discord, disturbances in parent–child attachment, large family size, and inadequate spacing between children. Although social isolation has been implicated as a contributing factor in physical abuse in several studies, others have argued that social isolation is more strongly associated with child neglect. Environmental and familial factors that are likely to mitigate the potential for physical abuse include middle-income status, low-stress work environment, small family or at least 2-year spacing in the ages of children, and two caregivers in the home with a stable marriage. Belsky (1993) reviewed research suggesting that at-risk parents who are fortunate enough to experience "emotionally corrective" close relationships with a nonabusive parent, close friend, therapist, or spouse may be protected from perpetrating abuse.

As mentioned earlier, the overwhelming majority of perpetrators of physical abuse against preschoolers are parents. A common misconception is that child abusers are seriously disturbed individuals with major psychopathology. In fact, the perpetrator is a seriously disturbed parent in only about 10% of cases (Kempe & Helfer, 1972). Substance abuse is implicated as a major factor in increasing numbers of both abuse and neglect cases (NCPCA, 1993). Other parent factors cited in the literature as contributing to the risk of physical abuse include negative maternal attitudes toward pregnancy, anger-control problems, negative affectivity including depression and anxiety, low educational achievement, low intellectual level, unrealistic developmental expectations, deficiency in child management skills, and parent history of childhood physical abuse. According to Kaufman and Zigler (1987), parental history of maltreatment during childhood may enhance risk, but its importance as a risk factor has been inflated because of the retrospective nature of most investigations. Belsky (1993) has been critical of this interpretation and suggests that better designed prospective studies clearly document a linkage between a history of physical abuse and perpetration of abuse. Although little empirical work has examined protective factors, those that may be inferred to operate at the level of the parent include positive attitudes toward parenting, average or higher intellectual functioning, high educational achievement, good understanding of early child development, repertoire of positive parenting skills, strong personal coping skills, and access to family-planning resources.

Caution against victim-blaming is warranted, but several child characteristics have been associated with an increased risk for abuse and will be noted for their etiological significance and to highlight populations that may be especially appropriate for prevention services. Preschoolers with developmental problems and histories of prematurity are at higher risk for physical abuse. For example, children with histories of low birth weight make up 20% to 30% of the physically abused population but comprise only 10% of the newborn population (Solomons, 1979). Some have conceptualized normal but difficult stages of child development as risk factors for abuse. According to Schmitt (1987), children are particularly vulnerable to abuse during developmental transitions that already stressed parents may not be prepared to handle. During the preschool years, such developmental challenges might include oppositionality, poor appetite, waking in the night, and resistance to toilet training. Child factors that may serve a protective function include flexibility, ability to play independently, average or higher intellectual functioning, high level of compliance with parental commands, smooth acquisition of developmental milestones, and access to a nurturing individual who provides love and affection (Mrazek & Mrazek, 1987).

Theoretical models for how these risk and protective factors interact are just beginning to emerge as researchers adopt a multivariate approach to examining the etiology of child physical abuse (see Culbertson and Schellenbach, 1992, for a promising recent model). In summarizing our current understanding of the etiology of abuse, Belsky (1993) asserts that there is no single cause of child maltreatment, there are no necessary or sufficient causes, and there are many pathways to child abuse and neglect. On a more positive note, Belsky observes that these findings are promising from the standpoint of prevention and remediation. With no single solution to the problem of maltreatment, "a variety of targets exist, ranging from the specific caregiving behavior of a parent to the social conditions that make it difficult for parents to be emotionally sensitive and psychologically available to their offspring" (Belsky, 1993, p. 413).

Correlates and Effects of Physical Abuse in Preschoolers

Because most physically abused children grow up in families with multiple stressors and dysfunctions, it is difficult to determine which of the psychosocial deficits noted in abused preschoolers are directly attributable to the abuse and which are more accurately described as correlates. Physically abused preschoolers may be oppositional, aggressive, hyperactive, and distractible; score lower on measures of intelligence; show problems adjusting to the classroom environment and interacting with peers; and score lower on measures of self-esteem. The social difficulties of physically abused children may be due in part to inaccurate perceptions of other children's emotions. For example, During and McMahon (1991) found that physically abused preschoolers were less accurate than nonabused children in the identification of emotional expression and did not have an age-appropriate understanding of emotional concepts.

Very little is known about the mechanisms through which physical abuse has its long-term consequences. Although a significant relationship has been documented between physical abuse in childhood and later juvenile delinquency, Lewis, Mallouh, and Webb (1989) cautioned that fewer than 20% of abused children become delinquent. In a recent review of the long-term outcome of childhood physical abuse, Malinosky-Rummell and Hansen (1993) concluded that physical abuse has been associated with battering in college students' dating relationships, spouse battering, self-injurious and suicidal behaviors, and emotional problems, such as somatization, anxiety, depression, dissociation, and psychosis. Approximately 30% of physically abused or neglected individuals abuse their own children (Kaufman & Zigler, 1987). According to Malinosky-Rummell and Hansen (1993), divorce, occupational status, alcoholism rates, and commission of exclusively nonviolent crimes do not differ between adult males with and without histories of abuse during childhood. However, childhood history of more than one type of abuse may predict greater risk of substance abuse problems in adulthood. Age at onset of abuse has not been sufficiently examined to determine whether it moderates long-term effects.

Clearly, not all physically abused children demonstrate major adjustment problems, and there has been an increasing recognition of the need to examine factors that may predict resiliency (Mrazek & Mrazek, 1987). Although little empirical work on resiliency has been reported to date, there is emerging support for the significant buffering role that the presence of another supportive, nurturing adult may play (Zimrin, 1986). Based on clinical observations, Mrazek and Mrazek (1987) describe a number of "adaptive personality characteristics" that may serve to buffer the effects of abuse including dissociation, hypervigilance in order to respond rapidly to danger, and precocious maturity to enhance self-esteem and internal locus of control. This information is preliminary and should be interpreted with caution. As Starr, MacLean, and Keating (1991) note, some of these buffering factors are viewed negatively by many clinicians, and these characteristics may or may not be appropriate targets for clinical intervention. Participation in therapy and relatively fewer stressful life events have also been suggested as predictors of resiliency (Malinosky-Rummell & Hansen, 1993).

Assessment of Physically Abused Preschoolers and Their Families

Assessment of whether abuse occurred and whether the child requires immediate removal from the caregiver's household (or removal of the alleged perpetrator from the family home) is most often conducted by child protection agencies, and factors specific to assessing the need for immediate protective intervention will not be addressed here. However, most referrals to mental health professionals occur after protective services intervention and involve requests for intervention recommendations and suggestions for secondary prevention of subsequent incidents of physical abuse. Because abusive families are a heterogeneous group with unique combinations of risk and protective factors, assessment should be both broad-based and tailored to the individual circumstances of each family (Wolfe, 1988). Although an in-depth discussion of child abuse assessment is beyond the scope of this chapter, we will highlight procedures we find particularly useful with preschoolers and their families. See Walker, Bonner, and Kaufman (1988) for a more complete review of assessment issues. In assessing the parent(s), information concerning environmental risk factors (such as financial and job-related stressors), proximal antecedents of the abusive incident(s), childhood experiences of abuse, and attitudes toward physical punishment may be obtained through a sensitive clinical interview. The interview information may be supplemented with standardized measures of parental personality functioning (e.g., MMPI-2), areas of perceived support (Perceived Social Support Questionnaire; Procidano & Heller, 1983), stress (e.g., Parenting Stress Index [PSI]; Abidin, 1990), distress and attitudes toward child rearing (Child Abuse Potential Inventory; Milner, 1986), and quality of the preschooler's home environment

(Home Observation for Measurement of the Environment [HOME]; Bradley & Caldwell, 1979).

Because many physically abused young children are developmentally delayed, a thorough evaluation of the child's current developmental status should be conducted including measures of both adaptive functioning and intelligence. To assess for aggression, overactivity, distractibility, and internalizing problems, the test battery should include standardized parent-report (e.g., Child Behavior Checklist-Parent Form [CBCL]; Eyberg Child Behavior Inventory) and teacher-report measures of child behavior (e.g., Sutter-Eyberg Student Behavior Inventory). Research has demonstrated that abusive parents may overreport conduct problems in their children (Reid, Kavanagh, & Baldwin, 1987), so comparison data should be collected from a nonabusive caregiver. Evaluations of peer interactional skills may include both parent report and preschool teacher report of social skills (e.g., Social Skills Rating System; Gresham & Elliott, 1990) and direct observation via school visits. Developmentally sensitive play interviews with preschoolers may also be used to provide children with an opportunity to disclose other abusive episodes.

Measures of marital functioning (e.g., Dyadic Adjustment Scale; Spanier, 1976) and the parent–child relationship should also be used. We recommend direct observation of parent–child interactions because it may yield important information concerning the quality of attachment and parenting style. Not surprisingly, studies comparing abusive and nonabusive parents find that abusive parents overrely on strategies such as threats and criticism, are more controlling, and display less evidence of positive parenting such as praise and descriptive statements relevant to the child's activity (Kavanagh, Youngblade, Reid, & Fagot, 1988). Although a number of structured observational coding systems are available for use with young children, we have found the Dyadic Parent–Child Interaction Coding System (Eyberg & Robinson, 1983) to be particularly useful for soliciting a wide range of both parent and child behaviors along meaningful dimensions using a relatively brief clinic-based observation. Both formal and informal parent–child interaction observations may be used to evaluate the child's attachment to caregivers. Physical abuse and neglect during infancy has been associated with insecure attachment relationships that persist during the preschool years. In parent–child interaction observations, anxious–avoidant children have been noted to interact little with their parents while in their presence, show little preference for their parents over a stranger, and actively avoid the parents when reunited after a separation (Cicchetti, 1987). In contrast, anxious–resistant children do not freely explore their environment, cling to their parents, yet resist comforting. Both patterns of insecure attachment have been associated with declines in developmental abilities such as those observed in physically abused children (Egeland & Farber, 1984).

Prevention of Physical Abuse in Preschoolers

Given the steady rise in reports of child abuse and overburdening of the child welfare system, attention to prevention methods seems timely. Based on our current understanding of risk factors, prevention efforts might best be directed toward low-income, multiproblem families. The disproportionate number of very young children who are seriously abused indicates that these programs should be initiated prenatally and be ongoing throughout the preschool years to help parents with limited resources cope with the stress associated with early child development.

Approaches to prevention of physical abuse have included public service announcements, community crisis hot lines, and family support services for high-risk groups such as low-income teenage parents. However, general parenting education may fall short of providing the level of specific information necessary for some parents to implement effective and developmentally appropriate parenting practices. Altepeter and Walker (1992) proposed that parent-training programs with demonstrated efficacy for managing a variety of childhood behavior problems (e.g., Winning!, Dangel & Polster, 1984; Parent–Child Interaction Therapy, Eyberg & Boggs, 1989 and Hembree-Kigin & McNeil, in press) be implemented in a preventive capacity with groups of high-risk parents. More specifically, these authors suggest that primary prevention may be addressed through time-limited group parent training programs available to all parents in the community. In a secondary prevention effort, parents who fall into any of several risk groups may be recruited for more intensive group or individual family parent training using the same empirically based models. At the tertiary prevention level, parents with a known history of abusing their children would be offered an individualized, intensive, multimodal parent-training service such as the one Wolfe, Sandler, and Kaufman (1981) describe. Compared to a waiting list control group, families with young children completing the program by Wolfe et al. (1981) have been shown to improve on child management skills, child behavior problems, and caseworker ratings of risk for reabuse.

A more comprehensive program, Project 12 Ways (Lutzker & Rice, 1984), has gathered preliminary evidence that it has reduced the incidence of abuse in the counties in which it has been implemented. Project 12 Ways works with low-income families identified by child protective services as being at high risk for child abuse or neglect, and provides them with in-home services from a menu of literally 12 different modalities (e.g., parent training, stress reduction, job placement services, marital counseling).

Treatment of Physically Abused Preschoolers

The intervention plan may involve multiple components that are prioritized in order to avoid overwhelming an already stressed family. Often, deficits in parenting skills or problems with oppositional child behavior will emerge as contributors to abusive parent–child interactions. In such cases, it is recommended that parents participate in an empirically validated parent-training program such as those based on the Hanf (1969) model (see Chapter 8 for a more detailed description of parent training for conduct problems). These programs have been shown to decrease parenting stress, as well as improve disruptive and noncompliant child behavior in clinic-referred, low-income families (Eisenstadt, Eyberg, McNeil, Newcomb, & Funderburk, 1993). They may be particularly suitable to crisis-oriented, lower income families because they are action oriented and time limited and rely heavily on direct coaching of parenting skills. However, substance abuse, parental psychopathology, and marital discord are problems that have been associated with less favorable outcome in parent training and should be addressed either before or concurrent with parenting skills deficits.

If during the initial evaluation it becomes evident that the parent engages in maladaptive attributions concerning the child's motivation for misbehavior or expresses inappropriate developmental expectations, the family should be involved in a cognitive-behavioral parent-training intervention such as the one Azar (1989) describes. Azar suggests combining child management skills training, cognitive restructuring and problem-solving training, and stress management and anger control training in a 10-week group treatment package. In the first session, groundwork is laid to instill the expectation that sessions will involve discussions of both behavior and thoughts, and much of the focus is on communicating that children are not just little adults and that their abilities are typically less than parents expect. Sessions two through five focus on basic child management skills (including rewards and punishments) and modification of misattributions concerning child behavior, while sessions six through eight focus on anger control techniques using guided imagery, relaxation, and group problem solving. The last two sessions are spent solidifying skills through group problem solving and identification of dysfunctional cognitions that may still occur in response to child behavior problems. A home trainer is often used to permit more individual tailoring of skills and promote generalization to the home setting. In a study of treatment effectiveness, Azar and Twentyman (1984) found no recidivism at a 1-year follow-up for their cognitive behavioral group with the home trainer, compared to 21% recidivism for the same intervention without the home trainer, and 38% recidivism for an insight-oriented group.

As mentioned earlier, many physically abused preschoolers have at least mild developmental delays warranting intervention. Depending on the degree and nature of the delay, developmental stimulation may be accomplished via parent training in developmental enhancement or placement in a developmental preschool setting. The respite provided by preschool placement may be an added benefit for stressed parents and may also help to address social skills deficits. Some of these developmentally delayed children are eligible for free special education services through the school system under the 1991 Individuals with Disabilities Education Act (IDEA), or Public Law 102-119, and many qualify for Social Security income (SSI) benefits. Assisting qualified low-income parents in obtaining these benefits is one way of providing an immediate and tangible service that may reduce financial stress (a risk factor for abuse) as well as enhance therapeutic rapport and parental compliance with treatment recommendations.

When assessment results indicate that the preschooler is experiencing significant anxiety or fears, one of the approaches to anxiety reduction reviewed in Chapter 10 should be considered. Individual play therapy may be helpful for providing a stable therapeutic relationship, teaching self-protection skills, and addressing affective issues; however this approach has received little empirical evaluation. For an excellent clinical description of issues and techniques in play therapy with abused children, the reader is referred to Gil (1991).

SEXUAL ABUSE OF PRESCHOOLERS

Nature and Scope of the Problem

The National Center on Child Abuse and Neglect (NCCAN, 1978, p. 2) defined child sexual abuse as "contacts or interactions between a child and an adult when the child is being used for the sexual stimulation of the perpetrator or another person." According to a 1986 review (Peters, Wyatt, & Finkelhor), the median rate of sexual abuse across studies is 20% of girls and 7% of boys. In contrast to physical abuse, the incidence of child sexual abuse appears to decline with younger age. However, preschoolers are not immune. Several reports indicate that one-third to one-half of sexual abuse victims are children under the age of 7 (e.g., Berliner & Stevens, 1982). Some prevalence studies have suggested a bimodal age distribution peaking at ages 4 and 14 to 15 (American Association for Protecting Children, 1985).

Etiology, Risk, and Protective Factors

Characteristics that may make young children vulnerable to sexual abuse include their social isolation, submissiveness to authority figures, limited knowledge about sexuality and sexual abuse, and strong needs for attention, affection, and approval (Wurtele & Miller-Perrin, 1992). Perpetrators are heterogeneous and have not been found to differ from nonperpetrators with respect to rates of severe psychopathology or intellectual level. Some have been reported to be shy, unassertive, deficient in heterosexual skills, immature, dependent, or lonely, and to have inadequate impulse control (Wurtele & Miller-Perrin, 1992). The overwhelming majority are male, and most are relatives or family acquaintances. In the Finkelhor and Lewis (1988) national survey, between 4% and 17% of the male population acknowledged having molested a child. Although most offenders are in their mid- to late 30s, recent attention has focused on the increasing numbers of adolescent and child offenders (Wurtele & Miller-Perrin, 1992). According to some reports, over 50% of sexually abused boys were assaulted by teenagers (e.g., Showers, Farber, Joseph, Oshins, & Johnson, 1983), and 15% to 25% of sexually abused girls were assaulted by a juvenile (Farber, Showers, Johnson, Joseph, & Oshins, 1984). A history of childhood sexual victimization may contribute to perpetrating sexual abuse as an adult, but it is clear that most sex abuse victims, particularly girls, do not grow up to abuse children (Hanson & Slater, 1988). According to Wurtele and Miller-Perrin (1992), family characteristics that may contribute to the risk for sexual abuse include marital conflict, power imbalance between parents, family isolation, financial and other major stressors, inadequate supervision of children, overly stimulating or repressive sexual milieu of the family, maternal absence due to employment outside the home, and the presence of a male caregiver in the home, especially if he is not the biological father. Family caretaking patterns may also enhance risk. Waterman (1986) suggests that fathers of preschool children may have greater opportunity for sexual contact than fathers of older children because of the children's developmental status. High-risk times for the sexual abuse of preschoolers include bathing, cleaning up, changing clothes, and bedtime. It is not unusual for perpetrators to gradually desensitize preschoolers to sexual touch by blurring the boundaries between appropriate caretaking tasks and sexual intimacy. Cultural factors that have been implicated include the attitude that children are possessions, availability of child pornography, cultural supports for sexual coercion by men, and the low rate of conviction of child molesters.

Wurtele and Miller-Perrin (1992) describe a multifactor model for the etiology of child sexual abuse (CSA):

> CSA is seen as occurring in a context consisting of a person predisposed to viewing children as sexual objects, who has access to children who are vulnerable to exploitation (related to inadequate supervision and/or the child's lack of knowledge or need for attention), and who functions in an environment that promotes (or condones) the sexual activity. These individual, familial, and environmental factors interact to lower the threshold for perpetrating CSA (p. 46).

Just as is the case in physical abuse, empirical information about protective factors lags behind what is known about risk factors. However, we would expect individuals with a sexual attraction to children to be at reduced risk for perpetrating sexual abuse if they have little access to unsupervised potential victims, are not experiencing significant stress, have good heterosexual social skills, and have access to an appropriate adult partner.

Correlates and Effects of Sexual Abuse in Preschoolers

Mounting evidence suggests that sexual abuse has the potential to profoundly affect the adjustment of young children throughout their lives (Cole & Putnam, 1992). In a recent review of studies evaluating the effects of childhood sexual abuse, Kendall-Tackett, Williams, and Finkelhor (1993) summarized the findings for children by age group. One of the most robust findings is that over one-third of sexually abused preschoolers demonstrate inappropriate sexual behaviors. Sexualized behaviors in preschoolers include frequent and overt masturbation, sexual overtures toward both children and adults, and preoccupation with sexual themes in play (Kendall-Tackett et al., 1993). In considering developmental changes in sexualized behaviors, Kendall-Tackett and colleagues (1993, p. 168) state that "sexualized behaviors may be prominent for preschool-age children, submerge during latency (or the school-age period), and re-emerge during adolescence as promiscuity, prostitution, or sexual aggression. These same symptoms might manifest themselves as sexual dysfunctions or sex offending in adulthood, although this has yet to be demonstrated empirically." Anxiety and behavior problems were evident for a substantial percentage of children studied. One-half to two-thirds of preschoolers showed symptoms of posttraumatic stress disorder such as sleep disturbance, hypervigilance, and traumatic play. There has been some suggestion that preschoolers' adaptation to chronic sexual abuse using dissociation may produce symptoms associated with borderline and multiple personality disorders in adulthood (McNally, 1991).

Notable in the results by Kendall-Tackett and colleagues (1993) was the one-third of children who showed no apparent indicators of ill effects. This may reflect genuine resiliency in a substantial portion of children, or be a function of inadequate assessment procedures, or reflect a course of symptomatology in which effects ebb and wane depending on developmental factors. For example, although preschoolers may show little evidence of guilt associated with their victimization, guilt may intensify over time as young children gain a clearer understanding of cultural norms (Lusk & Waterman, 1986) and experience the family upheaval that may result from an abuse disclosure. In fact, part of the negative impact of sexual abuse on preschoolers results from the ways in which the disclosure is responded to by family members and the array of professionals involved. Much of our information about the long-term effects of child sexual abuse comes from comparisons of adults with and without histories of childhood victimization. Starr and colleagues (1991) reviewed a number of recent studies demonstrating that adults who were sexually abused as children showed somewhat higher rates of a diverse set of disturbances than did comparison groups of adults who did not experience childhood sexual abuse. The disturbances included depression, suicidal ideation, anxiety disorders, alcohol or substance abuse, poor self-esteem, high levels of stress, and sleep disturbances. Nevertheless, these problems were not universally present in all adult survivors and are clearly present in individuals who did not experience sexual victimization in childhood. This pattern of findings suggests that child sexual abuse may best be viewed as a major stressor that amplifies the probability of developing a disturbance in an area of individual vulnerability. Research is needed addressing whether the age at time of abuse is differentially associated with particular types of adult dysfunction.

Short-term longitudinal studies of preschoolers who have been sexually abused are beginning to emerge and offer an encouraging picture. In their longitudinal work, Hewitt and Friedrich (1991) found that 65% of preschool-age children improved over a period of 1 year after the abuse, and abatement of symptoms was associated with a supportive family environment. However, it is currently unclear whether this is truly trauma resolution or developmental changes in the expression of trauma. Unfortunately, as Kendall-Tackett and colleagues (1993) noted, a significant portion of children appear to get worse over time (estimated to be 10% to 24%). Fears and somatic symptoms seem to abate the most quickly, while aggressive and sexualized behaviors are the most likely to remain or increase.

Sexual Abuse in Day-Care or Preschool Settings

Because of highly publicized day-care center abuse cases, there is a public perception of day care as a high-risk setting for sexual abuse. However, based on a review of sexual abuse incidence and settings, Finkelhor, Williams, and Burns (1988) concluded that children are at greater risk of being abused in their own homes than at day care. More recently, the National Committee for the Prevention of Child Abuse reported that day-care center abuse accounted for less than 1% of child maltreatment allegations during 1992 (NCPCA, 1993). Nevertheless, sexual abuse does occur in day-care settings, and there are certain aspects that set this type of abuse apart from what clinicians usually encounter with intrafamilial sexual abuse cases.

Day-care center sexual abuse is more likely to involve multiple perpetrators (17% of cases in Finkelhor et al., 1988). Cases with multiple perpetrators have the most serious impact on victims and are more likely to involve allegations of sexual penetration, pornography and ritualistic abuse, forced sexual acts between children, physical abuse, and women as co-perpetrators. Most of these children are subjected to several different sexual acts and are abused on more than one occasion over a period of up to 1 year (Kelley, Brant, & Waterman, 1993).

To keep young children from making disclosures, most perpetrators use threats of physical harm, as opposed to the threats of separation from family members often used in incest cases. Kelley et al. (1993) conclude that "threats used in day care center cases may go beyond what is usually needed to silence victims, and may in some instances be made for purposes of psychological terror in and of itself" (p. 74). Finkelhor and colleagues (1988) examined patterns and timing of disclosure and reported that only 20% of cases were disclosed on the same day of the abuse; almost 50% were disclosed within a month after the onset of the abuse; and 32% were not disclosed for at least 6 months. Most disclosures (63%) were precipitated by questions from suspicious parents who noticed that their preschoolers were experiencing sleep disorders, sexual acting out, or fears. Although abuse in day-care settings is clearly less prevalent than sexual abuse within the home, parents should be counseled to visit their child's day-care center often, to participate in the program as much as they are able, and to avoid concluding that location in a "good" neighborhood eliminates the risk of sexual victimization (Finkelhor et al., 1988). Many states now have registries of convicted or substantiated offenders that can be accessed by the public and used by child-care agencies to screen potential employees (NCPCA, 1993).

Suggestibility of Preschoolers' Abuse Allegations

Claims about the reliability of young children's reports of sexual abuse have ranged from the position that preschoolers are so suggestible that they cannot distinguish between fantasy and reality and nothing they say should be relied on as forensic evidence, to the point of view that very young children do not have the sexual knowledge or cognitive sophistication to fabricate sex abuse allegations, so all the information they provide must be accurate. In a recent review of research on the suggestibility of child witnesses, Ceci and Bruck (1993) concluded that (1) although everyone is vulnerable to suggestion, preschool-age children are significantly more vulnerable than both school-age children and adults; (2) even preschoolers sometimes lie or "keep secrets" when motivated to do so, and the ability to lie seems to increase with the age of the child; and (3) although preschoolers are much more likely to make errors of omission than commission, they are capable of recalling the majority of information presented to them, particularly if it is personally relevant. Ceci and Bruck (1993) summarize the suggestibility of preschoolers:

> It seems particularly important to know the circumstances under which the initial report of concern was made, how many times the child was questioned, the hypotheses of the interviewers who questioned the child, the kinds of questions the child was asked, and the consistency of the child's report over a period of time. If the child's disclosure was made in a nonthreatening, nonsuggestible atmosphere, if the disclosure was not made after repeated interviews, if the adults who had access to the child prior to his or her testimony are not motivated to distort the child's recollections through relentless and potent suggestions and outright coaching, and if the child's original report remains highly consistent over a period of time, then the young child would be judged to be capable of providing much that is forensically relevant. The absence of any of these conditions would not in and of itself invalidate a child's testimony, but it ought to raise cautions in the mind of the court (p. 433).

Assessment

Mental health professionals may be asked to participate in the investigation of an abuse allegation by interviewing the child victim. Discussion of the considerations involved in substantiating abuse allegations and techniques for conducting an investigative interview (including use of anatomically detailed dolls) are beyond the scope of this chapter, and the interested reader is referred to the American Professional Society on the Abuse of Children (1990) *Guidelines for Psychosocial Evaluation of Suspected Sexual Abuse in Young Children.*

More often, mental health professionals are called on following an abuse investigation to evaluate the correlates or effects of abuse and offer placement and treatment recommendations. Comprehensive family assessment following substantiation of a sexual abuse allegation includes individual child assessment, assessment of siblings, assessment of family relationships (marital, parent–child), assessment of the offending (in cases of incest) and nonoffending parent, and assessment of environmental variables that may serve as risk or protective factors.

Evaluation of the preschool victim of sexual abuse should include a developmentally sensitive interview. If the abuse allegation has already been substantiated, it is not recommended that the child be subjected to further inquiry concerning the details of the abuse, and few preschoolers will share this information without direct questioning. Rather, the clinical play interview may be used as a vehicle for assessing the child's understanding of the events that have transpired since the disclosure, attitudes toward the perpetrator and the nonoffending parent(s), fearfulness of strangers, and other behavioral and emotional responses. Many preschoolers will have particular difficulty separating from the safety of their caregiver, and the interview may need to be conducted in the caregiver's presence. In conducting a developmentally sensitive interview, Steward, Bussey, Goodman, and Saywitz (1993) suggest using several short questions instead of long, complex questions, and trying always to use names in place of pronouns to avoid confusion. Questions should be initially open-ended. These authors caution that "yes/no" questions can be problematic with preschoolers because they involve auxiliary verbs that are slow to develop such as "have," "can," "do," and "may." When "yes/no" questions are used, interviewers need to be careful to ask follow-up questions (e.g., "What makes you think so?" or "Tell me more about that") to clarify the meaning of the child's response (Saywitz, Nathanson, & Snyder, 1993). By age 3, children begin to understand the "what," "where," and "who" questions, but cannot consistently answer "why," "when," or "how" questions until they are 5 or 6 years old (Steward et al., 1993). It is not unusual for young children to recant their allegations after experiencing the trauma of family upheaval following disclosure, even in well-substantiated cases (Walker et al., 1988).

The play interview should be supplemented with standardized tests of emotional and behavioral functioning that tap correlates of sexual victimization in preschool-age children. On most child-report measures of self-concept, anxiety, and depression, the responses of sexually abused preschoolers do not differ significantly from those of their nonabused peers. However, the Louisville Fear Survey (Miller, Barrett, Hampe, & Noble, 1971) has been reported to be sensitive to the fearfulness of preschoolers commonly reported following sexual abuse (Waterman, Kelly, Oliveri, & McCord, 1993). On the CBCL, the measure most commonly used with young victims of sexual abuse, parents generally rate sexually abused children as more disturbed on both the externalizing and internalizing dimensions than nonclinical children, but no more pathological than non-abused clinical comparison groups (Waterman & Lusk, 1993). However, sexual problems are typically rated as worse for sexually abused children, and ritualistic and other severe forms of abuse appear related to more severe behavioral problems on the CBCL. A norm-referenced measure of young children's sexual behavior may also be useful if it has been shown to discriminate between traumatic sexualization and the normal sexual behavior of young children. It should be noted that during the course of normal development, preschoolers who have not been sexually abused show considerable curiosity about sexual body parts; most attempt to touch their parents' genitals and breasts (Rosenfeld, Bailey, Siegel, & Bailey, 1986) and show curiosity about the private parts of playmates. Although still in the early stages of standardization, the Child Sexual Behavior Inventory (Friedrich et al., 1992) is a promising measure for discriminating between developmentally appropriate types and amount of sexual behavior and traumatic sexualization in children between the ages of 2 and 6.

Because sexual abuse affects the entire family, siblings of the victim should be included both in the evaluation and in treatment planning. In intrafamilial abuse, it is not unusual for one or more siblings to have been victimized, and younger siblings in particular continue to be at risk if the perpetrator remains in the home. Depending on the ages of the siblings, many of the instruments and procedures used with the identified victim will be appropriate. Additional themes that may be addressed during the interview include attitudes toward the abuse victim, whether the siblings were aware of the abuse, attributions concerning responsibility for the abuse, and blaming of the victim for family upheaval resulting from disclosure.

Both offending and nonoffending caregivers should be evaluated in order to screen for factors that may enhance the risk of future abusive episodes, as well as areas of strength that may be bolstered to reduce risk. A detailed discussion of considerations for evaluating adult and juvenile offenders is beyond the scope of this chapter, and the interested reader is referred to Barnard, Fuller, Robbins, and Shaw (1989) and Ross and Loss (1991).

Prevention of Sexual Abuse in Preschoolers

Most prevention programs have focused on enhancing the self-disclosure and assertiveness skills of vulnerable children. This approach has been criticized on several grounds (Melton, 1992). First, this emphasis may place undue responsibility on potential victims for preventing their own abuse, with the experience of abuse interpreted as the child's failure to prevent his or her own victimization. Second, some question the developmental appropriateness of expecting very young children to resist a powerful adult authority figure. Third, these programs have generally taught abstract concepts that are difficult for young children to grasp, such as "confusing touches," "secrets," and "stranger." And fourth, most fail to teach children that the most likely perpetrators will be family members or friends, rather than strangers. Concern has been expressed about the wholesale adoption of sexual abuse prevention programs in the absence of documentation that they reduce the incidence of sexual abuse and do not harm children (Roberts, Alexander, & Fanurik, 1990).

Preschoolers can learn many sex abuse concepts and personal safety skills, particularly if these skills are presented in a concrete, action-oriented fashion making use of modeling and role-plays (Wurtele & Miller-Perrin, 1992). Feelings-based programs that teach children to identify touches that feel "bad," "good," or "confusing" have been generally unsuccessful with preschoolers, and much more favorable outcomes are obtained with behaviorally based programs that emphasize protection of genitals (Wurtele, Kast, Miller-Perrin, & Kondrick, 1989). The outcome of these programs appears to improve significantly with greater time spent, more one-on-one rehearsal, frequent "boosters," and involvement of the parents to reinforce cross-setting generalization. However, there is currently no empirical evidence that preschoolers actually use these skills in real-life situations, that disclosures of abuse are facilitated, or that sexual abuse prevention or personal safety programs reduce the incidence of sexual abuse (Melton, 1992). Despite the concerns raised by some researchers, according to Wurtele and Miller-Perrin (1992) these programs have not been demonstrated to result in significant short- or long-term negative effects on participants, and the majority of parents support the inclusion of sex abuse prevention programs in preschools (Wurtele, Kvaternick, & Franklin, in press). Wurtele and Miller-Perrin (1992) contend that greater focus should be placed on the prevention role of parents, professionals who interact with children, policy makers, community leaders, and the general public. Readers who are interested in learning more about child abuse prevention efforts are directed to recent volumes by Willis and colleagues (1992) and Wurtele and Miller-Perrin (1992).

Treatment of Preschool Sexual Abuse Survivors

A variety of models are available for treating young children who have been sexually abused; unfortunately, little empirical information is available concerning their effectiveness. Treatment models that have been described as clinically useful with preschoolers include parent counseling, individual play therapy, group therapy with parallel group therapy for mothers, therapeutic preschools, and bibliotherapy. These models have been designed to address a diverse set of treatment goals including acquisition of personal safety skills, education of the nonoffending parent on proper precautions to prevent revictimization, reduction of oppositional child behavior, reduction of inappropriate sexual behavior, strengthening of the parent–child relationship, reduction of fears and anxiety, age-appropriate sex education, coping with family disruption, coping with foster care placement, and preparing young children for court proceedings.

For preschoolers who are engaging in significant disruptive behavior or inappropriate sexual behavior, parent-counseling approaches for the nonoffending parent may be particularly helpful. Most parents will have basic questions about sexual abuse and its impact on children, and this information can be provided in the context of parent counseling or through bibliotherapy (e.g., Hagans & Case, 1988). Sometimes parents of sexually abused preschoolers are reluctant to set appropriate limits on disruptive behavior because of their child's victim status or guilt over their failure to adequately protect their child. In other cases, the parents are simply not equipped with effective child management skills. Participation in a parent-training program with demonstrated effectiveness in reducing oppositional and disruptive behavior while increasing positive parenting and mother–child bonding may be indicated for these families. Parents may also need to be educated concerning early childhood sexual development and effective ways of reducing excessive masturbation or inappropriate sexual behaviors. Such counseling is likely to involve exploring parental feelings about their child's sexuality, establishing rules for when self-stimulation is acceptable (e.g., alone and in the privacy of the child's bedroom), redirection, reinforcement for engaging in behaviors incompatible with masturbation, setting limits on sexual overtures toward both adults and children, and enhancing supervision of the child to reduce opportunities for sex play with other children.

Individual play therapy may be recommended for preschoolers who are showing evidence of internalizing problems such as anxiety or fears, those who have been further traumatized by separation from caregivers and out-of-home placement, those who are at continued risk because of their family's chaotic and stressful lifestyle, or those who need support through participation in court proceedings. Topics that may be addressed in play therapy include development of affective labels, discussion of feelings toward the perpetrator and family members, expression of anger, age-appropriate sex education, visitation issues, and personal safety skills.

For an excellent discussion of play therapy techniques with abused children, the reader is referred to Gil (1991). Long (1986) initially conducts individual play therapy with young children and later makes a transition into mother–child relationship enhancement. In our experience, this sequencing facilitates termination by allowing for a gradual reduction in the child's dependency on the therapist, with an appropriate transfer of dependency to the caregiver.

Some therapists have used individual therapy as a vehicle for preparing children for testifying in court. Preschoolers appear to benefit from preparation that provides concrete information about what a courtroom looks like, who will be there, how people will be dressed, who will ask questions, where they will sit, and how one behaves in a courtroom. According to Steward et al. (1993), it should be remembered from a developmental perspective that the younger the child, the less well he or she can generalize from toy models of courtrooms to the real thing, and the more the child benefits from a preliminary site visit. Drawing on the pediatric psychology literature on preparation for medical procedures, it may be inferred that preschool children should be informed only a day or two prior to their courtroom testimony in order to best retain the preparation information and not be subjected to extended anticipatory anxiety (Steward et al., 1993). Techniques for anxiety reduction such as deep breathing may be taught in individual therapy and then used by the child in response to adult cuing during the courtroom experience.

A number of books are available to use directly with young children who have been sexually abused. Bibliotherapy is typically employed in the context of play therapy or parent counseling, and may target basic concepts associated with play therapy (e.g., Nemiroff & Annunziata, 1990), sex and sex abuse education (e.g., Kehoe, 1987), teaching of self-protection skills (Freeman, 1982), and preparation for courtroom experiences (e.g., Caruso & Pulcini, 1988).

12

Depression and Reaction to Loss

It has only been within the last 20 years that there has been a general recognition of the existence of depression in prepubertal children, much less in preschoolers. The reasons for this failure to acknowledge the presence of major affective disturbances in young children are multiple. One factor is the earlier pervasive influence of psychoanalytic theory. Freud (1917) viewed depression as the inward turning of aggressive impulses resulting from object loss, and psychoanalytic theorists did not believe that children possessed sufficiently developed superegos, or stable enough self-concepts, to engage in this process and truly experience depression. Children were acknowledged to experience transient sadness, but this was viewed as trivial and qualitatively different from adult depression. Additional problems contributing to the failure to seriously consider the existence of depression in young children were the absence of adequate assessment instruments for that age group, and the difficulty obtaining and interpreting verbal self-reports from preschoolers.

Despite this general failure prior to the early 1970s to acknowledge the possibility that young children might suffer from depression, there was considerable research and clinical activity in related areas that would contribute to the later acceptance of the concept of childhood depression. Lowery (1940) was among the first to describe the effects of institutionalization on infants. He studied 28 children below the age of 1 year who were removed from their homes and put in institutional care, where they would remain for several years. Despite the absence of abuse and adequate nutrition and physical care, all of the children below the age of 6 months who were placed in institutional care demonstrated inadequate personality development and could not express affection or relate to others. Bakwin (1942) described similar findings in infants who were hospitalized for extended periods of time. They smiled and cooed less than they did before hospitalization and frequently demonstrated significant weight loss. Almost invariably, these problems disappeared when the children were returned home.

Spitz (1945) assessed the cognitive and personality development of infants who were placed in a "foundling home" and found that they developed cognitive retardation and abnormal social responses. As mentioned in Chapter 5, Spitz termed this phenomenon "hospitalism," and that syndrome became the precursor of nonorganic failure to thrive.

Spitz and Wolf (1946) then focused attention specifically on the mother's (or other primary caretaker's) relationship with the infant. They found that one-third of children who were deprived of contact with their primary caretaker for substantial periods of time during their first year of life developed behaviors indicative of affective disturbance, including sad facial expression, crying, social withdrawal, loss of appetite, and cognitive retardation. Spitz and Wolf (1946) recognized the affective similarity of these symptoms to adult depression and termed the syndrome the children demonstrated "anaclitic depression," both to acknowledge its affective qualities and to differentiate it from "regular" depression, which psychoanalytic theory insisted was impossible for children that age. If the separation from the caretaker did not last longer than 3 months, the effects were reversible; if the caretaker and the child were reunited after a longer period of time, the infant failed to respond to her on reunion (all primary caretakers in these cases were women), and the affective and cognitive symptoms continued, at least partially. Spitz and Wolf (1946) also found, interestingly, that no cases of anaclitic depression occurred in cases in which the infant–caretaker relationship was poor prior to the separation. Spitz viewed "hospitalism" and anaclitic depression as existing on a continuum of severity, with hospitalism requiring longer and more complete emotional deprivation and having more severe effects.

A number of case studies of anaclitic depression or similar syndromes have been presented in the mental health literature since Spitz and Wolf (1946) coined the term. Engel and Reichsman (1956) described the case of a girl who endured two early hospitalizations and demonstrated physical and mental retardation, loss of appetite, and depressed affect. She improved when reunited with her family but continued to demonstrate some symptoms. Later, it was noted that she was very noninteractive when feeding her own children as an adult (Engel, Reichsman, Harway, & Hess, 1985). Meyendorf (1971) described a case in which a 19-month-old girl demonstrated depression, weight loss, and developmental retardation after being separated from her parents and siblings. She showed improvement after being reunited with her family. A subsequent 1-hour trial readmission to the hospital nursery resulted in a reemergence of the depressive symptomatology. Gaensbauer (1980) described a case in which a girl was removed from her mother at the age of 3 months because of suspected abuse. Within 3 weeks she demonstrated rumination of her food and became lethargic and apathetic. Davidson (1968) followed a child diagnosed with anaclitic depression at 7 months of age and found that she still demonstrated significant depressive affect at age 15. Harmon, Wagonfield, and Emde (1982) also followed a child diagnosed with anaclitic depression as an infant and found a pattern of repeated depressive episodes throughout infancy and young childhood. Separation from a primary caretaker seemed to be the precipitating factor in each of these episodes.

Interest in, and recognition of, the characteristics of childhood depression broadened in time to include depressive phenomena other than anaclitic depression (which nonanalysts relabeled reactive attachment disorder of infancy). Feighner et al. (1972) were among the first to offer a set of diagnostic criteria for depression, and considerable debate ensued over the existence and symptoms of childhood depression. Some researchers continued to maintain that there was no such thing as depression in children, only transient sadness. Some authorities (Lesse, 1974) maintained that depression in young children was "masked," or hidden by a multitude of other symptoms, ranging from hyperactivity and hostility to encopresis. Carlson and Cantwell (1979) assessed this concept of masked depression by studying children who met diagnostic criteria for depression and found that in virtually no cases was the depression completely masked by other symptomatology. Other researchers (Weinberg, Rutman, Sullivan, Penick, & Dietz, 1973) espoused the view that depression in children had many of the same characteristics it demonstrated in adults, but that there were also some differences between adult and childhood depression. This view is the one most researchers and practitioners hold today.

The clinical characteristics of depressed preschoolers appear to be largely similar to those of older children and adults who are suffering from depression. When Kashani et al. (1987) evaluated the percentage of depressed preschoolers who demonstrated the 13 specific DSM-III symptoms of adult depression, they found that over 40% of the children demonstrated every symptom except "psychomotor agitation or hyperactivity" (33%) and "pervasive loss of interest" (22%). All of the children reported sadness, had appetite and sleep disturbance, and demonstrated somatic complaints. These data appear to argue strongly against preschool depression being effectively "masked," or substantially different from depression in adults. Interestingly, 67% of the depressed preschoolers reported having suicidal thoughts. All of the depressed preschoolers in this sample had been abused and/or neglected, suggesting that the correlation between disruptions in the child–caretaker relationship and anaclitic depression noted earlier may also hold true for preschool depression.

The DSM-III-R (APA, 1987) spells out the diagnostic criteria for major depression, with only minor modifications for application to children. These diagnostic criteria are presented in Table 12-1.

Rapoport and Ismond (1990) suggest that these criteria are appropriate for the diagnosis of depression in children and are supported by the failure to find validation for the concept of masked depression. They question whether the specification of irritable mood as equivalent to depressed mood creates difficulty in differentiating depression from oppositional defiant disorder. Rapoport and Ismond also point out that the duration criterion for another mood disorder, dysthymic disorder, is shortened from 2 years to 1 year for children and adolescents, and that seasonality has been demonstrated in pediatric depression.

There are a number of etiological theories concerning childhood depression (in addition to the psychoanalytic literature on anaclitic depression) that focus on both psychological and biological factors. Lewinsohn (1974) viewed depression as resulting from the lack of positive reinforcement (or excess of punishment) in the environment, which in turn could

Table 12-1. Symptoms Required for Major Depression in DSM-III-R

At least five of the following symptoms must be present during the same 2-week period; at least one of the symptoms is either (1) depressed mood or (2) loss of interest or pleasure.
  1. Depressed mood (or can be irritable mood in children and adolescents) most of the day, nearly every day, as indicated by either subjective account or observation by others
  2. Loss of interest or pleasure in all or almost all activities nearly every day, as indicated either by subjective account or observation by others of apathy
  3. Significant weight loss or weight gain when not dieting or binge eating (e.g., more than 5% of body weight in a month), or decrease or increase in appetite nearly every day (in children, consider failure to make expected weight gains)
  4. Insomnia or hypersomnia nearly every day
  5. Psychomotor agitation or retardation nearly every day (observable by others, not merely subjective feelings of restlessness or being slowed down [in children under 6, hypoactivity]
  6. Fatigue or loss of energy nearly every day
  7. Feelings of worthlessness or excessive or inappropriate guilt (either may be delusional) nearly every day (not merely self-reproach or guilt about being sick)
  8. Diminished ability to think or concentrate, or indecisiveness, nearly every day (either by subjective account or as observed by others)
  9. Thoughts that he or she would be better off dead or suicidal ideation, nearly every day; or suicide attempt

Note: Several exclusion criteria must be met as well (e.g., to distinguish depressive disorder from other conditions such as bereavement). Adapted from Kazdin, A. E. (1990). Childhood depression. *Journal of Child Psychology and Psychiatry, 31* (1), 121–160.

result from social skills deficits. Research has established that such social skills deficits do exist in depressed children (Vosk, Forehand, Parker & Rickard, 1982).

Another behavioral theory that has been advanced is Seligman's model of "learned helplessness" (Seligman & Maier, 1967). This model originated in animal research in which dogs were exposed to unavoidable shock and eventually stopped trying to escape, but rather simply sat and endured the shock, without even whimpering. Seligman noted the similarity between this reaction and the behavior of depressed humans and postulated that the same process might be involved in both conditions. A later reformulation of Seligman's core thesis (Abramson, Seligman, & Teasdale, 1978) specified that learned helplessness will result when an individual believes that aversive outcomes are likely and that nothing he or she can do will change this likelihood. The conversion of specific learned helplessness into generalized depression is dependent on the globality and stability of the attribution for helplessness and the degree that the individual views himself or herself as responsible for this helplessness.

Although most research concerning the learned helplessness model has been done with adults, some has involved children, although not preschoolers. Seligman and Peterson (1986) report two studies investigating attributions related to learned helplessness in children. In one study, boys and girls from 9 to 13 years of age were given a test for depression (the CDI, which is discussed later) and a test that assessed a child's causal explanations for positive and negative events on the dimensions of globality, stability, and internality. Depressed children made more internal, stable, and global attributions for negative events and more external, unstable, and specific attributions for positive events, thus supporting a learned helplessness explanation of the depression. The relationship between attributions and level of depression was even stronger in these children than it had been found to be in adults. Another study reported by Seligman and Peterson (1986) found significant correlations between mother's and children's attributions and depressive symptomatology, suggesting that an "attributional learning process" may be operating. One shortcoming in this research is its failure to establish attributional style as a true cause of depression, rather than simply a correlate.

Another psychological theory of depression that emphasizes attributional and cognitive factors is the cognitive model of Aaron Beck (1970). Beck proposed that depressed individuals, including children, have negative views of themselves, the future, and the world that are maintained by errors in perceiving and interpreting events. Hammen, Adrian, and Hiroto (1988) found some support for this idea in a study of children with depressed mothers. These children had more depression and more negative cognitions than children of nondepressed mothers. Again, however, the causal direction of this relationship is unclear, and the negative cognitions could be the product of, rather than the cause of, the depression.

A number of researchers have focused on genetic variables as causal in childhood depression. Gershon, Hamovit, and Guroff (1983) found that 27% of the children with one parent who was depressed had a depressive disorder, while 74% of those who had two depressed parents were themselves depressed. Although these figures are strongly suggestive of genetic causation, again it must be emphasized that behavioral modeling was not excluded as a factor in this study. Relevant to this point is the study by Weissman, Paykel, and Klerman (1972), which found that depressed mothers were less involved with their children, had impaired communication with them, and demonstrated less affection for them. Orvaschel, Walsh-Allis, and Ye (1988) also examined the link between parental depression and childhood mental illness. They compared children with at least one parent who had been diagnosed with depression to children whose parents had no identified mental illness. They found that 41% of the children with a depressed parent had a mental health disorder themselves, while only 15% of the children whose parents did not have any psychiatric illness were diagnosed with such a disorder. The differences between the two groups were particularly great with regard to the diagnosis of affective disorder (21% versus 4%) and attention-deficit disorder (20% versus 6%). Three children in the study had attempted suicide; all had parents who were depressed. Although these results are compelling with regard to the greater risk for mental illness in children of depressed parents, they do little to differentiate genetic from psychosocial causal factors.

Cantwell (1982) reported a concordance rate of 76% for depression in monozygotic twins, versus 19% for dyzygotic twins, and 67% for monozygotic twins reared apart. These figures certainly suggest the importance of genetic transmission as a primary, if not sole, causal factor in depression. Mendlewicz and Ranier (1977) found that 31% of the biological parents of adopted children with bipolar disorders had affective disorders versus only 12% of the adoptive parents. Cadoret (1978) found that 38% of the biological children of women with affective disorders were depressed versus 5% of the biological children of mothers with nonaffective mental illness.

Other research has focused on nongenetic, biological causal factors in childhood depression. Puig-Antich et al. (1984) found that prepubertal children with endogenous depression showed a blunted increase in growth hormone in response to insulin-induced hypoglycemia. Prepubertal children with depression, but not adolescents, have also been noted to hypersecrete growth hormone during sleep (Puig-Antich, 1987). Although the Dexamethasone Suppression Test (DST) has demonstrated considerable promise with adult depressives (Roy, Pickar, DeJong, Karoum, & Linnoila, 1988) there is much less clarity regarding its usefulness with children. Some researchers (Puig-Antich, 1987) report no differences in cortisol secretion on the DST between depressed and nondepressed children, while others (Klee & Garfinkel, 1984) have found significant correlations between cortisol suppression and depressive symptomatology. Nocturnal melatonin secretion was also found to be significantly decreased during sleep in depressed children (Cavallo, Holt, Hejazi, Richards, & Meyer, 1987), although the data on REM activity during sleep in depressed children are contradictory (Puig-Antich, 1987).

Comorbidity is a significant issue with regard to depression in young children. Kovacs, Feinberg, Crouse-Novak, Paulauskas, and Finkelstein (1984) found that 79% of prepubertal children diagnosed with major depression also have other concurrent psychiatric diagnoses. More children (38%) were found to have depression combined with dysthymic disorder than had depression alone. This finding makes some sense when one considers the similarity in diagnostic criteria for dysthymic disorder and major depressive disorder, and the difficulty identifying and differentiating affective symptoms in children. Kovacs has even suggested that they may represent variations of the same disorder in children. Anxiety has also been found to commonly co-exist with depression in children. Kovacs et al. (1984) found that one-third of the children with major depression in their study also had anxiety disorders. Estimates of the percentage of depressed children who meet the criteria for conduct disorder range from 7% (Kovacs et al., 1984) to 37% (Puig-Antich, 1982), although research has shown virtually no comorbidity between childhood depression and attention-deficit/hyperactivity disorder (Kovacs et al., 1984).

The prevalence of childhood depression in the general child population appears to range between 2% and 5%, depending on the age range surveyed (Anderson, Williams, McGhee, & Silva, 1987; Kashani et al., 1987). Studies of the preschool age range has shown that approximately 1% of children in regular preschools meet the diagnostic criteria for major depressive disorder (Kashani, Holcomb, & Orvaschel, 1986). There also appear to be differences in the characteristics of childhood depression at different ages. For example, Ryan et al. (1987) found that young depressed children were more likely to present with somatic complaints, agitation, hallucinations, and obviously depressed appearance than adolescents, while adolescents showed greater hypersomnia, hopelessness, anhedonia, and weight change than younger children. The frequency and lethality of suicide attempts also differ tremendously between depressed young children and adolescents, with such attempts being rare and seldom successful in young children (Kazdin, 1990). Most studies that have examined the long-term adjustment of young children diagnosed with major depression have determined that they are more likely to be diagnosed with affective disorders in adolescence, but have only a slightly higher risk of depression as adults (Kovacs et al., 1984).

ASSESSMENT

Traditionally, assessment of affective states in preschool children has relied heavily on the unstructured clinical interview with child and parents, and the use of such projective personality measures as the Rorschach Test, the Thematic Apperception Test, the Children's Apperception Test, and the Draw-A-Person Test (Kazdin, 1988). Unfortunately, there is little empirical evidence that supports the ability of these procedures to differentiate depressed from nondepressed preschoolers (Kazdin, 1990). Relatively few standardized psychological assessment instruments have been validated with, and are appropriate for use with, a preschool population. The most widely used instrument for assessing depression in children is probably the Children's Depression Inventory (CDI), a self-report scale developed by Kovacs and Beck (1977). Unfortunately, the CDI is only standardized for use with children as young as 7 years old. The only other widely used self-report measure that has been designed for use with younger children is the Center for Epidemiological Studies Depression Scale (modified for children), which was published by Weissman, Ovaschel, and Padian (1980), and this measure is only standardized for use with children as young as 6. It appears that self-report alone is not viewed as reliable and valid enough in preschoolers for diagnosis of depression, and more attention has been paid to behavioral rating scales completed by parents and structured interviews with children and parents. This is unfortunate, because in older children, parent and child measures often show little correlation (Kazdin, French, Unis, Esveldt-Dawson, & Sherick, 1983), and children's self-reports have been found to be more strongly related to suicidal thoughts and helplessness than parent ratings (Kazdin, Rodgers, & Colbus, 1986). A number of these measures are in the form of structured or semistructured interviews with children and parents. Usually, following the interview, the clinician rates the child's affective status on a number of items. Examples of such interview measures that are standardized for use with children 6 years of age and older include the Bellevue Index of Depression (BDI; Petti, 1978), the Bellevue Index of Depression-Modified (Kazdin, French, Unis, Esveldt-Dawson, & Sherick, 1983), the Children's

1983), the Children's Depression Rating Scale (CDRS; Poznanski, Cook, & Carroll, 1979), the Schedule for Affective Disorders and Schizophrenia for School-Age Children (K-SADS; Chambers et al., 1985), the Diagnostic Interview for Children and Adolescents (DICA; Herjanic & Reich, 1982), and the Diagnostic Interview Schedule for Children (DISC; Costello, Edelbrock, & Costello, 1985). An additional rating scale based on an interview with the child, which is standardized for children as young as 5 years of age, is the Children's Affective Rating Scale (CARS; McKnew, Cytryn, Efron, Gershon, & Bunney, 1979). These interview-based measures appear to have considerable value in the diagnosis of depression in young children, with perhaps the K-SADS receiving the most research and clinical attention at this point (Chambers et al., 1985).

Another assessment instrument that has only been standardized with older children but could have utility with preschoolers who are in an organized day-care or nursery school setting is the Peer Nomination Inventory of Depression (PNID; Lefkowitz & Tesiny, 1980). This measure asks children to identify others in their group who demonstrate behaviors indicative of affective disorder (e.g., "Who worries a lot?").

Two broad-based measures of childhood psychopathology that index depression and rely solely on parent report are the Personality Inventory for Children (PIC; Wirt, Lachar, Klinedinst, & Seat, 1984) and the Child Behavior Checklist (CBCL; Achenbach & Edelbrock, 1983), although the CBCL also has a self-report form. These instruments are among the most widely used and best standardized assessment measures used with children, and are also virtually the only assessment instruments standardized for use with younger preschool children that include a depression factor. The PIC is standardized for use with children as young as 3 years old and has been shown to be capable of discriminating depressed from nondepressed children (Lobovitz & Handal, 1985). The CBCL is standardized for children as young as 4, and also has been shown to be effective in detecting depression in children (Seagull & Weinshank, 1984). Research with the CBCL has also revealed developmental differences in depressive symptomatology in preschool children. For example, Achenbach and Edelbrock (1983) found that suicidal talk was associated with other depressive symptoms in boys aged 6 to 11, but not in boys aged 4 to 5. Similarly, for girls aged 6 to 11, anxiety and feeling persecuted were part of the constellation of depressive symptoms, while they were absent for girls aged 4 to 5. A number of other good behavioral rating scales exist for use with preschool populations (e.g., the Eyberg Child Behavior Inventory; the Conners Parent Rating Scale; the Preschool Behavior Questionnaire), but these do not include specific subscales indexing depressive symptomatology.

TREATMENT

Models of dynamic psychotherapy for depression have even been described for use with infants, although the evidence for their effectiveness is solely anecdotal (Fraiberg, 1980). Play therapy (Axline, 1947) is the psychodynamic treatment modality usually employed with preschool children. The stated goal of such therapy is to help the depressed child "play out" internal thoughts, worries, and concerns (often reenacting parent–child interactions) and develop the ability to more effectively express feelings and relate to others. Again, most reports of the effectiveness of this approach are anecdotal case studies (e.g., Bodtker, 1972). Psychodynamic practitioners (Sours, 1978) have proposed that children as young as 3 can participate in, and benefit from, verbal psychoanalysis. More traditionally, supportive psychotherapy is focused on the parents in cases of depression in preschool children, with the goal of improving the affective interaction between parent and child (Minde & Minde, 1981).

Cognitive–behavioral therapies have been shown to have considerable effectiveness in treating depression in preadolescent children. Positive self-statement training has reportedly been successful (Craighead, Wilcoxin-Craighead, & Meyers, 1978), for instance, and Butler, Miezitis, Friedman, and Cole (1980) evaluated role-playing and cognitive restructuring interventions with elementary school children and found significant treatment benefits, particularly with the role-playing intervention. Spivack, Platt, and Shure (1976) have developed a model for interpersonal problem-solving therapy that is applicable to preschool children. They report that this approach, which emphasizes the analysis and remediation of problematic social interactions, is effective in increasing social interaction in inhibited, withdrawn children, thus leading to greater opportunities for positive reinforcement (Lewinsohn, 1974). Dweck (1975) found that "attribution retraining," in which children were taught to attribute failure to a lack of effort rather than a lack of ability, was effective in improving children's persistence and performance when faced with failure feedback. This approach appears to address a significant causal factor in depression according to Seligman's (Seligman & Maier, 1967) and Beck's (1970) models. Cole and Kazdin (1980) propose the use of a therapeutic approach called self-instruction training to treat depression in children. This approach, which has not been empirically evaluated, entails teaching children to self-monitor, compare their performance to a realistic criterion, and administer self-reinforcement. Another cognitive approach called self-control training (Rehm, 1977), which focuses on self-monitoring, self-instruction, and self-reinforcement, was compared to training in behavioral problem solving and no treatment. The results indicated that both approaches were significantly and equally effective.

Social skills training has also proven effective in treating depression in children, although there are few empirical demonstrations with preschoolers. Calpin and Cinciripini (1978) were successful in using directed training of both specific (e.g., eye contact) and general social skills to decrease depressive behaviors in two children. Similarly, Matson et al. (1980) reported that use of social skills training modalities such as instruction, information feedback, modeling, and role-playing were effective in improving social interactions in depressed children as young as 9. Other interventions that have proven effective in treating the social skills deficits and social withdrawal of depressed children include modeling (O'Conner, 1972) and the use of individual and group contingencies and social reinforcement (Weinrott, Corson, & Wilchesky, 1979).

Medication has been increasingly used to treat depression in young children in recent years. Most of the attention has been focused on the tricyclic antidepressants, particularly imipramine and nortriptyline. Weller, Weller, and Preskorn (1983) evaluated the effect of imipramine on 20 hospitalized depressed children between the ages of 6 and 12. They found that none of the children showed a remission in their depressive symptoms during an initial 2-week period when they received only counseling. Following that phase, the children were treated with imipramine at a dosage of 75 milligrams per day. There was a remission rate of 80% for children whose plasma drug levels were within the range of 125 to 225 nanograms per milliliter at the end of 3 weeks, while the remission rate was zero for children whose drug levels were outside this range. After 3 additional weeks of medication treatment, children whose drug levels were within the therapeutic range showed a 93% remission rate, while those outside this range showed a 25% remission rate. Puig-Antich et al. (1987) have also reported that imipramine is effective in treating depression in preadolescent children, although they found that children with psychotic symptoms in addition to depression required higher plasma levels and generally showed less response to the medication. Wilson and Staton (1984), in a study using children as young as 5, found that not only did imipramine treatment result in improvement in a variety of internalizing and externalizing behaviors, it also produced improvement in neuropsychological functioning and IQ test performance.

Geller, Perel, Knitter, Lycaki, and Farooki (1983) found that nortriptyline was effective in treating depression in preadolescent children, and that it produced fewer side effects and required lower dosages to reach therapeutic levels than imipramine. Similarly, Dugas, Mouren, Halfon, and Moron (1985) investigated mianserin, a tetracyclic antidepressant, and found that it was effective in reducing depressive symptomatology within 1 week after administration was begun.

It is clear from the above research that psychotropic medications have considerable potential for the treatment of depression in young children. However, for the most part, these medications have not been investigated with, or approved for, younger preschoolers. In addition, significant negative side effects, including cardiac complications and neurological changes, can occur with tricyclic antidepressants, and the dangers of toxicity mandate the need for frequent blood monitoring (Trad, 1987). For these reasons, medication treatment of depression in preschoolers is probably not the treatment of choice, except in severe cases that have proven resistant to other interventions.

REACTION TO LOSS

Divorce

As mentioned earlier in this chapter, one causal factor that has been identified in connection with early childhood depression is disruption or loss of the parent–child relationship. Undoubtedly the most common event bringing about such loss in the lives of preschoolers is divorce. Every year the parents of over 1 million children in the United States get divorced (Everly, 1977). Each divorce involves an average of 1.2 children (Clingempeel & Repucci, 1982), and when permanent separations and desertions are included, the totals indicate that one out of every six children is living in a single-parent home (Everly, 1977).

Research has indicated that parental divorce has significant emotional and behavioral effects on children. These effects may be particularly strong when the divorce occurs during the preschool years. McDermott (1968) assessed 3- to 5-year-old children whose parents were in the process of divorcing and found that over half demonstrated abnormal emotional and behavioral reactions that had not previously been evident. These reactions included grief, depression, anger, and emotional detachment. Wallerstein and Kelly (1975) also studied the reactions of preschoolers to their parents' divorce and noted that effects differed by age. The youngest children (2- and 3-year-olds) demonstrated regression, irritability, and increased aggressiveness, while slightly older children (3- and 4-year-olds) demonstrated increases in irritability, fearfulness, and aggression. Most of the younger group showed a significant decrease in symptoms after 1 year, while most of the older children were worse after a year. Even older preschoolers (5- and 6-year-olds) became anxious, moody, and aggressive, and approximately one-third of these children later exhibited depression. No initial differences were noted between boys' and girls' reactions; however, after 1 year, twice as many girls as boys were still experiencing emotional problems. Hetherington, Cox, and Cox (1979) found that preschoolers whose parents divorced had significant adjustment problems during the first year after the divorce, but that by the second year children from divorced homes were better adjusted than children from intact homes with high levels of parental discord. Hodges, Wechsler, and Ballantine (1979), however, compared preschoolers from divorced and nondivorced homes and found that there were no significant differences in emotional adjustment, although both parents and teachers believed that the children from divorced homes had been negatively affected by the experience. Kelly and Wallerstein (1976) assessed a slightly older group of children (7- and 8-year-olds) whose parents had divorced or separated and found that most of them were experiencing grief, sadness, and anxiety. After a year, these emotional difficulties had improved in only 40% of the children.

A number of factors have been identified as significant in determining preschoolers' short-term adjustment to divorce. Jacobson (1978a) found a significant correlation between maladjustment and loss of time spent in activities with a noncustodial father in 3- to 6-year-olds. Jacobson (1978b) also found that there was a significant relationship between the amount of hostility expressed between the parents prior to the divorce and the child's adjustment after the divorce, for children as young as 3. Physical conflict between the parents was an especially strong predictor of later child maladjustment. Finally, Jacobson (1978c) investigated the relationship between parent–child communication and the child's adjustment to the divorce and found that the more parents discussed the divorce or separation with the child and the more they attended to the child's concerns, the better the child's postdivorce adjustment. It appeared to make little difference whether the marital separation was discussed in advance or at the time it occurred.

The longer-term effects of divorce on preschoolers were evaluated by Wallerstein and Kelly (1980), who assessed the emotional effects of divorce after 5 years on children as young as 3 at the time of the divorce. They found that long-term adjustment was less affected by the child's age than by the quality of the child's life following the divorce and the relationship between the child and the custodial mother. Five years after the divorce, approximately 40% of the children were experiencing moderate to severe depression, most often secondary to a poor relationship with the noncustodial father. Wallerstein (1986) also assessed the adjustment of children 10 years after the divorce and found that children who were preschoolers at the time had little memory for the events. Half of these children had a good relationship with their custodial mothers, and two-thirds had at least irregular contact with their fathers. Many of the children felt the desire for a closer relationship with their fathers, however. In terms of overall adjustment, Wallerstein found that girls who were preschoolers at the time of the divorce had the best adjustment 10 years later, while boys who were older at the time of the divorce had the poorest later adjustment. Generally, preschoolers were better adjusted after 10 years, although they had shown the poorest initial adjustment to the divorce. Regular contact with the noncustodial father and the absence of chronic anger or psychopathology in the custodial mother were related to good adjustment. The relationship between the child and the mother was found to be related to both short-term and long-term adjustment, while the relationship with the father was found to be related only to long-term adjustment.

Psychological interventions in cases of divorce and separation can involve parents alone, children alone, or both parents and children. Individual psychotherapy with one of the parents frequently focuses on the emotional reactions the adult is having to the divorce and the resolution of feelings of guilt, anger, depression, and/or anxiety. Frequently, the parent is concerned about how to tell the child that a marital separation is imminent, or if it has already occurred, how to reassure the child concerning his or her lack of responsibility for the divorce, and continued security in the future. When parents are seen together, either before or after the divorce, a frequently useful focus is the need to support the child's relationship with the other parent, and the necessity of not expressing anger toward each other through the children or in their presence. Counseling with both parents can also become focused on the logistics and responsibilities of visitation and financial support, although these issues are often better left to legal practitioners. Play or activity therapy is often the most appropriate treatment modality when working with the preschooler; however, older preschool children often benefit from a verbal interaction with a therapist in which they can express their feelings and concerns and receive reassurance, along with clear answers to their questions. There are a number of published materials that can be beneficial in helping children understand the divorce process and identify and resolve their feelings about what they're going through. Examples include *Mommy and Daddy Are Divorced* (Perry & Lynch, 1978), *Divorce Is...A Kid's Coloring Book* (Magid & Schriebman, 1980), and *The Dinosaur's Divorce* (Brown & Brown, 1986). Preschoolers will need someone to read these materials to them and help them process the contents.

Group interventions have also been implemented with school-age children from divorced families. Stolberg and Garrison (1985) found that a school-based, 12-session psychoeducational group intervention was effective in improving self-esteem and increasing adaptive social skills in participants. Pedro-Corrall and Cowan (1985) reported a decrease in problem behaviors and increased interpersonal competency following an identical intervention. Kalter and Rubin (1989) used both play therapy and verbal interventions in a school-based group intervention with children from divorced families. After eight sessions, participants demonstrated increased feelings of self-competence, better ability to identify emotions, and more positive feelings toward both parents. It appears that such group interventions could be effectively applied to preschool children, if age-appropriate adjustments were made to the content and format of the sessions.

Parental Death

An even more dramatic form of disrupted parent–child relationship occurs in cases of parental death. Traditionally, preschool children have been viewed as being unable to understand the finality, irreversibility, and universality of death because of their cognitive limitations. Since they are in the Preoperational Stage of cognitive development (Piaget, 1963), and thus, egocentric in their thought processes, they are thought to be only able to comprehend death in terms of things they have experienced, such as sleep, illness, and injury (Koocher & Gudar, 1992). Research suggests that this view is not necessarily accurate, and that children as young as 2 are able to comprehend the essential nature of death (Stambrook & Parker, 1987). Even when preschool children do not understand the concept of death, they seem to be capable of learning about it. Schonfeld and Kappelman (1990) provided children as young as 4 with educational presentations concerning death and found that their subsequent understanding of the concept significantly exceeded that of a control group. Duncan (1979) has designed a death education curriculum appropriate for use with young school-age children. Preschool children who have had a parent, sibling, or peer die also have a more complete and mature concept of death than those who have not had such exposure (Jay, Green, Johnson, Caldwell, & Nitschke, 1987).

Although research has attempted to correlate losses due to death in childhood with depression and psychopathology in later life, the relationship appears far from clear, posssibly because of the importance of subsequent actions in determining the impact of the death itself (Fleming, 1980). Ragan and McGlashan (1986) reported that mentally ill adults who had had a parent die when they were adolescents had more severe psychopathology than mentally ill adults who had had a parent die when they were younger children. A number of confounds exist in this study, however (e.g., stability of home environment), and it is unclear if the results have much significance for understanding the impact of death on children. A contradictory finding by Sheras (1983), that death of a parent before the age of 12 was associated with later suicide attempts, further confuses the issue. A review by Crook and Eliot (1980) concluded that there was little evidence that the death of a parent played any role in the etiology of adult depression.

Although the long-term impact of parental death on a young child is unclear, there appears to be little question that there are significant effects on short-term psychological adjustment. Black and Urbanowicz (1987) found that 92% of a sample of children whose parent had died demonstrated signs of emotional and behavioral disturbance in the weeks following the death. Such symptoms can include sleep and appetite disturbances, anxiety and fearfulness, depression, crying, distractibility, and conduct problems. In most children, these symptoms gradually decrease over 6 months to a year, suggesting uncomplicated and normal bereavement (DSM-III-R; APA, 1987). In some children, however, these symptoms continue without significant diminution for a longer period of time, indicating the possibility of pathological bereavement and subsequent depression. Kaffman and Elizur (1983) found that 50% of a sample of Israeli children whose fathers had been killed in battle were demonstrating significant symptoms of emotional maladjustment 18 months after the death, and 39% still showed symptoms at 42 months after the death. Among the symptoms demonstrated by the younger children were nightmares, anxiety, and dependency. The authors suggested that the children who showed extended maladjustment were those whose mothers were also not coping well, and who had not given their children much attention and assistance in dealing with their father's death.

The prevention of pathological bereavement in children whose parents have died begins with frank and open discussion with them (at their level of comprehension) about the death. Children (especially preschool children) frequently have misconceptions about events and their causes and effects, and these misconceptions may be the source of significant anxiety and upset. Typical misconceptions include concerns about the health of the surviving parent or themselves, worry that they may become homeless or have to leave school, and worry that they somehow caused the death. The best immediate intervention is to have a sensitive and caring adult who is close to the child (preferably the surviving parent) talk with him or her and offer direct answers to both spoken and unspoken questions and concerns. Schaefer and Lyons (1986) offer specific suggestions concerning the content and format of such a discussion and a number of published materials exist to help explain death to children (e.g., Lombardo & Lombardo, 1986; Mellonie & Ingpen, 1983). The involvement of a clergyperson may be useful, but the connection between death and religion is not as apparent to young children as it is to adults, and a minister may simply be another stranger to a child who does not have a strong preexisting church affiliation. If no one is available to talk with the child, or no one feels comfortable doing so, a therapist experienced in such work should be contacted. A number of the therapeutic approaches described earlier for dealing with depression in children are also appropriate for helping them cope with the death of a parent. Koocher (1983) suggests that the child should be given a choice about attending the funeral, and Schowalter (1970) suggests that attending the funeral in the company of an attentive adult will (even for a preschooler) provide a sense of closure and inclusion.

Masterman and Reams (1988) conducted an 8-week group intervention for preschoolers whose parents had died, and reported that it resulted in decreases in problem behaviors at home and improved communication between the child and the surviving parent concerning death-related issues. These group sessions included therapeutic play, storytelling, and role-playing around issues of death. Black and Urbanowicz (1987) implemented a series of family therapy sessions for children and surviving parents. The sessions focused on promoting appropriate mourning by discussion of the deceased parent and improving communication between family members about the death and their feelings in response to it. Follow-up evaluation after 2 years indicated that both parents and children who had participated in the sessions had fewer adjustment problems than a control group who had not received such treatment.

It appears that depression and emotional reactions to parental loss are significant issues with preschool children. Although most of the literature in these areas is fairly new, assessment and treatment procedures have been developed and empirically validated. Further research needs to be done, however, to elucidate the causal relationships in childhood depression, and to ensure that identification and treatment of affective problems in preschoolers are done in a way that will maximize positive outcomes.

References

Abel, E. L., & Sokol, R. J. (1987). Incidence of fetal alcohol syndrome and economic impact of FAS-related anomalies. *Drug and Alcohol Dependence, 19*(1), 51–70.

Abidin, R. (1990). *Parenting Stress Index manual* (3rd ed.). Charlottesville, VA: Pediatric Psychology Press.

Abraham, S., & Nordsieck, M. (1960). Relationship of excess weight in children and adults. *Public Health Reports, 75,* 263–273.

Abrams, J. C. & Kaslow, F. (1977). Family systems and the learning disabled child: Intervention and treatment. *Journal of Learning Disabilities, 10,* 27–31.

Abramson, L. Y., Seligman, M. E. P., & Teasdale, J. D. (1978). Learned helplessness in humans: Critique and reformulation. *Journal of Abnormal Psychology, 87,* 49–74.

Achenbach, T. M. (1991). *Integrative guide for the 1991 CBCL/4–18, YSR, and TRF profiles.* Burlington, VT: University of Vermont, Department of Psychiatry.

Achenbach, T. M. (1992). *Manual for the Child Behavior Checklist/2–3 and 1992 Profile.* Burlington, VT: University of Vermont, Department of Psychiatry.

Achenbach, T. M. & Edelbrock, C. S. (1983). *Manual for the Child Behavior Checklist and Revised Child Behavior Profile.* Burlington, VT: University Associates in Psychiatry.

Ack, M., Norman, M. E., & Schmitt, B. D. (1985). Enuresis: Alarms and drugs. (P. D'Epiro, Ed.). *Patient Care, 1.*

Acredolo, L. P., & Hake, J. L. (1982). Infant perception. In B. B. Wolman & G. Stricker, (Eds.), *Handbook of developmental psychology.* Englewood Cliffs, NJ: Prentice-Hall.

Ainsworth, M. (1979). Infant-mother attachment. *American Psychologist, 34,* 932–937.

Alexander, A. B., Chai, H., Creer, T. L., Miklich, D. R., Renne, C. M., & Cardoso, R. (1973). The elimination of chronic cough by response suppression shaping. *Journal of Behavior Therapy and Experimental Psychiatry, 4,* 75–80.

Alexander, A. B., Miklich, D. R., & Hershkoff, H. (1972). The immediate effects of systematic relaxation training on peak expiratory flow rates in asthmatic children. *Psychosomatic Medicine, 34,* 388–394.

Allen, J., & Phelan, P. D. (1980). Death from cystic fibrosis. *Australian Paediatric Journal, 16,* 128.

Allgeier, A. R. (1976). Minimizing therapist supervision in the treatment of enuresis. *Journal of Behavior Therapy and Experimental Psychiatry, 7,* 371–372.

237

Altepeter, T. S., & Walker, C. E. (1992). Prevention of physical abuse of children through parent training. In D. J. Willis, E. W. Holden, & M. Rosenberg (Eds.), *Prevention of child maltreatment: Developmental and ecological perspectives* (pp. 226–248). New York: Wiley.

Altman, P. J., & Schwartz, A. D. (1983). *Malignant diseases of infancy, childhood and adolescence.* Philadelphia: Saunders.

Ambrose, N. G., Yairi, E., & Cox, N. (1993). Genetic aspects of early childhood stuttering. *Journal of Speech and Hearing Research, 36,* 701–706.

American Association for Protecting Children. (1985). *Highlights of official child abuse and neglect reporting 1983.* Denver, CO: American Humane Association.

American Professional Society on the Abuse of Children. (1990). *Guidelines for psychosocial evaluation of suspected sexual abuse in young children.* Chicago: Author.

American Psychiatric Association. (1980). *Diagnostic and statistical manual of mental disorders* (3rd ed.). Washington, DC: Author.

American Psychiatric Association. (1987). *Diagnostic and statistical manual of mental disorders* (3rd ed., revised). Washington, DC: Author.

American Psychiatric Association. (1993). *DSM-IV draft criteria.* Washington, DC: Author.

Anders, T., & Chalemian, R. (1974). The effect of circumcision on sleep-wake states in human neonates. *Psychosomatic Medicine, 36,* 174–179.

Anderson, J. C., Williams, S., McGhee, R., & Silva, P. A. (1987a). The prevalence of DSM-III disorders in pre-adolescent children: Prevalence in a large sample from the general population. *Archives of General Psychiatry, 44,* 69–76.

Anderson, J. C., Williams, S. McGhee, R., & Silva, P. A. (1987b). DSM-III disorders in preadolescent children: Prevalence in a large sample from the general population. *Archives of General Psychiatry, 44,* 69–76.

Andolsek, K., & Novik, B. (1980). Use of hypnosis with children. *Journal of Family Practice, 3,* 503–508.

Apgar, V. (1953). A proposal for a new method of evaluation in the newborn infant. *Current Research in Anesthesia and Analgesia, 32,* 260.

Apley, J. (1975). *The child with abdominal pains.* Oxford: Blackwell Scientific.

Appelbaum, A. S. (1978). Validity of the Revised Denver Developmental Screening Test for referred and nonreferred samples. *Psychological Reports, 43,* 227–233.

Aragona, J. Cassady, J., & Drabman, R. S. (1975). Treating overweight children through parental training and contingency contracting. *Journal of Applied Behavior Analysis, 8,* 269–278.

Aram, D. M., Ekelman, B., & Nation, J. E. (1984). Preschoolers with language disorders: 10 years later. *Journal of Speech and Hearing Research, 27,* 232–244.

Ashkenazi, Z. (1975). The treatment of encopresis using a discriminative stimulus and positive reinforcement. *Journal of Behavior Therapy and Experimental Psychiatry, 6,* 155–157.

Axline, V. M. (1947). *Play therapy.* Boston: Houghton Mifflin.

Ayer, W. A. (1973). Use of visual imagery in needle phobic children. *Journal of Dentistry for Children, 28,* 41–43.

Ayllon, T., Simon, S. J., & Wildman, R. W. (1975). Instructions and reinforcement in the elimination of encopresis: A case study. *Journal of Behavior Therapy and Experimental Psychiatry, 6,* 235–238.

Azar, S. T. (1989). Training parents of abused children. In C. E. Schaefer & J. M. Briesmeister (Eds.), *Handbook of parent training: Parents as co-therapists for children's behavior problems* (pp. 414–441). New York: Wiley.

Azar, S. T., & Twentyman, C. T. (1984, November). *An evaluation of the effectiveness of behaviorally versus insight oriented group treatments with maltreating mothers.* Paper presented at the annual meeting of the Association for the Advancement of Behavior Therapy, Philadelphia.

Azrin, N. H., & Foxx, R. M. (1974). *Toilet training in less than a day.* New York: Simon & Schuster.

Azrin, N. H., Sneed, T. J., & Foxx, R. M. (1973). Dry bed: A rapid method of eliminating bed-wetting (enuresis) of the retarded. *Behaviour Research and Therapy, 11,* 427–434.

Azrin, N. H., Sneed, T. J., & Foxx, R. M. (1974). Dry-bed training: Rapid elimination of childhood enuresis. *Behaviour Research and Therapy, 12,* 147–156.

Azrin, N. H., & Thienes, P. M. (1978). Rapid elimination of enuresis by intensive learning without a conditioning apparatus. *Behavior Therapy, 9,* 342–354.

Bach, R., & Moylan, J. J. (1975). Parents administer behavior therapy for inappropriate urination and encopresis: A case study. *Journal of Behavior Therapy and Experimental Psychiatry, 6,* 239–241.

Bakal, D. A. (1982). *The psychobiology of chronic headache.* New York: Springer.

Bakwin, H. (1942). Loneliness in infants. *American Journal of Disabled Children, 63,* 30–40.

Bakwin, H. (1973). The genetics of bed wetting. In I. Kolvin, R. MacKeith, & R. S. Meadow (Eds.), Bladder control and enuresis (pp. 73–77). *Clinics in Developmental Medicine, Nos. 48/49.*

Bakwin, H., & Bakwin, R. M. (1972), *Behavior disorders in children* (4th ed.). Philadelphia: W. B. Saunders.

Ball, T. S., Hendrickson, H., & Clayton, J. A. (1974). Special feeding for chronic regurgitation. *American Journal of Mental Deficiency, 74,* 486–493.

Baller, W. R. (1975). *Bed-wetting: Origin and treatment.* New York: Pergamon.

Bandura, A. (1977). Self-efficacy: Toward a unifying theory of behavioral change. *Psychological Review, 84,* 191–215.

Barkley, R. A. (1987). *Defiant children: A clinician's manual for parent training.* New York: Guilford.

Barkley, R. A. (1989). Attention-deficit hyperactivity disorder. In E. J. Mash & R. A. Barkley (Eds.), *Treatment of childhood disorders* (pp. 39–72). New York: Guilford.

Barkley, R. A. (1990). *Attention deficit hyperactivity disorder: A handbook for diagnosis and treatment.* New York: Guilford.

Barkley, R. A., McMurray, M. B., Edelbrock, C. S., & Robbins, K. (1990). Side effects of methylphenidate in children with attention deficit hyperactivity disorder: A systematic, placebo-controlled evaluation. *Pediatrics, 86,* 184–192.

Barkley, R. A., Swanson, J., Gadow, K., Gittelman, R., Sprague, R., Conners, C. K., & Barclay, A. (1990). Task force report: The appropriate role of clinical child psychologists in the prescribing of psychoactive medication for children. *Journal of Clinical Child Psychology, 19*(Suppl.), 1–38.

Barlow, C. F. (1984). *Headaches and migraine in childhood.* London: Spastics International Medical Publications.

Barnard, G. W., Fuller, A. K., Robbins, L., & Shaw, T. (1989). *The child molester: An integrated approach to evaluation and treatment.* New York: Brunner/Mazel.

Barnett, D. W., & Carey, K. T. (1992). *Designing interventions for preschool learning and behavior problems.* San Francisco, CA: Jossey-Bass.

Baroff, G. S. (1986). *Mental retardation: Nature, cause, and management* (2nd ed.). New York: Hemisphere Publishing Corporation.

Baron-Cohen, S. (1989). Joint-attention deficits in autism: Towards a cognitive analysis. *Development and Psychopathology, 1,* 185–189.

Barr, R. G., & Feuerstein, M. (1983). Recurrent abdominal pain syndrome: How appropriate are our basic clinical assumptions? In P. J. McGrath & P. Firestone (Eds.), *Pediatric and adolescent behavioral medicine: Issues in treatment* (pp. 13–27). New York: Springer.

Barrett, J. (1977). *I hate to go to bed.* New York: Four Winds Press.

Barrios, B. A., & O'Dell, S. (1989). Fears and anxieties. In E. J. Mash & R. A. Barkley (Eds.), *Treatment of childhood disorders* (pp. 167–221). New York: Guilford.

Bates, E., Bretherton, I., & Snyder, L. (1988). *From first words to grammar: Individual differences and dissociable mechanism.* Cambridge, England: Cambridge University Press.

Baum, D. (1983). *Medication compliance in children with asthma.* Unpublished doctoral dissertation, Ohio University, Athens.

Baumeister, A. A. (1967). The effects of dietary control on intelligence in phenylketonuria. *American Journal of Mental Deficiency, 71,* 840–847.

Baumrind, D. (1980). New directions in socialization research. *American Psychology, 35,* 639–652.

Bayley, N. (1969). *Bayley Scales of Infant Development.* New York: Psychological Corporation.

Bayley, N. (1993). Bayley Scales of Infant Development: Second Edition. New York: Psychological Corporation.

Beardslee, W., Kerman, G., Keller, M., Lavori, P., & Podorefsky, D. (1985). But are they cases? Validity of DSM-III major depression in children identified in a family study. *American Journal of Psychiatry, 142,* 687–691.

Beck, A. T. (1970). Cognitive therapy: Nature and relation to behavior therapy. *Behaviour Research and Therapy, 7,* 184–200.

Beck, A. T., Ward, C. H., Mendelson, M., Mock, J., & Erbaugh, J. (1961). An inventory for measuring depression. *Archives of General Psychiatry, 4,* 561–571.

Becker, W. C. (1964). Consequences of different kinds of parental discipline. In M. L. Hoffman & L. W. Hoffman (Eds.), *Review of child development research* (Vol. 1). New York: Sage.

Behar, D., & Stewart, M. A. (1981). Fears and phobias. In S. Gabel (Ed.), *Behavior problems in childhood: A primary care approach* (pp. 333–340). New York: Grune & Stratton.

Beidel, D. C., & Stanley, M. A. (1993). Developmental issues in measurement of anxiety. In C. G. Last (Ed.), *Anxiety across the lifespan: A developmental perspective* (pp. 167–203). New York: Springer.

Beitchman, J. H., Nair, R., Clegg, M., Ferguson, B., & Patel, P. G. (1986). Prevalence of psychiatric disorders in children with speech and language disorders. *Journal of the American Academy of Child and Adolescent Psychiatry, 25,* 528–535.

Bellisari, A. (1985, March). *Beating CF: Patient compliance with chest physiotherapy in cystic fibrosis.* Paper presented at meeting of the Society of Behavioral Medicine, New Orleans.

Bellman, M. (1966). Studies on encopresis. *Acta Paediatrica Scandinavica, 170*(Supplement No. 70).

Belsky, J. (1993). Etiology of child maltreatment: A developmental–ecological analysis. *Psychological Bulletin, 114,* 413–434.

Beltramini, A. U., & Hertzig, M. E. (1983). Sleep and bedtime behavior in preschool-aged children. *Pediatrics, 71,* 153–158.

Bemporad, J. R., Pfiefer, C. M., Gibbs, L., Cortner, R. H., & Bloom, W. (1971). Characteristics of encopretic patients and their families. *Journal of the American Academy of Child Psychiatry, 10,* 272–292.

Benjamin, L. S., Serdahely, W., & Geppert, T. V. (1971). Night training through parents' implicit use of operant conditioning. *Child Development, 42,* 963–966.

Bentovim, A. (1970). The clinical approach to feeding disorders of childhood. *Journal of Psychosomatic Research, 14,* 267–276.

Berg, I. (1993). Aspects of school phobia. In C. G. Last (Ed.), *Anxiety across the lifespan: A developmental perspective* (pp. 78–93). New York: Springer.

Berg, I., & Jones, K. V. (1964). Functional fecal incontinence in children. *Archives of Diseases in Childhood, 39,* 465–472.

Bergman, A. (1982). Use of education in preventing injuries. *Pediatric Clinics of North America, 29,* 331–338.

Berko, J. (1958). The child's learning of English morphology. *Word, 14,* 5–17.

Berline, I. N., McCullough, G., Lisha, E. S., & Szurek, S. (1957). Intractable episodic vomiting in a three year old child, *Psychiatric Quarterly, 31,* 228–249.

Berliner, L., & Stevens, D. (1982). Clinical issues in child sexual abuse. *Journal of Social Work and Human Sexuality, 1,* 93–108.

Bernal, M. E. (1972). Behavioral treatment of a child's eating problem. *Journal of Behavior Therapy and Experimental Psychiatry, 3,* 43–50.

Berry, H. K., O'Grady, D. J., Perlmutter, L. J., & Bofinger, L. H. (1979). Intellectual development and academic achievement of children treated early for phenylketonuria. *Developmental Medicine and Child Neurology, 21,* 311–320.

Biller, H. B. (1974). Paternal and sex-role factors in cognitive and academic functioning. In J. K. Cole & R. Dienstbier, (Eds.), *Nebraska symposium of motivation.* Lincoln, NE: University of Nebraska Press.

Bindelglas, P. M., Dee, G. H., & Enos, F. A. (1968). Medical and psychosocial factors in enuretic children treated with imipramine hydrochloride. *American Journal of Psychiatry, 124(3),* 125–130.

Bing, S. B., & Bing, J. R. (1985). Comparison of the K-ABC and PPVT-R with Head Start children. *Psychology in the Schools, 22,* 245–249.

Bishop, D. V. M., & Edmundston, A. (1987). Language-impaired 4-year olds: Distinguishing transient from persistent impairment. *Journal of Speech and Hearing Disorders, 52,* 156–173.

Bitgood, S. C., Crowe, M. J., Suarez, Y., & Peters, R. D. (1977). Immobilization: Effects and side effects on stereotyped behavior in children. *Behavior Modification, 4,* 187–208.

Black, D., & Urbanowicz, M. A. (1987). Family intervention with bereaved children. *Journal of Child Psychology and Psychiatry, 28,* 467–476.

Blechman, E. A. (1985). *Solving child behavior problems at home and at school.* Champaign, IL: Research Press.

Blinick, G., Wallach, R. C., Jerez, E., & Ackerman, B. D. (1976). Drug addiction in pregnancy and the neonate. *American Journal of Obstetrics and Gynecology, 125,* 135–142.

Block, J. (1979). *Socialization influence of personality development in males and females.* American Psychological Association Master Lecture, Convention of the American Psychological Association, New York City, September 1979.

Block, R. W., & Rash, F. C. (1981). *Handbook of behavioral pediatrics.* Chicago: Year Book Medical Publishers.

Bloodstein, O. (1984). *Speech pathology: An introduction* (2nd ed.). Boston: Houghton Mifflin.

Blount, R. L., Powers, S. W., & Sturges, J. W. (1988, November). The Child–Adult Medical Procedure Interaction Scale-Revised (CAMPIS-R). Poster presented at the convention of The Association for Advancement of Behavior Therapy, New York.

Bodtker, J. S. (1972). Psychotherapy of anaclitic depression with severe autistic withdrawal (Report from a long term psychotherapy). In A. L. Annell, *Depressive states in childhood and adolescence*, (pp. 405–411). New York: Halstead.

Boggs, S. R., Geffken, G. R., Johnson, S. B., & Silverstein, J. (1992). Behavioral treatment of nocturnal enuresis in children with insulin-dependent diabetes mellitus. *Journal of Pediatric Psychology, 17*, 111–118.

Boggs, S. R. (1990, August). *Generalization of treatment to the home setting: Direct observation analysis*. Paper presented at the meeting of the American Psychological Association, Washington, DC.

Bollard, J. (1982). A 2-year follow-up of bedwetting treated by dry-bed training and standard conditioning. *Behaviour Research and Therapy, 20*, 571–580.

Bollard, J., & Nettelbeck, T. (1981). A comparison of dry-bed training and standard urine-alarm conditioning treatment of childhood bedwetting. *Behaviour Research and Therapy, 19*, 215–226.

Bollard, J., & Nettelbeck, T. (1982). A component analysis of dry-bed training treatment of bedwetting. *Behaviour Research and Therapy, 20*, 383–390.

Bollard, J., & Woodroffe, P. (1977). The effect of parent administered dry-bed training on nocturnal enuresis in children. *Behaviour Research and Therapy, 15*, 159–165.

Bolter, J. K. (1984). *Neuropsychological impairment and behavioral dysfunction in children with chronic epilepsy*. Unpublished doctoral dissertation, Memphis State University, Memphis, TN.

Bonner, B. L., Kaufman, K. L., Harbeck, C., & Brassard, M. R. (1992). Child maltreatment. In C. E. Walker & M. C. Roberts (Eds.), *Handbook of clinical child psychology* (2nd ed.). New York: Wiley.

Bornstein, M. H., Kessen, W., & Weiskopf, S. (1976). Color vision and hue categorization in young human infants. *Science, 191*, 201–202.

Bornstein, P. H., Balleweg, B. J., McLellarn, R. W., Wilson, G. L., & Sturm, C. A. (1983). The "bathroom game": A systematic program for the elimination of encopretic behavior. *Journal of Behavior Therapy and Experimental Psychiatry, 14*, 67–71.

Bowden, M. L., & Hopwood, N. J. (1982). Psychosocial dwarfism: Identification, intervention and planning. *Social Work in Health Care, 7*(3), 15–36.

Bower, T. G. R. (1977). *The perceptual world of the child*. Cambridge, MA: Harvard University Press.

Bowlby, J. (1969). *Attachment and loss*. Vol. 1: *Attachment*. New York: Basic Books.

Bowlby, J. (1973). *Attachment and loss*. Vol. 2: *Separation*. New York: Basic Books.

Bradley, R. H., & Caldwell, B. M. (1979). Home Observation for Measurement of the Environment: A revision of the preschool scale. *American Journal of Mental Deficiency, 84*, 235–244.

Braswell, L., & Kendall, P. C. (1988). Cognitive-behavioral methods with children. In K. Dobson (Ed.), *Handbook of cognitive-behavioral therapies* (pp. 167–213). New York: Guilford.

Brazelton, T. B. (1962). A child-oriented approach to toilet training. *Pediatrics, 29*, 121–128.

Brazelton, T. B. (1967). Sucking in infancy. In Y. Brackbill & G. G. Thompson (Eds.), *Behavior in infancy and early childhood*. New York: The Free Press.

Brazelton, T. B. (1973). *Neonatal Behavioral Assessment Scale.* Clinics in Developmental Medicine (No. 50). Philadelphia: Spastics International Medical Publications, J. B. Lippincott.

Brazelton, T. B. (1976). Early mother-infant reciprocity. In V. C. Vaughn III & T. B. Brazelton, (Eds.), *The family—Can it be saved?* Chicago: Yearbook Medical Publishers.

Brewin, C. (1985). Depression and causal attributions: What is their relationship? *Psychological Bulletin, 98,* 297–309.

Brierley, J. (1976). *The growing brain.* London: NFER Publishers.

Bristol, M. M. (1987). Mothers of children with autism or communication disorders: Successful adaptation and the double ABCX model. *Journal of Autism and Developmental Disabilities, 17,* 469–486.

Bristol, M. M., Gallagher, J. J., & Schopler, E. (1988). Mothers and fathers of young developmentally disabled and nondisabled boys: Adaptation and spousal support. *Developmental Psychology, 24,* 441–451.

Bristol, M. M., & Schopler, E. (1993). Introduction to preschool issues in autism. In E. Schopler, M. E. Van Bourgondien, & M. M. Bristol (Eds.), *Preschool issues in autism* (pp. 17–37). New York: Plenum.

Brock, W. A., & Kaplan, G. W. (1980). Voiding dysfunction in children. *Current Problems in Pediatrics, 10,* 1–63.

Bronheim, S. P. (1978). Pulmonary disorders: Asthma and cystic fibrosis. In P. R. Magrob (Ed.), *Psychological management of pediatric problems* (Vol. 1). Baltimore: University Park Press.

Brown, J., & Lloyd, H. (1975). A controlled study not speaking in school. *Journal of the Association of Workers for Maladjusted Children, 3,* 49–63.

Brown, L. K., & Brown, M. (1986). *The dinosaur's divorce.* Boston: Little, Brown.

Brownell, K. D. (1982). Obesity: Understanding and treating a serious, prevalent, and refractory disorder. *Journal of Consulting and Clinical Psychology, 50,* 820–840.

Bruch, H. (1957). *The importance of overweight.* New York: W. W. Norton.

Bryson, S. E., Clark, B. S., & Smith, I. M. (1988). First report of a Canadian epidemiological study of autistic syndromes. *Journal of Child Psychology and Psychiatry, 29,* 433–445.

Bussey, K. (1992). Lying and truthfulness: Children's definitions, standards and evaluative reactions. *Child Development, 63,* 129–137.

Butcher, J. N., Dahlstrom, W. G., Graham, J. R., Tellegen, A. M., & Kraemmer, B. (1989). *MMPI-2: Manual for administration and scoring.* Minneapolis: University of Minnesota Press.

Butler, L., Miezitis, S., Friedman, R., & Cole, E. (1980). The effect of two school-based intervention programs on depressive symptoms in preadolescents. *American Educational Research Journal, 17,* 111–119.

Butler, N. R., & Golding, J. (Eds.). (1986). *From birth to five. A study of the health and behaviour of Britain's five year olds.* London: Pergamon.

Butler, N. R., & Goldstein, H. (1973). Smoking in pregnancy and subsequent child development. *British Medical Journal, 4,* 573–575.

Butterworth, G., & Castillo, M. (1976). Coordination of auditory and visual space in newborn infants. *Perception, 5,* 155–161.

Byring, R., & Jarvilehto, T. (1985). Auditory and visual evoked potentials of school boys with spelling disabilities. *Developmental Medicine and Child Neurology, 27,* 141–148.

Cadoret, R. S. (1978). Evidence for genetic inheritance of primary affective disorder in adoptees. *American Journal of Psychiatry, 135,* 463–466.

Cahalane, S. F. (1989). Screening for genetic disease. In G. B. Reed, A. E. Claireaux, & A. D. Bain (Eds.), *Diseases of the fetus and newborn: Pathology, radiology and genetics* (pp. 559–614). St. Louis: Mosby.

Caldwell, B., & Bradley, R. (1984). *Home observation for measurement of the environment.* Little Rock: University of Arkansas at Little Rock.

Calpin, J. P., & Cinciripini, P. M. (1978). *A multiple baseline analysis of social skills training in children.* Paper presented at the Midwestern Association for Behavior Analysis, Chicago, IL, May 1978.

Campbell, M., Adams, P., Small, A. M., Tesch, L. M., & Curren, E. L. (1988). Naltrexone in infantile autism. *Psychopharmacology Bulletin, 24,* 135–139.

Campbell, M., Deutsch, S. I., Perry, R., Wolsky, B. B., & Palij, M. (1986). Short-term efficacy and safety of fenfluramine in hospitalized preschool-age autistic children: An open study. *Psychopharmacology Bulletin, 22,* 141–147.

Campbell, M., Green, W. H., Caplan, R., & David, R. (1982). Psychiatry and endocrinology in children: Early infantile autism and psychosocial dwarfism. In P. J. V. Beumont & G. D. Burrows (Eds.), *Handbook of psychiatry and endocrinology* (pp. 15–62). Amsterdam: Elsevier Biomedical Press.

Campbell, S. B. (1986). Developmental issues in childhood anxiety. In R. Gittelman (Ed.), *Anxiety disorders of childhood* (pp. 24–57). New York: Guilford.

Campbell, S. B. (1990). *Behavior problems in preschool children: Clinical and developmental issues.* New York: Guilford.

Campbell, S. B., & Breaux, A. M. (1983). Maternal ratings of activity level and symptomatic behavior in a non-clinical sample of young children. *Journal of Pediatric Psychology, 8,* 73–82.

Campbell, S. B., Breaux, A. M., Ewing, L. J., & Szumowski, E. K. (1986). Correlates and predictors of hyperactivity and aggression: A longitudinal study of parent-referred problem preschoolers. *Journal of Abnormal Child Psychology, 14,* 217–234.

Campbell, S. B, Endman, M., & Bernfeld, G. (1977). A three-year follow-up of hyperactive preschoolers into elementary school. *Journal of Child Psychology and Psychiatry, 18,* 239–250.

Campbell, S. B., & Ewing, L. J. (1990). Follow-up of hard to manage preschoolers: Adjustment at age 9 and predictors of continuing symptoms. *Journal of Child Psychology and Psychiatry, 31,* 871–889.

Cantwell, D. P. (1982). Childhood depression: A review of current research. In B. B. Lahey & A. E. Kazdin (Eds.), *Advances in clinical child psychology* (Vol. 5). New York: Plenum.

Cantwell, D., & Baker, L. (1987). *Developmental speech and language disorders.* New York: Guilford.

Capute, A. J., Accardo, P. J., Vining, E. P. G., Rubenstein, J. E., & Harryman, S. (1978). *Primitive reflex profile.* Baltimore: University Park Press.

Carlson, G. A., & Cantwell, D. P. (1979). A survey of depressive symptoms in a child and adolescent psychiatric population. *Journal of the American Academy of Child Psychiatry, 18,* 587–599.

Carney, R. M., Schechter, D., & Davis, T. (1983). Improving adherence to blood glucose testing in insulin-dependent diabetic children. *Behavior Therapy, 14,* 247–254.

Carrow, E. (1974). *Carrow elicited language inventory.* Austin, TX: Learning Concepts.

Carrow-Woolfolk, E. (1985). *Test of auditory comprehension of language (TACL)-Revised.* Austin, TX: Learning Concepts.

Caruso, K. R., & Pulcini, R. J. (1988). *Chris tells the truth*. Redding, CA: Northwest Psychological.

Case, R., Kurland, D. M., & Goldberg, J. (1982). Operational efficiency and the growth of short-term memory span. *Journal of Experimental Child Psychology, 33,* 386–404.

Cashman, M. A., & McCann, B. S. (1988). Behavioral approaches to sleep/wake disorders in children and adolescents. In M. Hersen, R. Eisler, & P. Miller (Eds.), *Progress in behavior modification,* (Vol. 22, pp. 215–283). New York: Academic Press.

Cassel, S. (1965). Effects of brief puppet therapy upon the emotional responses of children undergoing cardiac catheterization. *Journal of Consulting and Clinical Psychology, 29,* 1–8.

Catalina, D. A. (1976). Enuresis: The effects of parent contingent wake-up. *Dissertation Abstracts, 37,* 28025.

Catts, H. W. (1991). Facilitating phonological awareness: Role of speech-language pathologists. *Language, Speech, and Hearing Services in Schools, 22,* 196–203.

Caulfield, M. B., Fischel, J. E., DeBaryshe, B. D., & Whitehurst, G. J. (1989). Behavioral correlates of expressive language delay. *Journal of Abnormal Child Psychology, 17,* 187–201.

Cavallo, A., Holt, K., Hejazi, M., Richards, G. E., & Meyer, W. J. (1987). Melatonin circadian rhythm in childhood depression. *Journal of the American Academy of Child and Adolescent Psychiatry, 26*(3), 395–399.

Ceci, S. J., & Bruck, M. (1993). Suggestibility of the child witness: A historical review and synthesis. *Psychological Bulletin, 113,* 403–439.

Centers for Disease Control. (1988). AIDS profile update. *The AIDS Record, 2,*11.

Chamberlain, R. W. (1974). Management of preschool behavior problems. *Pediatric Clinics of North America, 21,* 33–47.

Chambers, W. J., Puig-Antich, J., Hirsch, M., Paez, P., Ambrosini, P. J., Tabrizi, M. A., & Davies, M. (1985). The assessment of affective disorders in children and adolescents by semistructured interview: Test-retest reliability. *Archives of General Psychiatry, 43,* 696–702.

Charache, S., Lubin, B., & Reid, C. D. (1989). *Management and therapy of sickle cell disease* (NIH Publication No. 89–2117). Washington, DC: U. S. Government Printing Office.

Charney, E., Chamblee, H., McBride, M., Lyon, B., & Pratt, R. (1976). The childhood antecedents of adult obesity: Do chubby infants become obese adults? *New England Journal of Medicine, 195,* 6–9.

Chesler, M. A., Paris, J., & Barbarin, O. A. (1986). "Telling" the child with cancer: Parental choices to share information with ill children. *Journal of Pediatric Psychology, 11*(4), 497–516.

Chess, S., Korn, S. J., & Fernandez, P. B. (1971). *Psychiatric disorders of children with rubella*. New York: Brunner/Mazel.

Chess, S., Thomas, A., & Hassibi, M. (1983). Depression in childhood and adolescence: A prospective study of six cases. *Journal of Mental and Nervous Disease, 171,* 411–420.

Children With Attention Deficit Disorders (CHADD) Education Committee. (1988). *Attention deficit disorders: A guide for teachers*. (Available from CHADD., 499 N. W. 70th Avenue, Suite 308, Plantation, FL 33317.)

Children with Specific Learning Disabilities Act 1969 Public Law 91–230, Taylor, 1989.

Chong, T. M. (1977). The management of bronchial asthma. *Journal of Asthma Research, 14*(2), 73–89.

Christ, A. E. (1981). Psychotherapy of the adolescent with true brain damage. In R. Ochroch (Ed.), *The diagnosis and treatment of minimal brain dysfunction in children* (pp. 255–271). New York: Human Sciences Press.

Christensen, M. F., & Mortensen, O. (1975). Long-term prognosis in children with recurrent abdominal pain. *Archives of Disease in Childhood, 50*, 110–114.

Christoffel, K. K., & Forsyth, B. W. C. (1985). *The ineffective parent, childhood obesity syndrome.* Abstract, 25th Annual Meeting of the Ambulatory Pediatric Association.

Christophersen, E. R, & Rainey, S. K. (1976). Management of encopresis through a pediatric outpatient clinic. *Journal of Pediatric Psychology, 4*, 38–40.

Christophersen, E. R., & Rapoff, M. A. (1983). Toileting problems of children. In C. E. Walker & M. C. Roberts (Eds.), *Handbook of clinical child psychology.* New York: Wiley.

Christophersen, E. R. (1988). *Little people: Guidelines for common sense child rearing.* Kansas City, MO: Westport Publishers.

Christophersen, E. R., & Hall, C. L. (1978). Eating patterns and associated problems encountered in normal children. *Issues in Comprehensive Pediatric Nursing, 3*, 1–16.

Cicchetti, D. (1987). Developmental psychopathology in infancy: Illustration from the study of maltreated youngsters. *Journal of Consulting and Clinical Psychology, 55*, 837–845.

Clarke-Stewart, K. A. (1989). Day care: Maligned or malignant. *American Psychologist, 44*, 266–273.

Clements, P. R., Bates, M. V., & Hafer, M. (1976). Variability within Down's syndrome (trisomy-21): Empirically observed sex differences in IQs. *Mental Retardation, 14*, 30–31.

Clingempeel, W. G., & Repucci, N. D. (1982). Joint custody after divorce: Major issues and goals for research. *Psychological Bulletin, 91*, 102–127.

Coates, T. J., & Thoresen, C. E. (1978). Treating obesity in children and adolescents: A review. *American Journal of Public Health, 68*, 143–151.

Coates, T. J., & Thoresen, C. E. (1981). Behavior and weight changes in three obese adolescents. *Behavior Therapy, 12*, 383–399.

Cohen, D. J. (1977). Minimal brain dysfunction: Diagnosis and therapy. In J. H. Masserman, (Ed.), *Current psychiatric therapies.* New York: Grune & Stratton.

Cohen, D. J., Paul, R., & Volkmar, F. R. (1987). Issues in the classification of pervasive developmental disorders and associated conditions. In D. J. Cohen & A. M. Donnellan (Eds.), *Handbook of autism and pervasive developmental disorders* (pp. 20–40). New York: Wiley.

Cohen, E. A., Gelfand, D. M., Dodd, D. K., Jensen, J., & Turner, C. (1980). Self-control practices associated with weight loss maintenance in children and adolescents. *Behavior Therapy, 11*, 26–37.

Cohen, P., Velez, N., Kohn, M., Schwab-Stone, M., & Johnson, J. (1987). Child psychiatric diagnoses by computer algorithm: Theoretical issues and empirical tests. *Journal of the American Academy of Child and Adolescent Psychiatry, 26*, 631–638.

Cole, P. M., & Kazdin, A. E. (1980). Critical issues in self-instruction training with children. *Child Behavior Therapy, 2*, 1–21.

Cole, P. M., & Putnam, F. W. (1992). Effect of incest on self and social functioning: A developmental psychopathology perspective. *Journal of Consulting and Clinical Psychology, 60*, 174–184.

Coleman, M. (1990). Is classical Rett syndrome ever present in males? *Brain and Development, 12*, 31–32.

Collins, R. W. (1973). Importance of the bladder-cue buzzer contingency in the conditioning treatment of enuresis. *Journal of Abnormal Psychology, 82*, 299–308.

Connor, W. N. J., & Doerring, P. L. (1968). Meanings of death to young children. *Offspring (Fall)*, 5–14.

Conners, C. K. (1989). *Manual for Conners Rating Scales.* Toronto, Ontario: Multi-Health Systems.

Consortium for Longitudinal Studies. (1983). *As the twig is bent: Lasting effects of preschool programs.* Hillsdale, NJ: Erlbaum.

Cooper, E. B., & Cooper, C. S. (1985). *Personalized fluency control therapy-revised.* Hingham, MA: Teaching Resources.

Costello, E. J., Edelbrock, C. S., & Costello, A. J. (1985). Validity of the NIMH Diagnostic Interview Schedule for Children: A comparison between psychiatric and pediatric referrals. *Journal of Abnormal Child Psychology, 13*, 579–595.

Craighead, W. E., Wilcoxin-Craighead, L. W., & Meyers, A. W. (1978). New directions in behavior modification with children. In M. Hersen, R. M. Eisler, & P. M. Miller (Eds.), *Progress in behavior modification* (Vol. 6). New York: Academic Press.

Crain-Thoreson, C., & Dale, P. S. (1992). Do early talkers become early readers? Linguistic precocity, preschool language, and emergent literacy. *Developmental Psychology, 28*, 421–429.

Crasilneck, H. B., & Hall, H. A. (1973). Clinical hypnosis in problems of pain. *American Journal of Clinical Hypnosis, 14*, 55–60.

Creasy, R. K. (1990). Preterm labor. In R. D. Eden & F. H. Boehm (Eds.), *Assessment and care of the fetus: Physiological, clinical, and medicolegal principles* (pp. 617–630). Norwalk, CT: Appleton & Lange.

Creer, T. L. (1970). The use of time-out from positive reinforcement procedure with asthmatic children. *Journal of Psychosomatic Research, 14*, 117–120.

Creer, T. L. (1977). Psychologic aspects of asthma. *Respiratory Therapy, 7*, 15–18.

Creer, T. L., & Davis, M. H. (1975). Using a staggered wakening procedure with enuretic children in an institutional setting. *Journal of Behavior Therapy and Experimental Psychiatry, 6*, 23–25.

Creer, T. L., Harm, D. L., & Marion, R. J. (1988). Childhood asthma. In D. K. Routh (Ed.), *Handbook of pediatric psychology* (pp. 162–185). New York: Guilford.

Creer, T. L., Marion, R., & Creer, P. P. (1983). The Asthma Problem Behavior Checklist: Parental perceptions of the behavior of asthmatic children. *Journal of Asthma, 20*, 97–104.

Creer. T. L., & Winder, J. A. (1986). Asthma. In K. A. Holroyd & T. L. Creer (Eds.), *Self-management of chronic disease: Handbook of clinical interventions and research.* Orlando, FL: Academic Press.

Crnic, K. A. (1988). Mental retardation. In E. J. Mash & L. G. Terdal (Eds.), *Behavioral assessment of childhood disorders* (2nd ed., pp. 317–354). New York: Guilford.

Crome, L., & Stern, J. (1967). *The pathology of mental retardation.* London: Churchill.

Crook, T., & Eliot, J. (1980). Parental death during childhood and adult depression. *Psychological Bulletin, 87*, 252–259.

Crowell, J., Keener, M., Ginsburg, N., & Anders, T. (1987). Sleep habits in toddlers 18 to 36 months old. *Journal of the American Academy of Child and Adolescent Psychiatry, 26*, 510–515.

Crowley, C. P., & Armstrong, P. M. (1977). Positive practice, overcorrection, and behavior rehearsal in the treatment of three cases of encopresis. *Journal of Behavior Therapy and Experimental Psychiatry, 8*, 411–416.

Crowther, J. K., Bond, L. A., & Rolf, J. E. (1981). The incidence, prevalence, and severity of behavior disorders among preschool-aged children in daycare. *Journal of Abnormal Child Behavior, 9,* 23–42.

Culbertson, J. L., & Schellenbach, C. J. (1992). Prevention of maltreatment in infants and young children. In D. J. Willis, E. W. Holden, & M. Rosenberg (Eds.), *Prevention of child maltreatment: Developmental and ecological perspectives* (pp. 47–77). New York: Wiley.

Cullen, K. J. (1966). Clinical observations concerning behavior disorders in children. *Medical Journal of Australia, 2,* 533–543.

Cunningham, C. E. (1989). A family-systems-oriented training program for parents of language-delayed children with behavior problems. In C. E. Schaefer & J. M. Briesmeister (Eds.), *Handbook of parent training: Parents as co-therapists for children's behavior problems* (pp. 133–175). New York: Wiley.

Cunningham, C. E., Cataldo, M. F., Mallion, C., & Keyes, J. B. (1983). A review and controlled single case evaluation of behavioral approaches to the management of elective mutism. *Child and Family Behavior Therapy, 5,* 25–49.

Curzon, M. E. J. (1974). Dental implications of thumb-sucking. *Pediatrics, 54,* 196.

Dahlquist, L. M., Czyzewski, D. I., Copeland, K. G., Jones, C. L., Taub, E., & Vaughan, J. (1993). Parents of children newly diagnosed with cancer: Anxiety, coping and marital distress. *Journal of Pediatric Psychology, 18*(3), 365–376.

Dangle, R. F., & Polster, R. A. (1984). WINNING!: A systematic, empirical approach to parent training. In R. F. Dangel & R. A. Polster (Eds.), *Parent training: Foundations of research and practice.* New York: Guilford.

Daro, D., & Mitchell, L. (1990). *Current trends in child abuse reporting and fatalities: The results of the 1989 annual 50 state survey.* Chicago: National Committee for Prevention of Child Abuse.

Dash, J. (1981). Rapid hypno-behavioral treatment of a needle phobia in a five-year-old cardiac patient. *Journal of Pediatric Psychology, 6,* 34–42.

Davidson, M. (1980). Constipation. In S. Gellis & B. Kagan (Eds.), *Current pediatric therapy.* Philadelphia: Saunders.

Davidson, J. (1968). Infantile depression in a "normal" child. *Journal of the American Academy of Child Psychiatry, 37,* 67–94.

Dawson, G., & Castelloe, P. (1992). Autism. In C. E. Walker & M. C. Roberts (Eds.), *Handbook of clinical child psychology* (2nd ed., pp. 375–397). New York: Wiley.

Dawson, G., & Lewy, A. (1989). Reciprocal subcortical–cortical influences in autism: The role of attentional mechanisms. In G. Dawson (Ed.), *Autism: Nature, diagnosis, and treatment* (pp. 144–177). New York: Guilford.

Dawson, G., Hill, D., Spencer, A., Galpert, L., & Watson, L. (1990). Affective exchanges between young autistic children and their mothers. *Journal of Abnormal Child Psychology, 18,* 335–345.

DeFries, J. C., Fulker, D. W., & LaBuda, M. C. (1987). Evidence for a genetic etiology in reading disability of twins. *Nature, 329,* 537–539.

DeJonge, G. A. (1973). Epidemiology of enuresis: A survey of the literature. In I. Kolvin, R. C. MacKeith, & S. R. Meadow (Eds.), *Bladder control and enuresis.* Philadelphia: J. B. Lippincott.

Delacato, C. H. (1966). *Neurological organization and reading.* Springfield, IL: Charles C. Thomas.

Delamater, A. M., Smith, J. A., Lankester, L., & Santiago, J. V. (1988, April). *Stress and metabolic control in diabetic adolescents.* Paper presented at the annual meeting of the Society of Behavioral Medicine, Boston.

Delaney, E., & Hopkins, T. (1987). *Examiner's handbook: An expanded guide for fourth edition users.* Chicago: Riverside Publishing.

DeLeon, G., & Mandel, W. (1966). A comparison of conditioning and psychotherapy in the treatment of functional enuresis. *Journal of Clinical Psychology, 22,* 326–330.

DeLeon, G., & Sacks, S. (1972). Conditioning functional enuresis: A four-year follow-up. *Journal of Consulting and Clinical Psychology, 39,* 299–300.

Delprato, D. J., & McGlynn, F. D. (1984). Behavioral theories of anxiety disorders. In S. M. Turner (Ed.), *Behavioral treatment of anxiety disorders* (pp. 63–122). New York: Plenum.

Denckla, M. B., LeMay, M., & Chapman, C. A. (1985). Few CT scan abnormalities found even in neurologically impaired learning disabled children. *Journal of Learning Disabilities, 18,* 132–135.

De Mille, R. (1973). *Put your mother on the ceiling: Children's imagination games.* New York: Viking-Compass.

DeVilliers, J. G., & DeVilliers, P. A. (1978). *Language development.* Cambridge, MA: Harvard University Press.

Dietz, W. H. (1988). Metabolic aspects of dieting. In N. A. Krasnegor, G. D. Grave, & N. Kretchmer (Eds.), *Childhood obesity: A biobehavioral perspective* (pp. 173–182). Caldwell, NJ: Telford Press.

DiLavore, P., Lord, C., & Rutter, M. (1992). *Prelinguistic Autistic Diagnostic Observation Schedule.* Unpublished manuscript.

DiLorenzo, T. M., & Matson, J. L. (1987). Stuttering. In M. Hersen & V. B. Van Hasselt (Eds.), *Behavior therapy with children and adolescents: A clinical approach* (pp. 263–278). New York: Wiley.

Dinoff, M., Rickard, H. C., & Colwick, J. (1974). Weight reduction through successive contracts. In H. C. Rickard & M. Dinoff (Eds.), *Behavior modification in children: Case studies and illustrations from a summer camp* (pp. 104–109). University, AL: The University of Alabama Press.

Doleys, D. M. (1977). Behavioral treatments for nocturnal enuresis in children: A review of the recent literature. *Psychological Bulletin, 84,* 30–54.

Doleys, D. M., Ciminero, A. R., Tollison, J. W., Williams, C. L., & Wells, K. C. (1977). Dry-bed training and retention control training: A comparison. *Behavior Therapy, 8,* 541–548.

Doleys, D. M., McWhorter, A. Q., Williams, S. C., & Gentry, R. (1977). Encopresis: Its treatment and relation to nocturnal enuresis. *Behavior Therapy, 8,* 105–110.

Doleys, D. M., Schwartz, M. S., & Ciminero, A. R. (1981). Elimination problems: Enuresis and encopresis. In E. J. Mash & L. G. Terdal (Eds.), *Behavioral Assessment of Childhood Disorders.* New York: Guilford.

Doleys, D. M., & Wells, K. C. (1975). Changes in functional bladder capacity and bed-wetting during and after retention control training: A case study. *Behavior Therapy, 6,* 685–688.

Dolgin, M. J., & Jay, S. M. (1989a). Childhood cancer. In T. H. Ollendick & M. Hersen (Eds.), *Handbook of child psychopathyology,* (2nd ed.). New York: Plenum.

Dollinger, S. J. (1986). Childhood sleep disturbances. In B. B. Lahey & A. E. Kazdin (Eds.), *Advances in clinical child psychology,* (Vol. 9, pp. 279–332). New York: Plenum.

Donenberg, G., & Baker, B. L. (1993). The impact of young children with externalizing behaviors on their families. *Journal of Abnormal Child Behavior, 21,* 179–198.

Douglas, J. (1989). Training parents to manage their child's sleep problem. In C. E. Schaefer & J. M. Briesmeister (Eds.), *Handbook of parent training: Parents as co-therapists for children's behavior problems* (pp. 13–37). New York: Wiley.

Drash, P. W., Greenberg, N. E., & Money, J. (1968). Intelligence and personality in four syndromes of dwarfism. In D. B. Cheek (Ed.), *Human growth: Body composition, cell growth, energy and intelligence* (pp. 568–581). Philadelphia: Lea & Febiger.

Drillien, C. M., (1967). The incidence of mental and physical handicaps in school age children of very low birth weight. II. *Pediatrics, 39,* 238–247.

Duffner, P. K., Cohen, M. E., Thomas, P. R. M., & Lansky, S. B. (1985). The long-term effects of cranial irradiation on the central nervous system. *Cancer, 56,* 1841–1846.

Dugas, M., Mouren, M. C., Halfon, O., & Moron, P. (1985). Treatment of childhood and adolescent depression with mianserin. *Acta Psychiatrica Scandinavica, 72*(Suppl. 320), 48–53.

Duncan, C. (1979). *Teaching children about death: A rationale and model for curriculum.* Unpublished doctoral dissertation, Boston College.

Dunn, H. G., McBurney, A. K., Ingram, S., & Hunter, C. M. (1977). Maternal cigarette smoking during pregnancy and the child's subsequent development: II. Neurological and intellectual maturation to the age of 6 1/2 years. *Canadian Journal of Public Health, 68,* 43–50.

Dunn, J. (1983). Sibling relationships in early childhood. *Child Development, 54,* 787–811.

Dunn, L. M., & Dunn, L. M. (1981). *Peabody Picture Vocabulary Test-Revised.* Circle Pines, MN: American Guidance Services.

Dunst, C. J. (1976). *The handicapped infant: Is there justification for cognitive intervention?* Paper presented at American Association of Mental Deficiency, Chicago.

Durand, V. M. (1982). A behavioral/pharmacological intervention for the treatment of severe self-injurious behavior. *Journal of Autism and Developmental Disorders, 12,* 243–251.

During, S. M., & McMahon, R. J. (1991). Recognition of emotional facial expressions by abusive mothers and their children. *Journal of Clinical Child Psychology, 20,* 132–139.

du Verglas, G., Banks, S. R., & Guyer, K. E. (1988). Clinical effects of fenfluramine on children with autism: A review of the research. *Journal of Autism and Developmental Disorders, 18,* 297–308.

Dweck, C. S. (1975). The role of expectations and attributions in the alleviation of learned helplessness. *Journal of Personality and Social Psychology, 31,* 674–685.

Earls, F. (1982). Application of DSM-III in an epidemiological study of preschool children. *American Journal of Psychiatry, 139,* 242–243.

Edelman, R. F. (1971). Operant conditioning treatment of encopresis. *Journal of Behavior Therapy and Experimental Psychiatry, 2,* 71–73.

Edelstein, B. A., Keaton-Brasted, C., & Burg, M. M. (1984). Effects of caffeine withdrawal on nocturnal enuresis, insomnia, and behavior restraints. *Journal of Consulting and Clinical Psychology, 52,* 857–862.

Edlund, L. D., French, R. W., Herbst, J. J., Ruttenberg, H. D., Ruhling, R. O., & Adams, T. D. (1986). Effects of a swimming program on children with cystic fibrosis. *American Journal of Diseases in Children, 140,* 80–83.

Education of the Handicapped Act, P. L. 99–457, 20 U. S. C. 1471–1485, C. F. D. A.: 84.181.

Egeland, B. (1988). Breaking the cycle of abuse: Implications for prediction and intervention. In K. D. Browne, C. Davies, & P. Stratton (Eds.), *Early prediction and prevention of child abuse*. New York: Wiley.

Egeland, B., & Farber, E. A. (1984). Infant-mother attachment: Factors related to its development and changes over time. *Child Development, 55*, 753–771.

Egeland, B., Kalkoske, M., Gottesman, N., & Erickson, M. F. (1990). Preschool behavior problems: Stability and factors accounting for change. *Journal of Child Psychology and Psychiatry, 31*, 891–909.

Egermark-Eriksson, I. (1982) Prevalence of headache in Swedish school-children. *Acta Paediatrica Scandinavica, 71*, 135–140.

Egley, L. C. (1991). What changes the societal prevalence of domestic violence? *Journal of Marriage and the Family, 53*, 885–897.

Eimas, P., & Miller, J. (1980). Discrimination of information for manner of articulation. *Infant Behavior and Development, 3*, 367–375.

Eisenberg, R. (1976). *Auditory competence in early life: The roots of communicative behavior*. Baltimore: University Park Press.

Eisenstadt, T. H., Eyberg, S. M., McNeil, C. B., Newcomb, K., & Funderburk, B. (1993). Parent–child interaction therapy with behavior problem children: Relative effectiveness of two stages and overall treatment outcome. *Journal of Clinical Child Psychology, 22*, 42–51.

Elias, M. F., Nicolson, N. A., Bora, C., & Johnston, J. (1986). Sleep/wake patterns of breast-fed infants in the first two years of life. *Pediatrics, 77*, 322–329.

Elizabeth, J. (1988). *Caring for babies at night*. New Zealand: Longman Paul.

Elkins, P. D., & Roberts, M. C. (1984). A preliminary evaluation of hospital preparation for nonpatient children: Primary prevention in a "Let's Pretend Hospital." *Children's Health Care, 13*, 31–36.

Elliott, C. H., Jay, S. M., & Woody, P. (1989). An observational scale for measuring children's distress during medical procedures. *Journal of Pediatric Psychology, 6*, 232–246.

Elliott, C. H., & Olson, R. A. (1983). The management of children's behavioural distress in response to painful medical treatment for burn injuries. *Behaviour Research and Therapy, 21*, 675–683.

Emslie, G., Roffwarg, H., Rush, A., Weinberg, W. A., & Parkin-Feigenbaum, L. (1987). Sleep EEG findings in depressed children and adolescents. *American Journal of Psychiatry, 144*, 668–670.

Engel, G. L., & Reichsman, F. (1956). Spontaneous and experimentally induced depressions in an infant with gastric fistula: A contribution to the problem of depression. *Journal of the American Pediatric Association, 4*, 428–452.

Engel, G. L., Reichsman, F., Harway, V. T., & Hess, D. W. (1985). Monica: Infant-feeding behavior of a mother gastric fistula-fed as an infant: A 30-year longitudinal study of enduring effects. In E. J. Anthony, & G. H. Pollock (Eds.), *Parental influences in health and disease*. Boston: Little, Brown.

Epstein, L. H., Wing, R. R., Koeske, R., Ossip, D. J., & Beck, S. (1982). A comparison of lifestyle change and programmed aerobic exercise on weight and fitness changes in obese children. *Behavior Therapy, 13*, 651–665.

Epstein, L. H., Woodall, K., Goreczny, A. J., Wing, R. R., & Robertson, R. J. (1984). The modification of activity patterns and energy expeditions in obese young girls. *Behavior Therapy, 15*, 101–108.

Epstein, L. H., Wing, R. R., Koeske, R., & Valoski, A. (1986). Effect of parent weight on weight loss in obese children. *Journal of Consulting and Clinical Psychology, 54*, 400–401.

Epstein, L. H., Marshall, W. R., & Masek, B. J. (1978). A nutritionally based school program for control of eating in obese children. *Behavior Therapy, 9*, 766–778.

Epstein, L. H., Parker, L., McCoy, J. F., & McGee, G. (1976). Descriptive analysis of eating regulation in obese and nonobese children. *Journal of Applied Behavior Analysis, 9*, 407–415.

Epstein, L. H., Beck, S., Fiqueroa, J., Farkas, G., Kazdin, A. E., Daneman, D., & Becker, D. (1981a). The effects of targeting improvements in urine glucose on metabolic control in children with insulin dependent diabetes. *Journal of Applied Behavior Analysis, 14*, 365–375.

Erikson, E. H. (1963). *Childhood and society* (2nd Ed.). New York: W. W. Norton.

Eriksson, M., & Zetterstom, R. (1979). Neonatal convulsions: Incidence and causes in the Stockholm Area. *Acta Paediatrica Scandinavica, 68*, 807–811.

Everly, G. S. (1977). New directions in divorce research. *Journal of Clinical Child Psychology, 6*, 7–10.

Eyberg, S. M. (1974). *Eyberg Child Behavior Inventory*. (Available from Sheila Eyberg, Department of Clinical and Health Psychology, Box 100165 HSC, University of Florida, Gainesville, FL 32610.)

Eyberg, S. M. (1992). Parent and teacher behavior inventories for the assessment of conduct problem behaviors in children. In L. VandeCreek, S. Knapp, & T. L. Jackson (Eds.), *Innovations in clinical practice: A source book* (Vol. 11, 261–270). Sarasota, FL: Professional Resource Exchange.

Eyberg, S. M., & Boggs, S. R. (1989). Parent training for oppositional–defiant preschoolers. In C. E. Schaefer & J. M. Briesmeister (Eds.), *Handbook of parent training: Parents as co-therapists for children's behavior problems* (pp. 105–132). New York: Wiley.

Eyberg, S. M., & Matarazzo, R. G. (1980). Training parents as therapists: A comparison between individual parent–child interaction training and parent group didactic training. *Journal of Clinical Psychology, 36*, 492–499.

Eyberg, S. M., & Robinson, E. A. (1982). Parent–child interaction training: Effects on family functioning. *Journal of Clinical Child Psychology, 11*, 130–137.

Eyberg, S. M., & Robinson, E. A. (1983). Dyadic Parent–Child Interaction Coding System: A manual. *Psychological Documents, 13*, Ms. No. 2582. (Available from Social and Behavior Sciences Documents, Select Press, P. O. Box 9838, San Rafael, CA 94912.)

Eyberg, S. M., & Ross, A. W. (1978). Assessment of child behavior problems: The validation of a new inventory. *Journal of Clinical Child Psychology, 7*, 113–116.

Fagan, J. (1973). Infants' delayed recognition memory and forgetting. *Journal of Experimental Child Psychology, 16*, 425–450.

Faller, K. C. (1988). The spectrum of sexual abuse in day care: An exploratory study. *Journal of Family Violence, 3*, 283–298.

Fantz, R. L. (1961). The origin of form perception. *Scientific American, 204*, 66–72.

Farber, E. D., Showers, J., Johnson, C. F., Joseph, J. A., & Oshins, L. (1984). The sexual abuse of children: A comparison of male and female victims. *Journal of Clinical Child Psychology, 13*, 294–297.

Farwell, J. R., Dodrill, C. B., & Batzel, L. W. (1977). Neuropsychological abilities of children with epilepsy. *Epilepsia, 26*, 395–400.

Farwell, J. R., Dohrmann, G. J., & Flannery, J. T. (1977). Central nervous system tumors in children. *Cancer, 40,* 3123–3132.

Feighner, J. P., Robins, E., Gauze, S. B., Woodruff, R., Winokur, G., & Munoz, R. (1972). Diagnostic criteria for use in psychiatric research. *Archives of General Psychiatry, 26,* 57–63.

Fentress, D. W., Masek, B. J., Mehegan, J. E., & Benson, H. (1986). Biofeedback and relaxation-response training in the treatment of pediatric migraine. *Developmental Medicine and Child Neurology, 28,* 139–146.

Ferber, M. D., & Rivinus, T. M. (1979). Practical approaches to sleep disorders in children. *Medical Times, 107,* 71.

Ferber, R. (1985). *Solve your child's sleep problems.* New York: Simon & Schuster.

Ferber, R. (1989a). Sleeplessness in the child. In M. H. Kryger, T. Roth, & W. C. Dement (Eds.), *Principles and practice of sleep medicine* (pp. 633–639). Philadelphia: Saunders.

Ferber, R. (1989b). Sleepwalking, confusional arousals, and sleep terrors in the child. In M. H. Kryger, T. Roth, & W. C. Dement (Eds.), *Principles and practice of sleep medicine* (pp. 633–639). Philadelphia: W. B. Saunders.

Ferholt, J. B., Rotnem, D. L., Genel, M., Leonard, M., Carey, M., & Hunter, D. E. K. (1985). A psychodynamic study of psychosomatic dwarfism: A syndrome of depression, personality disorder, and impaired growth. *Journal of the American Academy of Child Psychiatry, 24,* 49–57.

Ferinden, W., & Van Handel, D. (1970). Elimination of soiling behavior in an elementary school child through the application of aversive techniques. *Journal of School Psychology, 8,* 267–279.

Feuerstein, M., & Dobkin, P. A. (1990). Recurrent abdominal pain in children: Assessment and treatment. In A. M. Gross & R. S. Drabman (Eds.), *Handbook of clinical behavioral pediatrics* (pp. 291–309). New York: Plenum.

Fiedler, P. A., & Standop, R. (1983). *Stuttering: Integrating theory and practices.* Rockville, MD: Aspen.

Field, T., Cohen, D., Garcia, R., & Greenberg, R. (1984). Mother–stranger face discrimination by the newborn. *Infant Behavior and Development, 7,* 19–27.

Fielding, D. (1980). The response of day- and night-wetting children and children who wet only at night to retention control training and the enuresis alarm. *Behaviour Research and Therapy, 18,* 305–317.

Finkelhor, D., & Lewis, I. A. (1988). An epidemiological approach to the study of child molestation. *Annals of the New York Academy of Sciences, 528,* 64–78.

Finkelhor, D., Williams, L. M., & Burns, N. (1988). *Nursery crimes: Sexual abuse in day care.* Newbury Park, CA: Sage.

Finley, W. W., & Besserman, R. L. (1973). Differential effects of three reinforcement schedules on the effectiveness of the conditioning treatment for enuresis nocturna. *Proceedings of the American Psychological Association, 8,* 923–924.

Finney, J. W., Russo, D. C., & Cataldo, M. F. (1982). Reduction of pica in young children with lead poisoning. *Journal of Pediatric Psychology, 7,* 197–207.

Finney, J. W., Christophersen, E. R., Friman, P. C., Kalnins, I. V., Maddux, J. E., Peterson, L., Roberts, M. C., & Wolraich, M. (1993). Society of pediatric psychology task force report: Pediatric psychology and injury control. *Journal of Pediatric Psychology, 18,* 499–526.

Fischer, K., Hand, H., & Russell, S. (1984). The development of abstractions in adolescence and adulthood. In M. Commons, F. Richards, & C. Armon (Eds.), *Beyond formal operations: Late adolescent and adult cognitive development*. New York: Praeger.

Fischoff, J., Whitten, C. F., & Pettit, M. G. (1971). A psychiatric study of mothers and infants with growth failure secondary to maternal deprivation. *Journal of Pediatrics, 79*, 209–215.

Fisher, B. E., & Wilson, A. E. (1987). Selected sleep disturbances in school children reported by parents: Prevalence, interrelationships, behavioral correlates and parental attributions. *Perceptual and Motor Skills, 64*, 1147–1157.

Fitch, M. J., Cadol, R. V., Goldson, E., Wendell, T., Swartz, D., & Jackson, E. (1976). Cognitive development of abused and failure-to-thrive children. *Journal of Pediatric Psychology, 1*, 32–36.

Fitzgerald, M. T., & Karnes, D. E. (1987). A parent-implemented language model for at-risk and developmentally delayed children. *Topics in Language Disorders, 7*, 31–46.

Fitzsimmons, S. C. (1990, September 12). *Cystic fibrosis patient registry, 1989: Preliminary data*. Bethesda, MD: Cystic Fibrosis Foundation.

Flavell, J., Green, F., & Flavell, E. (1986). Development of knowledge about the appearance–reality distinction. With commentaries by M. Watson & J. Campione. *Monographs of the Society for Research on Child Development, 51* (1, Serial No. 212).

Fleming, S. (1980). Childhood bereavement. In R. Lonetto (Ed.), *Children's concepts of death* (pp. 178–187). New York: Springer.

Forehand, R. L., & McMahon, R. J. (1981). *Helping the noncompliant child: A clinician's guide to parent training*. New York: Guilford.

Forehand, R. L., & Wierson, M. (1993). The role of developmental factors in planning behavioral interventions for children: Disruptive behavior as an example. *Behavior Therapy, 24*, 117–141.

Forehand, R., Wierson, M., Frame, C. L., Kemptom, T., & Armistead, L. (1991). Juvenile firesetting: A unique syndrome or an advanced level of antisocial behavior? *Behavior Research and Therapy, 29*, 125–128.

Forsythe, W. I., Gillies, D., & Sills, M. A. (1984). Propranolol in the treatment of childhood migraine. *Developmental Medicine and Child Neurology, 26*, 737–741.

Forsythe, W. I., & Redmond, A. (1974). Enuresis and spontaneous cure rate. *Archives of Diseases of Childhood, 49*, 259.

Foxx, R. M. (1976). The use of overcorrection to eliminate the public disrobing (stripping) of retarded women. *Behaviour Research and Therapy, 14*, 53–61.

Foxx, R. M., & Azrin, N. H. (1972). Restitution: A method of eliminating aggressive–disruptive behavior of retarded and brain damaged patients. *Behaviour Research and Therapy, 10*, 15–27.

Foxx, R. M., & Shapiro, S. T. (1978). The timeout ribbon: A non-exclusionary timeout procedure. *Journal of Applied Behavioral Analysis, 11*, 125–136.

Fraiberg, S., Shapiro, V., & Cherniss, D. S. (1980). Treatment modalities, in clinical studies. In S. Fraiberg (Ed.), *Clinical studies in infant mental health: The first year of life* (pp. 53–61). New York: Basic Books.

France, K. G. (1992). Behavior characteristics and security in sleep-disturbed infants treated with extinction. *Journal of Pediatric Psychology, 17*, 467–475.

Francis, G. (1989). Anxiety disorders. In M. Hersen (Ed.), *Innovations in child behavior therapy* (pp. 209–227). New York: Springer.

Frankenburg, W. K. (1986). *Revised Denver Prescreening Developmental Questionnaire*. Denver: Denver Developmental Materials.

Frankenburg, W. K., Dodds, J. B., & Fandal, A. (1970). *The Revised Denver Developmental Screening Test Manual*. Denver: University of Colorado Press.

Frankenburg, W. K., Dodds, J. B., Fandal, A., Kazuk, E., & Cohrs, M. (1975). *Denver Developmental Screening Test* (rev. ed.). Denver: Denver Developmental Materials.

Freeark, K., Frank, S. J., Wagner, A. E., Lopez, M., Olmsted, C., & Girard, R. (1992). Otitis media, language development, and parental verbal stimulation. *Journal of Pediatric Psychology, 17*, 173–185.

Freedman, D. G. (1971). Behavioral assessment in infancy. In G. A. B. Stoelinga & J. J. Van Der Werff Ten Bosch (Eds.), *Normal and abnormal development of brain and behavior*. Leiden, the Netherlands: Leiden University Press.

Freeman, T. (1982). *It's my body*. Seattle, WA: Parenting Press.

French, T. M., & Alexander, F. (1941). Psychogenic factors in bronchial asthma. *Psychosomatic Medicine Monograph, 4*, 2–94.

Freud, S. (1916). *Three contributions to the theory of sex*. New York: Nervous and Mental Disease Publishing.

Freud, S. (1917). Mourning and melancholia, in *The standard edition of the complete psychological works of Sigmund Freud*, (Vol. 14. pp. 243–258). Ed. and trans. by J. Strachey. London: Hogarth Press, 1957.

Freud, S. (1965). *New introductory lectures on psychoanalysis*. Ed. and trans. by J. Strachey. New York: Norton.

Friedman, A. R. (1968). Behavior training in a case of enuresis. *Journal of Individual Psychology, 24*, 86–87.

Friedrich, W. N. (1990). *Psychotherapy of sexually abused children and their families*. New York: W. W. Norton.

Friedrich, W. N., Grambsch, P., Damon, L., Hewitt, S. K., Koverola, C., Lange, R. A., Wolfe, V., & Broughton, D. (1992). Child sexual behavior inventory: Normative and clinical comparisons. *Psychological Assessment, 4*, 303–311.

Friman, P. C. (1988). Eliminating chronic thumb sucking by preventing a covarying response. *Journal of Behavior Therapy and Experimental Psychiatry, 19*, 301–304.

Friman, P. C., & Hove, G. (1987). Apparent covariation between child habit disorders: Effects of successful treatment for thumb sucking on untargeted chronic hair pulling. *Journal of Applied Behavior Analysis, 20*, 421–427.

Friman, P. C., & Leibowitz, J. M. (1990). An effective and acceptable treatment alternative for chronic thumb- and finger-sucking. *Journal of Pediatric Psychology, 15*, 57–65.

Friman, P. C., Mathews, J. R., Finney, J. W., Christophersen, E. R., & Leibowitz, J. M. (1988). Do encopretic children have clinically significant behavior problems? *Pediatrics, 82*(3), 407–409.

Funderburk, B., & Eyberg, S. M. (1989). Psychometric characteristics of the Sutter-Eyberg Student Behavior Inventory: A school behavior rating scale for use with preschool children. *Behavioral Assessment, 11*, 297–313.

Furman, E. (1974). *A child's parent dies. Studies in childhood bereavement*. New Haven: Yale University Press.

Gaensbauer, T. J. (1980) Anaclitic depression in a three-and-one-half-month-old child. *American Journal of Psychiatry, 137*, 841–842.

Galvin, M. (1988). *Otto learns about his medicine*. New York: Magination Press.

Gardner, M. F. (1979). *Expressive one-word picture vocabulary test*. Novato, CA: Academic Therapy.

Garn, S., Cole, P. E., & Baily, S. M. (1976). Effect of paternal fatness levels on the fatness of biological and adoptive children. *Ecology of Food and Nutrition, 6*, 1–34.

Geller, B., Perel, J. M., Knitter, E. F., Lycaki, H., & Farooki, Z. Q. (1983). Nortriptyline in major depressive disorder in children: Response, steady-state plasma levels, predictive kinetics, and pharmacokinetics. *Psychopharmacology Bulletin, 19*, 62–65.

Gershon, E. S., Hamovit, J., & Guroff, J. J. (1983). A family study of schizoaffective, bipolar I, bipolar II, unipolar, and normal control probands. *Archives of General Psychiatry, 39*, 1157–1167.

Gesell, A., & Thompson, H. (1929). Learning and growth in identical twins. *Genetic Psychology Monographs, 6*, 1–124.

Gil, E. (1991). *The healing power of play: Working with abused children*. New York: Guilford.

Gillberg, C. (1989). The borderland of autism and Rett syndrome: Five case histories to highlight diagnostic difficulties. *Journal of Autism and Developmental Disorders, 19*, 545–559.

Gillberg, C., Ehlers, S., Schaumann, H., Jakobsson, G., Dahlgren, S. O., Lindblom, R., Bagenholm, A., Tjuus, T., & Blidner, E. (1990). Autism under age 3 years: A clinical study of 28 cases referred for autistic symptoms in infancy. *Journal of Child Psychology and Psychiatry, 31*, 921–934.

Gillberg, J. C., & Gillberg, C. (1989). Asperger's syndrome—some epidemiological considerations: A research note. *Journal of Child Psychology and Psychiatry, 30*, 631–638.

Gillberg, J. C., Gillberg, C., & Steffenburg, S. (1990). Reduced optimality in the pre-, peri-, and neonatal periods is not equivalent to severe peri- or neonatal risk: A rejoinder to Goodman's technical note. *Journal of Child Psychology and Psychiatry, 31*, 813–815.

Gillberg, C., & Steffenburg, S. (1987). Outcome and prognostic factors in infantile autism and similar conditions. *Journal of Autism and Developmental Disorders, 17*, 271–285.

Gittelman, R., & Koplewicz, H. S. (1986). Pharmacotherapy of childhood anxiety disorders. In R. Gittelman (Ed.), *Anxiety disorders of childhood* (pp. 188–203). New York: Guilford.

Gittelman-Klein, R., & Klein, D. F. (1980). Separation anxiety in school refusal and its treatment with drugs. In L. Hersov & I. Berg (Eds.), *Out of school* (pp. 321–341). New York: Wiley.

Glaser, H. H., Heagarty, M. C., Bullard, D. M., & Pivchik, E. C. (1968). Physical and psychological development of children with early failure to thrive. *Journal of Pediatrics, 73*, 690–698.

Glenn, J. (1978). The psychoanalysis of prelatency children. In J. Glenn (Ed.), *Child analysis and therapy* (pp. 163–203). New York: Jason Aronson.

Glennon, B., & Weisz, J. R. (1978). An observational approach to the reassessment of anxiety in young children. *Journal of Consulting and Clinical Psychology, 46*, 1246–1257.

Gliner, C. R. (1967). Tactual discrimination thresholds for shape and texture in young children. *Journal of Experimental Child Psychology, 5*, 536–547.

Goodman, J. F., Greenberg, J., & Pollak, E. (1993). Learning language in early intervention programs. *Early Education and Development, 4*, 204–216.

Goodman, R. (1990). Technical note: Are perinatal complications causes or consequences of autism? *Journal of Child Psychology and Psychiatry, 31*, 809–812.

Gordon, B. N., Schroeder, C. S., & Hawk, B. (1992). Clinical problems of the preschool child. In C. E. Walker & M. C. Roberts (Eds.), *Handbook of clinical child psychology* (2nd ed., pp. 215–233). New York: Wiley.

Goyette, C. H., Conners, C. K., & Ulrich, R. F. (1978). Normative data on revised Conners parent and teacher rating scales. *Journal of Abnormal Child Psychology, 6*, 221–236.

Grannel de Aldaz, E., Vivas, E., Gelfand, D. M., & Feldman, L. (1984). Estimating the prevalence of school refusal and school-related fears: A Venezuelan sample. *Journal of Nervous and Mental Disease, 172*, 722–729.

Graziano, A. M., & Mooney, K. C. (1980). Family self-control instruction for children's nighttime fear reduction. *Journal of Consulting and Clinical Psychology, 48*, 206–213.

Green, W. H., Campbell, M., Hardesty, A. S., Grega, D. M., Padron-Gayol, M., Shell, J., & Erlenmeyer-Kimling, I. (1984). A comparison of schizophrenia and autistic children. *Journal of the American Academy of Child Psychiatry, 23*, 399–409.

Greening, L., & Dollinger, S. J. (1989). Treatment of a child's sleep disturbance and related phobias in the family. In M. C. Roberts & C. E. Walker (Eds.), *Casebook of child and pediatric psychology* (pp. 94–111). New York: Guilford.

Gresham, F. M., & Elliott, S. N. (1990). *Social Skills Rating System: Preschool level*. Circle Pines, MN: American Guidance Service.

Griffiths, P., Medrum, C., & McWilliam, R. (1982). Dry-bed training in the treatment of nocturnal enuresis in childhood: A research report. *Journal of Child Psychology and Psychiatry, 23*, 485–495.

Grinnel, M., Detamore, K., & Lippke, B. (1976). Sign it successful—manual English encourages expressive communication. *Teaching Exceptional Children, 8*, 123–124.

Grolnick, W. S., Cole, R. E., Laurenitis, L., & Schwartzman, P. I. (1990). Playing with fire: A developmental assessment of children's fire understanding and experience. *Journal of Clinical Child Psychology, 19*, 128–135.

Gross, A. M., Heimann, L., Shapiro, R., & Schultz, R. (1983). Social skills training and hemoglobin A(1c) levels in children with diabetes. *Behavior Modification, 7*, 151–184.

Gross, A. M., & Johnson, W. G. (1981). The Diabetes Assertiveness Test: A measure of social coping skills in pre-adolescent diabetics. *The Diabetes Educator, 7*, 26–27.

Gross, A. M., Johnson, W. G., Wildman, H., & Mullett, N. (1981). Coping skills training with insulin dependent pre-adolescent diabetics. *Child Behavior Therapy, 3*, 141–153.

Gross, A. M., Magalnick, L. J., & Richardson, P. (1985). Self-management training with families of insulin-dependent diabetic children: A controlled long-term investigation. *Child and Family Behavior Therapy, 7*, 35–50.

Grossman, H. J. (Ed.). (1983). *Manual on terminology and classification in mental retardation* (4th ed.). Washington, DC: American Association on Mental Deficiency.

Gryboski, J. D. (1969). Suck and swallow in the premature infant. *Pediatrics, 43*, 96–102.

Guess, D., Sailor, W., & Baer, D. M. (1976). Children with limited language. In R. L. Schiefelbusch (Ed.), *Bases of language intervention*. Baltimore: University Park Press.

Gyurke, J. S. (1991). The assessment of preschool children with the Wechsler Preschool and Primary Scale of Intelligence-Revised. In Bruce H. Bracken (Ed.), *The Psychoeducational Assessment of Preschool Children, 6* (pp. 86–106). Boston: Allyn & Bacon.

Hagans, K. B., & Case, J. (1988). *When your child has been molested: A parent's guide to healing and recovery*. Lexington, MA: Lexington Books.

Hagberg, B. (1985). Rett syndrome: Swedish approach to analysis of prevalence and cause. *Brain and Development, 7,* 277–280.

Hagberg, B., & Witt-Engerstrom, I. (1986). Rett syndrome: A suggested staging system for describing impairment profile with increasing age towards adolescence. *American Journal of Medical Genetics, 24*(Suppl. 1), 47–59.

Hagman, E. R. (1932). A study of fears of children of pre-school age. *Journal of Experimental Education, 1,* 110–130.

Hahn, W. W. (1966). Automatic responses of asthmatic children. *Psychosomatic Medicine, 28,* 323–332.

Halle, J. W., Baer, D. M., & Spradlin, J. E. (1981). Teachers' generalized use of delay as a stimulus control procedure to increase language use in handicapped children. *Journal of Applied Behavior Analysis, 14,* 389–409.

Ham, R. E. (1990). *Therapy of stuttering: Preschool through adolescence.* Englewood Cliffs, NJ: Prentice-Hall.

Hamilton, D. V., Mundier, S. S., & Lister, J. (1976). Mode of presentation of juvenile diabetes. *British Medical Journal, 2*(6029), 211–212.

Hammen, C., Adrian, C., & Hiroto, D. (1988). A longitudinal test of the attributional vulnerability model in children at risk for depression. *British Journal of Clinical Psychology, 27,* 37–46.

Hanf, C. (1969). *A two-stage program for modifying maternal controlling during mother–child (M–C) interaction.* Paper presented at the meeting of the Western Psychological Association, Vancouver.

Hanson, R. K., & Slater, S. (1988). Sexual victimization in the history of child sexual abusers: A review. *Annals of Sex Research, 3,* 187–232.

Hargett, R. D., Hansen, F. G., & Davidson, P. O. (1970). Chronic thumbsucking: A second report on treatment and its psychological effects. *American Journal of Orthodontics, 57,* 164–178.

Harmon, R. J., Wagonfield, S., & Emde, R. N. (1982). Anaclitic depression: A follow-up from infancy to puberty. *The Psychoanalytic Study of the Child, 37,* 67–94.

Harris, L. S., & Purohit, A. P. (1977). Bladder training and enuresis: A controlled trial. *Behaviour Research and Therapy, 15,* 485–490.

Harris, S. L., & Romanczyk, R. G. (1976). Treating self-injurious behavior of a retarded child by overcorrection. *Behavior Therapy, 7,* 235–239.

Hartsough, C. S., & Lambert, N. M. (1985). Medical factors in hyperactive and normal children: Prenatal, developmental, and health history findings. *American Journal of Orthopsychiatry, 55,* 190–201.

Hartz, A., Giefer, E., & Rimm, A. A. (1977). Relative importance of the effect of family environment and heredity on obesity. *Annals of Human Genetics, 41,* 185–193.

Hatcher, R. P. (1979). Treatment of food refusal in a two-year-old. *Journal of Behavior Therapy and Experimental Psychiatry, 10,* 363–367.

Hayden, A. H., & Haring, W. G. (1977). The acceleration and maintenance of developmental gains in Down's syndrome school age children. In P. Mittler (Ed.), *Research to practice in mental retardation. Vol. 1. Care and intervention.* Baltimore: University Park Press.

Hedrick, D., Prather, E., & Tobin, A. (1984). *Sequenced Inventory of Communication Development-Revised.* Seattle: University of Washington Press.

Hefter, R., Worthington, J., Worthington, S., & Howe, S. (1982). *The stickybear ABC* [Computer program]. Middletown, CT: Xerox Education.

Heller, R. F., & Strang, H. R. (1973). Controlling bruxism through automated aversive conditioning. *Behaviour Research and Therapy*, 11, 327–328.

Hembree-Kigin, T. L., & McNeil, C. B. (in press). Parent–child interaction therapy: A step-by-step guide for clinicians. New York: Plenum.

Herjanic, B., & Reich, W. (1982). Development of a structured psychiatric interview for children: Agreement between child and parent on individual symptoms. *Journal of Abnormal Child Psychology*, 10, 307–324.

Hetherington, E. M., Cox, M., & Cox, R. (1979). Family interaction and the social, emotional and cognitive development of children following divorce. In V. Vaughn & T. Brazelton (Eds.), *The family: Setting priorities*. New York: Science and Medicine.

Hewitt, S. K., & Friedrich, W. N. (1991, January). *Preschool children's responses to alleged sexual abuse at intake and one year follow-up*. Paper presented at the meeting of the American Professional Society on the Abuse of Children, San Diego, CA.

Hilburn, W. B. (1968). Encopresis in childhood. *Journal of the Kentucky Medical Association*, 66, 978.

Hinshaw, S. P. (1992). Externalizing behavior problems and academic underachievement in childhood and adolescence: Causal relationships and underlying mechanisms. *Psychological Bulletin*, 111, 127–155.

Hobbs, S. A., Stratton, R., Geiss, S. K., Kramer, J. C., & Ozturk, A. (1987, March). *Effects of programmed exercise on children with cystic fibrosis*. Paper presented at the meeting of the Society of Behavioral Medicine, Washington, DC.

Hodges, P., Sauriol, D., Mann, S. F., Reichart, A., Grace, R. M., Talbot, T. W., Brown, N., & Thompson, A. B. (1984). Nutrient intake of patients with cystic fibrosis. *Journal of American Dietetic Association*, 84, 664–669.

Hodges, W., Wechsler, R., & Ballantine, C. (1979). Divorce and the preschool child: Cumulative stress. *Journal of Divorce*, 3, 55–67.

Hodson, B. (1986). *The Assessment of Phonologic Processes-Revised*. Danville, IL: PhonoComp.

Hodson, B., & Paden, E. (1983). *Targeting intelligible speech: A phonological approach to remediation*. San Diego, CA: College Hill Press.

Hoff, R., Berardi, V. P., Weiblen, B. J., Mahoney-Trout, L., Mitchell, M. L., & Grady, G. F. (1988). Seroprevalence of human immunodeficiency virus among childbearing women. *New England Journal of Medicine*, 318, 525–530.

Holden, E. W., Willis, D. J., & Corcoran, M. M. (1992). Preventing child maltreatment during the prenatal/perinatal period. In D. J. Willis, E. W. Holden, & M. Rosenberg (Eds.), *Prevention of child maltreatment: Developmental and ecological perspectives* (pp. 17–46). New York: Wiley.

Holden, K. R., Mellits, E. D., & Freeman, J. M. (1982). Neonatal seizures: I. Correlation of prenatal and perinatal events with outcomes. *Pediatrics*, 70, 165.

Holm, V. A., & Varley, C. K. (1989). Pharmacological treatment of autistic children. In G. Dawson (Ed.), *Autism: Nature, diagnosis, and treatment* (pp. 386–404). New York: Guilford.

Holroyd, K. A. (1986). Recurrent headache. In K. A. Holroyd & T. L. Creer (Eds.), *Self-management of chronic disease: Handbook of clinical interventions and research*. New York: Academic Press.

Hoppes, K., & Harris, S. (1990). Perceptions of child attachment and maternal gratification in mothers of children with autism and Down syndrome. *Journal of Clinical Child Psychology*, 19, 365–370.

Hopwood, N. J., & Becker, D. J. (1979). Psychosocial dwarfism: Detection, evaluation and management. In A. W. Franklin (Ed.), *Child abuse and neglect* (Vol. 3, pp. 439–447). London: Pergamon Press.

Horn, J., Loehlin, J., & Willerman, L. (1975, March). *The Texas Adoption Project*. Paper presented at the meeting of the Behavior Genetics Association, Austin, TX.

Houts, A. C. (1982). Relaxation and thermal biofeedback treatment of child migraine headache: A case study. *American Journal of Clinical Biofeedback, 5*, 154–157.

Howard-Peebles, P. M., & Markiton, R. I. (1979). A tetra-X female: Cytogenetic testing, dermatoglyphic studies, and speech impairment. *American Journal of Mental Deficiency, 84*, 252–255.

Howie, V. M. (1980). Developmental sequelae of chronic otitis media: A review. *Developmental and Behavioral Pediatrics, 1*, 34–38.

Hufton, I. W., & Oates, R. K. (1977). Nonorganic failure to thrive: A long-term follow-up. *Pediatrics, 59*, 73–77.

Hushka, M. (1942). The child's response to coercive toilet training. *Psychosomatic Medicine, 4*, 301–308.

Huston, A. (1983). Sex-typing. In P. Mussen (Ed.), *Handbook of child psychology* (Vol. 4). New York: Wiley.

Huszti, H. C. (1987). *The effects of educational programs on adolescents' knowledge and attitudes about acquired immunodeficiency syndrome (AIDS)*. Unpublished dissertation, Texas Tech University.

Hutt, M. L., & Gibby, R. G. (1979). *The mentally retarded child* (4th ed.). Boston: Allyn & Bacon.

Huttenlocher, J., Haight, W., Bryk, A., Seltzer, M., & Lyons, T. (1991). Early vocabulary growth: Relation to language input and gender. *Developmental Psychology, 27*, 236–248.

Hynd, G. W., & Willis, W. G. (1988). *Pediatric neuropsychology*. Orlando, FL: Grune & Stratton.

Illingworth, R. S. (1954). Three months' colic. *Archives of Disease in Childhood, 29*, 165–174.

Imhof, B. (1956). Bettnasser in der erziehingsberatung. *Heilpaedagogische Werkblaetter, 25*, 122–127.

Inhelder, B., & Piaget, J. (1958). *The growth of logical thinking from childhood to adolescence*. New York: Basic Books.

Israel, A. C., Stolmaker, L., Sharp, J. P., Silverman, W., & Simon, L. G. (1984). An evaluation of two methods of parental involvement in treating obese children. *Behavior Therapy, 15*, 266–272.

Jacklin, C., & Maccoby, E. (1978). Social behavior at 33 months in same-sex and mixed-sex dyads. *Child Development, 49*, 557–569.

Jacobson, D. (1978a). The impact of marital separation/divorce on children: I. Parent-child separation and child adjustment. *Journal of Divorce, 1*, 341–360.

Jacobson, D. (1978b). The impact of marital separation/divorce on children: II. Interparent hostility and child adjustment. *Journal of Divorce, 2*, 3–19.

Jacobson, D. (1978c). The impact of marital separation/divorce on children: III. Interparent hostility and child adjustment. *Journal of Divorce, 2*, 175–193.

Jacobson, R. R. (1985). The subclassification of child firesetters. *Journal of Child Psychology and Psychiatry and Allied Disciplines, 26*, 769–775.

Jason, L. A. (1977). A behavioral approach in enhancing disadvantaged children's academic abilities. *American Journal of Community Psychology, 5*, 413–421.

Jay, S. M. (1988). Invasive medical procedures: Psychological intervention and assessment. In D. K. Routh (Ed.), *Handbook of pediatric psychology* (pp. 401–425). New York: Guilford.

Jay, S. M., & Elliott, C. H. (1988). *Multimodal assessment of children's distress during medical procedures.* Manuscript submitted for publication.

Jay, S. M., Elliott, C. H., Katz, E. R., & Siegel, S. E. (1987). Cognitive-behavioral and pharmacologic interventions for children undergoing painful medical procedures. *Journal of Consulting and Clinical Psychology, 55,* 860–865.

Jay, S. M., Elliott, C. H., & Varni, J. W. (1987). Acute and chronic pain in adults and children with cancer. *Journal of Consulting and Clinical Psychology, 54,* 601–607.

Jay, S. M., Green, V., Johnson, S., Caldwell, S., & Nitschke, R. (1987). Differences in death concepts between children with cancer and physically healthy children. *Journal of Clinical Child Psychology, 16,* 301–306.

Jehu, D., Morgan, R. T., Turner, R. K., & Jones, A. (1977). A controlled trial of the treatment of nocturnal enuresis in residential homes for children. *Behaviour Research and Therapy, 15,* 1–16.

Jenkins, S., Bax, M., & Hart, H. (1980). Behaviour problems in preschool children. *Journal of Child Psychology and Psychiatry, 21,* 5–18.

Jersild, A. T., & Holmes, F. B. (Eds.). (1935). *Children's fears* (Child Development Monograph No. 20). Chicago: University of Chicago Press.

Johnson, C. M. (1991). Infant and toddler sleep: A telephone survey of parents in one community. *Developmental and Behavioral Pediatrics, 12,* 108–114.

Johnson, F. L. (1984). Bone marrow transplantation. In W. W. Sutow, D. J. Fernbach, & T. J. Vietti (Eds.), *Clinical pediatric oncology* (3rd ed.). St. Louis: Mosby.

Johnson, J. H., & Van Bourgondien, M. E. (1977). Behavior therapy and encopresis: A selective review of the literature. *Journal of Clinical Child Psychology, 6,* 15–19.

Johnson, M. R., Whitt, J. K., & Martin, B. (1987). The effect of fantasy facilitation of anxiety in chronically ill and healthy children. *Journal of Pediatric Psychology, 12(2),* 273–284.

Johnson, R. C. (1969). Behavioral characteristics of phenylketonurics and matched controls. *American Journal of Mental Deficiency, 74,* 17–19.

Johnson, V. M., & Werner, R. A. (1975). *A step-by-step learning guide for retarded infants and children.* Syracuse, NY: Syracuse University Press.

Kaffman, M., & Elizur, E. (1983). Bereavement responses of kibbutz and nonkibbutz children following death of father. *Journal of Child Psychology and Psychiatry, 24,* 435–442.

Kagan, J. (1979). Structure and process in the human infant: The otogeny of mental representation. In M. Bornstein & W. Kessen (Eds.), *Psychological development from infancy: Image to intention.* Hillsdale, NJ: Erlbaum.

Kagan, J. (1984). *The nature of the child.* New York: Basic Books.

Kahn, J. V. (1978). Acceleration of object permanence with severely and profoundly retarded children. *AAESPH Review, 3,* 15–22.

Kahn, J. V. (1979). Applications of the Piagetian literature to severely and profoundly mentally retarded persons. *Mental Retardation, 17,* 273–280.

Kahn, J. V., Staerk, M., & Bonk, C. (1973). Role of counter conditioning in the treatment of asthma. *Journal of Psychometric Research, 17,* 389–392.

Kalichman, S. C. (1993). *Mandated reporting of suspected child abuse: Ethics, law, and policy.* Washington, DC: American Psychological Association.

Kalter, N., & Rubin, S. (1989). *School-based therapy groups for children of divorce.* Paper presented at the annual meeting of the American Psychological Association, New Orleans.

Kamphaus, R. W., & Reynolds, C. R. (1987). *Clinical and research applications of the K-ABC.* Circle Pines, MN: American Guidance Service.

Kanner, L. (1943). Autistic disturbances of affective contact. *Nervous Child, 2,* 217–250.

Kanner, L. (1972). *Child psychiatry,* (4th ed.). Springfield, IL: Charles C. Thomas.

Kaplan, R. M., Chadwick, M. W., & Schimmel, L. E. (1985). Social learning intervention to promote metabolic control in type 1 diabetes mellitus: Pilot experimental results. *Diabetes Care, 8,* 152–155.

Kashani, J. H., & Carlson, G. A. (1987). Seriously depressed preschoolers. *American Journal of Psychiatry, 144*(3), 348–350.

Kashani, J. H., Carlson, G. A., Beck, N. C., Hoeper, E. W., Corcoran, C. M., McAllister, J. A., Fallahi, C., Rosenberg, T. K., & Reid, J. C. (1987). Depression, depressive symptoms, and depressed mood among a community sample of adolescents. *American Journal of Psychiatry, 144,* 931–934.

Kashani, J. H., Holcomb, W. R., & Orvaschel, H. (1986). Depression and depressive symptoms in preschool children from the general population. *American Journal of Psychiatry, 143*(9), 1138–1143.

Kastrup, M. (1976). Psychic disorders among pre-school children in a geographically delimited area of Aarhus county, Denmark. *Acta Psychiatrica Scandinavica, 54,* 29–42.

Kaufman, A. S. (1982). An integrated review of almost a decade of research on the McCarthy Scales. In T. R. Kratochwill (Ed.), *Advances in school psychology,* (Vol. II, pp. 119–170). Hillsdale, NJ: Erlbaum.

Kaufman, A. S., & Kaufman, N. (1983). *Kaufman Assessment Battery for Children (K-ABC) interpretative manual.* Circle Pines, MN: American Guidance Service.

Kaufman, J., & Zigler, E. (1987). Do abused children become abusive parents? *American Journal of Orthopsychiatry, 57,* 186–192.

Kaufman, K., Coury, D., Pickrell, E., & McCleery, J. (1989). Munchausen syndrome: A survey of professionals' knowledge. *Child Abuse and Neglect, 13,* 141–148.

Kavanagh, K. A., Youngblade, L., Reid, J. B., & Fagot, B. I. (1988). Interactions between children and abusive versus control parents. *Journal of Clinical Child Psychology, 17,* 137–142.

Kazdin, A. E. (1984). *Behavior modification in applied settings.* Homewood, IL: Dorsey Press.

Kazdin, A. E. (1988). Childhood Depression. In E. J. Mash & L. G. Terdal (Eds.), *Behavioral assessment of childhood disorders* (2nd ed., pp. 157–195). New York: Guilford.

Kazdin, A. E. (1990). Childhood depression. *Journal of Child Psychology and Psychiatry, 31* (1), 121–160.

Kazdin, A. E, French, N. H., Unis, A. S., & Esveldt-Dawson, K. (1983). Assessment of childhood depression: Correspondence of child and parent ratings. *Journal of the American Academy of Child Psychiatry, 22,* 157–164.

Kazdin, A. E, French, N. H., Unis, A. S., Esveldt-Dawson, K., & Sherick, R. B. (1983). Hopelessness, depression and sucidal intent among psychiatrically disturbed inpatient children. *Journal of Consulting and Clinical Psychology, 51,* 504–510.

Kazdin, A. E., Rodgers, A., & Colbus, D. (1986). The Hopelessness Scale for Children: Psychometric characteristics and concurrent validity. *Journal of Consulting and Clinical Psychology, 54,* 241–245.

Keane, W. M. (1980, August). *Hypnosis with pediatric cancer patients: Giving control in an uncontrollable situation.* Paper presented at the meeting of the American Psychological Association, Montreal.

Kearsley, R. B., & Sigel, I.E. (Eds.). (1979). *Infants at risk: Assessment of cognitive functioning.* Hillsdale, NJ: Erlbaum.

Keener, M. A., Zeanah, C. H., & Anders, T. (1988). Infant temperament, sleep organization and nighttime parental interventions. *Pediatrics, 81,* 762–771.

Kehoe, P. (1987). *Something happened and I'm scared to tell.* Seattle, WA: Parenting Press.

Kelley, S. J. (1989). Stress responses of children to sexual abuse and ritualistic abuse in day care centers. *Journal of Interpersonal Violence, 4,* 502–513.

Kelley, S. J., Brant, R., & Waterman, J. (1993). Sexual abuse of children in day care centers. *Child Abuse and Neglect, 17,* 71–89.

Kelly, C. K. (1976). Play desensitization of fear of darkness in preschool children. *Behavior Research and Therapy, 14,* 79–81.

Kelly, J. B., & Wallerstein, J. S. (1976). The effects of parental divorce: I. The experience of the child in early latency. *American Journal of Orthopsychiatry, 46,* 20–32.

Kempe, C., & Helfer, R. (1972). *Helping the battered child and his family.* Philadelphia: J. B. Lippincott.

Kendall-Tackett, K. A., Williams, L. M., & Finkelhor, D. (1993). Impact of sexual abuse on children: A review and synthesis of recent empirical studies. *Psychological Bulletin, 113,* 164–180.

Kerby, F. D., & Tolar, H. C. (1970). Modification of preschool isolate behavior: A case study. *Journal of Applied Behavior Analysis, 3,* 309–314.

Kerr, A., & Stephenson, J. B. P. (1986). A study of the natural history of Rett syndrome in 23 girls. *American Journal of Medical Genetics, 24,* 77–83.

Kessler, J. W. (1966). *Psychopathology of childhood.* Englewood Cliffs, NJ: Prentice-Hall.

Kimmel, H. D., & Kimmel, E. (1970). An instrumental conditioning method for the treatment of enuresis. *Journal of Behavior Therapy and Experimental Psychiatry, 1,* 121–123.

King, N. J. (1993). Simple and social phobias. In T. H. Ollendick & R. J. Prinz (Eds.), *Advances in clinical child psychology* (Vol. 15). New York: Plenum.

Kinzynski, L., Kochanska, G., Radke-Yarrow, M., & Girnius-Brown, O. (1987). A developmental interpretation of young children's noncompliance. *Developmental Psychology, 23,* 799–806.

Kirk, S., McCarthy, J., & Kirk, W. (1968). *The Illinois Test of Psycholinguistic Abilities.* Urbana, IL: University of Illinois Press.

Klackenberg, G. (1949). Thumbsucking: Frequency and etiology. *Pediatrics, 4,* 418–424.

Klackenberg, G. (1971). Rhythmic movements in infancy and early childhood. *Acta Paediatrica Scandinavica, 224,* 74–83.

Klackenberg, G. (1982). Sleep behaviour studied longitudinally: Data from 4–16 years on duration, night-awakening, and bed-sharing. *Acta Paediatrica Scandinavica, 71,* 501–506.

Klauber, G. T. (1989). Clinical efficacy and safety of desmopressin in the treatment of nocturnal enuresis. *Journal of Pediatrics, 114,* 719–722.

Klee, S., & Garfinkel, B. (1984). Identification of depression in children and adolescents: The role of the DST. *Journal of the American Academy of Child Psychiatry, 4,* 410–415.

Kleinknecht, R. A. (1991). *Mastering anxiety: The nature and treatment of anxious conditions.* New York: Plenum.

Klesges, R. C., Malott, J. M., & Ugland, M. (1984). The effects of graded exposure and parent modeling on the dental phobias of a four-year-old girl and her mother. *Journal of Behavior Therapy and Experimental Psychiatry, 15,* 161–164.

Klinger, L. G., & Dawson, G. (1992). Facilitating early social and communicative development in children with autism. In S. F. Warren & J. Reichle (Eds.), *Causes and effects in communication and language intervention* (pp. 157–186). Baltimore: Paul H. Brookes.

Kochanska, G., Kuczynski, L., & Radke-Yarrow, M. (1989). Correspondence between mother's self-reported and observed child-rearing practices. *Child Development, 60,* 56–63.

Koegel, R. L., Schreibman, L., Britten, K. R., Burke, J. C., & O'Neill, R. E. (1982). A comparison of parent training to direct clinic treatment. In R. L. Koegel, A. Rincover, & A. L. Egel (Eds.), *Educating and understanding autistic children.* San Diego: College Hill Press.

Kohen, D. P., Olness, K. N., Cornwell, S. D., & Heimel, A. (1984). The use of relaxation-mental imagery (self-hypnosis) in the management of 505 pediatric behavioral encounters. *Journal of Developmental and Behavioral Pediatrics, 5,* 21–25.

Kohlenberg, R. J. (1973). Operant conditioning of human anal sphincter pressure. *Journal of Applied Behavior Analysis, 6,* 201–208.

Kolb, B., & Whishaw, I. Q. (1991). *Fundamentals of human neuropsychology* (3rd ed.). New York: W. H. Freeman.

Kolko, D. J., & Kazdin, A. E. (1990). Matchplay and firesetting in children: Relationship to parent, marital, and family dysfunction. *Journal of Clinical Child Psychology, 19,* 229–238.

Kolko, D. J., & Richard-Figuero, J. L. (1985). Effects of video games on the adverse corollaries of chemotherapy in pediatric oncology patients: A single-case analysis. *Journal of Consulting and Clinical Psychology, 53,* 223–228.

Kolvin, I. (1971). Studies in childhood psychoses: I. Diagnostic criteria and classification. *British Journal of Psychiatry, 118,* 381–384.

Kolvin, I., & Fundudis, T. (1982). Elective mute children: Psychological, developmental and background factors. *Annual Progress in Child Psychiatry and Child Development, 22,* 484–501.

Kolvin, I., Humphrey, M., & McNay, A. (1971). Studies in childhood psychoses: VI. Cognitive factors in childhood psychoses. *British Journal of Psychiatry, 118,* 415–419.

Konstantareas, M. M., & Homatidis, S. (1989). Assessing child symptom severity and stress in parents of autistic children. *Journal of Child Psychology and Psychiatry, 30,* 459–470.

Koocher, G. P. (1980). Initial consultations with the pediatric cancer patient. In J. Kellerman (Ed.), *Psychological aspects of childhood cancer* (pp. 231–237). Springfield, IL: Charles C Thomas.

Koocher, G. P. (1983). Grief and loss in childhood. In C. E. Walker & M. C. Roberts (Eds.), *Handbook of clinical child psychology* (pp. 1273–1284). New York: Wiley.

Koocher, G. P., & Gudar, L. J. (1992) Grief and loss in childhood. In C. E. Walker & M. C. Roberts (Eds.), *Handbook of clinical child psychology* (2nd ed., pp. 1025–1034). New York: Wiley.

Kotelchuck, C. M. (1980). Nonorganic failure to thrive: The status of interactional and environmental etiologic theories. In B. Camp (Ed.), *Advances in behavioral pediatrics.* Greenwich, CT: JAI Press.

Kotelchuck, M. (1977). *Child abuse: Prediction and misclassification.* Presented at the Conference on Prediction of Child Abuse, Wilmington, DE.

Kovacs, M., & Beck, A. T. (1977). An empirical clinical approach towards a definition of childhood depression. In J. G. Schulterbrandt & A. Raskin (Eds.), *Depression in children: Diagnosis, treatment, and conceptual models* (pp. 1–25). New York: Raven Press.

Kovacs, M., Feinberg, T. L., Crouse-Novak, M. A., Paulauskas, S. L., & Finkelstein, R. (1984). Depressive disorders in childhood: I. A longitudinal prospective study of characteristics and recovery. *Archives of General Psychiatry, 41,* 229–237.

Kratochwill, T. R. (1981). *Selective mutism: Implications for research and treatment.* Hillsdale, NJ: Erlbaum.

Krause, M. K., & Mahan, L. K. (1984). *Food, nutrition, and diet therapy: A textbook of nutritional care* (7th ed.) Philadelphia: Saunders.

Krieger, I. (1982). *Pediatric disorders of feeding, nutrition, and metabolism.* New York: Wiley.

Kushkin, K. (1981). *Night again.* Boston: Little, Brown.

Kuttner, L. (1984). *Psychological treatment of distress, pain, and anxiety for young children with cancer.* Unpublished doctoral dissertation, Simon Frazer University, Burnaby, BC.

LaBaw, W., Holton, C., Tewell, K., & Eccles, D. (1975). The use of self-hypnosis by children with cancer. *American Journal of Clinical Hypnosis, 17,* 233–238.

Labbe, E. E., & Williamson, D. A. (1983). Temperature biofeedback in the treatment of children with migraine headaches. *Journal of Pediatric Psychology, 8,* 317–323.

Labbe, E. E., & Williamson, D. A. (1984). Behavioral treatment of elective mutism: A review of the literature. *Clinical Psychology Review, 4,* 273–292.

Ladd, G. W., & Price, J. M. (1987). Predicting children's social and school adjustment following the transition from preschool to kindergarten. *Child Development, 58,* 1168–1189.

Lake, C. R., Mikkelson, E. J., Rapoport, J. L., Zavadil, A. P., & Kopin, I. J. (1979). Effects of imipramine on norepinephrine and blood pressure in enuretic boys. *Clinical Pharmacology and Therapeutics, 26,* 647–653.

Lampley, D. A., & Rust, J. O. (1986). Validation of the Kaufman Assessment Battery for Children with a sample of preschool children. *Psychology in the Schools, 23,* 131–137.

Lang, P. J. (1979). A bio-informational theory of emotional imagery. *Psychophysiology, 16,* 495–512.

Lang, P. J., & Melamed, B. G. (1969). Avoidance conditioning therapy of an infant with chronic ruminative vomiting. *Journal of Abnormal Psychology, 74,* 139–142.

Langlois, J. H., & Downs, A. C. (1980). Mothers, fathers and peers as socialization agents of sex-typed play behaviors in young children. *Child Development, 51,* 1217–1247.

Last, C. G. (1992). Anxiety disorders in childhood and adolescence. In W. M. Reynolds (Ed.), *Internalizing disorders in children and adolescents* (pp. 61–106). New York: Wiley.

Last, C. G., & Francis, G. (1988). School phobia. In B. B. Lahey & A. E. Kazdin (Eds.), *Advances in clinical child psychology* (Vol. 11, pp. 193–222). New York: Plenum.

Last, C. G., Francis, G., Hersen, M., Kazdin, A. E., & Strauss, C. C. (1987). Separation anxiety and school phobia: A comparison using DSM-III criteria. *American Journal of Psychiatry, 144,* 653–657.

Last, C. G., Perrin, S., Hersen, M., & Kazdin, A. E. (1991). *DSM-III-R anxiety disorders in children: Sociodemographic and clinical characteristics.* Manuscript submitted for publication.

Last, C. G., Strauss, C. C., & Francis, G. (1987). Comorbidity among childhood anxiety disorders. *Journal of Nervous and Mental Disease, 175,* 726–730.

Lawton, C., France, K. G., & Blampied, N. M. (1991). Treatment of infant sleep disturbance by graduated extinction. *Child and Family Behavior Therapy, 13,* 39–56.

Learning Through Entertainment. (1993). *It's sleepy time*. Los Angeles, CA: Author. [Videotape available from Western Psychological Services, 12031 Wilshire Boulevard, Los Angeles, CA 90025–1251.]

Lebenthal, E., Rossi, T. M., Nord, K. S., & Branski, D. (1981). Recurrent abdominal pain and lactose absorption in children. *Pediatrics, 67*, 828–832.

Lefkowitz, M. M., & Tesiny, E. P. (1980). Assessment of childhood depression. *Journal of Consulting and Clinical Psychology, 48*, 43–50.

Lerner, J. A., Inui, T. S., Trupin, E. W., & Douglas, E. (1985). Preschool behavior can predict future psychiatric disorders. *Journal of the American Academy of Child Psychiatry, 24*, 42–48.

Lesse, S. (1974). *Masked depression*. New York: Jason Aronson.

Lester, B. M., & Zeskind, P. S. (1978). The organization of crying in the infant-at-risk. In T. Field (Ed.), *The high risk newborn*. New York: Spectrum.

Levine, M. D. (1981). Schoolchild with encopresis. *Pediatrics in Review, 2*(9), 285–290.

Levine, M. D. (1982). Encopresis: Its potentiation, evaluation, and alleviation. *Pediatric Clinics of North America, 29*, 315–329.

Levine, M. D., & Bakow, H. (1976). Children with encopresis: A study of treatment outcome. *Pediatrics, 58*, 845–852.

Levine, M. D., Mazonson, P., & Bakow, H. (1980). Behavioral symptom substitution in children cured of encopresis. *American Journal of Diseases of Children, 134*, 663–667.

Lewinsohn, P. H. (1974). A behavioral approach to depression. In R. J. Friedman & M. M. Katz (Eds.), *The psychology of depression: Contemporary theory and research*. New York: Holt, Rinehart & Winston.

Lewis, D. O., Mallouh, C., & Webb, V. (1989). Child abuse, delinquency, and violent criminality. In D. Cicchetti & V. Carlson (Eds.), *Child maltreatment: Theory and research on the causes and consequences of child abuse and neglect* (pp. 707–721). New York: Cambridge University Press.

Lewis, M., & Coates, D. L. (1980). Mother–infant interaction and cognitive development in twelve-week-old infants. *Infant Behavior and Development, 3*, 95–105.

Lewis, M., Stanger, C., & Sullivan, M. M. (1989). Deception in 3-year-olds. *Developmental Psychology, 25*, 439–443.

Lewy, A. L., & Dawson, G. (1992). Social stimulation and joint attention in young autistic children. *Journal of Abnormal Child Psychology, 20*, 555–566.

Lidz, C. S., & Ballester, L. E. (1986). Diagnostic implications of the McCarthy Scale General Cognitive Index/Binet IQ discrepancies for low-socioeconomic-status preschool children. *Journal of School Psychology, 24*, 381–385.

Lifshitz, M., & Chovers, A. (1972). Encopresis among Israeli Kibbutz children. *Israel Annals of Psychiatry and Related Disciplines, 4*, 326–340.

Lindqvist, B. (1972). Bruxism and emotional disturbance. *Odontologisk Revy, 23*, 231–242.

Linscheid, T. R. (1978). Disturbances in eating and feeding. In P. Magrab (Ed.), *Psychological management of pediatric problems* (pp. 189–203). Baltimore: University Park Press.

Linscheid, T. R. (1992). Eating problems in children. In C. E. Walker & M. C. Roberts (Eds.), *Handbook of clinical child psychology* (pp. 451–473). New York: Wiley.

Linscheid, T. R., Tarnowski, K. J., & Richmond, D. A. (1988). Behavioral approaches to anorexia nervosa, bulimia and obesity. In D. K. Routh (Ed.), *Handbook of pediatric psychology* (pp. 332–362). New York: Guilford.

Litrownik, A. J., & Freitas, J. L. (1980). Self-monitoring in moderately retarded adolescents: Reactivity and accuracy as a function of valence. *Behavior Therapy, 11,* 245–255.

Loadman, W., Arnold, K., Volmer, R., Petrella, R., & Cooper, L. (1987). Reducing the symptoms of infant colic by introduction of a vibration/sound based intervention. *Pediatric Research, 21,* 182A.

Lobovitz, D. A., & Handal, P. J. (1985). Childhood depression: Prevalence using DSM-III criteria and validity of parent and child depression scales. *Journal of Pediatric Psychology, 10,* 45–54.

Locke, H. J., & Wallace, K. M. (1959). Short-term marital adjustment and prediction tests: Their reliability and validity. *Journal of Marriage and Family Living, 21,* 251–255.

Loeber, R., Green, S. M., Lahey, B. B., Christ, M. A., & Frick, P. J. (1992). Developmental sequences in the age of onset of disruptive child behaviors. *Journal of Child and Family Studies, 1,* 21–41.

Loeber, R., & Schmalling, K. B. (1985). Empirical evidence for overt and covert patterns of antisocial conduct problems: A meta-analysis. *Journal of Abnormal Child Psychology, 13,* 337–352.

Lollar, D. J., Smits, S. J., & Patterson, D. L. (1982). Assessment of pediatric pain: An empirical perspective. *Journal of Pediatric Psychology, 7,* 267–277.

Lombardo, V. S., & Lombardo, E. F. (1986). *Kids grieve too!* Springfield, IL: Charles C. Thomas.

Londerville, S., & Main, M. (1981). Security of attachment, compliance, and maternal training methods in the second year of life. *Developmental Psychology, 17,* 289–299.

Long, S. (1986). Guidelines for treating young children. In K. MacFarlane, J. Waterman, S. Conerly, L. Damon, M. Durfee, & S. Long (Eds.), *Sexual abuse of young children* (pp. 220–243). New York: Guilford.

Lonigan, C. J., Fischel, J. E., Whitehurst, G. J., Arnold, D. S., & Valdez-Menchaca, M. C. (1992). The role of otitis media in the development of expressive language disorder. *Developmental Psychology, 28,* 430–440.

Lord, C. (1993). Early social development in autism. In E. Schopler, M. E. Van Bourgondien, & M. M. Bristol (Eds.), *Preschool issues in autism* (pp. 61–94). New York: Plenum.

Lord, C., Bristol, M. M., & Schopler, E. (1993). Early intervention for children with autism and related developmental disorders. In E. Schopler, M. E. Van Bourgondien, & M. M. Bristol (Eds.), *Preschool issues in autism* (pp. 61–94). New York: Plenum.

Lovaas, O. I. (1981). *Teaching developmentally disabled children: The ME book.* Austin, TX: Pro-Ed.

Lovaas, O. I. (1987). Behavioral treatment and normal educational and intellectual functioning in young autistic children. *Journal of Consulting and Clinical Psychology, 55,* 3–9.

Lovaas, O. I., & Simmons, J. Q. (1969). Manipulation of self-destruction in three retarded children. *Journal of Applied Behavioral Analyis, 2,* 143–157.

Lovaas, O. I., & Smith, T. (1988). Intensive behavioral treatment for young autistic children. In B. B. Lahey & A. Kazdin (Eds.), *Advances in clinical child psychology,* (Vol. 11, pp. 285–324). New York: Plenum.

Lowe, K., & Lutzker, J. R. (1979). Increasing compliance to a medical regime with a juvenile diabetic. *Behavior Therapy, 10,* 57–64.

Lowrey, L. G. (1940). Personality distortion and early institutional care. *American Journal of Orthopsychiatry, 10,* 576–585.

Lusk, R., & Waterman, J. (1986). Effects of sexual abuse on children. In K. MacFarlane, J. Waterman, S. Conerly, L. Damon, M. Durfee, & S. Long (Eds.), *Sexual abuse of young children* (pp. 101–120). New York: Guilford.

Lutzker, J. R., & Rice, J. M. (1984). Project 12 Ways: Measuring outcome of a large in-home service for the treatment of child abuse and neglect. *Child Abuse and Neglect, 8,* 141–155.

Lyon, M. A., & Smith, D. K. (1986). A comparison of at-risk preschool children's performance on the K-ABC, McCarthy Scales, and Stanford-Binet. *Journal of Psychoeducational Assessment, 4,* 35–43.

MacDonald, J. D., Blott, J. P., Gordon, K., Spiegel, B., & Hartmann, M. (1974). An experimental parent-assisted treatment program for preschool language-delayed children. *Journal of Speech and Hearing Disorders, 39,* 395–415.

MacFarlane, A. (1977). *The psychology of childbirth.* Cambridge, MA: Harvard University Press.

Madden, N. A., Russo, D. C., & Cataldo, M. F. (1980). Behavior treatment of pica in children with lead poisoning. *Child Behavior Therapy, 2,* 67–81.

Magid, D., & Schriebman, W. (1980). *Divorce is...: A kids' coloring book.* Gretna, LA: Pelican.

Magnusson, E., & Naucler, K. (1990). Reading and spelling in language-disordered children—linguistic and metalinguistic prerequisites: Report on a longitudinal study. *Clinical Linguistics and Phonetics, 4,* 49–61.

Mahoney, M. J., & Mahoney, K. (1976). Self-control techniques with the mentally retarded. *Exceptional Children, 42,* 338–339.

Malinosky-Rummell, R., & Hansen, D. J. (1993). Long-term consequences of childhood physical abuse. *Psychological Bulletin, 114,* 68–79.

Maloney, M. J., & Klykylo, W. M. (1983). An overview of anorexia nervosa, bulimia and obesity in children and adolescents. *Journal of the American Academy of Child Psychiatry, 22,* 99–107.

Mansdorf, I. J. (1977). Reinforcer isolation: An alternative to subject isolation in time-out from positive reinforcement. *Journal of Behavior Therapy and Experimental Psychiatry, 8,* 391–393.

Mansdorf, I. J., & Lukens, E. (1987). Cognitive-behavioral psychotherapy for separation anxious children exhibiting school phobia. *Journal of the American Academy of Child and Adolescent Psychiatry, 70,* 222–225.

Marcus, L. M., Lansing, M. D., Andrews, C. E., & Schopler, E. (1978). Improvement of teaching effectiveness in parents of autistic children. *Journal of the American Academy of Child Psychiatry, 17,* 625–639.

Marcus, L. M., & Schopler, E. (1989). Parents as co-therapists with autistic children. In C. E. Schaefer & J. M. Briesmeister (Eds.), *Handbook of parent training: Parents as co-therapists for children's behavior problems* (pp. 337–360). New York: Wiley.

Marcus, L. M., & Stone, W. L. (1993). Assessment of the young autistic child. In E. Schopler, M. E. Van Bourgondien, & M. M. Bristol (Eds.), *Preschool issues in autism* (pp. 149–173). New York: Plenum.

Marfo, K., & Kysela, G. M. (1984). Early intervention with mentally handicapped children: A critical appraisal of applied research. *Journal of Pediatric Psychology, 10,* 305–324.

Marion, R. J., Creer, T. L., & Burns, K. L. (1983). Training asthmatic children to use a nebulizer correctly. *Journal of Asthma, 20,* 183–188.

Maristo, A. A., & German, M. L. (1986). Reliability, predictive validity, and interrelationships of early assessment indices used with developmentally delayed infants and children. *Journal of Clinical Child Psychology, 4,* 327–332.

Marks, I. (1969). *Fears and phobias*. New York: Academic Press.

Marks, I. (1987). The development of normal fear: A review. *Journal of Child Psychiatry, 28*, 667–697.

Martinez, G., & Nalezienski, J. (1981). 1980 update: The recent trend in breastfeeding. *Pediatrics, 67*, 260.

Masek, B. J. (1982). *Behavioral medicine treatment of pediatric migraine*. Paper presented at the meeting of the Society of Behavioral Medicine, Chicago.

Masek, B. J., & Hoag, N. L. (1990). Headache. In A. M. Gross & R. S. Drabman (Eds.), *Handbook of clinical behavioral pediatrics* (pp. 291–309). New York: Plenum.

Mash, E. J., & Terdal, L. (1973). Modifications of mother–child interactions: Playing with children. *Mental Retardation, 11*, 44–49.

Masterman, S. H., & Reams, R. (1988). Support groups for bereaved preschool and school-aged children. *American Journal of Orthopsychiatry, 58*, 562–570.

Matson, J. L., & DiLorenzo, T. M. (1984). *Punishment and its alternatives*. New York: Springer.

Matson, J. L., Esvelt-Dawson, K., Andrasik, F., Ollendick, T. H., Petti, T. A., & Hersen, M. (1980). Observation and generalization effects of social skills training with emotionally disturbed children. *Behavior Therapy, 11*, 522–531.

McAuliffe, W. E., Doering, S., Breer, P., Silverman, H., Branson, B., & Williams, K. (1987, June). *An evaluation of using ex-addict outreach workers to educate intravenous drug users about AIDS prevention*. Paper presented at the 3rd International Conference on AIDS, Washington, DC.

McCarthy, D. A. (1972). *Manual for the McCarthy Scales of Children's Abilities*. San Antonio: Psychological Corporation.

McConaghy, N. (1969). A controlled trial of imipramine, amphetamine, pad-and-bell conditioning and nocturnal awakening in the treatment of nocturnal enuresis. *Medical Journal of Australia, 2*, 237–239.

McCormick, C. E., & Mason, J. M. (1986). Intervention procedures for increasing preschool children's interest in and knowledge about reading. In W. H. Teale & E. Sulzby (Eds.), *Emergent literacy: Writing and reading* (pp. 90–115). Norwood, NJ: Ablex.

McDermott, J. (1968). Parental divorce in early childhood. *American Psychologist, 124*, 1424–1432.

McElreath, L. H., & Eisenstadt, T. H. (1994). Child directed interaction : Family play therapy for developmentally delayed preschoolers. In C. E. Schaefer & L. Carey (Eds.), *Family play therapy*. New Jersey: Jason Aronson.

McFadden, E. R., Jr. (1980). Asthma: Pathophysiology. *Seminars in Respiratory Medicine, 1*, 297–303.

McGee, R., Partridge, F., Williams, S., & Silva, P. A. (1991). A twelve-year follow-up of preschool hyperactive children. *Journal of the American Academy of Child and Adolescent Psychiatry, 30*, 224–232.

McGee, R., Williams, S., & Feehan, M. (1992). Attention deficit disorder and age of onset of problem behaviors. *Journal of Abnormal Child Psychology, 20*, 487–502.

McGregor, H. G. (1937). Enuresis in children: A report of 70 cases. *British Medical Journal, 1*, 1061–1063.

McKendry, J. B. J., Stewart, D. A., Jeffs, R. D., & Mozes, A. (1972). Enuresis treated by an improved waking apparatus. *Canadian Medical Association Journal, 106*, 27–29.

McKnew, D. H., Cytryn, L., Efron, A. M., Gershon, E. S., & Bunney, E. W. (1979). Offspring of patients with affective disorders. *British Journal of Psychiatry, 134*, 148–152.

McMahon, R. J., & Forehand, R. (1988). Conduct disorders. In E. J. Mash and L. G. Terdal (Eds.), *Behavioral assessment of childhood disorders* (2nd ed., pp. 105–153). New York: Guilford.

McNally, R. J. (1991). Assessment of posttraumatic stress disorder in children. *Psychological Assessment, 3,* 531–537.

McNeil, C. B., Eyberg, S. M., Eisenstadt, T. H., Newcomb, K., & Funderburk, B. (1991). Parent-Child Interaction Therapy with behavior problem children: Generalization of treatment effects to the school setting. *Journal of Clinical Child Psychology, 20,* 140–151.

McReynolds, M. T. (1972). A procedure for the withdrawal of an infant oral pacifier. *Journal of Applied Behavior Analysis, 5,* 65–66.

McTaggert, A., & Scott., M. A. (1979). A review of twelve cases of encopresis. *Journal of Pediatrics, 54,* 762–768.

Meadow, R. (1977). Munchausen syndrome by proxy: The hinterland of child abuse. *Lancet, 11,* 343–345.

Meichenbaum, D. (1977). *Cognitive behavior modification.* New York, Plenum.

Melamed, B. G., & Siegel, L. J. (1975). Reduction of anxiety in children facing hospitalization and surgery by use of filmed modeling. *Journal of Consulting and Clinical Psychology, 43,* 511–521.

Mellonie, B., & Ingpen, R. (1983). *Lifetimes: The Beautiful Way to Explain Death to Children.* New York: Bantam Books.

Melton, G. B. (1992). The improbability of prevention of sexual abuse. In D. J. Willis, E. W. Holden, & M. Rosenberg (Eds.), *Prevention of child maltreatment: Developmental and ecological perspectives.* New York: Wiley.

Melyn, M. A, & White, D. T. (1973). Mental and developmental milestones of noninstitutionalized Down's syndrome children. *Pediatrics, 52,* 542–545.

Mendelson, M. (1974). *Psychoanalytic concepts of depression* (2nd ed.). New York: Spectrum.

Mendlewicz, J., & Rainer, J. D. (1977). Adoption study supporting genetic transmission in manic-depressive illness. *Nature, 268,* 327–329.

Menkes, J. H. (1985). *Textbook of child neurology* (3rd ed.). Philadelphia: Lea & Febiger.

Meyendorf, R. (1971). Infant depression due to separation from siblings syndrome or depression retardation starvation and neurological symptoms: A reevaluation of the concept of material deprivation. *Psychiatric Clinics, 4,* 321–335.

Meyers, L. F., & Fogel, P. (1985). Exploratory play [computer program]. Santa Monica, CA: Peal Software.

Mikkelsen, E. J., Rapoport, J. L., Nee, L., Gruenau, E., Mendelson, W., & Gillin, J. L. (1980). Childhood enuresis: Sleep patterns and psychopathology. *Archives of General Psychiatry, 37,* 1139–1145.

Miller, A. J., & Kratochwill, T. R. (1979). Reduction of frequent stomachache complaints by time out. *Behavior Therapy, 10,* 211–218.

Miller, J. F., & Yoder, D. E. (1974). An ontogenetic language teaching strategy for retarded children. In R. R. Schiefelbusch & L. L. Lloyd (Eds.), *Language perspectives—acquisition, retardation, and intervention.* Baltimore: University Park Press.

Miller, L. C. (1983). Fears and anxiety in children. In C. E. Walker & M. C. Roberts (Eds.), *Handbook of clinical child psychology* (pp. 337–380). New York: Wiley.

Miller, L. C., Barrett, C. L., Hampe, E., & Noble, H. (1971). Revised anxiety scales for the Louisville Behavioral Checklist. *Psychological Reports, 29,* 503–511.

Miller, L. C., Barrett, C. L., Hampe, E., & Noble, H. (1972a). Comparison of reciprocal inhibition psychotherapy and waiting list control for phobic children. *Journal of Abnormal Psychology, 79*, 269–279.

Miller, L. C., Barrett, C. L., Hampe, E., & Noble, H. (1972b). Factor structure of childhood fears. *Journal of Consulting an Clinical Psychology, 39*, 264–268.

Millichap, J. G. (1968). *Febrile convulsions.* New York: Macmillan.

Millican, F. K., & Lourie, R. S. (1970). The child with pica and his family. In E. Anthony & E. Koupernik (Eds.), *The child in the family* (pp. 48–61). New York: Wiley.

Milner, J. S. (1986). *The Child Abuse Potential Inventory: Manual (Revised).* Webster, NC: Psytec Corporation.

Minde, K. K., & Minde, R. (1981). Psychiatric intervention in infancy. *Journal of the American Academy of Child Psychiatry, 20*, 217–238.

Mira, M., & Cairns, C. (1981). Intervention in the interaction of a mother and child with nonorganic failure to thrive. *Pediatric Nursing, 7*(2), 41–45.

Mitchell, W. G., & Greenberg, R. (1980). Failure to thrive: A study in a primary care setting. *Pediatrics, 65*, 971–977.

Money, J., & Annecillo, C. (1976). I. Q. change following change of domicile in the syndrome of reversible hyposomatotropinism (psychosocial dwarfism): Pilot investigation. *Psychoneuroendocrinology, 1*, 427–429.

Money, J., & Ehrhardt, A. A. (1972). *Man and woman: Boy and girl: The differentiation and dimorphism of gender identity from conception to maturity.* Baltimore: Johns Hopkins University Press.

Moore, J. (1982). Project Thrive: A supportive treatment approach to the parents of children with nonorganic failure to thrive. *Child Development, 61*(6), 389–398.

Morris, T. N. (1980). *Goodnight, dear monster.* New York: Alfred A. Knopf.

Moustakas, C. (1966). *The child's discovery of himself.* New York: Ballantine.

Mowrer, O. H., & Mowrer, W. M. (1938). Enuresis: A method for its study and treatment. *American Journal of Orthopsychiatry, 8*, 436–459.

Mowrer, O. H. (1960). *Learning theory and behavior.* New York: Wiley.

Mrazek, P. J., & Mrazek, D. A. (1987). Resiliency in child maltreatment victims: A conceptual exploration. *Child Abuse and Neglect, 11*, 357–366.

Muellner, S. R. (1960). Development of urinary control in children: A new concept in cause, prevention and treatment of primary enuresis. *Journal of Urology, 84*, 714–716.

Mulhern, R. K., Fairclough, D. L., Smith, B., & Douglas, S. M. (1992). Maternal depression, assessment methods, and physical symptoms affect estimates of depressive symptomatology among children with cancer. *Journal of Pediatric Psychology, 17*(3), 313–326.

Mulick, J. A., Hoyt, P., Rojahn, J., & Schroeder, S. R. (1978). Reduction of a "nervous habit" in a profoundly retarded youth by increasing toy play. *Journal of Behavior Therapy and Experimental Psychiatry, 9*, 381–385.

Murray, P. L., & Mayer, R. E. (1988). Preschool children's judgements of number magnitude. *Journal of Educational Psychology, 80*, 206–209.

Nader, H. L., & Ben-Yoseph, Y. (1984). Genetics. In L. Taussig (Ed.), *Cystic fibrosis* (pp. 10–24). New York: Thieme Stratton.

Nadler, S. C. (1973). Facts about dental bruxism. *Journal of Dentistry, 43*, 153.

Naiman, J. L., Rolsky, J. T., & Sherman, S. B. (1976). The effects of fatal illness in the child on family life. In V. C. Vaughan & T. B. Brazelton, (Eds.), *The family—Can it be saved*. Chicago: Year Book Medical Publishers.

National Center on Child Abuse and Neglect. (1978). *Child sexual abuse: Incest, assault, and sexual exploitation. A special report*. Washington, DC: Author.

National Center on Child Abuse and Neglect. (1988). *Study of national incidence and prevalence of child abuse and neglect: 1988*. Washington, DC: Author.

National Committee for Prevention of Child Abuse (1993). *Current trends in child abuse reporting and fatalities: The results of the 1992 annual fifty state survey*. Chicago: Author.

National Institute of Neurological and Communicative Disorders and Stroke (NINCDS). (1979). *Technical document of the panel on developmental neurological disorders to the national advisory neurological and communicative disorders and stroke council*. Bethesda, MD: U.S. Department of Health and Human Services.

Neisworth, J. T., & Moore, F. (1972). Operant treatment of asthmatic responding with the parent as therapist. *Behavior Therapy, 3*, 95–99.

Nelson, K. B., & Ellenberg, J. H. (1978). Prognosis in children with febrile seizures. *Pediatrics, 61*, 720–727.

Nemiroff, M. A., & Annunziata, J. (1990). *A child's first book about play therapy*. Washington, DC: American Psychological Association.

Nettelbeck, T., & Langeluddecke, P. (1979). Dry-bed training without an enuresis machine. *Behaviour Research and Therapy, 17*, 403–404.

Newberger, E. H., Reed, R. R, Daniel, J. H., Hyde, J., & Kotelchuck, M. (1977). Pediatric social illness: Toward an etiological classification. *Pediatrics, 60*, 175–185.

New York State Department of Mental Hygiene. (1955). A special census of suspected and referred mental retardation in Onondaga County, New York. *Technical Report of the Mental Health Research Unit*. Syracuse: Syracuse University Press.

Nielson, J. (1970). Criminality among patients with Klinefelter's syndrome and XYY syndrome. *British Journal of Psychiatry, 117*, 365–369.

Nisley, D. D. (1976). Medical overview of the management of encopresis. *Journal of Pediatric Psychology, 4*, 33–34.

Niswander, K. R., & Gordon, M. (1972). *The women and their pregnancies* (Vol. 1). Philadelphia: Saunders.

Nitsche, R., Humphrey, G. B., Sexauer, C. L., Catron, B., Wunder, S., & Jay, S. (1982). Therapeutic choices made by patients with end-stage cancer. *Journal of Pediatrics, 101*, 471–476.

Norris, J. A., & Hoffman, P. R. (1990). Language intervention within naturalistic environments. *Language, Speech, and Hearing Services in Schools, 21*, 72–84.

O'Conner, R. D. (1972). Relative efficacy of modeling, shaping, and the combined procedures for modification of social withdrawal. *Journal of Abnormal Psychology, 79*, 327–334.

O'Donavan, J. D., & Bradstock, A. S. (1979). The failure of conventional drug therapy in the management of infantile colic. *American Journal of Diseases of Children, 133*, 999.

Ollendick, T. H. (1983). Reliability and validity of the Revised Fear Survey Schedule for Children (FSSC-R). *Behaviour Research and Therapy, 21*, 685–692.

Ollendick, T. H., & Cerny, J. A. (1981). *Clinical behavior therapy with children*. New York: Plenum.

Ollendick, T. H., & Francis, G. (1988). Behavioral assessment and treatment of childhood phobias. *Behavior Modification, 12*, 165–204.

Ollendick, T. H., Hagopian, L. P., & Hutzinger, R. M. (1991). Cognitive-behavior therapy with nighttime fearful children. *Journal of Behavior Therapy and Experimental Psychiatry, 22,* 113–121.

Ollendick, T. H., & King, N. J. (1991). Fears and phobias of childhood. In M. Hervert (Ed.), *Clinical child psychology. Social learning, development and behaviour* (pp. 309–329). Chichester, England: Wiley.

Ollendick, T. H., & Mayer, J. A. (1984). School phobia. In S. M. Turner (Ed.), *Behavioral treatment of anxiety disorders* (pp. 367–406). New York: Plenum.

Olley, J. G., Robbins, F. R., & Morelli-Robbins, M. (1993). Current practices in early intervention for children with autism. In E. Schopler, M. E. Van Bourgondien, & M. M. Bristol (Eds.), *Preschool issues in autism* (pp. 223–245). New York: Plenum.

Olness, K. (1981). Imagery (self-hypnosis) as adjunct therapy in childhood cancer: Clinical experience with 25 patients. *American Journal of Pediatric Hematology/Oncology, 3,* 313–321.

Olness, K., & MacDonald, J. (1981). Self-hypnosis and biofeedback in the management of juvenile migraine. *Developmental and Behavioral Pediatrics, 2,* 168–170.

Olson, R. A., Huszti, H. C., Mason, P. J., & Seibert, J. M. (1989). Pediatric AIDS/HIV infection: An emerging challenge to pediatric psychology. *Journal of Pediatric Psychology, 14,* 1–21.

Olson, S. L., & Brodfeld, P. (1991). Assessment of peer rejection and externalizing behavior problems in preschool boys: A short-term longitudinal study. *Journal of Abnormal Child Psychology, 19,* 493–503.

Opitz, J. M., & Lewin, S. (1987). Rett syndrome—A review and discussion of syndrome delineation. *Brain and Development, 9,* 445–450.

Orenstein, D., Henke, K., & Cherny, F. (1983). Exercise in cystic fibrosis. *Physician and Sports Medicine, 11,* 57–63.

Ornitz, E. M. (1985). Should autistic children be treated with haloperidol? *American Journal of Psychiatry, 142,* 883–884.

Orvaschel, H., Walsh-Allis, G., & Ye, W. (1988). Psychopathology in children of parents with recurrent depression. *Journal of Abnormal Child Psychology, 16,* 17–28.

Ott, J., Eisenstadt, T. H., Eugrin, C., & Frick, P. J. (in press). DSM-III-R and DSM-IV criteria for attention deficit disorders: Applicability to young children. *Journal of Child Psychology and Psychiatry.*

Ovellette, E. M., Rosett, H. L., Rosman, N. P., & Weiner, L. (1977). Adverse effects on offspring of maternal alcohol abuse during pregnancy. *New England Journal of Medicine, 297,* 528–530.

Ozonoff, S., Rogers, S. J., & Pennington, B. F. (1991). Asperger's syndrome: Evidence of an empirical distinction from high-functioning autism. *Journal of Child Psychology and Psychiatry, 32,* 1107–1122.

Paget, K. D., Philp, J. D., & Abramczyk, L. W. (1993). Recent developments in child neglect. In T. H. Ollendick & R. J. Prinz (Eds.), *Advances in Clinical Child Psychology, 15,* 121–174.

Palmer, S., Thompson, R. J., & Linscheid, T. R. (1981). Applied behavior analysis in the treatment of childhood feeding problems. *Developmental Medicine and Child Neurology, 17,* 333–339.

Paret, I. (1983). Night waking and its relation to mother–infant interaction in 9-month-old infants. In J. Call, E. Galenson, & R. L. Tyson (Eds.), *Frontiers of infant psychiatry* (pp. 171–177). New York: Basic Books.

Parmelee, A. H., Schulz, H. R., & Disbrow, M. A. (1961). Sleep patterns of the newborn. *Journal of Pediatrics, 58,* 241–250.

Part B, Education of the Handicapped Act as amended by P. L. 94–142, P. L. 99–457 and others. 20 U. S. C. 1419, C. F. D. A.: 84.173.

Paschalis, A. P., Kimmel, H. D., & Kimmel, E. (1972). Further study of diurnal instrumental conditioning in the treatment of enuresis nocturna. *Journal of Behavior Therapy and Experimental Psychiatry, 3,* 253–256.

Passman, R. H. (1987). Attachments to inanimate objects: Are children who have security blankets insecure? *Journal of Consulting and Clinical Psychology, 55,* 825–830.

Patterson, G. R. (1982). *Coercive family process.* Eugene, OR: Castalia.

Paul, R. (1991). Profiles of toddlers with slow expressive language development. *Topics in Language Disorders, 11,* 1–13.

Pedro-Corrall, J. L., & Cowan, E. L. (1985). The Children of Divorce Intervention Program: An investigation of the efficacy of a school-based prevention program. *Journal of Consulting Clinical Psychology, 53,* 603–611.

Perry, M. A. (1990). The interview in developmental assessment. In J. H. Johnson & J. Goldman (Eds.), *Developmental assessment in clinical child psychology: A handbook* (pp. 58–77). New York: Pergamon.

Perry, M. A., & Furukawa, M. J. (1980). Modeling methods. In F. H. Kanfer & A. P. Goldstein (Eds.), *Helping people change: A textbook of methods* (3rd ed., pp. 66–110). New York: Pergamon.

Perry, P., & Lynch, M. (1978). *Mommy and daddy are divorced.* New York: Dial Press.

Peters, S. D., Wyatt, G. E., & Finkelhor, D. (1986). Prevalence. In D. Finkelhor & Associates (Eds.), *A sourcebook on child sexual abuse* (pp. 15–59). Beverly Hills: Sage.

Peterson, L., Schultheis, K., Ridley-Johnson, R., Miller, D. J., & Tracy, K. (1984). Comparison of three modeling procedures on the presurgical and postsurgical reactions of children. *Behavior Therapy, 15,* 197–203.

Peterson, L., & Shigetomi, C. (1981). The use of coping techniques to minimize anxiety in hospitalized children. *Behavior Therapy, 12,* 1–14.

Petti, T. A. (1978). Depression in hospitalized child psychiatry patients: Approaches to measuring depression. *Journal of the American Academy of Child Psychiatry, 22,* 11–21.

Pfiffner, L. J., & Barkley, R. A. (1990). Educational placement and classroom management. In R. A. Barkley, *Attention deficit hyperactivity disorder: A handbook for diagnosis and treatment.* New York: Guilford.

Pflaunder, M. (1904). Demonstration of an apparatus for automatic warning of the occurence of bedwetting. *Verhandlungen der Gesellschaft fur Kinderheilpundl, 21,* 219–220.

Physicians' Desk Reference, 44th edition. (1993). Oradell, NJ: Medical Economics Company.

Piaget, J. (1963). *The origins of intelligence in children.* New York: Norton.

Piaget, J., & Inhelder, B. (1969). *The psychology of the child.* New York: Basic Books.

Pick, H. L., & Pick, A. D. (1970). Sensory and perceptual development. In P. H. Mussen (Ed.), *Carmichael's manual of child psychology* (Vol. 1, pp. 773–847). New York: Wiley.

Pierce, C. M. (1972). Enuresis. In A. M. Freedman & H. I. Kaplan (Eds.), *The child* (Vol. 1). New York: Atheneum.

Pierce, C. M., Lipcan, H. H., McLary, J. H., & Noble, H. F. (1956). Enuresis: Psychiatric interview studies. *United States Armed Forces Medical Journal, 7*(9), 1–12.

Pierson, D. E., Walker, D. K., & Tivnan, T. (1984). A school-based program from infancy to kindergarten for children and their parents. *Personnel and Guidance Journal, 62,* 448–455.

Pisterman, S., Firestone, T., McGrath, P., Goodman, J. T., Webster, I., Mallory, R., & Goffin, B. (1992). The role of parent training in treatment of preschoolers with ADDH. *American Journal of Orthopsychiatry, 62,* 397–408.

Plachetta, K. E. (1976). Encopresis: A case study utilizing contracting, scheduling, and self-charting. *Journal of Behavior Therapy and Experimental Psychiatry, 7,* 195–196.

Pollitt, E., & Eichler, A. W. (1976). Behavioral disturbances among failure to thrive children. *American Journal of Diseases of Childhood, 130,* 24–29.

Pollitt, E., Eichler, A. W., & Chan, C. K. (1975). Psychosocial development and behavior of mothers of failure-to-thrive children. *American Journal of Orthopsychiatry, 45,* 525–537.

Pollitt, E., & Thompson, C. (1977). Protein-calorie malnutrition and behavior: A view from psychology. In R. J. Wurtman & J. J. Wurtman (Eds.), *Nutrition and the brain* (Vol. 2, pp. 262–305). New York: Raven.

Poster, E. C., & Betz, C. L. (1983). Allaying the anxiety of hospitalized children using stress immunization techniques. *Issues in Comprehensive Pediatric Nursing, 6,* 227–233.

Powell, G. F., Brasel, J. A., & Blizzard, R. M. (1967). Emotional deprivation and growth retardation simulating idiopathic hypopituitarism. I. Clinical evaluation of the syndrome. *New England Journal of Medicine, 276,* 1271–1278.

Poznanski, E. O., Cook, S. C., & Carroll, B. J. (1979). A depression rating scale for children. *Pediatrics, 64,* 442–450.

Pratt, C. B. (1985). Some aspects of childhood cancer epidemiology. *Pediatric Clinics of North America, 32,* 541–556.

Preskorn, S. H., Weller, E. B., & Weller, R. A. (1982). Depression in children: Relationship between plasma imipramine levels and response. *Journal of Clinical Psychiatry, 43,* 450–453.

Prizant, B. M., & Wetherby, A. M. (1993). Communication in preschool autistic children. In E. Schopler, M. E. Van Bourgondien, & M. M. Bristol (Eds.), *Preschool issues in autism* (pp. 95–128). New York: Plenum.

Procidano, M., & Heller, K. (1983). Measures of perceived social support from friends and from family: Three validation studies. *American Journal of Community Psychology, 11,* 1–24.

Puig-Antich, J. (1982). Major depression and conduct disorder in prepuberty. *Journal of the American Academy of Child Psychiatry, 21,* 118–128.

Puig-Antich, J. (1987). Psychobiologic markers of prepubertal major depression. *Journal of Adolescent Health Care, 8,* 505–529.

Puig-Antich, J., & Gittelman, R. (1982). Depression in childhood and adolescence. In E. S. Paykel (Ed.), *Handbook of affective disorders.* New York: Guilford.

Puig-Antich, J., Goetz, R., Davies, M., Tabrizi, M. A., Novacenko, H., Hanlon, C., Sachar, E., & Weitzman, E. (1984, May). Growth hormone secretion in prepubertal depression II. *Archives of General Psychiatry, 41,* 463–466.

Puig-Antich, J., Novacenko, H., Davies, M., Chambers, W. J., Tabrizi, M. A., Krawiec, V., Ambrosini, P. J., & Schar, E. J. (1984, May). Growth hormone secretion in prepubertal children with major depression I. *Archives of General Psychiatry, 41,* 455–460.

Puig-Antich, J., Perel, J., Lumpatkin, W., Chambers, W. J., Tabrizi, M. A., King, J., Davies, M., Johnson, R., & Stiller, R. (1987). Imipramine in prepubertal major depressive disorders. *Archives of General Psychiatry, 44,* 81–89.

Purcell, K. (1975). Childhood asthma, the role of family relationships, personality, and emotions. In A. Davids (Ed.), *Child personality and psychopathology: Current topics* (Vol. 2). New York: Wiley.

Purcell, K., Brody, K., Chai, H., Muser, J., Molk, L., Gordon, N., & Means, J. (1969). A comparison of psychologic findings in variously defined asthmatic subgroups. *Journal of Psychosomatic Research, 31,* 144–164.

Purcell, K., & Weiss, J., (1970). Asthma. In C. G. Costello (Ed.), *Symptoms of psychopathology.* New York: Wiley.

Ragan, P. V., & McGlashan, T. H. (1986). Childhood parental death and adult psychopathology. *American Journal of Psychiatry, 143,* 153–157.

Ramey, C., & Campbell, F. A. (1984). Preventive education for high risk children: Cognitive consequences of the Abecedarian project. *American Journal of Mental Deficiency, 88,* 515–523.

Ramig, P. R. (1993). High reported spontaneous stuttering recovery rates: Fact or fiction? *Language, Speech, and Hearing Services in Schools, 24,* 156–160.

Ramsden, R., Friedman, B., & Williamson, D. (1983). Treatment of childhood headache reports with contingency management procedures. *Journal of Clinical Child Psychology, 12,* 202–206.

Rapoport, J. L., & Ismond, D. R. (1990). *DSM-III-R training guide for diagnosis of childhood disorders.* New York: Brunner/Mazel.

Rapoport, J. L., & Kruesi, J. P. (1985). Organic therapies. In H. I. Kaplan, & B. J. Sadock (Eds.), *Comprehensive textbook of psychiatry/IV* (Vol. 2, pp. 1793–1798).

Reding, G. R., Rulbright, W. C., & Zimmerman, S. O. (1966). Incidence of bruxism. *Journal of Dental Research, 45,* 1198–1204.

Reding, G. R., Zepelin, H., & Monroe, L. J. (1968). Personality study of nocturnal teeth-grinders. *Perceptual and Motor Skills, 26,* 523–531.

Reed, G. (1963). Elective mutism in children: A reappraisal. *Journal of Child Psychology and Psychiatry, 3,* 287–297.

Reed, L. J., Carter, B. D., & Miller, L. C. (1992). Fear and anxiety in children. In C. E. Walker & M. C. Roberts (Eds.), *Handbook of clinical child psychology* (2nd ed., pp. 237–260). New York: Wiley.

Rehm, L. P. (1977). A self-control model of depression. *Behavior Therapy, 10,* 429–442.

Reid, J. B., Kavanagh, K., & Baldwin, D. V. (1987). Abusive parents' perceptions of child problem behaviors: An example of parental bias. *Journal of Abnormal Child Psychology, 15,* 457–466.

Reilly, T. P., Drudge, O. W., Rosen, J. C., Loew, D. E., & Fischer, M. (1985). Concurrent and predictive validity of the WISC-R, McCarthy Scales, Woodcock-Johnson, and academic achievement. *Psychology in the Schools, 22,* 380–382.

Reilly, T. P., Hasazi, J. E., & Bond, L. A. (1983). Children's conceptions of death and personal mortality. *Journal of Pediatric Psychology, 8,* 21–31.

Renne, C. M., & Creer, T. L. (1976). The effects of training on the use of inhalation therapy equipment by children with asthma. *Journal of Applied Behavior Analysis, 9,* 1–11.

Renne, C. M., & Creer, T. L. (1985). Asthmatic children and their families. In M. L. Walraich & D. K. Routh (Eds.), *Advances in developmental and behavioral pediatrics* (pp. 41–81). Greenwich, CT: JAI Press.

Rheingold, H. L., & Eckerman, C. O. (1973). Fear of the stranger: A critical examination. In H. W. Reese (Ed.), *Advances in child development and behavior* (Vol. 8, pp. 186–222). New York: Academic Press.

Rhyner, P. M. P., Lehr, D. H., & Pudlas, K. A. (1990). An analysis of teacher responsiveness to communicative initiations of preschool children with handicaps. *Language, Speech, and Hearing Services in Schools, 21,* 91–97.

Richman, N. (1981). A community survey of characteristics of one- to two-year-olds with sleep disruptions. *Journal of the American Academy of Child Psychiatry, 20,* 281–291.

Richman, N., Stevenson, J., & Graham, P. J. (1982). *Preschool to school: A behavioural study.* London: Academic Press.

Richmond, J. B., Eddy, E., & Green, M. (1958). Rumination: A psychosomatic syndrome of infancy. *Pediatrics, 22,* 49–55.

Rickert, V. I., & Johnson, C. M. (1988). Reducing nocturnal awakening and crying episodes in infants and young children: A comparison between scheduled awakening and systematic ignoring. *Pediatrics, 81,* 203–212.

Rieser, J., Yonas, A., & Wilkner, K. (1976). Radical localization of odors by human newborns. *Child Development, 47,* 856–859.

Rinn, R. C. (1985). Children with behavior disorders. In M. Hersen & A. S. Bellack (Eds.), *Behavior therapy in the psychiatric setting* (pp. 365–395). Baltimore: Williams & Wilkins.

Risley, T., Reynolds, N., & Hart, B. (1970). The disadvantaged: Behavior modification with disadvantaged preschool children. In R. H. Bradfield (Ed.), *Behavior modification: The human effort.* San Rafael, CA: Dimensions Publishing.

Ritvo, E. R., Jorde, L. B., Mason-Brothers, A., Freeman, B. J., Pingree, C., Jones, M. B., McMahon, W. M., Petersen, P. B., Jenson, W. R., & Mo, A. (1989). The UCLA-University of Utah epidemiologic survey of autism: Recurrence risk estimates and genetic counseling. *American Journal of Psychiatry, 146,* 1032–1036.

Robertiello, R. C. (1956). Some psychic interrelations between the urinary and sexual systems with special reference to enuresis. *Psychiatric Quarterly, 30,* 61–62.

Roberts, M. C. (1986). *Pediatric psychology: Psychological interventions and strategies for pediatric problems.* New York: Pergamon.

Roberts, M. C., Alexander, K., & Fanurik, D. (1990). Evaluation of commercially available materials to prevent child sexual abuse and abduction. *American Psychologist, 45,* 782–783.

Rocklin, H., & Tilker, H. (1973). Instrumental conditioning of nocturnal enuresis: A reappraisal of some previous findings. *Proceedings of the American Psychological Association, 8,* 915–916.

Roff, M. F. (1974). Childhood antecedents of adult neurosis, severe bad conduct, and psychological health. In D. F. Ricks, A. Thomas, & M. Roff (Eds.), *Life history research in psychopathology* (Vol. 3). Minneapolis: University Press.

Roland, P. S., & Brown, O. (1990). Tympanostomy tubes: A rational clinical treatment for middle ear disease. *Topics in Language Disorders, 11,* 23–28.

Rolider, A., & Van Houton, R. (1985). Movement suppression time-out for undesirable behavior in psychotic and severely developmentally delayed children. *Journal of Applied Behavior Analysis, 18,* 275–288.

Rollings, J. P., & Baumeister, A. A. (1981). Stimulus control of stereotypic responding: Effects on target and collateral behaviors. *American Journal of Mental Deficiency, 86,* 67–77.

Rose, M. I., Firestone, P., Heick, H. M. C., & Faught, A. K. (1983). The effects of anxiety management training on the control of juvenile diabetes mellitus. *Journal of Behavioral Medicine, 6,* 381–395.

Rosenfeld, A., Bailey, R., Siegel, B., & Bailey, G. (1986). Determining incestuous contact between parent and child: Frequency of children touching parents' genitals in a nonclinical population. *Journal of the American Academy of Child Psychiatry, 25,* 481–484.

Rosenthal, N., Carpenter, C., James, S., Pany, B., Rogers, S., & Wehr, T. (1986). Seasonal affective disorder in childhood and adolescence. *American Journal of Psychiatry, 143,* 356–358.

Ross, D. M. (1984). Thought-stopping: A coping strategy for impending feared events. *Issues in Comprehensive Pediatric Nursing, 7,* 83–89.

Ross, J., & Loss, P. (1991). Assessment of the juvenile sex offender. In G. D. Ryan & S. L. Lane (Eds.), *Juvenile sexual offending: Causes, consequences, and correction* (pp. 199–251). Lexington, MA: Lexington Books.

Rothbart, M. K., & Rothbart, M. (1976). Birth order, sex of child, and maternal help-giving. *Sex Roles, 2,* 39–46.

Roy, A., Pickar, D., DeJong, J., Karoum, F., & Linnoila, M. (1988). Norepinephrine and its metabolites in cerebrospinal fluid, plasma, and urine. *Archives of General Psychiatry, 45,* 849–857.

Ruder, K. F., & Smith, M. D. (1974). Issues in language training. In R. L. Schiefelbusch & L. L. Lloyd (Eds.), *Language perspectives—acquisition, retardation and intervention*. Baltimore: University Park Press.

Rugh, J. D., & Solberg, W. K. (1975). Electromyographic studies of bruxist behavior before and during treatment. *Journal of the California Dental Association, 3,* 56–59.

Russell, A. B., & Trainor, M. (1984). *Trends in child abuse and neglect: A national perspective.* Denver, CO: American Humane Association.

Rutter, M. (1970). Autistic children: Infancy to adulthood. *Seminars in Psychiatry, 2,* 435–450.

Rutter, M. (1973). Indications for research: III. In I. Kolvin, R. C. MacKeith, & S. R. Meadow (Eds.), *Bladder control and enuresis*. Philadelphia: J. B. Lippincott.

Rutter, M., Macdonald, H., Le Couteur, A., Harrington, R., Bolton, P., & Bailey, A. (1990). Genetic factors in child psychiatric disorders—II. Empirical findings. *Journal of Child Psychology and Psychiatry, 31,* 39–83.

Rutter, M., Tizzard, J., & Whitemore, K. (1970). *Education, health, and behavior.* New York: Wiley.

Rutter, M., Yule, W., & Graham, P. (1973). Enuresis and behavioral deviance. In I. Kolvin, R. C. MacKeith, & S. R. Meadow (Eds.), *Bladder control and enuresis*. London: Heinemann.

Ryan, N. D., Puig-Antich, J., Ambrosini, P., Rabinovich, H., Robinson, D., Nelson, B., Iyengar, S., & Twomey, J. (1987). The clinical picture of major depression in children and adolescents. *Archives of General Psychiatry, 44,* 854–861.

Ryan, N. D., Puig-Antich, J., Cooper, T., Rabinovich, H., Ambrosini, P., Davies, M., King, J., Torrer, D., & Fried, J. (1986). Imipramine in adolescent major depression: Plasma level and clinical response. *Acta Psychiatrica Scandinavica, 73,* 275–288.

Rynders, J. E., Spiker, D., & Horrobin, J. M. (1978). Underestimating the educability of Down's syndrome children: Examination of methodological problems in recent literature. *American Journal of Mental Deficiency, 82,* 213–222.

Sajwaj, T., Libet, J., & Agras, S. (1974). Lemon juice therapy: The control of life threatening rumination in a six month old infant. *Journal of Applied Behavior Analysis, 7,* 557–563.

Sallustro, C., & Atwell, F. (1978). Jactatio capitis. *Journal of Pediatrics, 93,* 704–708.

Salzarulo, P., & Chevalier, A. (1983). Sleep problems in children and their relationship with early disturbances of the waking–sleeping rhythms. *Sleep, 6,* 47–51.

Sanders, M. R., Bor, B., & Dadds, M. (1984). Modifying bedtime disruptions in children using stimulus control and contingency management techniques. *Behavioural Psychotherapy, 12,* 130–141.

Sandford, D., & Nettlebeck, T. (1982). Medication and reinforcement within a token program for disturbed mentally retarded residents. *Applied Research in Mental Retardation, 3,* 21–36.

Sanger, M. D. (1955). *Language learning in infancy: A review of the autistic hypothesis and an observational study of infants.* Unpublished doctoral thesis, Harvard University.

Sank, L. I., & Biglan, A. (1974). Operant treatment of a case of recurrent abdominal pain in a 10 year old boy. *Behavior Therapy, 5,* 677–681.

Satz, P., & Fletcher, J. M. (1981). Emergent trends in neuropsychology: An overview. *Journal of Consulting and Clinical Psychology, 49,* 851–865.

Saywitz, K. J., Nathanson, R., & Snyder, L. S. (1993). Credibility of child witnesses: The role of communicative competence. *Topics in Language Disorders, 13,* 59–78.

Scadding, J. C. (1966). Patterns of respiratory insufficiency. *Lancet, 1,* 701–704.

Scandrett, F. R., & Ervin, T. H. (1973). Occlusion and preventive dentistry. *Journal of the American Dental Association, 87,* 1231–1233.

Scarborough, H. S., & Dobrich, W. (1990). Development of children with early language delay. *Journal of Speech and Hearing Disorders, 33,* 70–83.

Schaefer, C. E. (1979). *Childhood encopresis and enuresis: Causes and therapy.* New York: Van Nostrand Reinhold.

Schaefer, C. E. (1992). *Cat's got your tongue? A story for children afraid to speak.* New York: Magination Press.

Schaefer, C. E., & Petronko, M. R. (1987). *Teach your baby to sleep through the night.* New York: Penguin.

Schaefer, D., & Lyons, C. (1986). *How do we tell the children?* New York: Newmarket Press.

Scherr, M. S., Crawford, P. L., Sergent, C. B., & Scherr, C. A. (1975). Effect of biofeedback techniques on chronic asthma in a summer camp environment. *Annals of Allergy, 35,* 289–295.

Schiottz-Christensen, E., & Bruhn, P. (1973). Intelligence, behavior and scholastic achievement subsequent to febrile convulsions: An analysis of discordant twin pairs. *Developmental Medicine and Child Neurology, 15,* 565.

Schmitt, B. D. (1982). Nocturnal enuresis: An update on treatment. *Pediatric Clinics of North America, 29,* 9–20.

Schmitt, B. D. (1987). Seven deadly sins of childhood: Advising parents about difficult developmental phases. *Child Abuse and Neglect, 11,* 421–432.

Schonfeld, D. J., & Kappelman, M. (1990). The impact of school-based education on the young child's understanding of death. *Developmental and Behavioral Pediatrics, 11,* 247–252.

Schopler, E., Andrews, C. E., & Strupp, K. (1979). Do autistic children come from upper middle-class parents? *Journal of Autism and Developmental Disorders, 9,* 139–152.

Schopler, E., & Mesibov, G. (Eds.). (1988). *Diagnosis and assessment in autism.* New York: Plenum.

Schopler, E., Mesibov, G. B., & Baker, A. (1982). Evaluation of treatment for autistic children and their parents. *Journal of the American Academy of Child Psychiatry, 21,* 262–267.

Schopler, E., Reichler, R. J., Bashford, A., Lansing, M. D., & Marcus, L. M. (1990). *Individualized assessment and treatment for autistic and developmentally disabled children. Vol. 1, Psychoeducational profile revised.* Austin, TX: Pro-Ed.

Schopler, E., Reichler, R. J., & Renner, B. R. (1986). *The Childhood Autism Rating Scale (CARS).* Los Angeles: Western Psychological Services.

Schopler, E., Van Bourgondien, M. E., & Bristol, M. M. (Eds.). (1993). *Preschool issues in autism.* New York: Plenum.

Schowalter, J. E. (1970). How do children and funerals mix? *Journal of Pediatrics, 89*(1), 139–142.

Schreibman, L. Koegel, L. K., & Koegel, R. L. (1990). Autism. In M. Hersen (Ed.), *Innovations in child behavior therapy* (pp. 395–428). New York: Springer.

Schroeder, C. S., & Gordon, B. N. (1991). *Assessment and treatment of childhood problems: A clinician's guide.* New York: Guilford.

Schroeder, S. (1991). Self-injury and stereotypy. In J. L. Matson & J. A. Mulick (Eds.), *Handbook of mental retardation* (2nd ed., pp. 382–396). New York: Pergamon.

Schuler, A., & Prizant, B. (1985). Echolalia in autism. In E. Schopler & G. Mesibov (Eds.), *Communication problems in autism.* New York: Plenum.

Schulman-Galambos, C., & Galambos, R. (1979). Brain stem evoked response audiometry in newborn hearing screening. *Archives of Otolaryngology, 105,* 86–90.

Schwartz, L., & Chayes, C. M. (1968). *Facial pain and mandibular dysfunction.* Philadelphia: Saunders.

Seagull, E. A., & Weinshank, A. B. (1984). Childhood depression in a selected group of low-achieving seventh-graders. *Journal of Clinical Child Psychology, 13*(2), 134–140.

Seeburg, K. N., & DeBoer, K. F. (1980). Effects of EMG biofeedback on diabetes. *Biofeedback and Self-Regulation, 5,* 289–293.

Seifert, K. L., & Hoffnung, R. J. (1991). *Child and adolescent development* (2nd ed.). Boston: Houghton Mifflin.

Selan, B. H. (1979). Psychotherapy with the mentally retarded. *Social Work, 24,* 263.

Seligman, M. E. P. (1971). Phobias and preparedness. *Behavior Therapy, 2,* 307–320.

Seligman, M. E. P., & Maier, S. F. (1967). Failure to escape traumatic shock. *Journal of Experimental Psychology, 74,* 1–9.

Seligman, M. E. P., & Peterson, C. (1986). A learned helplessness perspective on childhood depression: Theory and research. In M. Rutter, C. E. Izard, & P. B. Read (Eds.), *Depression in young people: Developmental and clinical perspectives.* New York: Guilford.

Shaffer, D. (1985). Enuresis. In M. Rutter & L. Hersov (Eds.), *Child and adolescent psychiatry: Modern approaches* (pp. 465–481). Boston: Blackwell Scientific.

Shapiro, B. K., Palmer, F. B., Watchel, R. C., & Capute, A. J. (1983). Issues in the early identification of specific learning disability. *Developmental and Behavioral Pediatrics, 5*(1), 15–20.

Shapiro, E. S., Kazdin, A. E., & McGonigle, J. J. (1982). Multiple-treatment interference in the simultaneous- or alternating-treatments design. *Behavioral Assessment, 4,* 105–115.

Shapiro, E. S., McGonigle, J. J., & Ollendick, T. (1980). An analysis of self-assessment and self-reinforcement in a self-managed token economy with mentally retarded children. *Applied Research in Mental Retardation, 1,* 227–240.

Shea, J. D. C. (1981). Changes in interpersonal distances and categories of play behavior in the early weeks of preschool. *Developmental Psychology, 17,* 417–425.

Shea, V. (1984). Explaining mental retardation and autism to parents. In E. Schopler & G. Mesibov (Eds.), *The effects of autism on the family* (pp. 265–288). New York: Plenum.

Shea, V. (1993). Interpreting results to parents of preschool children. In E. Schopler, M. E. Van Bourgondien, & M. M. Bristol (Eds.), *Preschool issues in autism* (pp. 185–198). New York: Plenum.

Sheras, P. L. (1983). Suicide in adolescence. In C. E. Walker & M. C. Roberts (Eds.), *Handbook of clinical child psychology*. New York: Wiley.

Sherman, J., Barker, P., Lorimer, P., Swinson, R., & Factor, D. C. (1988). Treatment of autistic children: Relative effectiveness of residential, out-patient, and home-based interventions. *Child Psychiatry and Human Development, 19,* 109–125.

Sheslow, D. V., Bondy, A. S., & Nelson, R. O. (1982). A comparison of graduated exposure, verbal coping skills, and their combination in the treatment of children's fear of the dark. *Child and Family Behavior Therapy, 4,* 33–45.

Short, A. B. (1984). Short-term treatment outcome using parents as cotherapists for their own autistic children. *Journal of Child Psychology and Psychiatry and Allied Disciplines, 25,* 443–458.

Short, A. B., & Marcus, L. M. (1986). Psychoeducational evaluation of autistic children and adolescents. In P. J. Lazarus & S. S. Strichart (Eds.), *Psychoeducational evaluation of children and adolescents with low-incidence handicaps* (pp. 155–180). Orlando, FL: Grune & Stratton.

Showers, J., Farber, E. D., Joseph, J. A., Oshins, L., & Johnson, C. F. (1983). The sexual victimization of boys: A three-year survey. *Health Values: Achieving High-Level Wellness, 7,* 15–18.

Showers, P. (1961). *In the night.* New York: Thomas Y. Crowell.

Shriberg, L., & Kwiatkowski, J. (1988). A follow-up study of children with phonologic disorders of unknown origin. *Journal of Speech and Hearing Disorders, 53,* 144–155.

Siegel, L. J. (1982). Classical and operant procedures in the treatment of a case of food aversion in a young child. *Journal of Clinical Child Psychology, 11,* 167–172.

Sillanpaa, M. (1983). Changes in the prevalence of migrane and other headaches during the first seven school years. *Headache, 23,* 15–19.

Silva, P. A. (1980). The prevalence, stability, and significance of developmental language delay in preschool children. *Developmental Medicine and Child Neurology, 22,* 768–777.

Simeon, J. G., & Ferguson, H. B. (1987). Alprazolam effects in children with anxiety disorders. *Canadian Journal of Psychiatry, 32,* 570–574.

Simeonsson, R. J., Olley, J. G., & Rosenthal, S. L. (1987). Early intervention for children with autism. In M. J. Guralnick & F. C. Bennett (Eds.), *The effectiveness of early intervention for at-risk and handicapped children* (pp. 275–296). Orlando, FL: Academic Press.

Simon, J., Larson, C., & Lehrer, R. (1988). Preschool screening: Relations among audiometric and developmental measures. *Journal of Applied Developmental Psychology, 9,* 107–123.

Simonds, J. F. (1979). Emotions and compliance in diabetic children. *Psychosomatics, 20,* 10–14.

Simonds, J. F., & Parraga, H. (1984). Sleep behaviors and disorders in children and adolescents evaluated at psychiatric clinics. *Developmental and Behavioral Pediatrics, 5,* 6–10.

Siqueland, E. R., & Lipsitt, L. P. (1966). Conditioned headturning in human newborns. *Journal of Experimental Child Psychology, 3,* 356–376.

Smith, P. K., Eaton, L., & Hindmarch, A. (1982). How one-year-olds respond to strangers: A two-person situation. *Journal of Genetic Psychology, 140*(1), 147–148.

Smith, S. L. (1970). School refusal with anxiety: A review of sixty-three cases. *Canadian Psychiatric Association Journal, 126,* 815–817.

Solberg, W. K., & Rugh, J. D. (1972). The use of biofeedback devices in the treatment of bruxism. *Journal of the Southern California State Dental Association, 40,* 852–853.

Solomons, G. (1979). Child abuse and developmental disabilities. *Developmental Medicine and Child Neurology, 21,* 101–106.

Solyom, I., Beck, P., Solyom, C., & Hugel, R. (1974). Some etiological factors in phobic neurosis. *Canadian Psychiatry Association Journal, 19,* 69–78.

Sours, J. A. (1978). The application of child analytic principles to forms of child psychotherapy. In J. Glenn (Ed.), *Child analysis and therapy* (pp. 615–646). New York: Jason Aronson.

Spanier, G. B. (1976). Measuring dyadic adjustment: New scales for measuring the quality of marriage and similar dyads. *Journal of Marriage and the Family, 38,* 15–28.

Sparrow, S. S., Balla, D. A., & Cicchetti, D. V. (1984). *Vineland Adaptive Behavior Scales* (rev. ed.). Circle Pines, MN: American Guidance Services.

Spinetta, J. J., & Deasy-Spinetta, P. (1981). *Living with childhood cancer.* St. Louis: Mosby.

Spinetta, J. J., Swarner, J. A., & Sheposh, J. P. (1981). Effective parental coping following the death of a child from cancer. *Journal of Pediatric Psychology, 6,* 251–263.

Spitz, R. A. (1945). Hospitalism. An inquiry into the genesis of psychiatric conditions in early childhood. *Psychoanalytic Study of the Child, 1,* 53–74.

Spitz, R. A., & Wolf, K. M. (1946). Anaclitic depression. *Psychoanalytical Study of the Child, 2,* 313–342.

Spitznagel, A. (1976). *We will see you in the morning.* Unpublished manuscript, Chapel Hill, NC. [Available for $6 from Pediatric Psychology, 901 Willow Drive, Suite 2, Chapel Hill, NC 27514.]

Spivack, G., Platt, J. J., & Shure, M. B. (1976). *The problem-solving approach to adjustment.* San Francisco: Jossey-Bass.

Spock, B. (1963). *Baby and child care* (rev. ed.). New York: Pocket Books.

Sroufe, L. A., Fox, N., & Pancake, V. (1983). Attachment and dependency in developmental perspective. *Child Development, 54,* 1615–1627.

Stambrook, M., & Parker, K. C. H. (1987). The development of the concept of death in childhood: A review of the literature. *Merrill-Palmer Quarterly, 33,* 133–157.

Starfield, B., & Mellits, E. D. (1968). Increase in functional bladder capacity and improvements in enuresis. *Journal of Pediatrics, 72,* 483–487.

Stark, L. J., Miller, S. T., Plienis, A. J., & Drabman, R. S. (1987). Behavioral contracting to increase chest physiotherapy: A study of a young cystic fibrosis patient. *Behavior Modification, 11,* 75–86.

Stark, L. J., & Passero, M. A. (1987, November). The behavioral approach to nutrition support. In P. M. Farrell & C. C. Roy (Chairman), *Nutrition in cystic fibrosis.* Symposium conducted at the meeting at the North American Cystic Fibrosis Conference, Toronto, Canada.

Starr, R. H., MacLean, D. J., & Keating, D. (1991). Life-span developmental outcomes of child maltreatment. In R. H. Starr & D. A. Wolfe (Eds.), *The effects of child abuse and neglect.* New York: Guilford.

Stedman, J. M. (1972). An extension of the Kimmel treatment method for enuresis to an adolescent: A case report. *Journal of Behavior Therapy and Experimental Psychiatry, 3,* 307–309.

Stehbens, J. A. (1988). Childhood cancer. In D. K. Routh (Ed.), *Handbook of pediatric psychology* (pp. 135–161). New York: Guilford.

Steiner, S., & Larson, V. L. (1991). Integrating microcomputers into language intervention with children. *Topics in Language Disorders, 11*, 18–30.

Stephen, E., & Hawks, G. (1974). Cerebral palsy and mental subnormality. In A. M. Clarke and A. D. B. Clarke (Eds.), *Mental deficiency: The changing outlook* (3rd ed.). New York: Free Press.

Steward, M. S., Bussey, K., Goodman, G. S., & Saywitz, K. J. (1993). Implications of developmental research for interviewing children. *Child Abuse and Neglect, 17*, 25–37.

Stokes, T. F., Boggs, S. R., & Osnes, P. G. (1989). Separation anxiety disorder and school phobia. In M. C. Roberts & C. E. Walker (Eds.), *Casebook of child and pediatric psychology* (pp. 71–93). New York: Guilford.

Stolberg, A. L., & Garrison, K. M. (1985). Evaluating a primary prevention program for children of divorce. *American Journal of Community Psychology, 13*(2), 111–124.

Stone, W. L., Lemanek, K. L., Fishel, P. T., Fernandez, M. C., & Altemeier, W. A. (1990). Play and imitation skills in the diagnosis of young autistic children. *Pediatrics, 86*, 267–272.

Stores, G. (1992). Annotation: Sleep studies in children with a mental handicap. *Journal of Child Psychology and Psychiatry, 33*, 1303–1317.

Strain, P. S., & Hoyson, M. H. (1988, July). *Follow-up of children in LEAP.* Paper presented at the meeting of the Autism Society of America, New Orleans, LA.

Strain, P. S., Jamieson, B. J., & Hoyson, M. H. (1985). Learning experiences. An alternative program for preschoolers and parents: A comprehensive service system for the mainstreaming of autistic-like preschoolers. In C. J. Meisel (Ed.), *Mainstreamed handicapped children: Outcomes, controversies, and new directions* (pp. 251–269). Hillsdale, NJ: Erlbaum.

Strauss, C. C. (1988). Overanxious disorder. In M. Hersen & C. G. Last (Eds.), *Child behavior therapy casebook* (pp. 19–29). New York: Plenum.

Strauss, C. C. (1993). Developmental differences in expression of anxiety disorders in children and adolescents. In C. G. Last (Ed.), *Anxiety across the lifespan: A developmental perspective.* New York: Springer.

Strauss, C. C., Lease, C. A., Last, C. G., & Francis, G. (1988). Overanxious disorder: An examination of developmental differences. *Journal of Abnormal Child Psychology, 4*, 433–443.

Stunkard, A. J., d'Aquill, E., Fox, S., & Filion, R. D. L. (1972). Influence of social class on obesity and thinness in children. *Journal of the American Medical Association, 221*, 579–584.

Sullivan, R. C. (1984). Parents as trainers of legislators, other parents, and researchers. In E. Schopler & G. Mesibov (Eds.), *The effects of autism on the family: Current issues in autism* (pp. 237–246). New York: Plenum.

Szatmari, P., Bartolucci, G., Bremner, R., Bond, S., & Rich, S. (1989). A follow-up study of high-functioning autistic children. *Journal of Autism and Developmental Disabilities, 19*, 213–225.

Taft, L. T. (1993). Medical syndromes in young autistic children. In E. Schopler, M. E. Van Bourgondien, & M. M. Bristol (Eds.), *Preschool issues in autism* (pp. 175–183). New York: Plenum.

Tal, A., & Miklich, D. R. (1976). Emotionally induced decreases in pulmonary flow rates in asthmatic children. *Psychosomatic Medicine, 38*, 190–199.

Talbot, N. B., Sobel, E. H., Burke, B. S., Lindemann, E., & Kaufman, S. B. (1947). Dwarfism in healthy children. *New England Journal of Medicine, 236,* 783–793.

Tancer, N. K. (1992). Elective mutism: A review of the literature. In B. B. Lahey and A. E. Kazdin (Eds.), *Advances in clinical child psychology,* (Vol 14, pp. 265–288). New York: Plenum.

Tannock, R., & Girolametto, L. (1992). Reassessing parent-focused language intervention programs. In S. F. Warren & J. Reichle, *Causes and effects in communication and language intervention* (pp. 49–79). Baltimore, MD: Paul H. Brookes.

Tantam, D. (1988). Asperger's syndrome. *Journal of Child Psychology and Psychiatry, 29,* 245–255.

Tauber, M. A. (1979). Parental socialization techniques and sex differences in children's play. *Child Development, 50,* 225–234.

Tavormina, J. B. (1975). Relative effectiveness of behavioral and reflective group counseling with parents of mentally retarded children. *Journal of Consulting and Clinical Psychology, 43,* 22–31.

Taylor, H. G. (1989). Learning disabilities. In E. J. Mash & R. A. Barkley (Eds.), *Treatment of childhood disorders.* New York: Guilford.

Teele, D. W., Klein, J., & Rosner, B. (1984). Otitis media with effusion during the first three years of life and the development of speech and language. *Pediatrics, 74,* 282–287.

Templin, M., & Darley, F. (1968). *Templin-Darley Tests of Articulation* (2nd ed.). Iowa City: University of Iowa Bureau of Educational Research and Service.

Thiele, J. E. (1993). Federal legislation for young children with disabilities. In E. Schopler, M. E. Van Bourgondien, and M. M. Bristol (Eds.), *Preschool issues in autism* (pp. 247–260). New York: Plenum.

Thompson, E. D. (1987). *Pediatric nursing: An introductory text* (5th ed.). Philadelphia: W. B. Saunders.

Thorndike, R. L., Hagan, E., & Sattler, J. (1986). *Stanford-Binet Intelligence Scale: Fourth Edition.* Chicago: Riverside.

Thorpy, M. J., & Glovinsky, P. B. (1989). Headbanging (jactatio capitis nocturna). In M. H. Kryger, R. Roth, & W. C. Dement (Eds.), *Principles and practice of sleep medicine* (pp. 648–654). Philadelphia: Saunders .

Thyer, B. A. (1993). Childhood separation anxiety disorder and adult-onset agoraphobia: Review of evidence. In C. G. Last (Ed.), *Anxiety across the lifespan: A developmental perspective* (pp. 128–147). New York: Springer.

Tough, J. H., Hawkins, R. P., McArthur, M. M., & Van Ravensway, S. V. (1971). Modification of enuretic behavior by punishment: A new use for an old device. *Behavior Therapy, 2,* 567–574.

Trad, P. V. (1987). *Infant and childhood depression: Developmental factors.* New York: Wiley.

Travis, G. (1976). *Chronic illness in Children: Its impact on child and family.* Stanford, CA: Stanford University Press.

Trevathan, E., & Naidu, S. (1988). The clinical recognition and differential diagnosis of Rett syndrome. *Journal of Child Neurology, 3*(Suppl.), 6–16.

Tronick, E. Z. (1989). Emotions and emotional communication in infants. *American Psychologist, 44,* 112–119.

Turner, G., Daniel, A., & Frost, M. (1980). X-linked mental retardation, macro-orchidism, and the X 27 fragile site. *Journal of Pediatrics, 96,* 837–841.

Valdez-Menchaca, M. C., & Whitehurst, G. J. (1992). Accelerating language development through picture book reading: A systematic extension to Mexican day care. *Developmental Psychology, 28,* 1106–1114.

Van Acker, R. (1991). Rett syndrome: A review of current knowledge. *Journal of Autism and Developmental Disorders, 21,* 381–406.

van Kleek, A., & Richardson, A. (1990). Assessment of speech and language development. In J. H. Johnson & J. Goldman (Eds.), *Developmental assessment in clinical child psychology: A handbook* (pp. 132–172). New York: Pergamon.

Varni, J. W. (1981). Self-regulation techniques in the management of chronic arthritic pain in hemophilia. *Behavior Therapy, 12,* 185–194.

Varni, J. W. (1983). *Clinical behavioral pediatrics: An interdisciplinary biobehavioral approach.* New York: Pergamon.

Varni, J. W., Bessman, C. A., Russo, D. C., & Cataldo, M. F. (1980). Behavioral management of chronic pain in children: Case study. *Archives of Physical Medicine and Rehabilitation, 61,* 375–379.

Varni, J. W., Jay, S. M., Masek, B. J., & Thompson, K. L. (1986). Cognitive behavioral assessment and management of pediatric pain. In A. D. Holzman & D. C. Turk (Eds.), *Pain management: A handbook of psychological treatment approaches.* New York: Pergamon.

Varni, J. W., Thompson, K. L., & Hanson, V. (1987). The Varni-Thompson pediatric pain questionnaire: Chronic musculoskeletal pain in juvenile rheumatoid arthritis. *Pain, 28,* 27–38.

Vaughan, V. C., McKay, R. J., & Behrman, R. E. (1979). *Nelson textbook of pediatrics* (11th ed.). Philadelphia: Saunders.

Venter, A., Lord, C., & Schopler, E. (1992). A follow-up study of high-functioning autistic children. *Journal of Child Psychology and Psychiatry, 33,* 489–507.

Viorst, J. (1978). *My mama says there aren't any zombies, ghosts, vampires, creatures, demons, monsters, fiends, goblins, or things.* New York: Atheneum.

Volkmar, F. R. (1987). Diagnostic issues in the pervasive developmental disorders. *Journal of Child Psychology and Psychiatry, 28,* 365–369.

Volkmar, F. R., Cohen, D. J., & Paul, R. (1986). An elevation of DSM-III criteria for infantile autism. *Journal of the American Academy of Child Psychiatry, 25,* 190–197.

Vosk, B., Forehand, R., Parker, J. B., & Rickard, K. (1982). A multimethod comparison of popular and unpopular children. *Developmental Psychology, 18,* 571–575.

Wagner, W., Johnson, S. B., Walker, D., Carter, R., & Wittner, J. (1982). A controlled comparison of two treatments for nocturnal enuresis. *Journal of Pediatrics, 101,* 302–307.

Walco, G. A., & Dampier, C. D. (1990). Pain in children and adolescents with sickle cell disease: A descriptive study. *Journal of Pediatric Psychology, 15,* 643–658.

Walker, C. E., Bonner, B. L., & Kaufman, K. L. (1988). *The physically and sexually abused child: Evaluation and treatment.* New York: Pergamon.

Walker, C. W., Milling, L., & Bonner, B. (1988). Enuresis, encopresis, and related disorders. In D. K. Routh (Ed.), *Handbook of pediatric psychology.* New York: Guilford.

Walker, H. M., & Hops, H. (1973). The use of group and individual reinforcement contingencies in the modification of social withdrawal. In L. A. Hamerlynck, L. C. Handy, & E. J. Mash (Eds.), *Behavior change: Methodology, concepts, and practice.* New York: Academic Research Press.

Wallander, J. (1988). The relationship between attention problems in childhood and antisocial behavior eight years later. *Journal of Child Psychology and Psychiatry, 29,* 53–62.

Wallerstein, J. S. (1986). Children of Divorce Workshop presented at the Cape Cod Institute, Massachusetts.

Wallerstein, J. S., & Kelly, J. B. (1975). The effects of parental divorce: Experiences of the preschool child. *Journal of American Academy of Child Psychiatry, 14,* 600–616.

Wallerstein, J. S., & Kelly, J. B. (1980). *Surviving the breakup.* New York: Basic Books.

Ware, J. C., & Orr, W. C. (1992). Evaluation and treatment of sleep disorders in children. In C. E. Walker & M. C. Roberts (Eds.), *Handbook of clinical child psychology* (2nd ed., pp. 261–282). New York: Wiley.

Warren, F., & Kaiser, A. (1988). Research in early language intervention. In S. Odom & M. Karnes (Eds.), *Early intervention for infants and children with handicaps* (pp. 89–108). Baltimore: Paul H. Brookes.

Waterman, J. (1986). Family dynamics of incest with young children. In K. MacFarlane, J. Waterman, S. Conerly, L. Damon, M. Durfee, & S. Long (1986). *Sexual abuse of young children* (pp. 204–243). New York: Guilford.

Waterman, J., Kelly, R. J., Oliveri, M. K., & McCord, J. (1993). *Behind the playground walls: Sexual abuse in preschools.* New York: Guilford.

Waterman, J., & Lusk, R. (1993). Psychological testing in evaluation of child sexual abuse. *Child Abuse and Neglect, 17,* 145–159.

Waters, E., & Sroufe, L. A. (1983). Social competence as a developmental construct. *Developmental Review, 3*(1), 79–97.

Weber, R., & Shake, M. C. (1988). Teachers' rejoinders to students' responses in reading lessons. *Journal of Reading Behavior, 20,* 285–299.

Webster-Stratton, C. (1985). Predictors of treatment outcome in parent training for conduct disordered children. *Behavior Therapy, 16,* 223–243.

Wechsler, D. (1989a). *Manual for the Wechsler Preschool and Primary Scale of Intelligence-Revised.* San Antonio, TX: Psychological Corporation.

Wechsler, D. (1989b). *Wechsler Preschool and Primary Scale of Intelligence-Revised.* San Antonio, TX: Psychological Corporation.

Weinberg, W. A., Rutman, J., Sullivan, L., Penick, E. C., & Dietz, S. G. (1973). Depression in children referred to an educational diagnostic center: Diagnosis and treatment. *Journal of Pediatrics, 83,* 1065–1072.

Weinraub, M., & Lewis, M. (1977). The determinants of children's responses to separation. *Monographs of the Society for Research in Child Development, 42* (4, Serial No. 172).

Weinrott, M. R., Corson, J. A., & Wilchesky, M. (1979). Teacher-mediated treatment of social withdrawal. *Behavior Therapy, 10,* 281–294.

Weiss, A. R. (1977). A behavioral approach to the treatment of adolescent obesity. *Behavior Therapy, 8,* 720–726.

Weissbluth, M. (1987). Sleep and the colicky infant. In C. Guilleminault (Ed.), *Sleep and its disorders in children* (pp. 129–140). New York: Raven Press.

Weissman, M. M., Ovaschel, H., & Padian, N. (1980). Children's symptom and social functioning self-report scales: Comparison of mothers' and children's reports. *Journal of Nervous and Mental Disease, 168,* 736–740.

Weissman, M. M., Paykel, E. S., & Klerman, G. L. (1972). The depressed woman as a mother. *Social Psychiatry, 7,* 98–108.

Weller, E. B., Weller, R. A., & Preskorn, S. H. (1983). Depression in children. *Journal of the Kansas Medical Society, 84,* 117–119.

Wenar, C. (1990). *Developmental psychopathology from infancy through adolescence* (2nd ed.), New York: McGraw-Hill.

Wessel, M. A., Cobb, J. C., Jackson, E. B., Harris, G. S., & Detwiler, A. C. (1954). Paroxysmal fussing in infancy, sometimes called colic. *Pediatrics, 14,* 421.

Wheeler, M. E., & Hess, K. W. (1976). Treatment of juvenile obesity by successive approximation control of eating. *Journal of Behavior Therapy and Experimental Psychiatry, 7,* 235–241.

White, B. L., Watts, J. C. (Eds.). (1973). *Experience and environment: Major influences on the development of the young child.* Englewood Cliffs, NJ: Prentice-Hall.

White, E. A., Elsom, B., & Prawat, R. (1978). Children's conceptions of death. *Child Development, 49,* 307–310.

White, M. (1971). A thousand consecutive cases of enuresis: Results of treatment. *Child and Family, 10,* 198–209.

White, M. (1979). Structural and strategic approaches to psychosomatic families. *Family Processes, 18,* 303–314.

Whitehurst, G. J., Falco, F. L., Lonigan, C. J., Fischel, J. E., DeBaryshe, B. D., Valdez-Menchaca, M. C., & Caulfield, M. (1988). Accelerating language development through picture book reading. *Developmental Psychology, 24,* 525–559.

Whitehurst, G. J., Fischel, J. E., Arnold, D. S., & Lonigan, C. J. (1992). Evaluating outcomes with children with expressive language delay. In S. F. Warren & J. Reichle (Eds.), *Causes and effects in communication and language intervention* (pp. 277–313). Baltimore MD: Paul H. Brookes.

Whitehurst, G. J., Fischel, J. E., Caulfield, M. B., DeBaryshe, B. D., & Valdez-Menchaca, M. C. (1989). Assessment and treatment of early expressive language delay. In P. Zelazo & R. H. Barr (Eds.), *Challenges to developmental paradigms: Implications for assessment and treatment* (pp. 113–135). Hillsdale, NJ: Erlbaum.

Whitehurst, G. J., Fischel, J. E., Lonigan, C. J., Valdez-Menchaca, M. C., Arnold, D. S., & Smith, M. (1991). Treatment of early expressive language delay: If, when, and how. *Topics in Language Disorders, 11,* 55–68.

Wiener, J. M. (1984). Psychopharmacology in childhood disorders. *Psychiatric Clinics of North America, 7,* 831–843.

Wilkins, R. (1985). A comparison of elective mutism and emotional disorders in children. *British Journal of Psychiatry, 146,* 198–203.

Williamson, D. A., Kelley, M. L., Cavell, T. A., & Prather, R. C. (1988). Eating and eliminating disorders. In C. L. Frame & J. L. Matson (Eds.), *Handbook of assessment in child psychopathology: Applied issues in differential diagnosis and treatment evaluation.* New York: Plenum.

Willis, D. J., Holden, E. W., & Rosenberg, M. (1992). Child maltreatment prevention: Introduction and historical overview. In D. J. Willis, E. W. Holden, & M. Rosenberg (Eds.), *Prevention of child maltreatment: Developmental and ecological perspectives* (pp. 1–14). New York: Wiley.

Wilson, H., & Staton, R. D. (1984). Neuropsychological changes in children associated with tricyclic antidepressant therapy. *International Journal of Neuroscience, 24,* 307–312.

Wilson, M., & Fox, B. (1982). *First words* [computer program]. Burlington, VT: Laureate Learning Systems.

Wing, L., & Gould, J. (1979). Severe impairments of social interaction and associated abnormalities in children: Epidemiology and classification. *Journal of Autism and Developmental Disorders, 9,* 11–30.

Wing, R. R., Epstein, L. H., Nowalk, M. P., & Lamparski, D. M. (1986). Behavioral self-regulation in the treatment of patients with diabetes mellitus. *Psychological Bulletin, 99,* 78–89.

Wirt, R. D., Lachar, D., Klinedinst, J. K., & Seat, P. D. (1984). *Multidimensional description of child personality: A manual for the Personality Inventory for Children* (1984 rev. by David Lachar). Los Angeles: Western Psychological Services.

Wittmer, D., & Honig, A. (1989). Convergent or divergent? Teacher's questions to three-year-old children in day care. *Society for Research in Child Development Abstract, 6,* 402.

Wolf, M. M., Risley, T. R., & Mees, H. L. (1964). Application of operant conditioning procedures to the behavior problems of an autistic child. *Behaviour Research and Therapy, 1,* 305–312.

Wolfe, D. A. (1988). Child abuse and neglect. In E. J. Mash & L. G. Terdal (Eds.), *Behavioral assessment of childhood disorders* (2nd ed.). New York: Guilford.

Wolfe, D. A., Sandler, J., & Kaufman, K. (1981). A competency-based parent training program for child abusers. *Journal of Consulting and Clinical Psychology, 49,* 633–640.

Wolpe, J. (1958). *Psychotherapy by reciprocal inhibition.* Stanford, CA: Stanford University Press.

Wood, R. E., Boat, T. F., & Doershuck, C. F. (1976). Cystic fibrosis. *American Review of Respiratory Disorders, 113,* 833–877.

Woolston, J. L., & Forsyth, B. (1989). Obesity of infancy and early childhood: A diagnostic schema. In B. B. Lahey & A. E. Kazdin (Eds.), *Advances in clinical child psychology* (Vol. 12, pp. 179–192). New York: Plenum.

Wright, H., Miller, M. D., Cook, M. A., & Littman, J. R. (1985). Early identification and intervention with children who refuse to speak. *Journal of the American Academy of Child Psychiatry, 24,* 739–746.

Wright, L. (1977). Conceptualizing and defining psychosomatic disorders. *American Psychologist, 32,* 625–628.

Wright, L., Schaefer, A. B., & Solomons, G. (1979). *Encyclopedia of pediatric psychology.* Baltimore, MD: University Park Press.

Wright, L., & Walker, C. E. (1977). Treatment of the child with psychogenic encopresis: An effective program of therapy. *Clinical Pediatrics, 16,* 1042–1045.

Wurtele, S. K., Kast, L. C., Miller-Perrin, C. L., & Kondrick, P. A. (1989). A comparison of programs for teaching personal safety skills to preschoolers. *Journal of Consulting and Clinical Psychology, 57,* 505–511.

Wurtele, S. K., Kvaternick, M., & Franklin, C. S. (in press). Sexual abuse prevention for preschoolers: A survey of parents' behaviors, attitudes, and beliefs. *Journal of Child Sexual Abuse.*

Wurtele, S. K., & Miller-Perrin, C. L. (1992). *Preventing child sexual abuse: Sharing the responsibility.* Lincoln, NE: University of Nebraska Press.

Yairi, E., & Ambrose, N. (1992). Onset of stuttering in preschool children: Selected factors. *Journal of Speech and Hearing Research, 35,* 782–788.

Yeterian, E., & Pandya, N. (1988). Architectonic features of the primate brain: Implications for information processing and behavior. In H. Markowitsch (Ed.), *Information processing by the brain.* Toronto: Hans Huber.

Yirmiya, N., & Sigman, M. (1991). High functioning individuals with autism: Diagnosis, empirical findings, and theoretical issues. *Clinical Psychology Review, 11*, 669–683.

Young, G. C. (1969). The problem of enuresis. *British Journal of Hospital Medicine, 2*, 628–632.

Young, G. C. (1973). The treatment of childhood encopresis by conditioned gasto-ileal reflex training. *Behaviour Research and Therapy, 11*, 499–503.

Young, G. C., & Morgan, R. T. T. (1972). Overlearning in the conditioning treatment of enuresis: A long term follow-up study. *Behaviour Research and Therapy, 10*, 409–410.

Young, I. L., & Goldsmith, A. O. (1972). Treatment of encopresis in a day treatment program. *Psychotherapy: Theory, Research, and Practice, 9*, 231–235.

Young, J. L., Ries, L., Silverberg, E., Horm, J. W., & Miller, R. W. (1986). Cancer incidence, survival, and mortality for children younger than age 15 years. *Cancer, 58*, 598–602.

Yule, W., Gold, R. D., & Bush, C. (1982). Long-term predictive validity of the WPPSI: An 11 year old follow-up study. *Personality and Individual Differences, 3*, 65–71.

Zaleski, A., Gerrard, J. W., & Shokier, M. H. K. (1973). Nocturnal enuresis: The importance of a small bladder capacity. In I. Kolvin, R. C. MacKeith, & S. R. Meadow (Eds.), *Bladder control and enuresis*. Philadelphia: J. B. Lippincott.

Zegiob, L. W., Jenkins, J., Becker, J., & Bristow, A. (1976). Facial screening: Effects on appropriate and inappropriate behaviors. *Journal of Behavior Therapy and Experimental Psychiatry, 7*, 355–357.

Zeltzer, L. K., Dash, J., & Holland, J. P. (1979). Hypnotically induced pain control in sickle cell anemia. *Pediatrics, 64*, 533–536.

Zeltzer, L., & LeBaron, S. (1982). Hypnosis and non-hypnotic techniques for reduction of pain and anxiety during painful procedures in children and adolescents with cancer. *Journal of Pediatrics, 101*, 1032–1035.

Zeltzer, L., LeBaron, S., & Zeltzer, P. M. (1984). Paradoxical effects of prophylactic phenothiazine antiemetics in children receiving chemotherapy. *Journal of Clinical Oncology, 2*, 930–936.

Zimrin, H. (1986). A profile of survival. *Child Abuse and Neglect, 10*, 339–349.

Zoghbi, H. (1988). Genetic aspects of Rett syndrome. *Journal of Child Neurology, 3*(Suppl.), 76–78.

Zucker, S. G., & Copeland, E. P. (1988). K-ABC and McCarthy Scale performance among "at risk" and normal preschoolers. *Psychology in the Schools, 25*, 5–10.

Zuckerman, B., Stevenson, J., & Bailey, V. (1987). Sleep problems in early childhood: Continuities, predictive factors, and behavioral correlates. *Pediatrics, 80*, 664–671.

Index